Praise for *The Mathews Men*

"Vividly drawn and emotionally gripping, *The Mathews Men* shines a light on the mostly forgotten but astonishing role the U.S. Merchant Marine played in winning World War II. It brings back to life a breed of men who repeatedly risked all for their country. It chronicles the sagas of families that stoically endured heartrending losses. It honors a community that pulled together to support its sons as they set out—again and again—on deadly seas. And it reminds us how much we owe to the legions of ordinary Americans who quite literally saved the civilized world in the 1940s."
—Daniel James Brown, author of *The Boys in the Boat*

"William Geroux has written a classic American tale, a gripping story of courageous everyday heroes facing death in World War II."
—James Bradley, author of *Flags of Our Fathers*

"When a reporter who writes as elegantly as Geroux unearths such a dramatic and untold story, he must feel as if he's hit the mother lode. With *The Mathews Men*, Geroux gives us a rollicking read that plunges you into the middle of the ocean and seduces you into caring for the story's heroic seafarers. This is both a terrific and terrifying blow-by-blow of the actions of the sailors of the U.S. Merchant Marine as they dodged deadly U-boats during the course of World War II and who, as Lincoln put it, too often made the ultimate sacrifice upon the altar of freedom."
—Bob Drury and Tom Clavin, coauthors of *Halsey's Typhoon* and *The Heart of Everything That Is*

"Often overlooked and unsung, the men of the U.S. Merchant Marine risked all against stealthy German U-boats whether within sight of East Coast cities or on the Arctic run to Murmansk. Mr. Geroux has superbly chronicled the gripping and deeply personal story of brothers in blood as well as in mission."
—Walter R. Borneman, author of *The Admirals: Nimitz, Halsey, Leahy, and King—The Five-star Admirals Who Won the War at Sea*

"The German U-boat war against American merchant men was deadly and dramatic—in World War II, the U.S. Merchant Marine had twice the fatality rate of the U.S. Navy. William Geroux has unearthed a fascinating tale of one small coastal town caught in the thick of the fight, and he tells it with a sharp reporter's eye and a real feel for the heroic men who went down to the sea in ships."

—Evan Thomas, author of *Being Nixon* and *Sea of Thunder*

"William Geroux's *The Mathews Men* harkens to the war heroics of Laura Hillenbrand's *Unbroken* and the British detective drama *Foyle's War*. A little-known story about the brutal sacrifices made by Merchant Marines—and the tiny bayside community they left behind in Mathews County, Virginia—Geroux's book is a gripping account of hard-drinking and even harder-working seamen, and a fresh take on World War II history. Loaded with offbeat characters trying to survive against astonishingly impossible odds, Geroux gives these unheralded heroes their belated due in an account that is as meticulously researched as it is even-handed and poignant."

—Beth Macy, author of the *New York Times* bestseller *Factory Man: How One Furniture Maker Battled Offshoring, Stayed Local—and Helped Save an American Town*

"Poignant . . . A deep, compassionate group biography of these 'unsung heroes' of the Merchant Marines." —*Kirkus Reviews*

"Geroux combines the skills of a newsman and those of a scholar to tell the story of the vital and heroic role played by the U.S. Merchant Marines during World War II." —*Publishers Weekly*

"The valor and contributions of the U.S. Merchant Marines to victory in World War II has seldom been acknowledged. . . . Geroux presents an unflinching, inspiring, and long delayed tribute to the sacrifice of these men." —*Booklist* (starred review)

"A gripping tale of wartime heroics and an emotional family story, this is a must-read addition to World War II literature." —*Library Journal*

"A gripping, nearly lost story of World War II ('Hurry,' the author was told, while gathering names of possible interviewees) and a moving portrayal of family and community. Geroux brings a reporter's keen eye for detail and natural flair for storytelling to his account. . . . Readers experience both the terror at sea and the agonizing tension of families who waited for loved ones to return."
                                                                    —*BookPage*

"Fascinating . . . *The Mathews Men* redresses history's long slight, and it's well worth carrying to the beach this summer."
                                                    —*Richmond Times-Dispatch*

"Absorbing and affecting . . . [Geroux's] ability to compress an impressive amount of information into a story that moves quickly and holds the reader's interest is on a par with that of best-selling author Bill Bryson."
                                                    —*The Virginian-Pilot* (Norfolk)

"The men of Mathews County did their part and made their mark, daring the worst that nature and the Nazi navy could hurl against them. Though this modest volume concentrates on a handful of outstanding families, many more are well represented in such a stirring tale."
                                                    —*The Roanoke Times*

"[The U.S. merchant mariners'] seldom-related contribution to the war effort, along with their courage and fortitude in the face of terrible losses, should be the stuff of legend, and Geroux's fine book takes them a step in that direction. . . . One of the best books I have read [in] a very long time. . . . Don't miss this one."
                                                    —*Daily Herald* (Provo)

"Engrossing . . . At its heart, *The Mathews Men* is a story about duty, honor and sacrifice. . . . *The Mathews Men* gives credence to these World War II heroes who have been overlooked for far too long."
                                                    —*Virginia Living*

ABOUT THE AUTHOR

William Geroux wrote for the *Richmond Times-Dispatch* for twenty-five years. His writing has appeared in *The New York Times*, the Associated Press, Smithsonian.com, and Time.com and various regional magazines. He lives in Virginia Beach, Virginia. He is also the author of *The Ghost Ships of Archangel: The Arctic Voyage That Defied the Nazis*. A native of Washington, D.C., and a graduate of the College of William and Mary, he lives in Virginia Beach, Virginia.

williamgeroux.com

THE MATHEWS MEN

SEVEN BROTHERS AND THE WAR AGAINST HITLER'S U-BOATS

WILLIAM GEROUX

PENGUIN BOOKS

For my mother, Genevieve Blake Geroux

PENGUIN BOOKS
An imprint of Penguin Random House LLC
penguinrandomhouse.com

First published in the United States of America by Viking,
an imprint of Penguin Random House LLC, 2016
Published in Penguin Books 2017
This edition published 2022

LCCN Permalink: https://lccn.loc.gov/2016429937

ISBN 9780525428152 (hardcover)
ISBN 9780698184725 (ebook)
ISBN 9780593511367 (paperback)

Printed in the United States of America
1st Printing

Set in Warnock Pro
Designed by Daniel Lagin
Maps by Jeffrey L. Ward

CONTENTS

CONTENTS

A Gift from the Predators

One night in late July 1942, a hardscrabble Cuban fisherman hauled in a hulking shark from the Nicholas Channel off Cuba's northern coast. He gutted it and tore open its stomach with a knife. Out into the humid air spilled a mass of human remains. The fisherman, whose last name was Carillo, would have been surprised but not shocked.

The Nicholas Channel had been the Carillo family's prime shark-fishing grounds for years. The narrow passage branched off the Old Bahama Channel and the Straits of Florida, where the Gulf Stream ran deep and fast. Its dark-blue water teemed with fish. The sharks preyed on them, and the Carillos in turn preyed on the sharks. They set deep lines in the channel, suspending bloody chunks of meat on six-inch hooks from floating oil drums. When they caught big, dangerous sharks—tiger sharks or snout-nosed bull sharks—they beat them to death with long clubs or drove metal spikes through their gills. They gutted them to keep the meat fresh. The sharks made dinners for the fishermen, who could sell any extra to neighbors.

In recent months, a new predator had joined the sharks and the fishermen in these killing grounds. German U-boats crept among the islets and mangroves. The submarines did not waste time or torpedoes on fishing boats, but they attacked American merchant ships with single-minded focus. The fishermen had glimpsed the U-boats' thin silhouettes at dawn, and heard the rumble of their diesel engines in the dark. They had seen torpedoed vessels flaming like giant torches. And they had seen the U-boats' human victims. Only the previous day, another Cuban fishing boat had picked up survivors of the torpedoed American freighter *Onondaga*. Other men from that ship were still missing.

The Carillos spread out the contents of the shark's belly on the deck of the *Donatella*. They discovered two rings. One was a nondescript pale-yellow band of bone. The other was a heavy gold signet ring, cracked on the underside, bearing the initials "G.D.H." The Carillos could have simply crossed themselves and washed their discovery away with a bucket of sea-water. Instead, they pulled in their lines and pointed the *Donatella* toward the stone quays of Havana harbor, to hand over the remains to the authorities.

Port officials in Havana thought at first that the remains were leg bones, but closer analysis would reveal they were forearms. Word about them quickly spread around the harbor to the offices of shipping companies and other businesses. Several cargo ships had been torpedoed in nearby waters, including most recently the *Onondaga*.

The *Onondaga*'s captain—known as the ship's master—George Dewey Hodges, had understood the danger of sailing in the waters off Cuba. Dewey, as he was called, hailed from the tiny seafaring enclave of Mathews County, Virginia, on the western shore of the Chesapeake Bay. Mariners from Mathews had sailed the world's oceans since colonial times. Now, in the summer of 1942, seven months after the United States entered World War II, Mathews mariners were under attack by U-boats in the Atlantic Ocean, the Caribbean Sea, the Gulf of Mexico, the Mediterranean Sea, and the frigid Barents Sea in the Arctic Circle.

For the Mathews men aboard the *Onondaga*, the U-boat war was personal. Dewey's brother Leslie had been killed in a U-boat attack off Cuba

MATHEWS COUNTY

MIDDLESEX
COUNTY

Chesapeake Bay

Piankatank River

Cherry Point

Godfrey Bay

Cobbs Creek

Hills Bay

Gwynn's
Island

Hallieford

Callis Wharf

Queens Creek

Milford Haven

Point Breeze

MATHEWS COUNTY

Redart

Hole in the Wall

Stutts Cr.

Hudgins

Gales Neck

14

Moon

Chapel Neck

Mathews Courthouse

Garden Creek

North River

Put-in Creek

East River

Onemo

14

Winter Harbor

Port Haywood

Horn Harbor

GLOUCESTER
COUNTY

Shadow

New Point

Pepper Cr.

Motorun

Mobjack Bay

0 Miles   2   4

0 Kilometers   4

New Point Lighthouse ◆

© 2016 Jeffrey L. Ward

only eleven days before the *Onondaga* was attacked. Dewey's father and four of his six brothers were aboard merchant ships in waters already littered with torpedoed ships and the remains of men who had sailed them. The *Onondaga*'s second officer, Genious Hudgins Jr., also a Mathews man, had already survived one torpedoing, as had the bo'sun, William Hammond, whose two brothers were also at sea. Another Mathews sea captain, Mellin Respess, was sailing home aboard the *Onondaga* as a passenger after having had two ships torpedoed out from under him. The only Mathews man on the *Onondaga* who had not previously encountered a U-boat was the third officer, Russell Dennis. All the men had known the master, Dewey, for most of their lives.

Everyone seemed to know Dewey, a broad-shouldered man with an ever-present Lucky Strike cigarette burning between his fingers. Dewey was a veteran captain for the Ford Motor Co., which operated a fleet of ships that in peacetime delivered autos and auto parts from Ford plants on the East Coast to customers in the Caribbean and South America. At age forty-two, Dewey was a robust man with an infectious grin and a natural gift for conversation. He clapped men on the back and asked about their families. He tossed his spare change to children. "How he loved life!" a former shipmate wrote of him. "Possessing the happy faculty of making and keeping friends—friends the world over." Dewey loved to sing, although he was well aware he could not carry a tune. As a joke on his crew, he once cut a record of himself crooning his favorite song, "Mexicali Rose," a ballad about a man setting out on a journey without his beloved.

Dewey might well have been singing about his wife, Edna, and their four children. He was seldom home but doted on them from distant ports. "My darling and babys [*sic*]," he wrote in his last letter home. "I am not expecting anything to happen to me, but if it does, you should have enough with my insurance property to take care of you for a long time." He told Edna, "What you do with whatever I leave is all right with me as long as you take care of yourself and the children. I leave all of that to your judgment." He asked that his son finish college if the Army did not draft him first. He repeated, "Don't think that I think anything is going to happen. I am not even worried about it."

But he was worried about it. Everything about the trip felt wrong. It would be Dewey's first voyage after being idled for months by a serious illness. The *Onondaga* was not even his ship. He was substituting for her regular captain on a short but dangerous run from Mobile, Alabama, to Cuba. Dewey took time to inspect the *Onondaga* closely after flying into Mobile. The ship was a tiny freighter, only 231 feet long and displacing 2,309 tons. She was a "laker," designed for the Great Lakes rather than the open sea. Dewey noticed that the *Onondaga*'s life rafts were held to the deck by wire clamps. He replaced the clamps with ropes that could be cut with quick swipes of a knife to free the rafts in an emergency.

The *Onondaga* sailed out of Mobile on June 24, 1942, and made an uneventful passage from Mobile to the industrial port of Nuevitas on Cuba's northeast coast. She took on a load of heavy manganese ore, an ingredient of flares and incendiary bombs. Dewey waited until first light the next morning to leave Nuevitas. He was determined to reach the safety of Havana while the sun was still up. U-boats seemed to spend the daylight hours hiding on the bottom and then rise at night to hunt.

The *Onondaga* chugged through the Nicholas Channel between the Grand Bahama Bank and a string of barrier islands dotting the Cuban coast. Dewey posted two lookouts, though he knew the ship was doomed if a U-boat got close enough for them to spot it. The *Onondaga* was slow and unarmed. If she was unlucky enough to encounter Germans, her only real defense was her relative insignificance. She was such small fry that some U-boat commanders might hesitate to waste a precious torpedo on her.

The U-129's commander, Hans-Ludwig Witt, was not the type to hesitate. Witt was the most aggressive U-boat commander in the Caribbean. He had sunk ten merchant ships in six weeks, including a freighter commanded by another Mathews sea captain. Witt was not afraid to attack ships in daylight or close to shore. On July 23, he was ending his successful mission to the Caribbean. The U-129 was only passing through the

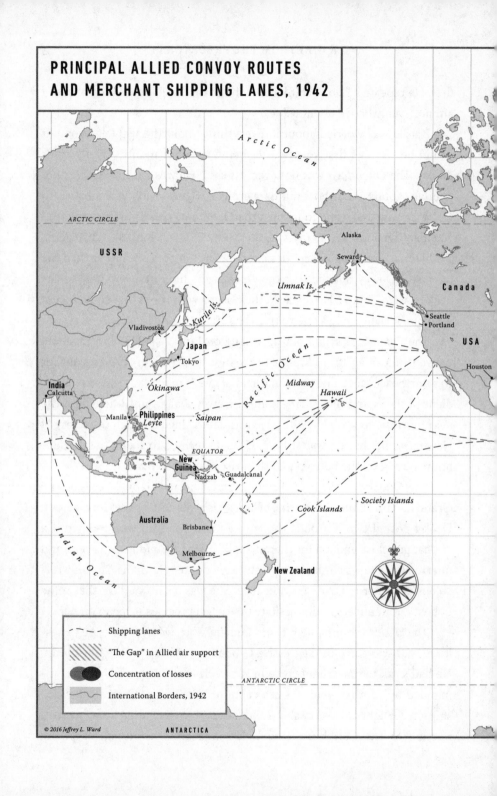

PRINCIPAL ALLIED CONVOY ROUTES
AND MERCHANT SHIPPING LANES, 1942

Arctic Ocean

ARCTIC CIRCLE

USSR

Alaska

Umnak Is.

Seward

Canada

Kurile Is.

Vladivostok

Seattle
Portland

Japan

USA

Tokyo

Houston

India
Calcutta

Okinawa

Pacific Ocean

Midway

Hawaii

Manila

Philippines
Leyte

Saipan

EQUATOR

New
Guinea

Nadzab

Guadalcanal

Society Islands

Cook Islands

Australia

Brisbane

Melbourne

Indian Ocean

New Zealand

Shipping lanes

"The Gap" in Allied air support

Concentration of losses

International Borders, 1942

ANTARCTIC CIRCLE

© 2016 Jeffrey L. Ward

ANTARCTICA

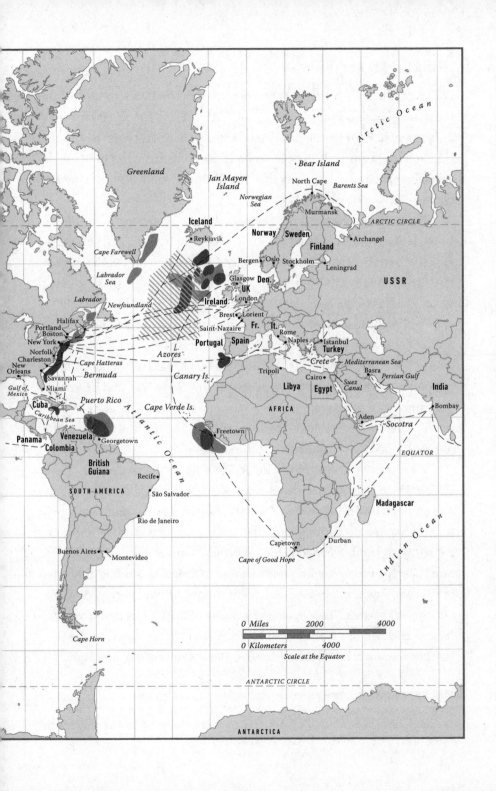

Nicholas Channel en route to the open Atlantic, and back to its base on the coast of Nazi-occupied France. But Witt had saved a torpedo in case a kill presented itself on the trip home. A little before 4:30 p.m., he spotted the *Onondaga* through his periscope as she passed Cayo Guillermo, a sparsely inhabited clump of sand where Ernest Hemingway later set the climax of a novel involving U-boats.*

The U-129 approached the *Onondaga* at periscope depth, unspotted by the lookouts. Witt ordered the sub slowed to its attack speed of 5 knots. He called out the target's range, speed, and course, and the depth to which the torpedo was to run. His torpedo officer entered the data into a steering system built into the torpedo tubes. Witt called *"Rohr los!"*—"Launch!"— and the U-boat shuddered as a torpedo burst from one of its bow tubes on a jet of compressed air. The torpedo raced through the water at approximately 50 miles per hour. Its tip contained an explosive charge of TNT, cyclonite, and aluminum flakes. It struck the *Onondaga* just below the waterline, with a bang and a white flash, and blew a hole in her three-quarter-inch-thick steel hull. The sea poured in and the heavy manganese ore she carried quickly pulled the little ship under.

"As soon as I heard the explosion I ran up to the boat deck," Third Officer Russell Dennis from Mathews told Navy investigators. "It was only six steps up a ladder from where I was standing, but by the time I got there, water was already rushing over the sides. The second mate [Genious Hudgins] hollered, 'Abandon ship,' and then jumped. I was right behind him." Dennis caught a glimpse of Dewey descending a ladder from the bridge, and saw Captain Respess "sawing at one of the ropes holding the life rafts to the deck." The *Onondaga* sank out of sight in less than a minute. "She went down like a brick," Dennis said. Nothing remained on the surface but some debris and three life rafts. Dennis and eight of his shipmates

---

* Hemingway's novel *Islands in the Stream* features a Hemingway-like protagonist, Thomas Hudson, who hunts U-boats off the coast of Cuba and dies in a firefight with a U-boat crew marooned on Cayo Guillermo.

swam to the life rafts and clambered aboard. They made it safely to an uninhabited barrier island, where they were spotted by a search plane, but Dewey and seventeen other men were listed as missing.

Thanks to the shark fishermen, however, Dewey was no longer missing.

The discovery of the rings caught the attention of R. M. Jenkins, who managed a business on the Havana waterfront. Jenkins knew Dewey and knew that he had been lost aboard the *Onondaga*, and recognized the initials "G.D.H." Jenkins examined the ring personally, and came away more convinced, but he was not sure who to tell. He wrote letters to the U.S. ambassador and various steamship companies, asking that someone contact Dewey Hodges's family. "If the widow of the good old man who went down with his ship knows this ring," he wrote, "I imagine it would be of great sentimental value to her."

He was wrong. It was not that simple. The rings would prove to be a thorny gift from the predators that took Dewey Hodges.

CHAPTER ONE

Born to the Water

Mathews County, Virginia, is not on the way to anywhere. "One only goes to Mathews when going to Mathews," the local saying went. The county is a peninsula spreading deep into the Chesapeake Bay, in the shape of a tattered sail. It clings to the western shore of the Bay by a four-mile border with Gloucester County. But the rest of Mathews's boundaries are tidal water.

To the east lies the Chesapeake Bay, one of the world's largest estuaries, which opens out like an inland sea from the outermost edges of the county. To the north, Mathews's shores are bathed by the brackish Piankatank River, and to the south by the North River and Mobjack Bay. That smaller bay joins the Chesapeake at a long shoal marked by the New Point Lighthouse, which was commissioned by President John Adams and completed in Thomas Jefferson's administration. The lighthouse stood on the mainland until August 24, 1933, when a ferocious hurricane flooded much of Mathews and carved a channel that stranded the lighthouse on its own rocky island. The interior of Mathews is gashed by dozens of creeks and streams, including the East River, which cuts a jagged swath through the geographic center of the county.

While Mathews lies only seventy miles from Virginia's capital city of Richmond, mileage never adequately captured the county's isolation. For much of Mathews's history, its roads were so awful that many citizens avoided them entirely and traveled by boat to shop, socialize, and attend church. Bad roads had literally forced the creation of Mathews in the first place. The county had been a parish of Gloucester County until 1791, when citizens complained that the thirteen-mile trip to the Gloucester courthouse was too daunting, especially in the mud of winter and early spring. "Those who have business in court [must walk] or resque their lives often over a wide & dangerous Bay in canoes," read a petition by a member of the Virginia House of Delegates, Thomas Mathews. He argued that the far-flung citizens should have their own county with a courthouse less perilous to reach. The Virginia legislature agreed, and the citizens of the new county thanked Thomas Mathews by naming it after him. The signers of the petition included men named Callis, Hudgins, Powell, Billups, Foster, Hunley, Marchant, Forrest, and Borum, whose descendants still live in the lonely community and sail in the Chesapeake and beyond.

By 1941, as the war in Europe was about to explode into World War II, Mathews was an isolated, tightly knit community of about 7,500 people, scattered in hamlets and tiny villages along the tidal creeks. Mathews was country. Everyone knew everyone else, or at least knew their families. Neighbors pitched in to help one another at harvest time and at hog-killing time—right after the first cold snap in late autumn, when the freshly butchered meat would set properly. Many Mathews families ventured into the city of Richmond only twice a year: to buy school clothes, and to take children to see Santa Claus at Thalhimers department store.

The only highway leading into Mathews, State Route 14, veered through thick maritime forest along half-hidden shorelines, past the redbrick Mathews courthouse, and down toward the lighthouse before ending abruptly, as if exhausted by the journey, in a confusion of back roads. The back roads narrowed into dirt lanes bordered by small, wood-frame houses and an occasional rotted-out boat or collapsed shed. Some lanes ended at weather-beaten docks, where workboats swung at anchor or rested in the muck, depending upon the tide. The air was filled with the cries of gulls and the sweet reek of the marsh.

One of about every ten citizens of Mathews was black, living almost completely segregated from the county's white population. Black children attended small schools, most of them connected to black churches. When the children grew up, their dealings with their white neighbors consisted mainly of laboring and cooking for them. Mathews was not spared the prejudices of many rural southern communities in the early twentieth century. The portraits in the Mathews courthouse were of Robert E. Lee and Thomas "Stonewall" Jackson. As late as the 1920s, hooded and robed Ku Klux Klansmen had marched in Mathews's Fourth of July parade.

By 1941, though, attitudes about race in Mathews varied widely from family to family. The Hodgeses were progressive. Dewey's father and mother, Captain Jesse and Henny, would have swatted any child who showed disrespect toward the black neighbors who helped out at Gales Neck. "Animosity toward blacks was not in my family, period," said Louise Hodges's daughter, Stormy Heart.* But the gulf between white and black in Mathews was wide enough that the weekly paper, the *Gloucester-Mathews Gazette-Journal*, relegated all news about blacks to the back pages, under the heading "Among the Colored."

The closest thing to a downtown in Mathews was the Main Street business district, which bordered the grassy courthouse green. About half of the county's 150 businesses were clustered along the adjoining streets in tidy, one-story brick buildings. The businesses included Richardson's Drug Store—whose lunch counter was the social center of the county—as well as the Farmers and Fishermen's Bank, two grocery stores, a dry-goods store, a car dealership, a gas station, a candy shop, two pool halls, and the BeJo theater, which showed films that had already played everywhere else.

---

* Stormy Heart got her name from a character in a magazine story that her mother, Louise Hodges, was reading while waiting for a midwife to help deliver her.

There was a public library and, in the courthouse green, a jail, a welfare office, and a stone monument with the names of Mathews's Confederate dead. An unimpressed visitor described the town as "straggling."

The only time the courthouse area really came alive was on Saturday nights, when more than two thousand people from all over Mathews put on their best clothes and converged at sunset on Main Street in a swirling promenade. They shopped, gossiped, politicked, did business, settled scores, and looked for romance. After about four hours, they climbed back into their Model A sedans and horse-drawn wagons and returned to their villages along the creeks.

Each village had its post office, usually contained in a general store that sold only those essentials that could not be handmade, grown, or caught in the Bay. Mathews villages were not named for European kings or colonial governors, as in Virginia counties with similar colonial pedigrees, but for the hardworking families who eked out their livings there. Several villages had been named just for the hell of it, including Shadow, Onemo ("one more" post office), Redart ("trader" spelled backward), Motorun (the home of a boat mechanic who could get any motor to run), and Moon (named by a postmaster while sitting on his front step one moonlit night). People in Mathews did not put on airs with names, or with anything else.

Mathews's far-flung communities were bound together by some twenty churches, most of them conservative Baptist, Methodist, and Episcopal, with two small Quaker congregations. The evangelical strains of the Quakers and Methodists held revivals wherein traveling preachers held the devout spellbound. In most Mathews churches, however, the pastors beseeched rather than thundered at their flocks to fill the benches on Sundays. The patriarchs of prominent Mathews families had founded those churches, but their children, by and large, were less devoted, and some already had drifted away. Every Sunday the Reverend Iris Elmon Belch of Gwynn's Island Baptist Church welcomed the visiting mariners he spotted in attendance, but the welcome was wistful. He knew those men probably would not see the inside of another church until they came home to the island again, if then. Life at sea did not lend itself to regular churchgoing.

Mathews was also bound together by its schools. While all white Mathews children attended one of the county's four primary schools, many of them never set foot in Mathews High School. They quit their studies to work to support their families. The Chesapeake Bay was too bountiful to allow anyone in Mathews to starve. But beyond basic sustenance, the prospects in Mathews were limited.

"There wasn't nothing in Mathews but the water," said Bill Callis, who grew up in Mathews on Gwynn's Island, a triangular dot in the Bay at the mouth of the Piankatank River. "You farmed, you fished the Bay, or you went to sea. Those were your only options."

Farming was hard in Mathews. The sandy loam soil was too poor to produce crops on a large scale, except for daffodils, which burst into silvery profusion every spring to be shipped by the thousands to florists in northeastern cities.

Working on the water came more naturally to people in Mathews. Every child in the county grew up handling boats. They learned to sail, and also to scull, a method of propelling a boat by twisting a single oar back and forth rapidly at the stern. Sculling was considered an art in Mathews. A capable sculler could outrace a small motorboat. Bill Callis was a commercial fisherman by the first grade, setting pots in the rivers to catch blue crabs and eels, and then selling them to neighbors. "By the time I was five or six, I could take a boat and make it do as I damn well pleased," Bill said. "I guess you could say I was born to the water."

Mathews fishermen favored pound nets, which were large nets staked into the bottom in a T shape. Fish swam into them and could not find their way out. When bulging nets happened to align with high market prices, fishing was lucrative. But fishing could also break your heart, bankrupt you, or even kill you. Catches plummeted without warning. Expensive gear broke. Fish houses burned. Boats sank. Men flayed or smashed their fingers while driving stakes for pound nets. And every year, the storms that boiled up suddenly on the Bay caught at least one fisherman too far out. Many fishermen never learned to swim, regarding it as a leisure activity.

For more than 250 years, the profession of choice in Mathews had been sailing merchant ships. To a Richmonder, Mathews might seem like a dead end at the water's edge, but to a mariner, Mathews was a portal, a jumping-off point to the world. Mathews had been a tobacco port and then a busy steamboat port. In 1941, steamboats still stopped in Mathews regularly on their way between Norfolk and Baltimore. A young man born to the water, with an urge to explore or simply nothing to lose, could pack some clothes into a seabag, present himself to a ship's captain on the dock, and change his life forever. Generations of Mathews men had done exactly that, running away from home or walking away with their families' blessings. During a grueling fall harvest in 1938, George Hudgins of Mathews announced he was leaving the family farm to go to sea. His father handed him $10 and said, "Good luck." George had never been much help on the farm, but he was a natural at the helm of a vessel. He would retire many years later as chief pilot on the Panama Canal.

The pinnacle of achievement in Mathews was to become a captain, to command a ship at sea. In some Mathews families, it was not enough for a young man to find steady work as a seaman or even a ship's officer. His birthright was to become a captain. Portraits of his ancestors in *their* white captain's caps stared down at him expectantly from the walls of his home.

Captains were celebrities in Mathews. When one came home from his ship for a visit, neighborhood boys orbited his house on their bicycles, hoping for a shout of greeting or maybe even a quarter flung to them. Captains always had money in their pockets, even during the worst years of the Great Depression. In 1941, an experienced captain could earn $350 a month. By most standards, that was hardly lavish pay. Captains were "the poorest paid executives in the country," wrote author and mariner Bruce Felknor. But captains made ten times more than able seamen, whose pay was $32.50 per month, and able seamen earned more than most other people in Mathews.

A few captains in Mathews always stood out from the crowd, either for their skill, their exploits, or their prodigious personalities. Captain Jesse Hodges stood out for all of those reasons and more. The Hodges family of Gales Neck was extraordinary.

In 1884, when Jesse was only ten years old, he had signed on as cabin boy on a neighbor's sailing schooner, the *Clemmie Travers*, which ran between Norfolk, Baltimore, and the Caribbean hauling everything from coal to pineapples. The captain taught Jesse to read by the light of swaying oil lanterns, using newspapers from ports of call as textbooks. According to a family history, Jesse "learned to read other things too, like tides, winds, stars, currents, charts, depth sounders and men."

Jesse could handle large vessels as if they were bathtub toys. He just had the touch. He started with sailing schooners and freighters but gravitated toward tugboats. Two of his brothers followed. At the age of twenty, Jesse was promoted to captain of an oceangoing tug, and he spent most of the rest of his life in the wheelhouse, shepherding ships and barges through busy harbors from New England to the Caribbean.

Captain Jesse had a barrel chest, enormous hands, and a piercing look that seemed to say, "Get off your ass." He would not employ men who drank too much or had too little ambition. He was accustomed to shouting orders and seeing them followed without discussion or delay.

Jesse's wife, Henrietta, was a tall, large-boned woman, as kind as Jesse was hard. Henny, as she was universally known, presided over the family's sixty-acre farm on Gales Neck at the head of the East River. Jesse knew little about the farm or other matters on dry land. He got off the tugboat only three or four times a year, for a few days at a stretch. When he was home, Henny waited on him hand and foot. She fixed him his favorite meal of baked alewives—oily fish that most people refused to eat. Jesse enjoyed a little activity, like hoeing his watermelon patch, but mostly he sat in the shade of a tall cedar near the riverbank, smoking a cigar or his corncob pipe, whittling, and waiting for the call back to his ship. He seemed lost at home in all respects except one.

Between 1895 and 1920, Jesse and Henny had fourteen children—nine sons and five daughters. "It seemed like every time he came home, he'd leave her with another child to care for," observed his daughter Louise. It wasn't enough for Henny, who joked that she wanted enough children for a steamship crew but that he had fathered only enough for a tugboat crew. And indeed, at one point Jesse employed five of his sons as officers on his tug.

The Hodges children accumulated quickly: Raymond, Seth, Dewey, Willie, Leslie, Alice, Elizabeth, Spencer, John, Coleman, David, Henrietta, Louise, and finally Hilda. By the time Hilda, the fourteenth and last child, arrived, Jesse and Henny had run out of names. They christened her Hilda Fourteen Hodges. She was the only one born in a hospital. Jesse lost count of his sons and named the ninth boy David in the mistaken belief he was the biblical "seventh son."

But Captain Jesse's career advice to his boys was as clear as the Gulf Stream. When his oldest, Raymond, turned thirteen, Jesse walked him to the dune at the edge of the Bay and pointed out at a ship chugging north to Baltimore. "When you are 14, you'll be old enough to work on a ship," he told Raymond. "By the time you are 21, I want you to be master of a ship like that."

Raymond would not disappoint. Six of Captain Jesse's sons would, in fact, become ship's captains, and a seventh would quit the sea only after hurting his back in a shipboard accident. Jesse and Henny reared two of their grandsons, who also went to sea. Three of the Hodges daughters married Mathews mariners.

When the seafaring Hodges sons married, they had to move their families to the home ports of their ships in Norfolk, Philadelphia, and New York, but whenever their ships docked for more than a day or two, they came home to Gales Neck to pay their respects to Henny, whom they all called "Mama." Even if they were no longer *from* Mathews, they would always be *of* Mathews. After they retired, they would return to Mathews to live out their final years. They would always be Mathews men.

The Hodges captains hired all the crew members from Mathews they could. Every time Captain Dewey Hodges came home to see his mother, he spread the word around Mathews of any jobs open on his ship or other vessels he knew. Any man who wanted work had only to meet him in front of Richardson's Drug Store at 1 p.m. on Sunday, and Dewey would drive him to the docks and sign him on to the crew. Dewey, like his father, encouraged men to apply themselves and advance. "My father wanted to help men from Mathews," Dewey's daughter Jean recalled. "He knew that with a little help, some of them could get out and make some money and see the world. That was what he had done, and he saw himself in them." Dewey also pushed them to be ambitious and rise through the ranks; he had once threatened to fire his second mate, Clayton Hammond of Mathews, if Clayton did not quit procrastinating and test for his first-mate's license. Hammond did as he was told, and became Dewey's second-in-command. At one of Mathews's darkest moments in the coming U-boat war, Clayton Hammond would repay Dewey's confidence in him.

The Hodges family may have been abundant, but it was only one of a dozen families in Mathews with a tradition of sailing merchant ships. The center of Mathews seafaring, in fact, was not the Hodges's community of Gales Neck but Gwynn's Island. The island was three miles long and a mile wide, heavily wooded, and linked to mainland Mathews by a steel drawbridge spanning a placid anchorage called Milford Haven. Gwynn's Island was home to about six hundred people, who were even more closely tied to the sea than were their neighbors across the water.

Gwynn's Island had been a cradle of merchant sea captains since colonial times, which was a great source of pride on the island. In 1924, the *Mathews Journal* printed a letter from "Father Neptune" listing twenty-four Gwynn's Islanders who were captains of merchant ships. The names included Callis, Hudgins, Borum, and Respess, the first families of island seafaring. The list included six island captains named Callis, including the brothers Homer, Rodney, and Robert Melville Callis, who had sailed the deep ocean for two decades.

Like most islanders, the three Callis brothers had quit school after ninth grade rather than scull across Milford Haven every morning to catch the bus to the high school. The sea seemed far more interesting. "I have seen many queer things and had many queer experiences," Captain Robert Melville Callis once said. He had stopped a ship in a Louisiana canal to let a cow swim across. He had seen a storm strip a man naked. He claimed to have seen mermaids, whose "eyes were blue, blue like the waters of old Milford Haven," and who were "built like the steeple on the Gwynn's Island Baptist Church."

Merchant mariners like the Mathews men were civilians, sailing privately owned cargo ships from port to port. Their employer, the U.S. Merchant Marine, was not a branch of the military, as its name seemed to suggest. It was, and is, an association of privately owned shipping companies operating under the American flag, employing American crews, and fighting like bull sharks over contracts to haul goods by sea.

Merchant shipping dated back to the world's earliest civilizations. Any ambitious nation with even a sliver of seacoast projected its economic strength through merchant ships. The U.S. Merchant Marine is as old as the nation itself. It helped build the United States into a global power. Merchant ships carried American goods abroad and foreign goods to America after the Revolution. They fought the young nation's sea battles, as privateers commissioned by the government to attack enemy ships, until the U.S. Navy grew strong enough to take over that job.

Throughout its history, the U.S. merchant fleet had grown and shrunk according to the laws of supply and demand and the strength of foreign competition. But the government never let it grow too feeble without reviving it through subsidies and exclusive contracts. The nation needed a functioning U.S. Merchant Marine. The need was not so clear during peacetime, when foreign ships could deliver goods to and from U.S. ports just as well and often more cheaply. But in times of war, the Merchant Marine was transformed into a vital part of America's arsenal—a fleet of ships the nation could rely on to carry men and supplies wherever they were needed. The Merchant Marine had always showed its true value to the country when the shooting started.

Most Mathews men joined the Merchant Marine at the lowest rungs of the shipboard job ladder, as cabin boys or ordinary seamen, and learned through experience. Climbing up through the ranks that way, rather than through study at maritime training academies, is called "coming up through the hawsepipe," which means coming up the hard way. A hawsepipe is the opening in a vessel's bow through which the anchor chain passes as the anchor is dropped and weighed; a sufficiently determined man could scramble up the greasy chain through the hawsepipe and onto the ship's deck. A hawsepipe mariner would rise through the ranks by logging enough time at each job on a ship to qualify for the next higher job. If the rank or job they aspired to required a certificate or license, they would sit for an exam by the U.S. Coast Guard to prove their knowledge. The job descriptions on merchant ships were as old as seafaring itself.

In the deck department, where Mathews men tended to work, the entry-level deckhands were Ordinary Seamen, who performed tedious work such as painting, scraping rust, washing the deck, and stowing cargo. After three years, they could become Able Seamen, skilled at handling lines, maintaining deck equipment, standing watch, and other duties essential to sailing a vessel. The deck crew was supervised by the Boatswain, or Bo'sun, the senior unlicensed man on the ship. The Ship's Carpenter, who was always nicknamed "Chips," built cargo containers and other wooden structures as needed. The radio operator, always called "Sparks," was responsible for communications.

The lowest-ranking licensed officer on the ship was the Third Mate, or Third Officer, who oversaw cargo operations and maintenance of safety equipment, including lifeboats. The Second Mate, or Second Officer, was in charge of navigation. He used a sextant to measure the angle from the sun or the stars to the horizon, and then used those readings to find the ship's position and chart its course. The First Mate, or First Officer, was second-in-command on the ship. He supervised the day-to-day performance of the vessel and the crew.

Roughly equal to the First Mate in rank was the Chief Engineer. He ruled the loud, hellishly hot engine room, which usually was located amidships just below the waterline. He oversaw one or more Assistant Engineers as well as the unlicensed Firemen, Oilers, and Wipers, who, respectively, kept the ship's engines fueled, lubricated, and wiped free of spilled oil and grime. The ship's Steward oversaw food service, supervising the Cooks who prepared the meals and the Messmen who served them to the crew and then cleaned up.

Every officer and crewman on the ship—somewhere between twenty-five and forty men—answered to the Captain. The captain was ultimately responsible for everything that happened aboard his vessel. He was not actually a member of the crew but an agent of the ship's owner. His job was to deliver the cargo to its destination as fast as possible, while keeping the crew sufficiently healthy and content to get it there. He did not stand regular watches at sea, as his officers did, but when the ship was in danger, the captain's duty was to stay on the bridge for as long as the threat lasted, or until he was too exhausted to continue. The captain might be easygoing, aloof, or a tyrant hated by every man on his ship. But his standing was undisputed and his authority absolute.

Mathews had a reputation for producing capable mariners, and some shipping companies went out of their way to hire Mathews men. An executive of the New York–based A. H. Bull & Co. shipping line explained in the 1930s: "From the beginning of the Line comes the tradition that natives of Mathews County, Virginia, should be in command of its ships. Applicants for positions in the company merely stated they were from [Mathews] and proved their contention, and were immediately employed. On the seven steamers now operated by the line, every deck officer is a native of Mathews County." Much of the Bull Line's hiring in Baltimore was handled by a retired sea captain from Gwynn's Island, Virgil Respess, who simply called around Mathews until he found men for the open jobs. All the hiring was supposed to go through the seamen's unions, with the mariners who had been ashore the longest getting the next available jobs for which they qualified. By 1941, every mariner had to join a union, but the unions were still consolidating their hold on the hiring process, and a savvy captain or hiring agent could still place a favored man on a ship.

Mariners from outside the county who did not enjoy the benefits of the Mathews job pipeline understandably resented it. They viewed Mathews men as clannish and ambitious to a fault. Bill Callis once signed on to a new ship and told the captain where he was from. "Oh, Christ!" the captain muttered. "If you're from Mathews County, I had better be careful or you'll have my job." He was not smiling.

Some Mathews mariners scoffed at outsiders who had impressive licenses or commands but no true feel for a ship. The Mathews captain of the Virginia state patrol boat *Commodore Maury* noted condescendingly that the crew of President Franklin D. Roosevelt's presidential yacht, though "immaculately uniformed," needed three tries to dock the vessel during a visit to Yorktown, Virginia. The *Commodore Maury*, by contrast, "eased up to the dock in perfect form on the first approach."

Mathews mariners who preferred to come home every night chose to work on patrol boats, harbor tugs, barges, and other vessels that stayed in and around the Bay. The more adventurous men chose vessels bound across the ocean. Bill Callis, like his father and uncles, loved bracing against a bulkhead while his ship climbed up and down thirty-foot storm seas. "When you're at the top of one of those seas," he said, "you can look out for twenty miles all around you and not see a speck or a soul, just rows and rows of giant rollers. It's a sight you can't see anywhere else except the middle of the ocean." Bill loved sipping strong coffee on the bridge during the morning watch as the rising sun reignited the colors of the sky.

Not everyone saw romance and adventure in the Merchant Marine, however. Daily life on a cargo ship was Spartan. Seamen often slept in coffin-sized bunks, sometimes twelve to thirteen men to a room, packed in like the cargo in the ship's holds. They bathed in the ocean and washed their clothes in buckets of salt water heated by steam from the ship's boilers. The ships had no doctors. Any ailment that could not be cured with iodine or castor oil had to wait for the next port call. The food on a ship was usually plentiful, but its quality depended on the cook's skills and mood.

A voyage might last for three weeks or six months. Most of the work was tedious and monotonous. Each mariner worked a four-hour watch and got the next two watches off. He had little to do in his free time except sleep, read, write letters, play cards or Chinese checkers, or listen to the same phonograph records over and over. He did not get to choose his shipmates, some of whom were sure to be drunks, idlers, or brawlers. "The unlicensed seamen were a bunch of rounders," said Captain Jesse's grandson, Horace "Brother" Hodges, who went to sea during World War II. "When we'd dock, they'd get drunk and chase each other around the deck with fire axes. In Puerto Rico, a guy came back aboard with a pig." By the time the ship finished a voyage, mariners always knew more than they wanted to know about some of their shipmates.

Mariners were paid in cash at the end of each voyage, the result of a law designed to protect them from dishonest shipowners who might otherwise offer them worthless IOUs. They also had to sign on to voyages—to "sign the articles"—in the presence of port officials, whose job was to make sure they were boarding the ships by choice rather than being taken aboard by force or because they were too drunk to know what they were doing.

"Most of us didn't go to sea because we loved it so much," said Captain Willard Hudgins Jr. of Gwynn's Island, who barely knew his sea captain father and yet followed his path. "It was a way to make a living, and it was better than the alternatives."

For some, going to sea was an act of economic desperation. Guy Hudgins of Mathews quit school and joined the Merchant Marine to support his mother and four siblings after his father disappeared. Joseph William Elliott of Mathews joined the Merchant Marine at age sixteen after his father left his mother with six children to feed. At first, Joseph did not meet the Merchant Marine's minimum weight requirement because he was so malnourished. He made weight two weeks later after gorging on bananas and gulping a gallon of water just before the weigh-in. Walter Stillman was an orphan who had been sent as a boy to live with relatives in Mathews. He spent his weekdays toiling in a sawmill and his weekends toiling on a farm. He earned money for his school clothes by gigging frogs—spearing them with a sharp pole at night in the marshes near his home—and selling the meat to neighbors. One blazing hot summer day, he was plowing a cornfield behind a mule when Dewey Hodges's brother Spencer spotted him and offered him a job on Dewey's freighter, the *East Indian*. Walter had never even been on a skiff, but he decided that nothing could be worse than "looking a mule in the butt."

Mathews mariners ran into one another on the docks of New York, London, Rotterdam, Rouen, Cape Town, and Istanbul. "The sun never sets on Mathews men," people in the county said. Brother Hodges once stepped off a freighter in Odessa, Russia, and saw his uncle Captain Raymond Hodges's ship docked nearby. One of Jesse's sons, Captain Coleman Hodges, was surprised to discover that his new second officer was his own nephew, J. W. Corbett. In a few cases, Mathews men's ships literally met at sea. The freighter *Grecian* and the passenger ship *City of Chattanooga*, both commanded by Gwynn's Islanders, collided in 1932 in dense fog off Rhode Island. Four men were killed, including a Mathews man who was second officer on the *Grecian*.

Collisions in the fog were among the common perils of the sea, which had changed little over time. Some twenty-first-century maritime insurance policies still enumerate those perils in nineteenth-century terms, bordering on poetry:

> They are of the Seas, Men-of-War, Fire, Lightning, Earthquake, Enemies, Pirates, Rovers, Assailing Thieves, Jettisons, Letters of Marque and Counter-Marque, Surprisals, Takings at Sea, Arrests, Restraints, Detainment of all Kings, Princes and Peoples of what

Nation, Condition or Quality Soever, Barratry [sabotage] of the Master and Mariners and of all other Like Perils, Losses and Misfortune.

For mariners, the perils also included malaria, smallpox, typhoid fever, and the like in distant ports. They also included a richer variety of shipboard accidents than even the most seasoned mariner could possibly anticipate. Reginald Deagle of Mathews was bitten in the neck by a half-drowned monkey he tried to pull from the ocean after a typhoon.

The mariners' families tried not to dwell on the dangers. They were used to the men being gone, and to having to wait weeks or even months to hear from them, and with farms and businesses and houses to run, they had little time to sit around and wonder what the men were up to. Mariners' wives learned out of necessity to be energetic and resourceful. Their husbands were absent for every crisis and every triumph, every birth, death, injury, birthday, and graduation, and every strange noise in the house at night. The wives singlehandedly maintained the homes and farms and reared the children. Some women secretly dreaded the return of their husbands, who barked orders at them as if they were ordinary seamen.

Henny Hodges, her daughter Louise recalled, "would work in the fields until dinnertime, put dinner on the table, say 'Give me 15 minutes,' and lie down, then get up and go back to the fields and work until dark. There was nothing she couldn't do. She sewed, quilted, milked the cows, fed the hogs and cured the meat." And when her husband came home, "her schedule didn't change except that he stood around telling her what to do."

Not every woman could stand that life. One lonely Mathews widow wrote a letter to the *Gazette-Journal* seeking a new husband, and expressed no preferences about his looks or his occupation, with one exception: "No man who follows a boat and is away from home for weeks need write."

At least the mariners' wives had known what they were getting into, or had thought they did when they married; they had made their own choices. But it was different for a mother when a son followed his father to sea. Saying good-bye to him was a wrenching experience, in which pride mingled with resignation that her life would be defined thereafter by the boy's absences. He would be gone most of the time. Then one day, he might be gone forever. The sea could create hazards that not even the finest mariner could survive. Every mother in Mathews knew a family that had lost a son to the ocean, if she hadn't lost her own. Scattered among the little cemeteries in Mathews were empty graves with footstones bearing the words "Lost at Sea."

War added perils to the sea, and Mathews mariners had fought in every American war since the Revolution. In 1776, the last British governor of Virginia, John Murray, Lord Dunmore, sailed his fleet to Gwynn's Island in search of a safe harbor. A colonial militia hauled cannons to a hill and opened fire on Dunmore's ships, wounding him with splintered wood. He sailed away, never to return. When the people of Mathews learned that His Lordship had dismissed the militiamen at first as "crickets," they named the hill where the cannons had been mounted "Cricket Hill." In another part of Mathews, a tide mill, powered by the ebb and flow of the tide, is said to have supplied grain to George Washington's troops at the decisive siege of Yorktown.*

In the War of 1812, Mathews carpenters built gunboats for the undermanned Continental Navy. The boatbuilders worked in secluded creek beds to avoid patrols by the British, whose blockade fleet for the upper Bay was anchored just off Mathews. In the Civil War, a swashbuckling Confederate naval officer used Mathews as his base of operations, dispatching two yin-and-yang gunboats, the black-painted *Raven* and the white-painted *Swan*, to raid Union shipping in the Bay. Union troops retaliated against the Mathews "guerillas and river pirates" by fanning out through

---

* In April 1980 the tide mill and the colonial estate to which it belonged, Poplar Grove, were purchased by John Lennon through a real estate company. After Lennon was murdered in December of that year, his widow, Yoko Ono, donated the property to a boys' home.

the county to hit Mathews where it hurt: sinking more than 150 boats and skiffs. Mathews also produced the Confederacy's only female officer, Captain Sally Tompkins. She received an honorary officer's commission to allow her to operate a private hospital for wounded soldiers. During the Spanish-American War, Captain Jesse hauled coal to U.S. troops in Cuba. He so admired the U.S. Navy hero of that war, Admiral George Dewey, that he named one of his boys after him.

During World War I, mariners from Mathews had faced the first generation of U-boats, slower and less powerful than those in World War II, but lethal nonetheless. Coles Frank Hudgins, a seaman from the Mathews hamlet of Laban, was killed when the British tanker *Healdton* was torpedoed in the middle of the North Atlantic in 1917. Soon after, Captain L. P. Borum of Gwynn's Island survived the sinking of his freighter *City of Memphis* off the coast of Scotland.

Borum had been returning from Britain with no cargo when a U-boat surfaced and fired warning shots across his bow. Borum ordered the crew and passengers into lifeboats, and they abandoned ship. The submarine approached the lifeboats and the German commander asked what cargo they carried. None, Borum informed him. "Well, captain," the U-boat commander said, "I have to sink your ship, you know that." Borum did not agree, but was in no position to argue. The U-boat sank the *City of Memphis*, and Borum, his crew, and the passengers endured a frigid night in the lifeboats before a British warship spotted them. When he got back to the United States, he was given command of the freight/passenger ship *City of Savannah*. He crossed the Atlantic eighteen more times, carrying thousands of American doughboys to the battlefields of France. By 1941, Borum was fifty-eight years old and approaching the end of his seafaring career. But he was still captain of a ship, and he was still not afraid of U-boats.

In the waning months of World War I, the Germans sent three U-boats to the coast of the United States to attack merchant ships. They were too late to accomplish much, and they found few choice targets, but in the course of a few weeks they sank a cruiser and dozens of unarmed vessels,

including a lightship—a floating lighthouse—off Cape Hatteras, North
Carolina. Captain Robert Melville Callis of Gwynn's Island recalled sailing
along the East Coast in 1918 and seeing "signs of death and destruction
every place. One eight-masted schooner was turned over, her sails set and
her masts sticking out . . ." It was a last-ditch attack by a defeated enemy,
but it was also a warning that U-boats could easily reach U.S. shores.

The Spanish Civil War, a prelude to World War II, is not remembered
for its sea engagements. But Captain Elvin "Bubba" Lewis of Mathews, a
fearless, hard-drinking, chain-smoking rooster of a man, ran his oil tanker
Nantucket Chief through a Fascist blockade in the Mediterranean to deliver fuel to besieged Loyalist forces in Barcelona. The job paid so well that
Lewis tried it again, but this time he was captured and thrown into a Fascist prison. He was beaten with rubber hoses every day for weeks until the
State Department negotiated his release. "My whole body is a mass of
bruises," Lewis told *The New York Times*. "I am fed up with the whole
business and will not go to Spain again."

In a separate effort, Mathews captain Stanley Ransome diverted his
freighter *Exeter* from a cargo run to evacuate Americans who were trapped
in Barcelona as Fascist forces closed in. While warplanes engaged in dogfights over his head, Ransome took aboard 162 American refugees and the
Exeter steamed out of the war zone through a cross fire between Fascist
shore batteries and Loyalist warships.

But nothing in Mathews's two hundred years of maritime conflict prepared the people of the county for the deadly confluence of events of World
War II.

By late 1941, fishing in the Chesapeake Bay was in decline. Catches of blue
crabs had plummeted for no apparent reason. The Bay's oysters, which
once had grown in clumps big enough to pose hazards to navigation, were
starting to suffer from diseases that eventually would decimate them. Shad
were so scarce that fishermen who had caught them for decades no longer
even bothered to set nets. Some fishermen turned to work in the shipyards

in nearby Norfolk and Newport News. Those yards had plenty of work, and many of the jobs were vital to the government's shipbuilding program and thus exempted the jobholders from being drafted into the Army.

To men accustomed to working on the water, however, the most obvious place to look for work in 1941 was the Merchant Marine. Experienced sailors had always been able to find regular work, but now jobs on ships were becoming so plentiful that any man who knew a bow from a stern was hired. Men from all over the country were streaming into maritime union halls on East Coast ports. The demand for American ships and mariners kept soaring as the war engulfed Europe.

The United States, while still officially a neutral nation, was already fighting in the Battle of the Atlantic on Britain's side. For two years, shipments of American supplies on British, American, and other nations' ships had kept Britain alive. German U-boats tried to sever Britain's lifeline to the outside world by sinking any vessel hauling food, fuel, and arms to the British Isles. They sank more than a thousand British merchant ships and killed more than twenty thousand British seamen—more than Britain could replace. British prime minister Winston Churchill called on Roosevelt for more help.

In 1940, Roosevelt ordered a government agency, the U.S. Maritime Commission, to build two hundred new cargo ships, which would be owned by the government but operated by private companies at government expense. The president then quickly upped the number to three hundred, and then four hundred. He gave the Commission all the money and political muscle it needed. The Commission built or expanded more than seventy American shipyards and then flooded them with orders for ships. The yards ran around the clock and hired thousands of men and women. The only thing that ever threatened to slow them down was having to compete for steel with the U.S. Navy, which even before Pearl Harbor was building 1.3 million tons of new warships, including aircraft carriers, battleships, cruisers, destroyers, submarines, and smaller vessels for fighting submarines. Some of the new ships were already sliding down the ways of shipyards into the water. They would be part of the greatest shipbuilding campaign in history, and a key to winning World War II, but most of the new ships would not be finished in time for the first and most dangerous phase of the war.

For that phase, the U.S. government requisitioned most of the existing U.S. merchant fleet, some 1,200 merchant ships from 131 shipping companies, and chartered them on a permanent basis to haul war cargo. The government paid the companies to operate the ships as before. But the Maritime Administration, and later the War Shipping Administration, decided what cargo the ships would carry and when and where they would sail. Roosevelt considered merging the Merchant Marine into the Navy, as he had done with the Coast Guard. But the maritime unions opposed it. After fighting for years to improve mariners' dismal pay and shipboard conditions, the unions feared losing those gains and the power they had amassed by winning them. Many rank-and-file union mariners also wanted no part of the Navy, which they associated with pointless rules and spit-and-polish.

So merchant mariners went to war as independent contractors, serving their country through a combination of necessity, patriotism, and collective bargaining. In exchange for giving up their right to strike during the war, they received bonuses for sailing in war zones and hauling hazardous cargo such as ammunition and gasoline. Those bonuses could double their wages, which led to complaints from enlisted military men that the mariners were better paid.

But mariners were compensated very differently than soldiers, sailors, or airmen. They were hired from voyage to voyage, and earned money only when they were sailing. Their wages did not start until they boarded a ship, and stopped as soon as the voyage ended, even if it ended with a torpedo strike in mid-ocean. Mariners would be off the clock when swimming for their lives, fending off sharks, or shivering in lifeboats. When they safely completed a voyage, they had to sign on to another ship within thirty days or become eligible to be drafted into the Army. Their only government

benefits were death benefits—a $5,000 check for their next of kin if they
were lost at sea.

By December 1941, America was on a knife-edge between peace and war
in the Atlantic. U-boats had already sunk eighteen American merchant
ships, supposedly by mistake. Hitler at first had made excuses for those
sinkings, but eventually he quit bothering. A U-boat also had sunk an
American destroyer, the USS *Reuben James*, while it was shielding a convoy
of merchant ships en route to Britain. Hitler had made no excuses for the
sinking of the destroyer. America seemed certain to enter the war, and the
moment she did, any merchant ship flying the American flag would become a prime target.

Those ships—the Mathews men's ships—were mostly freighters and
tankers built for the last war. Most of the companies that owned them had
been founded between 1900 and 1920 by entrepreneurs, many based in
New York, who shifted their vessels' routes from ocean to ocean as they
won or lost cutthroat competitions for cargo with their rivals. The A. H.
Bull & Co. shipping line, commonly known as the Bull Line, had been
started in 1902 by Archibald H. Bull, a character out of a Horatio Alger
rags-to-riches story. Sixteen-year-old Archibald had begged a job as a clerk
at a New York shipping firm after his father fell to a Confederate bullet at
the battle of Fredericksburg, and had hustled his way to ownership of a
fleet. One of the largest U.S. shipping companies, Moore-McCormack
Lines, bore the names of two founding partners who had gambled everything they owned to open a cargo and passenger service to South America.
The shipping companies were generous but demanding bosses. As far as
they were concerned, no captain ever delivered his cargo quite quickly
enough or deserved time off.

By the 1940s, some of the World War I–vintage cargo ships had dete-
riorated into rust buckets. Even those in the best shape were past their
prime. None of them were built to outrun U-boats, or to stand up against

attacks. If a torpedo blew a hole in the hull, no watertight bulkheads would slow the in-rushing sea. The old ships would sink fast.

The old seafaring families of Mathews recognized the danger building. In a sermon at Gwynn's Island Baptist Church in November 1941, the Reverend Iris Belch observed, "The prospect of war is being felt more keenly as our own boys and men go into the danger zone in their ships." The only real surprise was that the event that finally drew America into the war took place in the Pacific.

Mathews was preoccupied when war finally came. One week before Pearl Harbor, fire gutted an entire block of the Main Street business district, destroying a grocery store, a hardware store, and one of the pool halls. Black ash rained down on homes a mile away. The Mathews fire truck refused to start, so the flames spread unchecked until pumper trucks arrived from the neighboring towns of West Point and Urbanna. Firefighters prevented even worse damage by extending a hose to nearby Put-in Creek to draw water. By the next day, the failure of the Mathews fire truck was turning into a political scandal. Most citizens of Mathews were too caught up in the scandal and the growing tension in the Atlantic to pay much attention to Japan. The only harm the Japanese had ever done to Mathews was occasionally driving down the price of blue crabs by flooding the market with cheap Alaskan king crab meat.

For more than a year, however, Japanese soldiers had been rampaging through parts of Southeast Asia, seizing coastal regions of China, killing and raping thousands. Japan had allied itself with Nazi Germany. Japanese leaders spewed anti-Allied propaganda. In July 1941, after Japanese troops occupied former French territories in Indochina, America froze Japanese assets in the United States. A few weeks later, the United States halted the sale of oil and aviation fuel to Japan. The furious Japanese began negotiating to try to reverse those steps, while planning a devastating surprise attack. On the morning of December 7, more than 330 Japanese bombers took off from aircraft carriers in the Pacific Ocean and devastated the U.S.

fleet at the Pearl Harbor naval base in Hawaii. The bombers sank or severely damaged 14 American warships, including 4 battleships, and killed
2,490 people. Fortunately for the United States, all of its aircraft carriers
happened to be at sea on that day, beyond the bombers' reach.

News of the attack came to Mathews over the radio as people returned home from Sunday church services in a cold drizzle. Some of the
churches reopened for prayer. The next morning, a small group of veterans delivered patriotic speeches at the courthouse square. President Roosevelt called December 7 "a date which will live in infamy" in a speech that
did not mention Germany. The *Gazette-Journal* printed a list of men from
Mathews who were stationed with the Navy in the Pacific. They included
Bill Callis's big brother, Homer Verdayne Callis Jr., who was a quartermaster on the destroyer USS *Hazelwood*. Luckily, the *Hazelwood* had not been
at Pearl Harbor.

Hitler did not need to rush into war with America after Pearl Harbor,
but he did anyway, declaring war against the United States on December
11. He lifted all restrictions on U-boats' attacking American merchant
ships. Given what had happened at the end of World War I, it seemed certain that U-boats would return to the U.S. coast. The Navy asked citizens
living along the ocean and the Bay to help watch for them.

No one answered the Navy's call with more dedication than twelve-
year-old John Dixon of Gwynn's Island. John's big brother, Boyd, was
aboard a merchant ship. John did not know him well because Boyd was
mostly at sea. But John wanted to help. Some of his buddies had brothers
or fathers at sea. The boys established an observation post at Cherry Point,
on the northern tip of Gwynn's Island. Every day after school they hurried
to take up the watch. They leaped to their feet, breathless, at every passing
chunk of driftwood or trick of the light on the water. They stayed until it
was too dark to see, and came back the next day. They were inspired and
terrified. Nothing stirred their seafarers' blood like the specter of a U-boat,
the embodiment of stealthy death.

CHAPTER TWO

The Devil's Shovel

The first wave of U-boats crossing the Atlantic to America in January 1942 collided with a winter hurricane. Thirty-foot seas struck the steel hulls with audible clangs and swept over the U-boats' exposed conning towers. Men standing lookout on the towers ducked and held on for their lives, tethered to the rail by safety harnesses, their dirty hair and beards rimed with freezing salt water.

Breaking waves "swept away the few things they could seize on," wrote Peter Cremer, the commander of the U-333, which started out with the five U-boats that made up the attack force against the United States, but later split from them. Cremer's submarine "climbed the waves, broke through the crests, hung for a moment with its stern in the air, and plunged down the other side into the trough of the wave. When it buried its nose, the screws (propellers) in its stern seemed to be revolving in the air. The stern dropped down, the screws disappeared into the maelstrom and the exhaust broke off with a gurgle." The lookouts caught only glimpses of the horizon between buckshot bursts of spray.

Diving was an option, of course, but traveling submerged would reduce a U-boat's maximum speed from 17 knots to a plodding 7—from

18.5 mph to 8 mph—and prolong the voyage from two weeks to three or longer. The distances from the U-boats' bases on the coast of occupied France were 3,000 miles to New York and 3,500 miles to the mouth of the Chesapeake Bay.

So the U-boats stayed on the surface and absorbed the pounding until a freak wave engulfed one of the conning towers and wrenched loose an antiaircraft gun from its mounting. The gun spun into one of the lookouts and seriously injured him.* Reluctantly, Cremer and the other U-boat commanders gave the orders to submerge, and the submarines crawled underwater toward the United States, at a rate of about 25 to 30 miles per day.

Weather was the least of the challenges in the U-boats' first mission to America. So far from home, they had nowhere to turn for additional fuel or food, and could expect no help with medical or mechanical emergencies. Even the long-range, Type IXC U-boats carried only enough fuel to operate in U.S. waters for about two weeks between their long transatlantic voyages. Each sub could carry only fourteen to eighteen torpedoes, and circumstances often required a U-boat to fire several torpedoes in a fan-shaped pattern to be sure of sinking a single ship. Some of the torpedoes were virtually guaranteed to malfunction, either veering off course, exploding prematurely, or failing to detonate at all.

The commanders had no idea what antisubmarine defenses awaited them in American waters. They did not even possess detailed maps that showed the topography of the American coastline or the depths of the waters in which they would need to hide. The commander of the U-123, Reinhard Hardegan, carried a tourist guide to the 1939 World's Fair in New York, with a map of the New York coastline on one side and an image of the Statue of Liberty on the other.

---

* Standing lookout on a U-boat in rough seas was dangerous work. More than a dozen lookouts were swept overboard in storms during the war, including an entire four-man watch. But whenever a U-boat was on the surface, its commander had no choice but to post lookouts to watch for enemy planes and ships.

The whole mission to America was so fraught with risks and unknowns that it made sense only if the potential rewards were enormous. Admiral Karl Doenitz, the head of the German U-boat command, believed they were, and Doenitz usually got such calculations right.

At age fifty, Doenitz was a master of twentieth-century submarine warfare. He had served twenty-nine years in the German Navy, including time in the U-boat service during World War I. He had been commanding a U-boat in 1917 when its diving system malfunctioned. "[We] suddenly found ourselves submerged and standing on our heads," he recalled. "The batteries spilled over, the lights went out, and in darkness we plunged on into the depths." Doenitz ordered the water blown out of the ballast tanks, and the sub rocketed to the surface, where it bobbed helplessly in the middle of an Allied convoy. Doenitz was sent to a British prison camp, where he feigned insanity—"playing childish games with biscuit tins and little china dogs that could be bought in the canteen"—until he was transferred to an asylum, where he enjoyed softer treatment than his less devious boatmates.

At the beginning of World War I, U-boats such as the one commanded by Doenitz had come close to severing Britain's supply lines. The British had managed to neutralize the U-boats with convoys, a tactic dating back to Julius Caesar's time, in which groups of merchant ships sailed together under the protection of armed escorts.* At the end of the Great War, Winston Churchill had declared, "The submarine has been mastered," a boast he would regret making.

The Treaty of Versailles, which ended World War I, required Germany to abandon its U-boat program. More than 150 U-boats that survived the

---

* The U-boats' effectiveness in the early stages of World War I captured the public's attention. Sir Arthur Conan Doyle, the British creator of Sherlock Holmes, wrote a short story in which a small nation used submarines to starve Britain into defeat. The American humorist Will Rogers joked that the best way to hunt down the U-boats was to drain the Atlantic Ocean. "How?" he continued. "That is a detail. I am not a detail man."

Great War were destroyed, dismantled, or towed to Allied nations to be displayed like trophies at victory rallies. But Germany, bitter over the terms of the treaty, had no intention of abandoning submarine warfare and soon set out to rearm itself for the next war. In the 1920s, the German government secretly bought a Dutch company that designed and built submarines for other nations. In violation of the treaty, Germany operated the company as a cover to develop faster and more powerful U-boats. That new generation of U-boats would lead the assault across the Atlantic.

Doenitz was slender and pale, with birdlike features, but he projected authority with a rigid bearing and an incisive mind. Later, prosecutors at the Nuremberg trials said he had an IQ of 138, just short of "genius or near genius." Doenitz was given the task of running the U-boat force. He used his personal experience to teach his commanders how to take advantage of light and sea state to approach ships unseen, and how to outwait and outsmart pursuers. He cultivated personal relationships with his men in order to motivate them. He recruited pretty nurses to welcome them home at the docks with garlands of flowers, and treated them to dinners of lobster and champagne. When a child was born to a U-boat man at sea, Doenitz personally radioed the news to the new father in a code that referred to a newborn boy as an "arrival with a periscope" and a girl as "an arrival with no periscope." Doenitz promoted the U-boat force to the German public as the nation's elite warriors. One of his U-boat aces, Gunther Prien, enjoyed such rock-star status in Germany that after his submarine was lost, Germans for years reported sightings of Prien, the way Americans years later would report sightings of the long-departed Elvis Presley.

On a tactical level, Doenitz was a master improviser. He constantly shifted his subs and his tactics to capitalize on his U-boats' lethal capabilities and hide their glaring weaknesses.

U-boats were not submarines in the modern sense. They were not equipped to remain underwater for long periods without surfacing. Rather, they were diving vessels. They functioned far better on the surface, but could submerge for short periods to get into position to attack, elude pursuers, or escape rough weather. On the surface, they could outrun most merchant ships and some warships, but not destroyers and certainly not planes. When submerged, they were slow and nearly blind, but they could strike without warning and then withdraw without ever showing themselves, leaving their victims unsure whether they had been attacked or had struck a mine.

A U-boat was a cigar-shaped cylinder of high-tensile steel plates welded together. It had a raked bow, inclined at an angle to the water line and blunted at the tip. The standard Type VII C U-boat, the workhorse of the German submarine fleet, was 220 feet long and highly agile and maneuverable. The larger, long-range Type IXC was 250 feet long and more sluggish, but also more stable in heavy seas and capable of carrying more fuel and torpedoes. Doenitz much preferred the smaller subs.

U-boat hulls were designed to withstand depths of 500 feet, where the water pressure was roughly 16 tons per square foot, but U-boats dove deeper when desperate to avoid attack. On at least one occasion, a U-boat survived a dive to 850 feet. The U-boat hull's structural integrity was compromised by the hatches, air intakes, and exhaust vents necessary to sustain life inside. When a U-boat went deep, the water pressure on those weak points sent eerie creaks and groans echoing through the boat.

When on the surface, a U-boat ran on two thundering, 1,160-horsepower diesel engines located near the stern. The diesels gulped air from outside through an induction pipe high on the conning tower, and drew fuel from saddle tanks outside the hull. When the U-boat submerged, the diesels were shut down and the sub switched over to a pair of battery-powered 375-horsepower motor/generators. The batteries ran out of juice quickly when the sub had to maneuver or run at full speed underwater. Every day, the submarine had to surface and crank up its diesels to recharge the batteries. A full charge took more than two hours. No daily activity was more vital than charging the batteries, without which the sub could not keep its crew alive while submerged.

A typical U-boat commander spent his days in the *Zentrale*, or control room, just forward of the engine room. He peered up at the surface world through angled mirrors in the U-boat's two periscopes, which were mounted on a long metal shaft. He sat in a harness straddling the base of the shaft, and could spin the periscopes 360 degrees. He navigated while looking through the larger periscope but attacked while looking through the smaller one, which left almost no telltale wake on the surface. If a commander felt safe in a stretch of ocean, he might order the sub to surface so that he could look around and enjoy the sweet taste of fresh air.

When the U-boat was surfaced, as many as six lookouts peered through high-powered Zeiss binoculars at their assigned quadrants of the sky and sea. Men with the keenest eyesight were chosen to stand watch at dusk and dawn, when the light played tricks. Every seagull looked like a plane at first glance. A moment's delay in spotting an approaching ship or plane could doom them all. A crash dive, or emergency dive, took twenty-five to thirty seconds. U-boats crash-dived at any hint of trouble. The U-boat commander's manual advocated erring on the side of caution: "It is better to dive too soon, than too late—and [thus] to lose forever the chance to dive."

The U-boat's signature weapon was the torpedo, which resembled a miniature U-boat. Torpedoes were 23.5 feet long and 21 inches in diameter, with fins and a propeller at the tail. They were launched from horizontal tubes with blasts of compressed air, and traveled at speeds of 45 to 50 miles per hour. Torpedoes were named for the electric ray fish, genus *Torpedo*, which delivers a paralyzing shock to its prey, but U-boat crews called them "eels." Commanders were taught to fire them from a distance of 600 yards, calculating the target's speed and bearing and firing at a point in front of it, as a duck hunter fires ahead of a duck in flight. The first torpedoes were designed to explode on contact with a target, but they sometimes failed to detonate unless they hit straight on. The Germans developed magnetic torpedoes that exploded when they entered the magnetic field surrounding a ship's hull, sending shock waves through the water to "break the ship's back." Magnetic torpedoes proved unreliable, too, however, and the British learned to counter them by wrapping electrical cables around ships' hulls to neutralize their magnetic fields, a process known as degaussing.

Toward the end of the war, the Germans would introduce acoustic torpedoes, which homed in on the sound of a ship's propellers. The British would counter them with noisemakers called Foxers, which generated more noise than the propellers and could be towed behind ships to draw acoustic torpedoes harmlessly astern. The continual chess game in which the Germans developed new kinds of torpedoes and the British found ways to neutralize them typified the technological side of the U-boat war. Each engineering breakthrough gave one side an edge for only as long as it took the other side to counter it. "Strange how little time one side or the other can hold the upper hand thanks to a new weapon," observed the fictitious U-boat commander in Lothar-Günther Buchheim's classic World War II novel, *Das Boot*. "Nothing stimulates the brain cells like a desire to wipe out the other side."

As deadly as torpedoes were, they were undependable and hard to aim. The most successful U-boat of the war, U-48, launched 126 torpedoes and scored only 55 hits. U-boat commanders tried to conserve torpedoes by sinking merchant ships whenever possible with their deck cannons, fearsome-looking 88mm guns mounted on the sub's main deck, forward of the conning tower. The deck cannons could be used only when the U-boat was on the surface and the sea was calm enough for gun crews to venture out onto the narrow deck to man them and aim them. Each U-boat was also armed with an antiaircraft gun on the conning tower, two hand-held machine guns, and various small arms.

U-boats were equipped with defenses designed to thwart antisubmarine weapons, the most formidable of which was the Allies' sonar. Sonar (an acronym for SOund Navigation And Ranging) beamed sound waves through the water that bounced off any solid surfaces and sent back echoes. The speed of an echo's return revealed an object's distance from the ship, and the angle of its return revealed the object's bearing, or direction. Significantly, sonar could not determine an object's depth. All kinds of submerged objects besides U-boats returned sonar echoes, including schools of fish and thermal layers between warm and cold water. An experienced sonar operator could tell the echoes apart.

U-boats were equipped with passive sonar. It did not broadcast a sonar pulse—which could be traced back to the sub—but it gave warning when the U-boat was being detected by another vessel's sonar. The warning came in the form of a metallic "ping" that tolled ominously through the U-boat like a phone call in the depths of the night. If the ping was loud, the hunter was close to its prey, and the next sound in the ears of the U-boat's sonar operator might be the churning of a destroyer's propellers and the splash of depth charges into the ocean overhead.

Depth charges, invented by the British in World War I, haunted submariners' dreams. They were metal canisters about 18 inches in diameter and twice as long. Each contained about 300 to 500 pounds of explosives and could be set to blow up at a specific depth, such as 50, 100, 150, or even 500 feet. Sailors on destroyers called them ash cans. They could be rolled off racks on the stern or fired to either side. Destroyers dropped them in patterns to bracket a sonar target. The cans sank in silence at a rate of 8 to 12 feet per second until they reached their preset depth and then detonated, hurling plumes of water into the air and shock waves through the water. A depth charge exploding within 25 feet of a U-boat would cripple it, and a blast within 14 feet would crack its hull and send it to the bottom, usually with all hands.

Sonar's inability to detect an object's depth posed problems for U-boat hunters. They could only guess at how deep to set their depth charges to explode. In addition, a ship could not drop depth charges while performing delicate maneuvers; it had to drop them while racing full speed, in order to get beyond the range of the explosions. Depth-charge blasts also jumbled the water and "blinded" the sonar long enough to give the U-boat a chance to escape. A U-boat might also throw off its pursuers by activating its *Pillenwurfer*, or "bubble-thrower," which released a jet of sodium hydride that reacted with seawater to create a large chemical bubble with a sonar signature similar to a U-boat's.

If the U-boat did not escape, the pinging would start again. The cat-and-mouse game could last for hours. The air inside the pressurized hull would grow progressively thinner. Every underwater maneuver would further deplete the U-boat's batteries, which could only be recharged on the surface. Former U-boat commander Herbert A. Werner described one such experience:

> A series of 24 [depth] charges detonated in quick succession. The bellowing roar slammed against our boat. The explosions again pushed her into a sharp down tilt while the echo of the detonations rolled endlessly through the depths . . . A new spread [of depth charges] deafened us and took our breath away. The boat listed sharply . . . The steel knocked and shrieked and valves were thrown into the open position. The shaft packings leaked, and a constant stream of water soon filled the aft bilges. Pumps spouted, the periscope packings leaked, and water trickled into the cylinders, water everywhere. Its weight forced the boat deeper into the depths. In the meantime the convoy crawled in a thunderous procession over our boat.

The strain was too great for some submariners, who became hysterical during depth-charge attacks. Their boat-mates said they suffered from *Blechkiller*, or tin-can neurosis—a condition similar to the breakdowns that men on the waters above them suffered while sailing under the constant threat of a torpedo attack.

The Allies' sonar could not detect U-boats on the surface, but radar could. Radar, or RAdio Detecting And Ranging, operates on the same principle as sonar, beaming radio waves through the air—rather than the water—in search of solid objects. Radar could see through darkness and storms and spot a U-boat on the surface from a distance of seven miles. The Germans did not realize how effective radar was until after numerous U-boats had been ambushed by planes and ships.

American submarines were superior to U-boats in the critical capability of detecting and jamming enemy radar, and in other ways as well. The *Gato*-class American subs, which did most of the fighting in World War II, were faster and larger than U-boats and could carry more fuel and torpedoes. U.S. subs were also vastly more comfortable, with roomier living quarters and even air-conditioning. U-boats, on the other hand, were more nimble, especially when under attack. They could crash-dive faster, dive deeper, and run more quietly while submerged. They required fewer crewmen—fifty-five rather than the American subs' seventy to eighty-five. And the Germans' torpedoes, for all their persistent problems, were more reliable than American torpedoes.

U-boat crews had orders to prevent their vessels from being captured at all costs. If a U-boat was forced to the surface, the crew was trained to rig it with explosive charges and open valves to flood it. Then they were to fight off the enemy with small arms until the U-boat plunged into the depths, out of the reach of enemy salvage divers. Every measure designed to prevent the U-boat's capture also reduced the U-boat's crew's chances of surviving.

The crew comprised approximately fifty officers and men. Most of them had come up through the ranks of Nazi youth programs, which since the early 1920s had provided young Germans with physical training and psychological indoctrination. An angry Germany had been preparing for World War II while its victorious foes licked their wounds from World War I. But Germany's navy lagged behind its army and air force, which attracted most of Hitler's attention as well as German money and resources. Doenitz had hoped to start World War II with three hundred active U-boats, but ended up with only forty-four. As he slowly added U-boats to his fleet, he made the most of the relative few he had. Doenitz tried to confuse the Allies by giving U-boats numbers much larger than the number of U-boats he had. The U-506 and U-507, for example, would be operating in American waters long before Doenitz had five hundred U-boats.

The men of the German U-boat force ranged from hard-core believers in the Nazi philosophy to men who doubted Hitler's leadership but who resolved nonetheless to fight for their country. "Very few U-boat captains cared about all those dogmas of the Third Reich," U-boat commander Hans Georg Hess asserted. Another U-boat commander disparaged the Nazi leadership to his crew while at sea, only to be denounced by a subordinate upon his return, and then convicted of treason and executed by a firing squad.

The narrow confines of a U-boat offered no room for privacy, reflection, or even hygiene. Men slept in shifts, tuning out the pounding of the diesel engines and the hiss of the sea sliding past the hull. They never saw the sky or breathed fresh air except on lookout duty. They did not bathe or shave because freshwater was too precious; each man was allotted just enough of it to brush his teeth once a day. Crewmen wore black underwear to hide their filth, and used scented soap to mask their stink. A week or so into the voyage, the heat and humidity inside the hull broke down the fresh food. Fluffy white mold engulfed loaves of bread, and mildew coated sausages and fruit. The cook would scrape off the unwelcome layers and serve the food until no one could bear it. The air inside the hull was a miasma of spoiling food, unwashed bodies, diesel fumes, and overburdened toilets.

U-boat toilets were particularly despised. They did not work when the sub ran deep because the outside water pressure kept them from flushing. They could not be used when the sub was under attack, because the enemy might hear them flush. When the toilets did work, they demanded a precise operating sequence. The waste had to be transferred from the bowl to an intermediate chamber, then to an outer chamber, and then into the sea. Any deviation from that sequence could back up the toilet into the sub in a foul gush of waste and seawater. If the seawater reached the U-boat's batteries, it could react with battery acid to form poisonous chlorine gas.

At least one U-boat was sunk by just such a toilet malfunction. Forced to the surface to ventilate the poisonous chlorine, it was bombed by a British plane.

Few of the U-boat's operational systems tolerated error. If the engine crew failed to shut off the diesels before closing the main hatch in a dive, the exhaust system would suck all the oxygen from the hull. A malfunctioning fan could allow hydrogen to build up to explosive levels in the hull. Maintaining the U-boat's trim—the horizontal balance between its bow and stern—required constant readjustments for even small shifts in weight, such as a torpedo launch. The U-boat's operating systems were so interconnected that a mistake by anyone could kill everyone. Doenitz liked to call a U-boat crew a *Schickselgemeinschaft*—a community bound by fate. U-boat crews had a variety of descriptive names for their vessel, but the most unflattering—and also the most sinister—was "the devil's shovel."*

The main battleground in the Battle of the Atlantic was the North Atlantic convoy routes, a 2,400-mile wilderness of frigid, stormy ocean between Maritime Canada and the British Isles, where the water depth was measured not in feet but in miles. Mariners tried to avoid those waters even in peacetime. The North Atlantic run was known for gales that lasted for entire voyages, mountainous waves, shrieking winds, cold, snow, and ice. U-boats could attack at any point during the voyage, but the most dangerous segment was the "air gap," a 600-mile stretch of sea south of Greenland that was too far from either shore for Allied planes to reach. U-boats could operate freely in the air gap without fear of attack from above.

The convoys, organized by the British Admiralty and the Royal Cana-

---

* An American seaman from Texas named Archie Gibbs got a close look at life aboard a U-boat when he was taken prisoner aboard one for four days after his ship was torpedoed in the summer of 1942. Gibbs said the Germans acted like men who "knew they had a dirty job to do and wanted to get it over with and go home."

dian Navy, departed every eight days from either Halifax in Nova Scotia or Argentia in Newfoundland. A large convoy contained as many as sixty merchant ships loaded with food, arms, fuel, and supplies for Britain. The night before departure, the commodore in charge of the convoy, usually a retired British naval officer, called all the merchant captains and radio operators to a meeting on shore. He explained the convoy's structure, planned course, and precautions for avoiding U-boats. Those precautions always included a total blackout of the ships, as well as periodic zigzagging or changes of course to avoid torpedoes.

The next morning, the ships left the safety of the harbor and took their assigned positions in the convoy, which formed into a rectangle perhaps 6 miles wide and 2 miles deep. Convoys were designed to be much more wide than deep, with as few ships as possible following in a row, because a ship presented its biggest target from the side, and a long line of vessels presented a target few U-boats could miss. Inside the convoy, ships were to maintain distances of 600 feet from the vessels in front of and behind them, and distances of 1,000 yards between ships in the adjacent columns. Freighters full of ammunition and tankers full of oil or gasoline were assigned to the convoy's interior columns for added protection. Ships with less volatile cargo sailed closer to the edges. The exposed positions at the four corners of the convoy's rectangle were called the "coffin corners."

Once a convoy got under way, it was screened by a half dozen or more Allied destroyers, Coast Guard cutters, and smaller escort vessels such as corvettes, all of them equipped with sonar, depth charges, and deck guns. Each escort vessel guarded an assigned segment of the convoy's perimeter. Sometimes, larger Allied warships such as cruisers and even battleships formed an outer ring of protection against German surface warships and planes.

A convoy's best defense, however, was the vastness of the ocean. Even the largest convoys were just dots on the North Atlantic. The U-boats first had to find them, and then find a way past the escorts. Doenitz's answer was the *Rudeltaktik*, or wolf pack strategy. A wolf pack, consisting of eight to fifteen U-boats, spread out like a net across the North Atlantic convoy routes, with gaps of twenty miles between subs. Each U-boat stayed on the surface, weather permitting, watching for the telltale smoke or masts of an approaching convoy. When a U-boat found a convoy, the commander radioed its location to Doenitz, who directed a wolf pack to converge on it. The pack waited until dark and then struck as a unit to confuse and overwhelm the escorts. U-boats often attacked on the surface, darting through gaps in the escort screen into the heart of the convoy and rapid-firing torpedoes in all directions to hit as many ships as fast as possible. A wolf pack could strike a convoy repeatedly over the course of a single night, and then attack every night afterward until the convoy reached port. One wolf pack tore into two convoys heading in opposite directions through a remote stretch of ocean and sank a total of thirty-two ships.

Merchant seamen could only go about their duties and pray they would not be the next target. If their ship went down and they ended up in the water, the other ships in the convoy would not stop for them. Their only hope was that the single rescue vessel assigned to the convoy could reach them in the few minutes they could expect to stay alive in the icy water.

Behind the scenes, the Battle of the Atlantic turned back and forth on clandestine electronic surveillance and code breaking. Almost since the start of the war, the British had been able to pinpoint the locations of U-boats at sea by intercepting their daily radio transmissions. Doenitz required each U-boat to check in with headquarters every day by radio. Those radio transmissions were picked up by a British network of direction-finding stations scattered all along the Atlantic coast. Once two stations picked up the same U-boat's transmission, they could use the cross-bearings to pinpoint the sub's location. The British used the information to route convoys away from U-boats. Doenitz did not think the radio transmissions posed any risk unless the Allies broke the German Enigma code and could read the coded messages—something he thought could never happen. He and the rest of the German high command considered Enigma unbreakable.

The code relied on Enigma machines, which resembled complicated typewriters, to encrypt messages in a way that only other Enigma machines, set identically, could decrypt. The German Navy used an extra layer of encryption in its variation of the Enigma code, which made the naval Enigma code even more difficult to break. Each U-boat carried an Enigma machine, and Doenitz confidently sent all his orders to his U-boats through Enigma. British cryptologists broke the code in early 1941 after a captured U-boat yielded up an Enigma machine and codebook. By May, the British could read the Germans' most secret communications. That capability was so precious that the British used it sparingly to avoid giving the Germans any reason to suspect the code had been compromised. Unfortunately for the Allies, the Germans would soon seize the advantage in the code-breaking war.

Germany's conquest of France in 1940 had extended the U-boats' reach. Until France fell, U-boats had operated out of bases in Germany and occupied Norway. They had had to dodge British patrols in the North Sea just to reach the ocean. The coast of France, however, offered U-boats direct access to the North Atlantic. The Germans built U-boat bases in French fishing villages along the Bay of Biscay, including Lorient and Saint-Nazaire. The German construction firm, the Todt Organisation—the builder of the Autobahn— built three-foot-thick, steel-reinforced concrete bunkers to protect the U-boats from Allied bombs. Doenitz appropriated the waterfront estate of a sardine tycoon in Lorient and set up an operations center nearby. The walls of the center were papered with maps pinpointing the locations of all U-boats and all known or suspected convoys, as well as weather reports, tide charts, and up-to-date statistical breakdowns of U-boat kills and, especially, tonnage.

A ship's tonnage is the volume, in cubic meters, of all its enclosed spaces—its cargo capacity. Tonnage was the best measurement of a merchant ship's size and value. Doenitz called the U-boat campaign a tonnage war, or *Tonnageschlacht*. He maintained that if U-boats could sink 700,000 tons of Allied shipping per month, Germany would win the Battle of the Atlantic.

The U-boats had yet to hit Doenitz's target, but between 1939 and 1941, they had sunk more than 1,100 Allied merchant ships and killed 9,200 men. They had also sunk several British warships, including a battleship. The U-boat force had lost 50 submarines and about 2,200 men. It had come close several times to choking off Britain's lifeline.

The fall of France also set the U-boats on a collision course with the United States. Throughout the first two years of the war, most Americans had favored leaving the fight to the Europeans. Memories of American dough-boys dying by the thousands in World War I were still vivid, and all those deaths had purchased only twenty years of peace for Europe. Roosevelt had won a third term as president in 1940 by promising to keep America out of the war. But the newsreel images of German armored divisions rumbling down Paris's fair boulevards and Hitler posing in front of the Eiffel Tower raised questions about how much of the world the Führer might actually be able to conquer.

The isolationist spirit in America faded with the fall of France. Congress quickly supported Roosevelt's proposals for billions of dollars' worth of new warships and cargo ships. In March 1941, Roosevelt signed the Lend-Lease Act, which committed the United States to lending Britain and China millions of tons of supplies and weaponry—"all possible aid short of war." Roosevelt downplayed the significance of the Lend-Lease Act with the famous analogy that America was simply lending a garden hose to a neighbor whose house was on fire. He never really imagined America would get the fire hose back.

In August 1941, Roosevelt met with Churchill in Newfoundland and agreed that in case of war with Germany and Japan, they would focus on beating Germany first. Roosevelt and Churchill also signed the Atlantic Charter, agreeing to defend "freedom of the seas"—a euphemism for

America's freedom to haul war supplies across the ocean without attacks by U-boats. The following month, the U.S. Navy assumed responsibility for escorting North Atlantic convoys halfway across the ocean to a point south of Iceland—the so-called mid-ocean meeting point—where British warships met the convoys and escorted them the rest of the way to the British Isles. The U.S. Navy's expanded role led to increasingly deadly encounters between U-boats and "neutral" U.S. warships on the North Atlantic convoy routes.

Hitler had ordered his U-boats not to attack American warships and cargo ships despite the obvious aid they were providing Britain. Hitler was in no hurry to add America to his growing list of enemies so soon after invading his old ally Russia in June. But events overtook his uncharacteristic caution.

In the first week of September 1941, the World War I–vintage American destroyer *Greer* encountered a submerged U-boat en route to Iceland and tracked it with sonar. The U-boat commander, thinking he was under attack, fired two torpedoes at the *Greer* but missed. The *Greer* responded with a barrage of depth charges. The U-boat sustained minor damage but escaped.

In October, a U-boat mistook the U.S. destroyer *Kearney* for a British warship in the confusion of a nighttime wolf pack attack on a convoy south of Iceland, and torpedoed the *Kearney*, killing eleven American sailors and injuring twenty-four—the first American military casualties of the Atlantic war. The damaged *Kearney* limped into port in Iceland. Over the course of the next two weeks, the Germans sank two American merchant ships and damaged the U.S. Navy oiler *Salinas*—all with no loss of life.

But the crew of the old U.S. destroyer *Reuben James* would not be so fortunate. On October 31, the *Reuben James* was escorting a convoy near the mid-ocean meeting point when a torpedo from the U-552 smashed into its hull. The blast ignited the destroyer's magazine and blew the ship apart. Of the *Reuben James*'s 159 crew members, 115 were killed, some of them by the destroyer's depth charges, which exploded in the water beneath them as the *Reuben James* plunged into the depths. "Whether the country knows it or not, we are at war," the U.S. chief of naval operations, Admiral Harold R. Stark, told a fellow admiral.

Folksinger Woody Guthrie wrote a ballad titled "The Sinking of the *Reuben James*," with the chorus:

> *Tell me what were their names*
> *Tell me what were their names*
> *Did you have a friend*
> *On the good* Reuben James?

Five weeks later, the Japanese attacked Pearl Harbor. Hitler was as surprised as the Americans, but he seized his chance. Within four days, Germany and America were at war. The two nations' armies would not meet on the battlefield for almost a year—after the Allied invasion of North Africa—but the U-boats could carry the fight to America immediately.

Doenitz proposed sending fifteen of his ninety-one operational U-boats immediately into U.S. waters. But his superiors had other ideas. Hitler insisted on dispatching a large force of U-boats to Norway, wrongly expecting a British invasion there. Doenitz's immediate boss, Grand Admiral Erich Raeder, the head of the German Navy, ordered twenty-five U-boats into the eastern Mediterranean to support Germany's Afrika Corps against the British in North Africa. Still more U-boats were assigned to operate as weather spotters for German bombing raids on Britain. Doenitz privately stewed. His U-boats were wasted on such support missions. They were purely ship-sinking machines, and they were at their best against weak and inexperienced defenses, as America's were certain to be. But after satisfying all his superiors' demands, Doenitz was left with only six U-boats to send to the United States, and one of those broke down at the last minute.

Still, Doenitz believed that five U-boats could cause enough havoc to shock America and persuade Hitler to send more. He felt so confident that he code-named the mission to America *Paukenschlag*, which translated to a "roll of the kettledrums"—melodrama in the extreme.

During Christmas week, 1941, Doenitz called the five U-boat commanders he had chosen for *Paukenschlag* into his office for one-on-one conferences. The commanders were not his aces; two of the five had never led U-boats into combat. He assigned each commander a patrol area between New England and Cape Hatteras, North Carolina. Commander Hardegan took the U-123 out before Christmas and celebrated the holiday at sea. He wrote in his war diary:

> U-boat Christmas in the Bay of Biscay. Trees were placed in all compartments, decorated by the crew and provided with electric candles. Later the real trees were in some cases replaced by artificial trees. After a collective ceremony and subsequent meal, the letters, packets and goody bags were distributed. It was celebrated in the individual compartments and one could hear the old Christmas songs performed by the crew. The war was forgotten for a few hours by this simple but impressive Christmas festival.

Yuletide sentiments notwithstanding, Doenitz told the commanders to get into position off the U.S. coast and wait for his signal. He wanted all five to strike in unison at different points along the coast for maximum effect. The Americans would think their waters teemed with U-boats. Just after midnight on January 1, 1942, Doenitz broadcast a coded message to his crews: "Men of the U-boat Service: In the year anew we want to be like steel, harder, fiercer, stronger. Long live the Führer."

The winter hurricane that struck the first wave of U-boats en route to America kept them submerged for two days. The weather finally abated on January 10, and the subs resurfaced and resumed their voyage at top speed. The British direction-finding stations pinpointed their locations from their radio transmissions and decoded enough of their messages to determine where the subs were going. The British warned the U.S. Navy that five U-boats would be in American waters by January 13.

That was, in fact, the day Doenitz had chosen for the coordinated attack. The day before, however, Hardegan in the U-123 spotted the British freighter *Cyclops* steaming unprotected off Cape Cod, and could not resist torpedoing her. The *Cyclops* carried a crew of 30 and 151 British merchant mariners riding as passengers to meet their new ships. Ninety-eight of those men died, most from exposure in lifeboats on the wintry sea. Their shipmates survived by stacking the corpses of the dead to shield their own bodies from icy rain and spray.

Hardegan sank his second ship on the morning of January 14, torpedoing a Panamanian oil tanker 60 miles off Montauk Point on Long Island, New York. "I think the Americans are going to be very surprised to see us," he told his crew. The U-123 intercepted the tanker's radio distress call. The radioman said the ship was sinking after being struck by a torpedo or possibly a mine. "They're saying a mine?" Hardegan cried. "What assholes."

In the predawn hours of the following morning, the U-123 reached the shallow waters off Long Island. Hardegan, who had visited New York before the war, recognized the Ferris wheel at the Coney Island amusement park and the glow of New York City against the low clouds farther west. The U-123 cruised along the surface among fishing boats and harbor tugs, whose crews did not recognize the enemy in their midst. Every vessel in the harbor was burning its lights as if America were still at peace. Merchant captains talked freely over the radio about their ships' locations and the routes they planned to follow. Hardegan shook his head at their cluelessness.

He was about to bring the U-boat war home to Mathews County.

CHAPTER THREE

Missing

Henny Hodges was "a crier," all her children agreed. Four or five times a day, while she was cooking or working the family farm, her green eyes would glisten behind her Coke-bottle glasses and tears would slide down her cheeks. She cried softly, but eventually her broad shoulders shook and gave her away. "Mama, what's the matter?" the children would ask. Henny would cite a recent trivial event, such as an argument among her daughters, who argued all the time. But just as often, she cried without any provocation, and deflected questions with a shake of her head. Then she threw herself back into her chores until the feeling passed. Her children regarded her crying as just part of her makeup, like her big bones and her coarse brown hair. What the tears did not mean was that Henny Hodges was soft.

On the contrary, she worked harder than anyone they had ever seen. She had reared fourteen children and several of her twenty-seven grand-children with little help from her husband, Captain Jesse, who rarely came home from the sea. She ran the family's sixty-acre farm, which included forty acres of crops, a barn full of horses and cows, a hog pen and smoke-house, a chicken house, and two docks. Henny maintained the Hodges home, a two-story, white clapboard farmhouse that rose like a citadel from a marshy bank on the East River. The house offered a panoramic view of the river and its tributary creeks, but few other amenities. It had no electricity, running water, or indoor plumbing. Every drop of water for cooking, washing, and bathing had to be pumped from a well fifty feet from the house and lugged inside. The family outhouse had three seats angled for a pretty view of the river, but it was always wise to rattle a broom handle before entering, to dislodge the spiders. None of the Gales Neck inconveniences seemed to faze Henny, who had grown up just across the river in a log cabin with dirt floors.

Henny got up at three o'clock every morning, tied on an apron and a floppy, wide-brimmed bonnet, and rekindled the fire in the woodstove to start breakfast. Then for the next seventeen hours, she worked. Henny grew or raised all the food the extended family needed—corn, butter beans, collard greens, turnips, cucumbers, peppers, and tomatoes, as well as hogs, chickens, and cows for meat. The only items she ever bought at the store were salt, pepper, and coffee. Their self-sufficiency had insulated the Hodges, like a lot of Mathews families, against the Great Depression. The Depression's impact was muffled throughout the county, where most families already grew their own food and made do with little work that brought in wages. "People who grew up in Mathews during the Depression thought they were poor because of the Depression, but Mathews was poor before and afterward," said Roland Foster III, whose father went to sea.

Between Henny's cooking, child rearing, and toiling on the farm, she found time to carry on running quarrels with the U.S. Department of Agriculture over milk prices and limits on the amount of wheat she could grow. Jesse Carroll Thornton, who lived with her when he was a child, thought she was superhuman: "I really believed that if I had accidentally cut my arm off, she could have fixed it." Henny was the only person in the family—maybe the only person, period—who did not hesitate to buck Captain Jesse, even when he was in a nasty mood. Nothing in her makeup explained her tears.

But Henny's family sometimes wondered if her tears brimmed out of a reservoir of sadness too deep inside her for them to see. She had seen three of her children die in horrific ways. One stifling-hot summer day, her two oldest sons had raced into the house parched from working in the yard and snatched up containers of a white liquid they assumed was milk. It was toxic lye, which Henny used to make soap. The older boy, Raymond, recognized his mistake just in time and spat out the poison. But four-year-old Seth Hodges drank his down and died in agony while Henny watched helplessly. Captain Jesse was at sea, so Henny washed and dressed her son's body while her father-in-law fashioned a little casket from lumber he had brought from Savannah, Georgia, for building boats. Henny sewed a cloth lining for the casket. Six years later, the Hodges's one-year-old son, John, died, very likely of tuberculosis but possibly from fatal burns after falling into the family's fireplace. Jesse and Henny never spoke of him after his death. Fourteen years later, in 1918, their two-year-old daughter, Martha Henrietta, was killed when the car driven by her brother Leslie overturned while passing a truck on a sharp curve. Little Henrietta, who had been asleep on the seat, was thrown from the car and died two hours later at a hospital without ever regaining consciousness.

In addition to losing three children, Henny had lost a home. The family's previous house on Tick Neck, across the East River from Gales Neck, had burned to the ground in 1931. No one was in the house when the fire started in the chimney. Henny was outside hanging up clothes when she saw smoke pouring from an upstairs window. The family managed to salvage only a few pieces of furniture and a wooden shoe from a pair that one of the boys had brought back from a voyage to Holland.

Jesse and Henny immediately purchased the farm at the tip of Gales Neck. The land was not flat but a series of ridges and swales, like gentle waves on an ancient seabed. The East River once had been lined with wharves, shipyards, and seafood packinghouses, but by the 1940s the river was so silted in that only small boats could navigate its upper reaches. Some of Captain Jesse's neighbors wondered what had possessed him to settle his family in such an isolated place. "Maybe he saw himself becoming a gentleman farmer," said his grandson Horace Hodges. "The Hodges were always dreamers." But it was not the sort of question one asked Captain Jesse. And Henny seemed happy at Gales Neck.

Over the course of a decade, she had transformed Gales Neck into a working farm and the focal point of the family. The Hodges built a large kitchen onto the front of the house, lined with windows because Henny loved the sun. The aroma of fresh bread and biscuits hung perpetually in the air. The children loved the farm's secret places and idiosyncratic animals. The bad-tempered mule was terrified of storms and would scoot under the house into the crawl space at the sound of thunder. The Hodgeses' enormous sow crashed out of the hog pen every so often and, for reasons only she understood, led her piglets swimming across a creek to root in a neighbor's yard. The Hodges children would take a skiff to capture her, tie her front legs together, and tow her back across the creek, with the piglets again thrashing behind, while other family members cheered the flotilla from the dock. Henny's grandchildren often spent entire summers with her at Gales Neck.

Henny watched out for her friends and neighbors. She was tight with money, in the Hodges tradition, but gave freely of the family's time and possessions. When her sons were younger, Henny sent them around the neighborhood as a volunteer work team to help people at critical junctures in the year, such as hog-killing time, the onset of winter, and harvest season. She gave away clothes even if her family was still wearing them if she met someone who needed them more. She gave one son's only dress clothes to a poor black farm laborer to wear to the Mathews Farmers and Fishermen's Bank to apply for a loan to buy a home. Henny also accompanied him to the bank and vouched for him to make sure he got the loan.

It wasn't all work, all the time, though. Sometimes when Captain Jesse or one of the boys came home to Gales Neck from a voyage, Henny would order all the furniture moved out of the main downstairs room of the house and organize square dances. The man who drove the ice truck in

Mathews played the fiddle, accompanied by two of his cousins. Henny called the figures if no one else wanted to. Fishermen came in skiffs and clomped to the music in their work boots. Dancers competed to see who could stay on the floor the longest without collapsing. Across the creek, Edwin Jarvis's pious parents shook their heads at the unholy racket emanating from the Hodges place. Edwin only wished he could be there.

By the winter of 1942, however, Gales Neck was a lonely place. Chill northeast winds blew across the long fetch of the Bay. Captain Jesse was gone as usual on his tug, towing barges through the Caribbean. He had taken along his sixteen-year-old grandson J. W. Corbett as a member of his crew. Most of Jesse and Henny's sons had moved to port cities where their ships regularly docked. Raymond and Dewey commanded freighters. Willie was the captain of a seagoing tug. Leslie and Coleman were officers on Ford Motor Co. freighters, working their way up the hawsepipe. David worked in a Norfolk shipyard. All of them were exempt from being drafted into the Army because the nation needed capable mariners and shipyard workers more urgently than it needed a few more infantrymen. Spencer Hodges was the only brother to remain in Mathews, where he worked in a creamery. He had been forced ashore by a shipboard back injury, which also exempted him from the draft. All four of the Hodges daughters had married and moved, though they tended to move back in with Henny between marriages.

Henny's only constant companions at Gales Neck were her three-year-old grandson, Jesse Carroll Thornton, and Ammon Gwynn, a wiry black man with a frosting of gray in his hair. Ammon had worked for the family for years. He lived in a cabin several miles away and walked to the Hodges farm every day through the woods, checking his traplines for rabbits and other game. Ammon was a character. "He could curse the mule for a half hour and never use the same word twice," Jesse Carroll recalled. "He called the horse everything but a horse." But Ammon was kind to the Hodges children and respectful to Henny, with whom he worked side by side in the fields.

Twice a week, Ammon hitched the Hodgeses' horse and mule to a wagon and drove Henny to Main Street. She always took along a few clothes in case a telegram had arrived from Captain Jesse instructing her to meet him in a port somewhere. If no telegram awaited her, Henny settled into the rear booth at the Richardson's Drug Store lunch counter and held court for a couple hours. Friends from all over Mathews stopped to exchange the latest news and gossip with her.

Henny's trips to Main Street were her only regular contact with the world beyond Gales Neck. The farmhouse had no telephone or radio. Henny did not drive (or own) a car. The Hodges lived at the end of a mile-long dirt driveway that ran razor-straight through a dense forest and was riddled with deep ruts and potholes. Neighbors wondered whether the family simply neglected the driveway or kept it that way on purpose to discourage visitors. From the farmhouse at night, the headlights of a car bobbing up and down through the potholes resembled the lights of a ship pitching in heavy seas. Any news for Henny that was too urgent to wait for Saturday—any bad news—would come jouncing down the driveway.

Henny insisted she did not worry about Captain Jesse or her boys. The sea had been dangerous long before the U-boats. If a man's time was up, her worrying about him would not help him. "It's just the way of life that everybody dies," she told Jesse Carroll. "We're all going to die."

Once, when the boy had jumped off a dock and cut his knee on an oyster shell, Henny and her daughter Alice cleaned the wound and then caught a June bug and tied it to his finger with a piece of thread. He got so caught up watching the June bug trying to fly free that he forgot all about his knee. That was the Hodges way of dealing with pain: Turn your mind somewhere else.

Their detachment was about to be tested.

By late January 1942, the war had disrupted the rhythms of life in Mathews in ways that were impossible to ignore. The absence of so many young men at sea and in the military had left Mathews an enclave of women, old men, and children. Volunteers shivered around the clock in the Mathews fire tower and other observation posts, watching the skies for enemy planes. Each observer had a guide sheet showing the silhouette shapes of German warplanes. A Luftwaffe pilot would have to be very lost indeed to bomb Mathews, but a civil-defense film titled *Fighting the Fire Bomb* drew a large crowd at the high school. The annual Mathews daffodil show and formal ball were canceled "due to war conditions." Mathews held blackout drills, spreading the word by air-raid sirens and by church bells in hamlets too far from the sirens to hear them. The drills never went well because too many people in Mathews lived too far out to hear either the sirens or the church bells.

Life on the Bay had changed too. Lighthouse keepers could no longer broadcast weather reports to fishermen for fear the information would aid U-boats. The Navy said a U-boat had picked up a report of blue skies over Duluth, Minnesota, and used it to plan subsequent attacks in the shipping lanes. Commercial fishermen had to get special ID cards in order to take their boats offshore. But not all of them wanted to keep fishing, despite good catches. Many of the trawlers in the lower Bay stayed in port because they kept spotting U-boats in their fishing grounds.

Then, in the last week of January, the first Mathews mariner was killed by a U-boat. He simply vanished along with his ship.

Captain Ernest Jefferson Thompson was the forty-year-old son of a farmer from the Mathews hamlet of Hallieford, at the mouth of the Piankatank River across a bay from Gwynn's Island. At age fifteen, he had written a letter asking for a job from a neighbor who owned the sailing schooner *Clemmie Travers*—the same ship on which Captain Jesse had gone to sea at age ten. The shipowner told Thompson to meet the schooner in the Chesapeake Bay's main channel on her daily run to Baltimore. A friend sailed Thompson to the rendezvous point and he climbed aboard. He quickly rose through the ranks to become captain of the 253-foot freighter *Norvana*, operated by the North Atlantic and Gulf Steamship Company.

Thompson was a rugged, confident man with dark hair and eyes. He treated his crews fairly and showed a playful side. He always trailed a big meat hook in the water behind his ship, baited with a chunk of beef, to try to catch big sharks. But at home in Mathews, Captain Thompson was neither patient nor playful. "He was a very determined man, and when he made up his mind about something, he was going to do it," his son Ernest Travers Thompson said. "He had a habit that if anything went wrong, he'd whack you, and he did worse than whack me a couple of times. He had an iron fist, and you feared him, you didn't want to get beat by him. He'd beat the hell out of you." Travers had been relieved when his father divorced his mother, moved out of the house, and remarried.

On January 14, 1942, Captain Thompson sailed the *Norvana* out of Nuevitas, Cuba, bound for Philadelphia with a load of raw sugar. Some of the sugar was destined for American cooks and kitchens, but it was also an ingredient in the C rations produced for the troops. Cuban sugar was especially precious because the Japanese had cut off the sugar supply from the Philippines. The freighter's northern deep-ocean route took her hundreds of miles off Hatteras.

The *Norvana*'s sole link to the rest of the world, in a time before Global Positioning Systems (GPS) and Emergency Position-Indicating Radio Beacons (EPIRBs), was her wireless radio, which could broadcast a distress call for hundreds of miles. But if the radio operator failed to get the message off in time, or if no vessel was near enough to help, the sinking ship was alone on the face of the sea.

When the *Norvana* had been overdue in Philadelphia for a week, her owners started to worry. They could only hope she had been forced to put into a port unexpectedly along the way. The steamship company and the Navy inquired at all the ports the ship could possibly have reached. No one had seen the ship. First the *Norvana* was listed as "overdue," a term the seafaring novelist Joseph Conrad described as "an ominous threat of loss and sorrow trembling yet in the balance of fate . . . There is something sinister to a seaman in the very grouping of the letters which form this word, clear in its meaning, and seldom threatening in vain." There was no set timetable for declaring a ship overdue or missing; it depended on the ship, the weather, and the length of the voyage.

Next, the *Norvana* was classified as "missing"—an even more foreboding term for the insurers and next of kin. Conrad wrote, "Nobody ever comes back from a 'missing' ship to tell how hard was the death of the craft, and how sudden and overwhelming the last anguish of her men." Only one ship had ever returned safely from the "missing" list—a sailing schooner in the Pacific that had been delayed five months by unfavorable winds.

On the day the *Norvana* finally was declared lost, Thompson's son Travers was at Navy boot camp in Norfolk, having enlisted right after Pearl Harbor. He was standing in line to be issued his uniform when an officer called out his name, took him aside, and told him in a surprisingly gentle tone to call his mother. She came on the line sobbing and told him his father's ship was believed to have been sunk by a U-boat with the loss of all hands. She still thought the world of her husband. Travers could not muster any grief over his father's death, but he was "young and stupid and wanted revenge." He decided on the spot to join the American submarine force. He would spend the rest of the war on a U.S. sub in the South Pacific, stalking Japanese cargo ships in much the same way a U-boat had stalked his father's.

The only trace ever found of Ernest Thompson's ship was a battered lifeboat that drifted in, empty, among the shoals north of Hatteras. In Mathews, Thompson was described as "lost," which he literally was. But even when a mariner's body was found, or the cause of his death at sea was clear, people in Mathews would always call him lost, a term cloaked in ambiguity, hope, and faith.

U-boat logbooks captured after the war showed that Hardegan of the U-123 torpedoed the *Norvana* on January 22. Hardegan wrote that the torpedo jumped out of the water twice but blew up the ship with such force that men on the U-boat's bridge heard "the whistling of debris flying past and falling all around the [U-boat] into the water."

The *Gazette-Journal* article about Thompson's "loss" contained a piece of unrelated good news: Captain Bernard Blake of Mathews, whose ship had been rumored lost with all hands, had turned up safe with his vessel. A few weeks later, another ship rumored to have been sunk with two Mathews men aboard also reached port. Rumors of sinkings raced through the county with the terrifying speed of a marsh fire.

Some of those rumors proved true. Just as the news of Captain Thompson's death reached Mathews, a second Mathews man disappeared with his ship. George Ernest Harrison of Port Haywood was forty-five years old, powerfully built, with blue eyes and close-cropped black hair. He had fought in France during World War I and come home to Mathews to fish pound nets in the Bay with his father. But after a run of poor catches in 1935 he joined the Merchant Marine. He caught on with the Bull Line and was working his way up to second officer of the freighter *Major Wheeler* when America entered the war. In one of his last letters, he wrote his sister:

> I was in hopes I would never see any more wars in my time. But we have to make the best of things. How are the children making on? . . . I sure wish I could be home with you all Christmas. [My wife and I] have been married 19 years and this is the first time I haven't been home with the family. I shouldn't say this but I sure hate this going to sea. It is sure a dog's life. The work is not hard but being away from home all the time is bad . . . Think of me when you all are eating that old ham at Christmas. I will probably have a tough piece of cod.
>
> Lovingly, Bro.

Like the *Norvana*, the *Major Wheeler* was on the sugar run between Philadelphia and the Caribbean. She had been held in Puerto Rico for three days because of reports of U-boats along her route. She was finally allowed to sail on February 3, alone and unarmed. The Navy advised the captain to stay well offshore to avoid submarines. The *Major Wheeler* was never seen again. Not even a battered lifeboat remained of her. After the war, captured

U-boat records would reveal that the U-107 had torpedoed her in the deep ocean off Hatteras. She had sunk in only two minutes, taking the lives of all thirty-five officers and crew. Their killers were the only witnesses.

As with the *Norvana*, the first signs that the *Major Wheeler* would not return were an empty berth in Philadelphia and the ominous silence of her crew. Harrison's family had not heard from him since Puerto Rico. After a week, they and the family of Everett Callis, another Mathews man who was believed to have been on the ship, called the Bull Line office in New York. The company could tell them nothing. On February 17, the Bull Line manager, W. A. Kiggins Jr., wrote to Navy secretary Frank Knox about the *Major Wheeler*:

> Even allowing for an unduly long voyage, due to special routing instructions, this vessel is now considerably overdue, and no word has been received from her. Relatives and friends of personnel aboard the *Major Wheeler* are calling on us daily for information. The purpose of this letter is to inquire whether the Navy Department can give us any information as to the *Major Wheeler*, or advise us as to what we may tell the next of kin.

Declaring a vessel sunk with all hands was not a step to be taken hastily. On rare occasions, mariners who had been given up for dead reappeared months or even years later, after having been marooned or hospitalized with serious injuries. Everett Callis's family rejoiced when he telephoned them to report he had never boarded the *Major Wheeler*. He had, in fact, just gotten off a different ship before *that* ship was torpedoed. For Harrison's family, the silence continued. His wife drove to Baltimore and checked into a hotel near the docks. After two weeks of staring at the ship's empty berth, she went home to Mathews. The Navy informed the Bull Line that the *Major Wheeler* had not been seen at any port where she conceivably might have stopped. The ship first was classified as overdue and then as "missing—presumed sunk by a submarine."

The ship's disappearance received only a brief mention in the big-city newspapers, which were far more concerned about the possibility of America being bombed, invaded, or betrayed from within. On the East Coast, the FBI hunted spy rings. On the West Coast, the government prepared to force thousands of innocent Japanese Americans out of their homes and into bleak internment camps for the duration of the war, to prevent them from covertly aiding the enemy.

On February 20, another Bull Line ship popular with Mathews men, the *Lake Osweya*, vanished with all hands in the North Atlantic. She had been en route from New York to the Navy's new base in Iceland with a load of ammunition. Captured U-boat documents would later show she was torpedoed hundreds of miles off the northeast coast by the U-96. No Mathews men had sailed on the *Lake Osweya*'s last voyage. Louise Hodges's husband, Ralph Brooks, however, had been a regular member of the ship's crew. Brooks had made two trips to Iceland aboard the vessel, but had decided at the last moment to sit out what was her final trip. Brooks was so shaken by his close call that he quit the Merchant Marine and took a job splicing cables at a shipyard. Several other Mathews men who regularly sailed on *Lake Osweya* but had skipped her last voyage contacted the *Gazette-Journal* to spread the word they were still alive.

These would be no random incidents in the coming U-boat war. By war's end, 33 U.S. merchant ships would just vanish in the war zones, along with their 1,499 officers and crew. Some of the ships probably left no trace because they carried ammunition and were blown to bits. Most of them, however, were torpedoed in remote reaches of the ocean. Any survivors were left to die of exposure, thirst, hunger, or madness in open lifeboats. No other sinkings so clearly illustrated how U-boats were changing the traditional rules of war at sea.

Since the Age of Sail, maritime tradition had called for the captain of a ship that defeated another ship at sea to capture her as a "prize" rather than sink her, and to ensure the safety of her crew. Even at the height of a war, the captain of the victorious ship would dispatch a "prize crew" from his own vessel to sail the captive ship into port, where a judge could award it to a new owner or sell the vessel and divide the proceeds among the captors. If circumstances prevented a victorious captain from taking a defeated ship as a prize, he still had to ensure the safety of the crew before sinking her. As quaint as the prize rules may seem today, they had prevailed for centuries, preserving a degree of mercy in war at sea. But submarines simply could not follow the prize rules.

U-boats could survive only if they struck fast and then hid or fled. They could not expose themselves by leading captured prizes into harbors. They had no room to take aboard captured crews. "Submarine warfare, whoever wages it, will always be a ruthless, cold-blooded business following no rules except expediency," wrote U.S. Navy admiral Daniel V. Gallery, who hunted U-boats in World War II. Gallery regarded any effort to impose rules on submarine warfare as "pious hypocrisy . . . It was like agreeing that from now on when we drop bombs on cities we will kill only combatant males. Such rules of warfare make no more sense than a set of rules for rape."

Gallery's attitude prevailed in the Pacific war, on both sides. U.S. Navy submariners targeted Japanese merchant ships, recognizing that the island nation of Japan depended just as heavily on shipping as Britain did. Over the course of World War II, American subs would sink more than a thousand Japanese merchant ships—63 percent of the Japanese merchant fleet—and rarely offer help to the survivors. U.S. submarines would even copy Doenitz's wolf pack tactics against Japanese convoys. After the war, the brutal similarities between the German and American submarine campaigns would be part of Doenitz's defense at his war crimes trial at Nuremberg.

Japanese submarines did not routinely target Allied merchant ships. They were assigned primarily to protect Japanese warships. But when they happened upon unprotected Allied cargo ships, they sank them without regard for the safety of the crews, and sometimes tortured and murdered mariners. The commander of the Japanese sub I-8, Tetsunosuke Ariizumi, ordered his men to line up American seamen from the torpedoed freighter

Jean Nicolet on the sub's narrow deck, tie their hands, and assault them with bayonets and rifle butts. When a lookout spotted a plane, the I-8 crash-dived, leaving the bound and helpless prisoners on the sub's deck to drown.*

Hitler wanted his U-boats to kill as many merchant mariners as possible, gunning them down in lifeboats if necessary. "Once it gets around that most of the seamen are lost in the sinkings, the Americans will have great difficulty in enlisting new people," the Führer told the Japanese ambassador soon after Pearl Harbor. "We are fighting for our existence and cannot therefore take a humanitarian viewpoint." Hitler backed off after Doenitz assured him that new triggers on magnetic torpedoes would sink Allied ships faster and cause mariners' casualties to soar without forcing U-boat commanders to commit such overtly murderous acts. Doenitz was right: About 70 percent of the merchant ships sunk between 1940 and 1944 went to the bottom within fifteen minutes. But the moral question of how to treat survivors of sunken ships persisted in the U-boat force. In the historical novel *Das Boot*, a drunken U-boat officer complains to friends, "The whole thing is a farce . . . As long as a man has a deck under his feet you can shoot him down, but if the poor bugger is struggling in the water, your heart bleeds for him. Pretty ridiculous, isn't it?"

In the end, Hitler and Doenitz had little impact on the moral choices their U-boat commanders made thousands of miles from Berlin. Many U-boat commanders balanced their cold-blooded orders with the dictates of their consciences, and provided lifeboat survivors with food, water, medical attention, and directions to the nearest land. The U-boat ace Otto Kretschmer posted a standing order aboard his U-99: "Survivors are to be assisted if there is time and by doing so the submarine is not exposed to

---

* The ruthless commander of the I-8 rose through the ranks of the Japanese submarine force. At the time Japan surrendered he commanded a giant submarine designed for special missions. He shot himself as his sub was being escorted into port by American warships.

undue danger. The crew of U-99 . . . would expect to be rescued by the enemy, and that is precisely what the enemy have the right to expect from us." Circumstances also dictated how much help a U-boat crew offered its victims. One U-boat was en route to its assigned patrol station off the coast of the United States when it torpedoed a freighter far from land. The U-boat commander stuck to his schedule and did not stop to help survivors who had escaped the sinking ship in a lifeboat. But two weeks later, the U-boat was en route back to its base when it happened upon the same lifeboat. This time, the U-boat commander had no schedule to keep and plenty of supplies to get home. He stopped to give the men in the lifeboat food, water, chocolates, and cigarettes.

Another U-boat commander, Friedrich Guggenberger of the U-513, astonished a lifeboat full of survivors by asking how the Brooklyn Dodgers baseball team had been doing. Guggenberger had lived in Brooklyn with his parents before the war. Still another U-boat commander, Werner Winter of U-103, subjected lifeboat survivors to tirades against President Roosevelt. "I am sorry but you can thank Mr. Roosevelt for this," he told castaways from one torpedoed ship. On a different occasion, Winter refused a plea by lifeboat survivors for drinking water, telling them, "Roosevelt is to blame for this, he will give you water."

The U-boat captain was not far wrong. Roosevelt was partly to blame for the castaways' predicament, but the blame extended well beyond the White House, to the U.S. Navy and even the American public. The U-boats had taken over American coastal waters with little interference from the U.S. military. After three-quarters of a century of peace on its shores, the United States was unprepared to defend itself. The first of the Navy's new warships were just emerging from the yards. Half of the Navy's existing warships were in the Pacific, trying to hold back the Japanese, who had overrun Borneo, Singapore, Burma, Bali, Timor, and the Solomon Islands, and had cornered thousands of exhausted, starving American and Filipino troops on the Bataan peninsula in the Philippines.

The Navy had compounded its shortage of warships in 1940 by giving Britain fifty old World War I–vintage destroyers in exchange for ninety-nine-year leases for U.S. military bases on British territory in Newfoundland, Bermuda, and the British West Indies, which provided the United States with an outer ring of defense against a German attack on the American continent. Without those fifty destroyers, the only U.S. warships left to defend the East Coast were a dozen other old destroyers and a wide variety of smaller craft, including Coast Guard cutters, wooden-hulled subchasers from World War I, and pleasure boats of dubious value in a war. The Coast Guard's vessels at Ocracoke Island, North Carolina, included a sailboat rigged to drop depth charges from its stern. The sailboat's crew suspected the boat was too slow to get clear before the depth charges exploded, and that they would blow themselves up if they ever dropped them. Fortunately for the crew, the sailboat never got anywhere near a U-boat.

The Navy had no planes on the East Coast capable of flying patrols over distant sea lanes to protect merchant ships. The Army Air Forces was only slightly better equipped. Its assets included one long-range bomber, three torpedo bombers, three fighters, and various patrol and training planes incapable of carrying bombs or depth charges. Most of the planes lacked the radio equipment to communicate with American ships. Further compounding the problem, Army leaders did not want their planes flying routine patrols. They wanted them out hunting U-boats, which seemed like a more aggressive approach than babysitting coastal convoys. It would take the U.S. military months to figure out that the surest way to find and engage the elusive U-boats was to stay close to the merchant ships the subs had traveled thousands of miles to attack. For U-boats, merchant ships were irresistible bait.

A shortage of ships and planes was only part of the Americans' problem. Their sailors and aviators had no experience in antisubmarine warfare. Regular Navy and Army Air Forces training was of little use against seasoned U-boat commanders in the specialized world of sonar, magnetic torpedoes, and *Pillenwurfers.*

Before America entered the war, the Navy had handed the task of protecting U.S. coastal waters to Vice Admiral Adolphus Andrews, a capable, energetic officer with friends in Roosevelt's inner circle. Andrews struck some fellow officers as windy—"senatorial in port and speech," wrote the distinguished naval historian Samuel Eliot Morison. But Andrews was savvy, and he recognized at once that he had nowhere near enough forces to protect his assigned area of responsibility. That area encompassed 28,000 square miles of the Atlantic, extending from Maine to Florida, and for 200 miles out to sea. The Navy dubbed that zone the Eastern Sea Frontier, and set up other sea frontiers for the Caribbean and the Gulf of Mexico. They would be wild frontiers.

The shipping lanes in the sea frontiers were crowded with Allied merchant ships hauling every kind of war cargo. Tankers loaded with Venezuelan crude oil lumbered up the coast to Halifax to join North Atlantic convoys. Old freighters hauled manganese from Caribbean mines to defense plants in the United States, where it was used to harden steel. Other freighters carried powdery bauxite ore, an ingredient of aluminum, from open-pit mines in Brazil to American aircraft factories. Still other freighters carried staples of everyday American life such as rubber, sugar, and coffee—all of which would soon grow scarce enough to require rationing.

Andrews did not mince words with his superiors. Two weeks before Pearl Harbor, he wrote to them, "There is not a vessel [under my command] that an enemy submarine could not out-distance when operating on the surface. In most cases, the guns of [my] vessels would be out-ranged by those of the submarines. It is submitted that should enemy submarines operate off this coast, this command has no forces available to take adequate action against them, either offensive or defensive." Andrews set out to remedy the problem, shuttling between his headquarters in Manhattan and Washington, D.C., trying to leverage his connections into additional ships and planes. But his requests usually died at the desk of his formidable boss, Admiral Ernest J. King, the commander in chief of the U.S. fleet, who had operational control over the entire U.S. Navy.

King, a classmate of Andrews's at the Naval Academy, was on the cusp of a legendary career. He was a workaholic with a keen intellect. He had broad experience, having commanded a submarine base, a squadron of seaplanes, and an aircraft carrier. He had overcome career setbacks that would have discouraged many ambitious officers. But King was no sympathetic figure. He was an arrogant bully, a heavy drinker, and a strict disciplinarian—a "sundowner" in Navy slang. Roosevelt, who liked his toughness, joked that King "shaved with a blowtorch." But General Dwight D. Eisenhower, who found King difficult to work with, wrote in his diary that America would win the war faster if someone shot King. One of King's daughters described her father as "the most even-tempered man I know—always in a rage."

King faced the enormous challenge of managing wars in two oceans with a Navy unready to fight in even one. In the Pacific, he had to rally the U.S. fleet after the devastating losses at Pearl Harbor, and to prevent Japan from conquering still more territory. In the Atlantic, King had to defend the United States against a possible German invasion by sea, which seemed possible in 1942, and to provide destroyers and other escort vessels to protect the big North Atlantic convoys as far as mid-ocean. He also had to protect the troopships that were starting to carry American soldiers to Britain.

With so many demands on his resources, King did not regard protecting merchant ships in America's coastal waters as a priority. He was adamant in refusing to assign his few available ships and planes permanently to that task. King and his inner circle of advisers believed in running convoys only if those convoys had powerful enough escorts to fight off or scare off U-boats. In King's view, organizing convoys with weak escorts only made the U-boats' work easier, by assembling their targets in one place for them. King thought merchant ships were better off sailing alone, relying on luck to keep them from ever crossing paths with a U-boat. The Navy would help them by routing them away from waters where British intelligence and recent sinkings showed U-boats were operating.

At a glance, King's view seemed logical. But the British had learned over the course of two world wars that even the weakest escort was better than none. Lone, unarmed ships were the U-boats' favorite targets. They and their cargoes could be destroyed quickly with little risk. The only reason Doenitz was willing to send his U-boats all the way across the Atlantic to American waters was that the kills were so easy there. Any step the United States took to make those kills more difficult would force Doenitz to recalculate the costs versus benefits of the long-range mission.

King had misread the enemy, and he would stick to his misguided course for seven months—long after the terrible losses of merchant ships had proven him wrong. But he was adamant, and in case Admiral Andrews still had not gotten his message, King emphasized in a memo that the Eastern Sea Frontier's prospects for acquiring new escort ships and planes were "dependent on future production" of those ships and planes.

The U-boats wasted no time in confirming that the Eastern Sea Frontier was as vulnerable as Andrews had predicted. In January 1942, they sank thirty-five ships totaling more than 200,000 tons within the frontier's boundaries—three times the tonnage sunk on the North Atlantic convoy routes over the same period.

The American defenders were game but overmatched. At times the U.S. coastal defense resembled a deadly comedy of errors. Inexperienced American pilots often bombed and strafed whales, thinking they were U-boats.* An American submarine traveling from New London, Connecticut, to Norfolk to help with antisubmarine training was mistaken for a U-boat and attacked by two different U.S. warships. The submarine returned fire but none of the combatants hit anything. One dark night near the mouth of the Chesapeake Bay, jittery Navy gunners on a merchant ship

---

* The writer Theodore Taylor concluded, "The extent to which whales were machine-gunned, depth charged and subjected to aerial bombardment during World War II was such that their . . . survival was little short of miraculous. So many of the mammals were sent to the bottom that pilots, to ease their mortification, organized the 'Royal Order of the Whale Bangers,' and its members were legion."

opened fire on what they thought was a U-boat but was, in fact, the destroyer USS *Dickerson*. The rounds tore into the *Dickerson*'s bridge and critically wounded the captain. After the *Dickerson* raced into Norfolk to take the wounded to a hospital, the freighter that had mistaken the *Dickerson* for a U-boat was torpedoed by a real U-boat.

The United States neglected to employ even the most obvious antisubmarine measures. The merchant ships sailed blacked out at night in order to blend in with the darkness, but the glow of American coastal cities silhouetted them like targets in a carnival shooting gallery. U-boats had only to sit on the surface to the seaward side of the shipping lanes and wait for ships to reveal themselves against the lights. One U-boat commander wrote that "against this floodlight glare of a carefree new world," merchant ships were "recognizable in every detail and sharp as the outlines in a sales catalogue. Here they were formally presented to us on a plate: Please help yourselves! All we had to do was press the [torpedo launch] button."

Britain and Germany had blacked out their coastal cities since the start of the war, but American business owners complained a blackout would cost them money. Police warned it would increase crime. Roosevelt clearly understood the danger of coastal lights. On February 16, 1942, he signed an executive order giving the military the authority to control "all lighting on the seacoast as to prevent the silhouetting of ships and their consequent destruction by enemy submarines." But King took no steps to implement a blackout. He possessed all the real power in the Navy, and his opinion, and his orders, were the only ones that mattered.

U-boats attacked helpless merchant ships every night and sometimes by day. During February, they sank twenty-five Allied merchant ships in American waters. The victims included the tanker *W.D. Anderson*, which was torpedoed on February 22 within sight of the Florida coast. A crewman on the fantail of the tanker felt the ship shudder, and then glanced up to see a mass of fire racing along the length of the ship toward him. He saw a shipmate's hair burst into flames, and dove over the side. He would be the only survivor of the *W.D. Anderson's* thirty-six officers and crew. Tourists in beachfront hotels watched the tanker burn.

Unlike the *W.D. Anderson*, most merchant ships were torpedoed too far offshore for their destruction to be seen or heard from land. But the losses were too severe to remain secret from the mariners. In New York, some ship sailings were delayed due to shortages of crews. The press and public started asking the government why the sinkings could not be stopped or at least reduced. The Navy and the White House responded with secrecy and lies.

The Navy began to withhold the names of torpedoed ships, citing a need to keep that information from the Germans. Even official U.S. government telegrams announcing merchant mariners' deaths to their next of kin included a plea for secrecy: "TO PREVENT POSSIBLE AID TO OUR ENEMIES PLEASE DO NOT DIVULGE THE NAME OF HIS SHIP." But the Germans had their own sources of information. U-boat commanders took pains to find out the torpedoed ships' names, cargoes, and tonnages because Doenitz wanted that information. Some U-boats carried copies of Lloyd's of London's *Register of Ships*, which listed the specifications of the world's vessels. If all else failed, a U-boat commander would pry the information from men in lifeboats at the point of a machine gun. The only people kept in the dark by the government's secrecy were American citizens, who, in their enforced ignorance, had to assume their leaders knew what they were doing.

The government's iconic "Loose Lips Sink Ships!" campaign, launched in 1942, focused on a problem that barely existed. German spies did haunt some squalid waterfront taverns to try to coax drunken seamen to blurt out ship schedules and cargoes. But America's coastal waters were so crowded with merchant ships that U-boats needed no whispered secrets to find them. Spies would only have slowed the U-boats down. Most merchant mariners knew little about their own ships' cargo or itinerary anyway. "The total knowledge of one million seamen, sounding off in as many bars with 'scraps of information,' could never equal the sum of German Naval Intelligence knowledge of Allied merchant ship movements in World War II," the mariner and writer "Ferocious" O'Flaherty (S. J. Flaherty) declared.

The Allies' most damaging security breaches occurred far from the pierside bars. In February 1942, the Germans added a fourth rotor to the naval Enigma machines, complicating the encryption system and abruptly cutting off the Allies from reading the Germans' coded radio messages. A few weeks later, the German Navy's code-breaking service, B-dienst, penetrated a British code through which Allied convoy plans were transmitted. Soon the Germans knew most of the convoys' routes and could shift U-boats into position to intercept them. For the Allies, the one-two punch of suddenly losing access to the Germans' most sensitive messages while the Germans gained access to theirs was devastating. Tipsy seamen talking in dockside bars or among their friends in places like Mathews were the least of the Allies' worries.

The White House and Navy were not content to merely stonewall the public. Only two weeks after America entered the war, Navy Secretary Knox—the publisher of the *Chicago Daily News*—declared that U.S. warships "probably" had sunk or damaged at least fourteen U-boats. In fact, they had not sunk or even damaged any. Knox based his claims partly on wildly optimistic reports from Navy warships and Army planes. As the weeks passed, the Navy kept adding phony U-boat kills to Knox's total, even affecting a winner's swagger. "Some of the recent visitors to our territorial waters will never enjoy the return trip," the Navy bragged in a news release on January 23. A widely published news story described an Army pilot sinking a U-boat and then announcing his kill over the radio with a jaunty "Sighted sub—sank same." But he had only thought he had sunk a sub, and he had never spoken those memorable words. A military public affairs officer had made them up.

Rear Admiral Manley H. Simons would set a standard for malarkey when he declared in a speech in Elizabeth City, North Carolina, "I can tell you this—we have sunk plenty of submarines . . . the Axis has paid a terrible price in both submarines and men for the sinkings on the Atlantic Seaboard." In fact, at that point, the Axis had yet to pay any price at all, as Doenitz well knew from his daily radio communications with his U-boats.

Rear Admiral John Howard Hoover, Admiral Andrews's counterpart in the Caribbean Sea Frontier, maintained his credibility by refusing to make any public statements whatsoever. His standard comment to reporters was, "Gentlemen, I have nothing to say."

The Eastern Sea Frontier's war diary, an official record not accessible to the public, provided a more candid assessment of the U-boat war in the winter of 1942. The diarist Elting Morison, a naval reservist, professor at the Massachusetts Institute of Technology, and cousin of naval historian Samuel Eliot Morison, wrote that no antisubmarine strategy could possibly overcome America's shortage of escorts. Merchant ships and their crews would remain easy prey for U-boats until America produced enough new ships and planes to protect them. In the meantime, Morison wrote, "Whatever possible grounds there may be for optimism must be found in the hope that the forces available can be used in such fashion as to limit losses to bearable proportions."

To Morison and to America's military and political strategists, "bearable" losses meant losses of ships and cargo in small enough proportions that America could keep its factories and defense plants humming. Bearable losses meant losing no more ships than could be replaced by the new ships emerging from American shipyards. Bearable losses meant losing few enough mariners that their shipmates would be willing to keep sailing. All of those calculations were critical to winning the war.

But to seafaring families in Mathews and hundreds of other communities from Maine to Texas to California, the losses were not merely proportions or calculations, but husbands, fathers, sons, and brothers. Already, mariners' families had begun to dread the jangle of the telephone, the trip to the post office, and the clump of footsteps on the front porch. On Gwynn's

Island, nine-year-old Clarence Collier Jr., whose father and grandfather were both at sea, "prayed to the Lord every night to watch over my daddy, bring him home." It seemed to the boy that every ship on the sea was getting torpedoed.

A mariner's family would receive no letters for weeks, and then receive a thick stack of them. Any details a mariner might have written about his ship's voyage or his own activities would have been cut out of the letters by a censor. The letters were always too old to be of any comfort. The only time Lottie Mise of Gwynn's Island ever stopped worrying about her fiancé, Lester Smith, was when he telephoned her from a port. The moment he hung up, she resumed worrying. Lottie moved in with Lester's parents for company, but they were even more worried about Lester than she was. She would hear them in their bedroom at night, their voices hushed and anxious.

The losses in Mathews had just begun, and Henny Hodges and her neighbors would have to make their own calculations of what was bearable.

CHAPTER FOUR

Professional Survivors

Two months into the war, Raymond Hodges paid a rare visit to Gales Neck. Henny could not stop beaming. If she had a favorite son, he was Raymond. He was her first, and the only one of her children widely considered to be his father's equal at handling ships. And while Captain Jesse was rough and taciturn, Raymond was handsome, charming, and savvy in business. He was a senior captain with Moore-McCormack Transportation Co. of New York, one of the nation's most prominent shipping lines, and the master of the freighter *Mormacmoon*—the loftiest position any Hodges had ever achieved. "Raymond was above us," a family member recalled without a trace of sarcasm. And Raymond had a flair for the spotlight.

He mingled with shipping executives. A Hollywood studio chartered his ship as the set for the movie *His Woman*, starring Gary Cooper and Claudette Colbert. In 1936, Raymond nearly started his own war in the upper reaches of the Amazon jungle on behalf of the Colombian Navy. As he explained to *The New York Times*, the Colombian government bought his ship, the freighter *Commercial Traveler*, from Moore-McCormack in order to strengthen its navy for a border clash with Peru. The Colombians had no vessel anywhere near as big as the freighter, and they offered to double Raymond's salary if he stayed at the helm to lead their forces up the Amazon to a disputed patch of jungle. Command of the ship came with the temporary title of Admiral and Commander in Chief. After Moore-McCormack agreed to let Raymond stay aboard, he recruited a crew of American seamen in Philadelphia to sail the ship, which was renamed the *Cucata*. He sailed her down to the coast of South America and then more than 2,000 miles up the Amazon. Along the way, Raymond picked up Colombian troops, ammunition, and pompom guns to be fired from the deck of the freighter. The *Cucata* arrived at its destination and reinforced a small garrison of Colombian troops, but the League of Nations stepped in and resolved the border dispute before the Peruvian Navy arrived to join the fight. Raymond collected his pay, surrendered his title, and returned to Moore-McCormack. "It was fun, but I'm glad we never fired a shot," he told the *Christian Science Monitor* years later. "I don't know how I would have made out as an admiral." He charmed the *Monitor* reporter, who wrote that Raymond looked less like a sea captain than "a tycoon, a new ambassador off to some South American post, or perhaps a noted archaeologist southward bound to prod among Inca ruins."

When Raymond arrived at Gales Neck in February 1942, he wore a coat and tie, as usual. He wore a tie whenever he went out in public. "The only man I ever saw who went fishing with a tie on," one of his nieces joked. Raymond cared about appearances. When he caught his young sons slouching, he whacked them in the small of their backs with a paint-stirring stick. He once chewed out his brothers Dewey and Willie for dressing sloppily aboard his father's ship, only to see Captain Jesse clump into the wheelhouse in a grimy, sleeveless T-shirt, gnawing on a cigar.

Raymond had a barrel chest and a trim waist, unlike his brothers and sisters, who were squarely built, even pear-shaped. At his side was his wife, Ethel, whom the family had nicknamed Dolly. Dolly had grown up in New York City. She was tall and slender. She was not beautiful, but she wore elegant dresses and puffed cigarettes through a silver holder. The Hodges girls whispered that she had been a dancer for the Ziegfeld Follies. In fact, Dolly came from a prosperous family on Long Island but had been working as a telephone operator in Manhattan when Raymond first met her. After they married, he tried to talk her into moving to Mathews but she vetoed the idea, saying the county was "all marsh and salt water and ticks and dirt roads." The couple compromised and bought a home in neighboring Gloucester County on a bluff overlooking the York River. By late 1941 that home stood mostly empty. Raymond lived aboard his ship in New York Harbor; Dolly had moved back in with her parents. They sent their son Bill to boarding school in upstate New York.

Henny cried when Raymond arrived at Gales Neck, and cried harder when he rose to leave. He told her not to worry. He said he had not seen a single U-boat in several voyages between New York and South America, and if one came after him, the *Mormacmoon* was fast enough to outrun it. The *Mormacmoon* was only two years old, one of the newest American freighters on the ocean, and could make 18 knots. Raymond's easy confidence was contagious. Even in a war, he seemed in total control of events. Henny wanted to believe him.

About the time Raymond returned to his ship, the focus of the U-boat war on America shifted south. Doenitz sent his next wave of U-boats to Florida, the Caribbean, and the South Atlantic. Despite Admiral King's intransigence, Admiral Andrews had mustered enough Coast Guard cutters, smaller craft, and patrol planes to pose a nuisance to the U-boats, at least in the Atlantic. The sight of any plane usually forced a U-boat to crash-dive; the Germans did not have the luxury of waiting until they got a close look at the aircraft and determined how much of a threat it posed. Doenitz figured the waters farther south would have fewer defenses, and that the hunting would be just as good, if not better.

The Caribbean was a crossroads for ships hauling oil and raw materials from South America to North America. Britain had come to depend almost entirely on South American oil since the Germans had cut off the oil supply routes from the Middle East. Getting South American oil to

Britain was a challenge. The crude oil was pumped out of the vast fields under teardrop-shaped Lake Maracaibo on Venezuela's northern coast, and then hauled by shallow-draft tankers across a lagoon to refineries on the Dutch islands of Aruba and Curaçao. The refineries processed the crude oil into gasoline, aviation gas, and other essential fuels. Large, deep-ocean tankers then carried the refined products across the Caribbean, up the U.S. coast, and across the North Atlantic. The last, transatlantic leg of that journey was the only one protected by convoys.

The Caribbean and South Atlantic were also the sources of more than half the dry-cargo tonnage entering the United States, including bauxite, manganese, and other raw materials for American factories building ships, tanks, and planes. Manganese was precious to both sides. One of Hitler's main reasons for invading Russia had been to seize its manganese resources. Sir Thomas Holland, head of the University of Edinburgh, declared in 1942 that Germany needed manganese more than oil.

The six Caribbean U-boats announced their presence in the predawn hours of February 19, 1942, with the kind of coordinated mayhem Doenitz loved. One U-boat slipped into a coral lagoon at Aruba and shelled the refinery and the British base with its deck cannon, but had to retreat after a round exploded in the cannon barrel and killed a crewman. Another U-boat, commanded by a former merchant sea captain who knew the Caribbean well, squeezed into the harbor at Curaçao through a shallow inlet named the Dragon's Mouth and sank two ships right under the British guns. By daybreak, the six German submarines had sunk four ships and damaged three others. Over the next two weeks, they sank eighteen more ships in the Caribbean. The shaken Allies temporarily halted all tanker traffic. That left the U-boats to hunt lesser prey, such as the little Bull Line freighter *Mary.*

The *Mary* had long been a favorite of Mathews men. Captain Holly Bennett of Mathews had commanded her for years before switching to a different ship weeks before. The *Mary's* final crew included two twenty-one-year-old Gwynn's Islanders, Robert Lee Brown and Allenby Grimstead. Grimstead's father had died on a ship in Puerto Rico, and Grimstead eventually would suffer the same fate. But he and Brown would outlive the *Mary*.

The *Mary* had sailed out of New York on February 3 loaded with food, supplies, and airplanes—still unassembled in crates—for British troops in North Africa. The ship stopped in San Juan, Puerto Rico, and then steamed down the coast of South America. She eventually was to cross the ocean to Cape Town, South Africa, and then sail around the Cape of Good Hope and continue up the east coast of Africa and through the Suez Canal to Egypt. Instead, late in the morning of March 3, 160 miles off the coast of Brazil, she was struck by two torpedoes from the U-129.

Brown, an able seaman, was resting in his quarters when the first torpedo hit. He got up and struggled into his pants. Then a second torpedo shook the ship, and he took off his pants. He did not know why. Instinct may have told him he was going to have to swim for his life. But first he had to escape from his room. The force of the second explosion had thrown his bunk and locker against the exit door. Brown cleared a path to the door but found it jammed shut. Cold seawater gushed into the room through gaps in the bent door frame and swirled around his bare feet. Brown gave no thought to his belongings. He kicked out a panel in the door. A phonograph somewhere on the ship continued to play music as if nothing had happened, filling the passageways of the doomed ship with the twang of a cowboy love song by Gene Autry, "Be Honest with Me."

Brown reached the main deck and beheld "an awful sight." The 5,104-ton *Mary* was dead in the water and sinking. The weather was fair, but heavy swells persisted from a recent storm. The first torpedo had sent a mass of water flying into the air and thundering down onto the ship's bridge. It had wrecked the radio before a distress call could be sent, caved in part of the crew's quarters, and smashed one of the lifeboats, which hung in splinters from its davits. The *Mary* had two other lifeboats and six rafts. The rafts were nothing more than wooden platforms nailed to empty, buoyant barrels, but they were better than swimming.

Grimstead was the *Mary*'s third assistant engineer. He had been on watch in the engine room when a torpedo blew a hole in the hull big enough to "drive a truck into." Grimstead shut down the ship's engines, stopping the vessel so that the lifeboats could be launched safely. Then he scrambled up a ladder out of the engine room, just ahead of the rising water.

The *Mary*'s crew cut free the life rafts from the lines holding them to the deck, and lowered the rafts into the ocean near the ship. Brown and some other men leaped overboard and swam to the rafts, but the captain called them back to help launch the two intact lifeboats. The *Mary* was listing steeply, which complicated the launching process. Brown saw a friend, Edwin Fleming of Gloucester County, standing on deck wearing only his underclothes. Fleming had been asleep when the impact of the first torpedo threw him out of his bunk. He had stumbled to his feet, grabbed a life preserver, and run. Now, it occurred to him for the first time that he might have to survive a long voyage in an open boat. Fleming ran back inside his quarters and grabbed his seaman's papers, some clothing, and a hat. The captain also risked returning to his cabin. He fetched the secret Navy routing codes, stuffed them in a weighted bag, returned to the main deck, and threw the bag into the ocean.

The crew lowered two lifeboats and got into them without anyone falling overboard. That was critical, Grimstead said, because the turmoil in the water had attracted a large number of sharks, and anyone in the sea at that point "would have been devoured." A fire in the cargo holds was burning its way up through the main deck and engulfing the *Mary*. The oarsmen in the lifeboats pulled hard, but the waves kept driving the boats back to the freighter. A sinking ship was a deathtrap that could kill a man in a thousand ways. Falling masts and guy wires snagged mariners and pulled them under. Jagged debris swirled through the water. The ship's hot boilers could explode from contact with cold seawater. The *Mary*'s crew feared the ship would capsize onto the lifeboats.

A third torpedo drove the *Mary* under fast. The ship's whistle sounded two long, shrill blasts, followed by a short one. It seemed to repeat that sequence twice more. At first, the men in the lifeboats assumed the whistle cord had caught on something. Then they noticed that one of their shipmates was not in either lifeboat. Just before the first torpedo explosion, he had entered the crew's quarters to wake men for the next watch. Brown thought he had seen the man on deck afterward but was not certain. Had the man gotten trapped inside the ship? Was he blowing the whistle, calling them back to save him? They would never know.

The U-129 remained submerged and cruised slowly past the lifeboats. Its commander, Nicolai Clausen, swiveled the periscope to examine the castaways as he passed. Clausen had hunted convoys in the North Atlantic. Stalking lone, defenseless ships in the turquoise waters of the Caribbean was child's play for him. He brought the sub to the surface only twenty-five feet from the nearest lifeboat, nearly capsizing it. The U-boat's conning tower was a kiosk of painted messages, including "Westward Ho" written in English, "Das Kampf" ("the struggle"), and the U-129's unofficial symbol, a deck of playing cards. Clausen emerged from the main hatch, shirtless in the tropical heat and holding a submachine gun. He was described by the survivors as about thirty (he actually was thirty-one), blond, rugged, and speaking good English with a German accent. Three other Germans followed Clausen out onto the U-boat's bridge. They glared down at the Americans. Clausen demanded in English the name of their ship, its tonnage, cargo, and intended destination. The crew lied that they were carrying "general cargo" to Rio de Janeiro. Clausen probably did not believe them. The Germans could not have failed to notice the pieces of airplanes floating among the wreckage. But Clausen signaled they were free to go. He called out an incongruous "Cheerio" and waved as the Germans retreated down the hatch. The U-129 submerged and left the thirty-three castaways to their own devices.

The two lifeboats had plenty of room and supplies for the *Mary*'s survivors. A standard World War II–era lifeboat was twenty-eight feet long with a ten-foot beam, and could hold as many as thirty-six people. Most merchant ships carried at least four lifeboats. Both sides of each lifeboat were lined with buoyancy tanks, atop which lay wooden thwarts that served as benches. Four perpendicular cross-thwarts provided seats for the oarsmen. Each boat had four oars to a side, as well as a twenty-foot mast that could be stepped and fitted with a small sail. The boat was steered with a tiller in the stern. Unlike modern lifeboats, those in the 1940s were open at the top, offering no protection from the sun, rain, snow, wind, and spray.

Each lifeboat was required by the U.S. Bureau of Marine Inspection and Navigation to carry fifteen gallons of drinking water, the basic sustainer of life. A healthy adult requires at least three six-ounce cups of water a day. Without water, digestion begins to slow, toxins accumulate in the body, the blood thickens, circulation stops, and death arrives in as little as four days. Each lifeboat also was required to contain two weeks' worth of protein-rich foods such as biscuits, chocolate, dried milk, and pemmican, a concentrate of dried beef, flour, and molasses. The *Mary* castaways had extra food, because the captain had had the presence of mind to collect the supplies from a wrecked lifeboat before abandoning ship. The captain also had remembered to bring his compass and sextant for navigation. Unfortunately for the castaways, they could not bring the radio.

The rough seas made it hard to keep the two lifeboats together. Brown found rowing against the strong current exhausting. The wind came up, and the boats rigged their sails and set a course for the coast of French Guiana, almost 300 miles away. The sun and wind burned the men's skin. Nightfall brought a cold wind. Brown wished he had risked going back to his quarters to get more clothing. Big waves ambushed the lifeboats from unexpected directions in the dark, drenching everyone and jarring awake those who had managed to doze. During the second night, the men noticed a blinking red light in the water that seemed to be following them. They theorized it was a U-boat using them as bait to attract another ship. On the third night, a blue parachute flare lit up the sky and the object with the blinking light appeared to exchange signals with another vessel. Then the lights disappeared for good.

The wind and current kept pushing the lifeboats off course. By the fifth day, they had traveled and drifted for more than 540 miles. The captain rationed the food and water. One man in his boat caught a flying fish, tore off its scales with his teeth and ate it.* Grimstead got plenty to eat but never enough to drink. For years afterward, an intense thirst would seize him every time he thought about his lifeboat voyage.

The castaways finally drifted into the sea lanes off British Guiana—now Guyana—and were picked up by an old bauxite freighter, which looked to Brown "like a million-dollar hotel." The freighter dropped them at the U.S. Navy base in Trinidad. The island of Trinidad had become an ad hoc refugee camp for mariners whose ships had been sunk out from under them. At one point, more than seven hundred survivors of dozens of torpedoed ships were stranded at Trinidad, waiting for transportation back to the United States, living on burlap pallets in tents, swatting at insects and vermin.

The *Mary* survivors spent several weeks in Trinidad before a ship carried them and the survivors of seven other vessels to Miami. When Brown got back to Gwynn's Island, he visited his mother and then joined the Navy. He wanted to serve on a ship that could defend herself. Grimstead stayed in the Merchant Marine, as did the *Mary*'s captain, who kept sailing even after he lost two more ships to U-boats.

Less than a week after the *Mary* sinking, her sister ship the *Barbara* approached the Windward Passage under a bright Caribbean full moon.

The Windward Passage is a deep, fifty-mile-wide strait between Cuba and the island of Hispaniola, which Haiti and the Dominican Republic share. From the lush, green hills on either side of the strait, the lights on

---

*Throughout the war, castaways caught birds or fish to eat after their food ran out. The most obliging creatures were flying fish, which glided over the waves on winglike pectoral fins and sometimes slammed into the sides of lifeboats and knocked themselves senseless. Eating any sea creature other than fish was a gamble. Seaweed was plentiful and nutritious, but too salty if the water supply was unreliable. One starving mariner ate a jellyfish, became deathly sick, and then jumped out of his lifeboat and disappeared.

the other side are visible at night. The Windward Passage was the most direct sea route between the Caribbean and the U.S. East Coast. Its remoteness had made it a haven for eighteenth-century pirates, including Henry Morgan, Charles Vane, and Jack "Calico Jack" Rackham. Two centuries later, the Windward Passage attracted U-boats for the same reason it had attracted the pirates: It was an isolated chokepoint for merchant shipping.

The *Barbara*'s master was Captain Walter Gwynn Hudgins of Gwynn's Island. Walter was part of a vast network of Hudgins mariners that reached into every neck of Mathews, and seemingly onto every ship on the sea. Three Hudgins captains from Mathews once sailed their ships out of Baltimore harbor in a single afternoon. Walter was a big man with a balding pate and a ruddy complexion. He wore glasses that lent him a grandfatherly air. He was fifty-five and had been denied an officer's commission in the Navy because of his age. Besides, the Navy had informed him in a letter, "Your services [as a merchant captain] will be of just as much value to the war effort as if you were serving on some man-of-war."

Walter spoke commandingly at sea but softly at home. His son Elliott was shocked when he accompanied Walter on a voyage and heard him bellow at a crewman. Walter had moved his family from port to port while he worked his way up through the hawsepipe. He worked on colliers—coal ships—before landing a job with the Bull Line, which promoted him to master in 1918. By the time America entered World War II, he and his family had settled in Baltimore, though Walter seldom was there. His children wrote of him, "His one regret about his calling to sea was that it required him to be away from his family for extended times."

Walter's chief officer on the *Barbara* was twenty-one-year-old Charles Harold Davis, a slightly built bachelor from the hamlet of Bavon near the southeastern tip of Mathews. Harold chain-smoked Camels and closed out every day ashore with a six-pack of beer. He made a point of knowing every scrap of gossip in Mathews and buffeted his friends and family with jokes and silly stories about life at sea. But Harold was shy and soft-spoken among people he did not know well. He had no ambition to command a ship, and was content to sail under Walter, whom he had known most of his life.

The *Barbara* was a freight/passenger ship, built to carry cargo in its holds and dozens of passengers in private berths. Even in wartime, the ship employed three women as stewardesses to wait on the passengers. The passengers on the current voyage included twenty-seven military personnel en route to their duty station at the new U.S. Navy base in Guantanamo Bay, Cuba. Walter and Harold were both on the bridge on the night of March 7 as the ship approached the Windward Passage. Walter followed the Navy's routing instructions to the letter, zigzagging and hugging the coast of Haiti on the Hispaniola side of the strait. He kept the ship blacked out, even though the full moon illuminated the water and every ship on it in sharp relief.* Neither Walter nor Harold noticed the U-126 sitting on the surface a half mile ahead of them.

The U-126 commander, Ernest Bauer, was a veteran of the North Atlantic like Nicolai Clausen. He had sunk twelve ships, including a British warship, under much more difficult conditions than those in the Caribbean. He coolly watched three vessels enter the Windward Passage ahead of the *Barbara* before choosing her. He somehow mistook the *Barbara* for a tanker, to her great misfortune.

Bauer's first torpedo hit the *Barbara* amidships, blowing thirty feet of metal plating off the hull. The blast killed every man in the engine room, which was always the most dangerous place on a merchant ship because U-boats typically aimed their first torpedoes at engine rooms to disable their prey. The explosion also killed two of the *Barbara*'s three stewardesses, whose berths were directly above the engine room. The *Barbara*'s fuel tanks exploded, showering the ship with flaming bunker oil and set-

---

* The Caribbean full moon helped U-boats in early 1942, when the United States had only a few float planes and wooden-hulled subchasers to patrol the Windward Passage. But once the United States had enough ships and planes to patrol the strait regularly, the full moon made U-boats so easy to spot that Doenitz kept them out of the Windward Passage until the moon waned.

ting all four lifeboats on fire. Flames towered mast-high above the bridge.
The fire bell clanged incessantly. Passengers flung open their cabin doors
and were engulfed by fire and superheated gases. The radioman wrapped
a stewardess's fur coat around his nose and mouth to keep out the smoke
and ran into the crew's quarters to check if everyone had gotten out. Walter tried to retrieve the secret codes from the radio room but was driven
back by the heat. He gave the order to abandon ship. The lifeboats were
gone, but the crew managed to throw three rafts into the water. Some men
jumped overboard without life preservers or vests. A Navy report cited "a
complete lack of discipline and order" on the part of the crew, but a messman found no fault with his shipmates: "Some [were] plenty scared but
behaved all right."

Three swimming men pulled themselves onto a floating gangway. It
was barely buoyant enough to stay afloat beneath their weight, but they
dared not let go of it. Sharks flashed through the water around them. The
men splashed and kicked at them to keep them back.

Walter and Harold were the last men to leave the ship. They swam to
different rafts and took command of them. All around, men thrashed in
the water, crying for help. Harold tried to paddle his raft to them, but the
paddles were too small and the raft too unwieldy to maneuver. Some of the
drowning men recognized Harold on the raft by the light of the burning
ship and cried out to him by name, pleading with him to save them. Several
of them "went down screaming for help before the rafts could get to them,"
he recalled.

The men on the rafts picked up all the swimmers they could. The other
men left in the water soon fell silent. The survivors rowed the rafts toward
a thin sliver of Haitian coast, barely visible in the distance. They could hear
the dull booms of the U-126 firing its deck cannon at one of the ships that
had preceded the *Barbara* into the Windward Passage. On Harold's raft, the
men lay piled on top of one another so precariously that he was afraid to
sleep for fear he would tumble off the pile into the sea. On Walter's raft, the
only surviving stewardess, a middle-aged woman nicknamed "Grandma,"

took her turns at the paddles. She had survived the sinking by jumping overboard and then swimming to a raft, and she knew how to row. "The men would row for awhile and when they got tired, the woman would row and put them to shame," Walter recalled.

On the third day, the pilot of a Navy seaplane spotted Walter's raft, landed the plane on the ocean, and took all the people on the raft aboard, ignoring regulations against overloading the plane (and earning a medal for doing so). The other two rafts, including Davis's, drifted for another day before scraping ashore on the northern tip of Tortuga Island, a mountainous, turtle-shaped mass of rock and jungle that once had been a pirate stronghold. One seaman hiked for eighteen hours through the jungle to a native village for help. Harold was given a ride on a mule into the village, and then on a bus to Santo Domingo in the Dominican Republic, where he was entertained in the home of a wealthy family "in a way fitting to royalty."

The three men on the floating gangway were not so lucky. They had no water and were coated with thick bunker C fuel oil—"the blood of dead ships," in the words of the Caribbean historian Gaylord T. M. Kelshall. The oil weighed the men down and magnified the effects of the sun. On the second day, one of the men swam off in quest of food and drink that existed only in his mind. He apparently was a victim of heat stroke, which can disrupt the body's heat-regulating mechanisms and cause lethal fevers and bizarre visions.

Heat-stroke hallucinations often drove castaways in lifeboats to suicidal acts. Two men in one lifeboat joined hands and walked over the side into the ocean, saying, "We're going down to the hospital." In a lifeboat of the torpedoed freighter *Blink*, the first mate recalled, "One by one the men went mad. They would talk of a comfortable bed or a cup of coffee. [The captain] talked of his family just before he died. Several men tried to jump overboard but we kept them inside." One young seaman repeatedly jumped into the water to haul the hallucinating swimmers back into the lifeboat.

The two men on the *Barbara*'s floating gangway kept seeing planes fly directly overhead, but could not attract the pilots' attention; the gangway rode too low in the water. Finally, on the third day, a ship picked the men up. They had survived without food or water.

Hudgins's wife, Bessie, who worried about him constantly, first learned of the *Barbara*'s sinking in a phone call from a friend. The friend did not know if anyone on the ship had survived. Bessie was beside herself for several hours until the Bull Line called to report Walter was alive. Two days later, she received a postcard from Walter saying only that he was "well and happy" and asking her to tell Harold's mother that he, too, was safe. Walter had come through the sinking without a scratch. Even his gold pocket watch still kept time: His skin-tight life vest had kept any water from reaching it.

In all, thirty-seven of the *Barbara*'s eighty-eight crew and passengers died and fifty-one lived. The Bull Line flew Walter home from Santo Domingo and booked Harold a comfortable stateroom on a ship for the ride back. But Harold felt trapped inside the stateroom and barely set foot inside it. He spent his days on the ship's bridge and his nights on deck, sleeping in his clothes with his life vest fastened around him. Weeks later, a *Gazette-Journal* reporter interviewed him at home in Bavon and wrote that Harold "showed signs of having gone through a great struggle," and seemed haunted by the memories of drowning shipmates calling to him for help: "His thoughts were mirrored in his eyes." But as soon as the Bull Line assigned Walter a new ship, Harold signed back on with him and returned to sea, where another U-boat encounter awaited them both.

Hundreds of merchant mariners went right back to sea after harrowing experiences such as Walter's and Harold's. One hard-luck mariner, John Stanizewski, had a total of ten ships sunk out from under him over the course of the two world wars. The survivors of the ore carrier *Marore*, torpedoed off Norfolk in February, included two old seamen who had survived a total of seven sinkings. One of them told reporters he had tried driving a taxi and a streetcar but concluded "life was too short for such uninteresting professions." The experience of being torpedoed was so common that the president of the Boston Seaman's Club founded a "40-

Fathom Club" for men who had survived sinkings. "I hope the membership won't become too large," he added. But it grew larger every day as rescue ships brought exhausted, oil-soaked survivors to the docks of St. John's, Halifax, Boston, New York, Norfolk, Morehead City, Miami, and Havana.

Twenty-seven ships from six Allied nations were sunk off U.S. shores in March 1942. Statistically, U.S. coastal waters had become the most dangerous on earth, the scene of half the world's sinkings. The U-boat war was forcing mariners to become professional survivors. Their job description had expanded from navigation and cargo stowage to escaping from shipwrecks, avoiding fire and sharks, and surviving days or even weeks in open boats with no guarantee of rescue.

Surviving a sinking could be absurdly easy or agonizingly hard. All eighty-four men on one torpedoed ship made it into the lifeboats without even getting their feet wet, and spent their time adrift being entertained by a young seaman who played the flute. When a ship picked them up, the captain had a cow slaughtered in order to feed them a steak dinner. But the survivors of a Belgian freighter drifted in a lifeboat for three weeks in the North Atlantic cold. "Those of us who lived saw wounds, hunger, thirst and cold take 24 men one-by-one," the chief mate reported. "Two men went insane, stood up screaming and jumped overboard during that 25-day eternity, but men willingly gave up their rations to those weaker than themselves. They say there's an animal streak in all men. That's a damn lie."

All a merchant captain could do was to follow the route assigned to him by the Navy, and hope the Navy had gotten it right. The Navy received daily updates from the British Admiralty about the locations of U-boats in the Atlantic, and kept track of U-boat sightings and sinkings in U.S. waters. But the Navy's methods of tracking U-boats were still disjointed, and many ships, including the *Barbara*, followed their Navy routing instructions straight to the bottom of the sea.

Merchant captains also were told to keep their ships zigzagging in dangerous waters to make it harder for U-boats to line them up for torpedo strikes. But zigzagging extended a voyage, widening the window of opportunity for the ship to encounter a U-boat, and a ship might just as easily zigzag into a torpedo's path as out of it. "For every ship saved by a fortuitous zig, another is lost by an unfortunate zag," an American submariner concluded.

No captain was more conscientious than Homer Callis of Gwynn's Island. Homer, a trim man with a carefully groomed moustache, was one of three brothers commanding freighters for the Bull Line. Homer and his brothers Robert and Rodney all had reputations as fine seamen, but Homer stood out. He was a natural ship-handler like Jesse Hodges. But unlike Captain Jesse, Homer was a soft-spoken and benevolent boss. He took care of his crews and treated them with respect. Two of his crew members named their sons Homer after him. Shipowners and even the sea unions held Homer in high regard. Some mariners said that until they sailed with Captain Callis, they had never realized a sea captain could also be a gentleman.

Homer and his wife, Nancy, lived on Gwynn's Island in a white, two-story clapboard house on the shore of Milford Haven, near the drawbridge. Nancy named the house "Dunrovin'," as in the place Homer came when he was "done rovin'." The couple's two sons, Homer Jr. and Bill, had learned to sail and scull almost as soon as they could walk. Homer kept the captain's launch from his ship, the *Mae*, anchored in Milford Haven for the boys to use. Homer also took Homer Jr. and Bill on voyages to the Caribbean aboard the *Mae*, where they worked alongside the crew. Homer's crews always included several Mathews men. When Homer came back to the island, he always rounded up the local boys to play baseball, and then afterward treated them all to Cokes at the general store.

Since Pearl Harbor, Homer had sailed the *Mae* on short voyages in the Caribbean and Gulf of Mexico. He diligently followed the Navy's routing instructions, monitored all radio traffic, conducted daily lifeboat drills, and assigned extra lookouts. He was well aware that the *Mae* was on its own against U-boats. One day, a Coast Guard vessel escorted the *Mae* along the coast until nightfall, when the Coast Guard captain announced his ship was returning to port. Homer held his tongue, but as the Coast Guardsmen sped off, he said to himself, "But now is when I need you."

Homer spent every night on the bridge. At any hint of trouble he sounded the ship's general alarm, rousing the crew from their bunks to stand by the lifeboats. "Sometimes when you sailed with him you wouldn't get no sleep at all," said Jack Rowe of Gwynn's Island. "He'd call you to the lifeboats three or four times a night, the alarm going beep, beep, beep. I got so I would rather get torpedoed than wake up again and stand by the lifeboat. But I and all the other men on the crew appreciated Capt. Homer. He treated his ship and his crew like he was their daddy. He was an A-No. 1 captain, the best captain I ever sailed with." Mothers in Mathews wanted their sons to go to sea with Homer.

The only time Rowe ever saw Homer angry was on a gloomy night in the Caribbean in early 1942. The *Mae* was steaming blacked out through Stygian darkness when a light started blinking about a half mile away. The ship's third officer started to signal back with his own light in reply. "Stop, Goddamn it," Homer roared at him. "That light could be a trap by a U-boat." Homer ordered the *Mae* to run at full speed, zigzagging. He called down to the engine room to tell the firemen to keep the fuel temperature steady so the ship would not produce exhaust smoke.

Not every merchant captain took Homer's approach. Captain Jesse Hodges followed the Navy's instructions only when they did not conflict with his instincts. He tried to think like U-boat captains, who used the weather and the changing light to their advantage. "Twilight, that's when you've got to watch the boogers," he told a reporter. "That's when there's shadows. Early mornings, too."

The freewheeling Captain James Elvin "Bubba" Lewis of Mathews completely ignored the Navy and took his own precautions. Lewis—who had been captured by the Fascists in the Spanish Civil War and beaten with rubber hoses—did not trust the Navy to protect him. He avoided convoys even when assigned to them. He always sailed at night and alone. He never told the crew more than a couple hours in advance of when he planned to leave port. He was the kind of merchant captain who infuriated the Navy. But he sailed tankers across the Atlantic and Pacific throughout the course of the war without ever encountering an enemy submarine.

So many ships were being torpedoed that a publisher of mariners' textbooks hurried into print a 144-page book titled *How to Abandon Ship*, whose purpose was to reduce fatalities. One of the coauthors, John Banigan, had survived a torpedoing. The writers interviewed dozens of mariners who had lived through explosions, fires, and lifeboat voyages. They interviewed Navy survival experts, doctors, professors of chemistry and physiology, search-and-rescue coordinators, the inventor of the life suit, and even a polar explorer. *How to Abandon Ship* was a step-by-step primer for surviving a torpedoing, with vivid examples of self-sacrifice and ingenuity, including the case of a ship's engineer who saved everyone in his lifeboat by cobbling together plastic scraps and rubber tubing to build a still that converted seawater into drinkable water. *How to Abandon Ship* sought to encourage readers by evoking the eighteenth-century British captain William Bligh, who sailed a small boat 3,618 miles across the Pacific after being set adrift by mutineers on the HMS *Bounty*, and Sir Ernest Shackleton, who guided three lifeboats 346 miles through Antarctic waters in 1915 after polar ice crushed his ship, the *Endurance*.

How to Abandon Ship stressed in its opening chapter that the best way to survive was to prepare for the worst. The U-boat war punished those who flouted that rule, including Captain Levy Morgan of Gwynn's Island and the crew of the freighter *Colabee*.

Morgan was descended from an oysterman, a sailor, and a tugboat captain—his rough-hewn father, Napoleon Vaudie Morgan. Levy and his brother quit school to go to sea. Levy rose through the ranks to become a captain for the Hawaiian American Line. A family photo of him shows a big man flashing a grin beneath a wide-brimmed straw hat, as if on holiday.

The *Colabee*, however, was not a happy ship. Morgan's treatment of his crews had prompted the shipping line to take the unusual step of ordering him to "lean [over] backward in the treatment of the crew," his first officer said, and that leniency "ruined shipboard discipline." The crew never practiced launching the lifeboats.

The *Colabee* sailed out of Nuevitas, Cuba, on March 12 on the sugar run to Baltimore, laden with 38,600 bags of raw sugar. She crept along the northern coast of Cuba for two days before turning north. Morgan kept two lookouts posted, but the sea was choppy and they failed to spot the U-126 waiting in ambush on the surface ahead of them. The submarine drilled a torpedo into the *Colabee*'s starboard side, blowing a hole in the hull and raining sugar down on the deck. Steam pipes in the engine room ruptured, scalding the chief engineer as he tried to stop the engines. Morgan gave the order to launch the only remaining intact lifeboat. He lowered a suitcase full of documents to the boat on its way down. But the crew had committed the cardinal sin of launching the lifeboat while the ship was still moving. As soon as the boat reached the water, its bow nosed under and it flipped violently, hurling its occupants into the sea. Seven of them never came up. The briefcase sprang open and spilled the documents across the water. Some of the crew struggled to right the lifeboat. Others panicked and jumped overboard without life rings or life vests. "Leadership was lacking," one survivor recalled. "Each man looked out for himself." The *Colabee*'s momentum carried the ship into the shallows, where she ran aground. The U-126 prowled alongside the stranded freighter, shining a searchlight on the superstructure. The badly scalded chief engineer flattened himself against the deck as the searchlight beam swept back and forth over his head. The Germans fished one of the *Colabee*'s crew from the ocean and interrogated him. One U-boat officer spoke perfect English, having lived in America before the war. Bauer, the U-boat commander, expressed annoyance that the *Colabee* had been carrying only sugar. He let his prisoner slide down the U-boat's hull into the water near the lifeboat, which the men had finally managed to right. Then the U-126 submerged.

There was no sign of Levy Morgan. Several men said they had seen the captain jump into the ocean.

The Navy took possession of the damaged *Colabee* the next day. Intelligence officers searched in vain for her secret codebooks, and speculated ominously that the Germans had boarded the ship and captured them. The codes more likely had been in the briefcase and now lay at the bottom of the sea, but Morgan was not available to ask, and the night had been a debacle. Twenty-five of the *Colabee*'s thirty-seven officers and crew were dead, even though the ship had not sunk. A Navy report blamed the high death toll on "great confusion and lack of discipline among the crew." The Coast Guard was even more unsparing: "Had the crew remained onboard [*sic*] instead of trying to cast off precipitously in the port lifeboat, they would have all been saved, or could have left at their leisure in the [other] boat." It was a harsh critique from a government that had sent Levy Morgan and his volunteer crew into harm's way alone and unarmed. And it hinted at America's ambivalence toward the men of the 40-Fathom Club.

After the war, the merchant mariners' independent status would shut them out of a lifetime's worth of military veterans' benefits, including health care, money for a college education, and low-interest loans for homes and businesses. The mariners' reputation, and the Navy's wariness about them, was already a problem even as they faced the U-boats in 1942. "The sailor from the merchant ships was in those days known to America as a bum," the former mariner and author Felix Riesenberg wrote. "He was associated with rotgut whiskey, waterfront brawls and quickie strikes that held up big passenger ships at New York, New Orleans and San Francisco . . ." Mariners had been in such short supply at the start of the war that shipping companies had lowered their standards and hired drunks, idlers, thieves, brawlers, and card sharps to fill out their crews. The antics of those "performers," as the unions called them, had tarnished the Merchant Marine's reputation. The presence of Communists in the sea unions further eroded the mariners' public image, although most mariners, and certainly the Mathews men, had no interest in radical politics. Navy admirals deplored the mariners' refusal to bend to military discipline. Critics in the press railed that wartime bonuses raised mariners' pay higher than that of military men—ignoring the facts that mariners earned wages only when at sea, paid income tax, and received no government benefits. The Hearst newspaper columnists Walter Winchell and Westbrook Pegler, whose influence with the public far exceeded their understanding of the war, attacked mariners as greedy and unpatriotic. Pegler asserted in a column that merchant seamen had refused to unload supplies at Guadalcanal, forcing sick Marines to do the work—a baseless and easily disproven claim for which Hearst ended up paying libel damages. *Time* magazine declared that new recruits to the Merchant Marine greeted one another as "slacker," "draft-dodger," and "profiteer"—at a time when mariners were dying at a higher rate than men in any branch of military service except the U.S. Marines.

Not everyone piled on. President Roosevelt praised the Merchant Marine in speeches, and his wife, Eleanor, credited mariners with "supreme courage" and suggested they be issued uniforms. Helen Lawrenson, a writer for *Collier's* magazine, waded into a dingy seamen's bar in Greenwich Village and was charmed by a group of mariners who went by the names of Low Life McCormick, No Pants Jones, Screwball McCarthy, Foghorn Russell, Soapbox Smitty, Riff Raff, and Whiskey Bill. Ten of the twelve mariners she met had been torpedoed at least once, and one of the other two complained, "I feel so out of place. I'm a wallflower, a nobody." Lawrenson wrote that the mariners cut decidedly unromantic figures, guzzling "vast and formidable quantities of beer" while belting out sea ditties with raw lyrics. But beneath that surface, she found them intensely patriotic, casually fearless, and wise to the workings of the world. "They were the best informed, the most widely traveled, and the most truly sophisticated men I have ever met," she concluded.

The New York Times characterized merchant mariners as the war's unsung heroes: "No one steps up to the bar to buy them drinks. No moist-eyed old ladies turn to them in the subway to murmur 'God bless you.' The cop on the beat, gentle with the tipsy soldier or the unsteady gob [Navy man], is apt to put his nightstick to the britches of a merchant sailor who has tippled heavily in the town's bars to celebrate his rescue from the sea."

Few of the Mathews men read the columnists or listened to the Communists, the admirals, or the politicians. They were too focused on trying to reach the next port with their ships still beneath their feet. The tedium of sailing was now overlaid with a constant, corrosive fear of being attacked without warning. When their ships delivered badly needed supplies or arms, most of them felt as if they had achieved something. "The stuff had to go overseas," said J. W. Corbett. "It had to be done. We were the only ones who could do it, and we did it."

The fear receded in port but returned to the pit of the stomach as soon as the ship left the dock again. U-boats often waited just outside busy Allied harbors and sank ships at the start of their voyages. Standing lookout was nerve-racking at any time, but especially around dawn and dusk, when the colors of the sea and the sky merged into a gray haze, and any flash of color or ripple of motion might signal a U-boat waiting in ambush.

"I just tried to relax and think, if we get hit, we get hit," recalled Jack Rowe of Gwynn's Island. "You were taking a chance, that's for sure, but a lot of people were taking chances. You couldn't just say, 'Why me?' Somebody had to sail the ships." Raymond Edwards, a Gloucester mariner who survived a torpedoing, said of his shipmates: "[M]ost of them act as if they are not worried about or even thinking about submarines. Occasionally a man will get the jitters and will be noticed walking the deck at night when he should be asleep . . . usually the men laugh and joke, go through the routine of life aboard a ship as they did before the war, except for the precautions for lifesaving that are now required."

When a ship is torpedoed, Edwards added, "Even two seconds could mean the difference between life and death for any member of the crew. Running in the wrong direction might cut a sailor off from all means of escape. Jumping overboard at the wrong spot or at the wrong instant might easily cost a life. If a sailor is lucky enough to be alive after a torpedo hits his ship, it takes quick thinking and fast action to get him off the ship and into a lifeboat. Many are saved by sheer luck."

The job of professional survivor seemed to grow tougher all the time. The risk extended not only to men on freighters and tankers but to fishermen and tugboat men like Captain Jesse Hodges, his son Willie, and his grandson J. W. Corbett. If Henny Hodges had ever taken comfort in the idea that tugboats were too small for U-boats to attack, an incident in late March 1942 dispelled that assurance. On a misty night off a lonely uninhabited barrier island on the Virginia coast, a U-boat chased down the tug *Menominee*, blew it out of the water with point-blank blasts from its deck cannon, and then attacked three barges the tug had been towing. The attack killed sixteen men, including several from Virginia's Northern Neck, a peninsula on the Bay north of Mathews. The Hodges family had known several of the dead.

Henny's sons Raymond, Leslie, and Coleman were on freighters in the Caribbean, which was arguably the most dangerous place in the world to sail. Her son Dewey was at home with a serious illness, but he would soon be back at sea. In Dewey's absence, his ship the *East Indian*, commanded by a substitute captain, was shuttling between austere ports on the coast of West Africa, from Cameroon to Nigeria, Ivory Coast, Liberia, and Sierra Leone, stalked not only by U-boats but by malaria. The odds that all of the seafaring Hodges men would be lucky enough to survive the U-boat war seemed to grow longer every day.

No mariner in Mathews, however, would face longer odds than Captain Mellin Respess of Gwynn's Island, whose fate was soon intertwined with the Hodges family's.

Mellin had grown up on the island, the grandson of an oysterman and the son of a pound net fisherman. He had been named Mellin after a favorite brand of baby food, but everyone on Gwynn's Island called him "Choc" because he loved chocolate, and many islanders knew him by no other name. Mellin grew up fishing with his father but switched to the Merchant Marine in his late twenties. He was handsome, with dark hair and a sparkle in his brown eyes that women liked. "He was a ladies' man, sort of took life as a joke," recalled Bill Callis. Mellin traveled the world as a young man, leaving the island for years at a time. The only surviving photo of him shows him sitting on a camel in Giza, Egypt, with the Great Sphinx and the Second Pyramid in the background. But Mellin always came home to Gwynn's Island. In 1935 he took a job on a freighter commanded by a neighbor on the island, Captain J. T. Powell, who lived just down a dirt lane from the house where Mellin grew up. The ship hauled a load of ice from Baltimore to Fort Pierce, Florida, and returned with a cargo of fresh oranges. Mellin must have impressed Powell, because soon after they returned to the island, he married Powell's daughter Eleanor, whom he had barely known growing up. Eleanor was a pretty, whip-smart brunette with a serious demeanor. She taught math and later French at Mathews High School, where the boys nicknamed her "Poker" because she maintained a poker face no matter what pranks they pulled on her.

By 1942, Mellin was twenty-six years old and a licensed master. He sailed for the Bull Line—for which his cousin Virgil did the hiring—but worked for other companies too. Like many young masters, Mellin sometimes sailed as a first officer for lower pay while he waited for a ship of his own. He and Eleanor moved to Baltimore and hoped to start a family, but she miscarried. Once America entered the war, Eleanor moved back into her parents' two-story home at Cherry Point on the island's northern tip, not far from where twelve-year-old John Dixon and his friends kept watch for U-boats in the Bay. Eleanor rented rooms to the wives of Bill Callis and two other mariners, and the women fortified one another against the rumors and loneliness.

Mellin's first and lightest brush with death had come in February 1942. He had been among the half dozen Mathews men who got off the *Major Wheeler* just before it vanished. Even Eleanor had sailed on the *Major Wheeler*, having joined her husband on a harbor cruise before the war. Mellin had left the *Major Wheeler* to become first officer of the *Oakmar*, a 5,766-ton freighter owned by Calmar Steamship Co. of New York.

In late February, 1942, the *Oakmar* had steamed from Baltimore across the Atlantic and around the Cape of Good Hope to Calcutta, India, where she had taken on a cargo of leather and burlap. The ship recrossed the ocean to Trinidad to pick up a load of manganese ore. By mid-March, U-boats had sunk several ships in the waters off Trinidad, and the Navy, hoping to spare the *Oakmar* from a similar fate, instructed her captain to stay well offshore on the homebound voyage to Baltimore. The captain did as he was told. But on the morning of March 20, about 300 miles off Hatteras, the ship steamed into the crosshairs of the U-71.

The *Oakmar* was so alone and helpless that the U-71's commander, Walter Flachsenberg, decided to save his torpedoes and sink her by other means. The sea was too rough for the Germans to aim the deck cannon. So the U-71 charged the *Oakmar* and raked the freighter's bridge with machine-gun fire. The *Oakmar* was too slow to outrun the sub, so the captain gave the order to abandon ship. Flachsenberg had the U-71 hold its fire until the crew got away in two lifeboats. Despite his show of mercy, two of the freighter's crew members drowned while trying to board the lifeboats.

Flachsenberg reluctantly decided to spend a torpedo to sink the *Oakmar*. His first torpedo missed—or possibly was a dud—so he ended up having to use two. He did not stop to engage the men in the lifeboats. The boats became separated and the one without Mellin was never seen again. Mellin and twenty-nine of his shipmates drifted in the second lifeboat for two days before a Greek freighter picked them up and took them to Bermuda. Mellin spent almost a month in Bermuda "quite ill in a hospital" before finally catching a Pan Am flying boat to New York. He took a bus home to Gwynn's Island, arriving just in time for his twenty-seventh birthday. His family and friends held a birthday dinner for him.

After a couple of weeks, he had to start looking for a new ship. In Mathews, the thirty-day deadline for a mariner to either go back to sea or be drafted was strictly enforced. A representative of the local draft board, Ms. Moody, had a preternatural sense of how long each mariner had been back in Mathews. She sent them official letters when their time was near, and if they stayed too long, she reported them to the Selective Service and also gave their names to the newspaper. "She acted like it was her privilege and pleasure," fumed Charles "Pete" White of Mathews, who received a letter from her. His eyes still flashed at the memory seventy years later, at the age of ninety-two. During the war, some Mathews mariners took pains to avoid the courthouse area, where Ms. Moody worked in a lawyer's office.

Mellin did not hesitate when, after two weeks on the island, the Bull Line offered him command of the Liberty ship *Thomas McKean*. Getting torpedoed, coming home for a break, and then going back out into the war zone had become part of his job description.

The night before Mellin left Gwynn's Island to join his new ship in Baltimore, he stopped by the L.M. Callis & Son general store near the courthouse, where old-timers gathered around a woodstove every day to play cards and pass the time. Mellin was sharply dressed in a suit and hat, and lighthearted as always. Everyone wished him a good voyage. Nobody mentioned U-boats. Mellin shook hands all around and returned to the island for a last night with Eleanor.

His encounters with U-boats were only beginning. He would never see Gwynn's Island again.

An unidentified U-boat pursues a lone Allied ship in the Atlantic. U-boats were considerably faster when on the surface than most Allied merchant ships.

CREDIT: HUGO JAEGER/THE LIFE PICTURE COLLECTION/GETTY IMAGES

Captain Dewey Hodges's ring. It was discovered in the belly of a shark caught by fishermen near the spot where Dewey's ship was sunk.

CREDIT: COURTESY OF G. DEWEY HODGES III

Captain Dewey Hodges, one of seven Hodges brothers, was lost when his ship the *Onondaga* was torpedoed by the U-129 off Cuba in July 1942.

The freighter *Onondaga* was built to ply the Great Lakes but was pressed into service during World War II to haul ore and other war cargo.

The U-701 returns to its base in France after a patrol. Its final mission ended on the sea bottom off the North Carolina Outer Banks.

The Hodges' farmhouse, commanding the family's forty-acre farm on isolated Gales Neck along the East River in Mathews County.

A painting of Captain Jesse Hodges. The artist captured Jesse's intensity and his hard gaze, which seemed to say, "Get off your ass."

CREDIT: COURTESY OF THE HODGES FAMILY, VIA JESSE CARROLL THORNTON

Henny Hodges churns butter at Gales Neck. She toiled for long hours running the farm while Captain Jesse essentially lived on his tugboat.

CREDIT: COURTESY OF THE HODGES FAMILY, VIA JESSE CARROLL THORNTON

Several of the Hodges men playing baseball barehanded at Gales Neck. From left, they are J. W. Corbett (Captain Jesse's grandson), David, Dewey (in the background), and Spencer.

CREDIT: COURTESY OF THE HODGES FAMILY, VIA JESSE CARROLL THORNTON

Captain Raymond Hodges, the eldest Hodges son, was widely regarded as having inherited his father's extraordinary skill handling ships.

Raymond's freighter the *Mormacmoon*. Unlike most merchant vessels of its time, it was fast enough to outrun a U-boat, but that did not guarantee safety.

Captain Leslie Hodges. He was an outlier among the Hodges brothers, with dark hair, a quiet manner, and a family tragedy weighing on his conscience.

Captain Willie Hodges. He agreed to limit his wartime sailing to safe inland waters for the sake of his heartbroken mother.

Captain Coleman Hodges. His lighthearted, joking manner concealed an intensely driven man who was determined to command a merchant ship against the Germans.

Mr. and Mrs. Spencer Hodges. Spencer was the only Hodges brother not to pursue a career at sea, but he recruited mariners for his brothers' ships.

Captain David Hodges, the youngest Hodges brother. Known for his piercing wit, he worked in a shipyard during the war but afterward became a pilot.

Ammon Gwynn, a black neighbor of the Hodges family. He spent much of his adult life working on the farm at Gales Neck.

The oil tanker *Dixie Arrow* sinks in flames after being torpedoed off Cape Hatteras. Tankers were the U-boats' favorite targets.

CREDIT: NATIONAL ARCHIVES

This photo of the *Dixie Arrow* was taken just as a young helmsman sacrificed his life to save his shipmates from wind-driven flames.

CREDIT: NATIONAL ARCHIVES

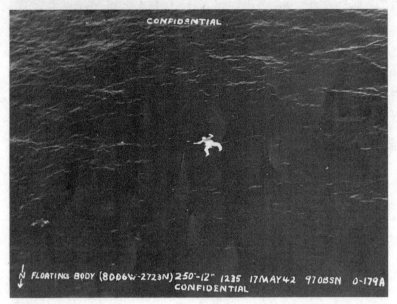

The body of an unidentified mariner floats off the coast of Florida, a prime hunting ground for U-boats in 1942.

CREDIT: NATIONAL ARCHIVES

An unidentified U-boat returns to its base on the French coast. Germany's conquest of France gave U-boats easy access to the Allied convoy routes.

CREDIT: THE OLD COAST GUARD STATION MUSEUM

Admiral Karl Doenitz, the head of the German U-boat force, was a gifted improviser who constantly shifted his submarines into weak areas in the Allies' defenses.

Doenitz welcomes a U-boat crew home after a mission. Doenitz took pains to reward returning crews with medals and special perks.

Doenitz (fourth from left) with Hitler and other Nazi leaders and Italian dictator Benito Mussolini (far left).

The cocky and capable U-boat commander Reinhard Hardegan, who distinguished himself in the U-boat assault on America. Hardegan's victims included two Mathews men.

Admiral Ernest J. King. Though acclaimed for leading the U.S. Navy during the war, he failed to protect merchant ships in U.S. waters in 1942.

CREDIT: NATIONAL ARCHIVES

Admiral Adolphus Andrews. He improvised after being handed the impossible task of protecting the U.S. East Coast from U-boats with aging, poorly equipped vessels and planes.

CREDIT: NATIONAL ARCHIVES

An Allied convoy plows through the North Atlantic carrying desperately needed supplies to Britain. The British called such convoys "the heartbeat of the war."

A U.S. Coast Guardsman watches the explosion of depth charges his ship has just dropped in an effort to sink a U-boat.

In this sequence of three photos, taken by a Nazi propaganda officer, the American oil tanker *Muskogee* sinks by the stern after being torpedoed by the U-123, and the U-boat approaches a raft carrying seven survivors. The castaways were hundreds of miles from land in the dead of winter and their expressions suggest they know they are doomed. Their families knew nothing of their fates until the late 1980s, when the son of the *Muskogee*'s captain tracked down the retired commander of the U-123, Reinhard Hardegan, who recounted the sinking and provided the photographs.

The only surviving photo of Captain Mellin Respess of Gwynn's Island shows him perched on a camel during a prewar voyage to Egypt.

LAUNCHING S·S· JOHN RUSSELL PO
FAIRFIELD, MD. SEPTEMBER 27, 19

Eleanor Respess, the widow of Captain Mellin Respess, christens a just-completed Liberty ship before it is launched at a Baltimore shipyard.

CHAPTER FIVE

"Off Hatteras the Tankers Sink"

The oil tanker *E.M. Clark* was approaching Cape Hatteras early on the morning of March 18, 1942, when a lightning storm swept across the Outer Banks of North Carolina. The tanker was running without exterior lights, and her portholes and passageways were draped with heavy curtains to prevent any light from leaking out and betraying the ship's position. But the storm made a cruel joke of the crew's precautions. The lightning flashes lit up the big tanker from bow to stern every few seconds, like a giant strobe light. Every man aboard the *E.M. Clark* knew U-boats haunted Hatteras, and that they were in grave danger. It is hard to imagine, however, that Boyd Dixon of Mathews was afraid.

Boyd led a hustling, devil-may-care life. He was a tinkerer and an entrepreneur. He built the fastest Soap Box Derby cars in Mathews. He built a telescope, grinding and polishing his own lenses. He grew miniature vegetables and raised a family of raccoons. He was a good student but a brilliant billiards player, and steadily gravitated from the classroom to his father's pool hall near the courthouse. By age fifteen he was playing exhibition matches against adult billiards champions in front of crowds in Richmond and elsewhere. When he lost, he laughed about it. In high school, he managed a local boxer, whom he insisted could challenge heavy-weight champ Max Baer. Boyd set up a ring in the local Odd Fellows Lodge. After his fighter won a couple of bouts, he talked the principal of Mathews High School into setting up a ring on the baseball diamond, with seating for hundreds of paying customers. He arranged for a doctor to oversee the fight and a man "with traveling-circus and professional ring experience" to referee. The upcoming fight was the talk of Mathews until the local prosecutor, a friend of the Dixon family, pointed out that sixteen-year-old Boyd was not a licensed boxing promoter.

After high school, Boyd signed on with the Bull Line as an able seaman. He loved the ocean and devoted his time ashore to smoking, drinking, and hustling pool to finance those vices. He lived too hard to ever rise above the rank of seaman, but he was no hoodlum. He "believed in the idea of helping everyone that he could, and to never hurt anyone or an animal," his brother John wrote of him. Boyd sailed on several voyages through war zones before signing on to the *E.M. Clark*, a 9,647-ton Standard Oil Co. tanker that carried heating oil from refineries in the Gulf of Mexico to cities in the Northeast.

Some mariners sailed exclusively on tankers, but others avoided them like the plague. Tankers offered roomy quarters, good food, and steady employment with chances for advancement. Tanker crews did not have to manhandle cargo or quarrel with stevedores on the docks. They had only to connect the hoses and turn on the valves and wait for the cargo to flow. The process was so fast that the crews complained they rarely got to spend any time in port. Tankers docked at remote piers at safe distances from the bustling waterfronts, in case their volatile cargo ignited or exploded.

The downside of serving on tankers was that their cargoes of oil and its refined products such as gasoline, aviation fuel, and kerosene, gave off flammable vapors that readily ignited.* Gasoline has a flash point of minus-

---

* Vapor is the only form of a substance that burns, because fire occurs when molecules of a flammable substance are virtually surrounded by oxygen molecules. The mole-

45 degrees Fahrenheit, which means a spark can ignite it under virtually any weather conditions. Crude oil has a far higher flash point of 400 degrees, but a fire burning out of control can reach that temperature quickly. An oil fire can generate temperatures exceeding 2,500 degrees, along with dense, black smoke laden with soot, particulates, and compounds like sulfur dioxide and carbon monoxide. The smoke alone can kill, wrecking a victim's lungs and causing chemical pneumonia or convulsions. Any oil spilled into the sea floats and gives off fumes that also can ignite, creating a moat of fire around the ship and sealing off escape. After one wreck, two mariners were burned to death when the self-igniting calcium flares on their life vests, designed to attract rescuers in the dark, ignited oil slicks around them. Other men fought fires in their lifeboats when oily water sloshing around their feet suddenly burst into flame from sparks or intense heat. One tanker captain recommended equipping lifeboats with fire extinguishers.

A quarter-inch-thick layer of oil can burn for thirty minutes, boiling the water under and around it. Even if spilled oil does not ignite, it can incapacitate swimmers by clogging their noses and mouths and plastering their eyelids shut. Even a man rescued from an oil slick might suffer long-term illness because of oil lodged in his lungs or eyes. Men drowned in 1942 because the oil coating their bodies made them too slippery for rescuers to pull from the water. No peril of the sea conjured more nightmare images than a tanker on fire.

Oil companies installed safety features such as fire-retardant chemical sprays to reduce the risk of catastrophe. Those features were fine for peacetime, but they could not stop torpedoes from transforming tankers into floating volcanoes. And that was exactly what Doenitz wanted his U-boats

---

cules of solids and liquids are too tightly packed to allow such encirclement. Heat applied to solids and liquids releases vapors into the air where they can ignite. Increasing heat releases more and more vapor, degrading the substance as the fire burns. That is why fire consuming an object often appears to be hovering just above the object. In fact, it is.

to do. He made it clear to his commanders that tankers were their No. 1 targets. Sinking a tanker was the single most telling blow a U-boat could strike against the Allies, and the surest path to medals and glory for a U-boat commander. No one understood that better than Johann Mohr, the cocky, twenty-eight-year-old commander of the U-124.

Mohr had entered American waters in early March 1942 as a part of a wave of eleven U-boats. Doenitz had given him the plum assignment of patrolling off Hatteras, where strong currents and the ever-shifting Diamond Shoals created a bottleneck for shipping. Mohr had sunk two ships on his way to Hatteras and two more after arriving on March 16. He had brazenly attacked in daylight and within sight of a U.S. destroyer and a Coast Guard cutter. The American ships had not pursued him, choosing instead to pick up survivors, but a plane had dropped depth charges that rattled the U-124 as it crash-dived. Mohr kept the sub on the bottom for several hours until night fell. He had just brought the U-124 to the surface when the lightning storm presented the *E.M. Clark* to him as a gift.

The U-124's first torpedo hit the tanker amidships on the starboard side, blowing a hole in the hull below the water line and leaving the *E.M. Clark* rattling "like a bunch of tin cans," a seaman recalled. The 118,725 barrels of heating oil in her tanks did not ignite. Dixon and his shipmates were climbing down rope ladders into the lifeboats when a second torpedo hit and the tanker sank fast. The men in the lifeboats felt hot rain patter down on them. Except it was not rain. The ship's cargo of heating oil, blown high into the air, was falling in a fine spray. "It seemed a miracle that the ship had not caught fire," the radioman said. The oil overspread the water around the ship. The fumes made some men vomit, but the crew was lucky. Had the oil been a few degrees hotter, or exposed to an open flame, they might all have died in a rain of fire. As it was, the oil calmed the ocean around them.

The *E.M. Clark*'s captain ordered the two lifeboats to circle the spot of the sinking, in case any survivors were still in the water. All they found was a shark floating belly up, apparently killed by the torpedo explosion.

The U-boat lingered at the scene and shined a spotlight in all directions, but the cresting waves concealed the lifeboats, and the submarine left after an hour. The men in one lifeboat were picked up a few hours later by a Venezuelan tanker. The occupants of the other boat were picked up shortly after dawn by a U.S. destroyer.

Forty of the *E.M. Clark*'s forty-one officers and crew survived, including Boyd Dixon. He went home to Mathews, collected some new clothes and a new pool cue, and soon went cheerfully back to sea. He would sail on tankers and freighters throughout the war, injuring his leg while abandoning ship after a torpedoing in the Caribbean, and suffering a shrapnel wound from a German bomb on the docks of North Africa.

Sinking Dixon's ship was only a warm-up for Mohr. In the space of five days off Hatteras, the U-124 sank five tankers and damaged three more. One of the victims, the tanker *Naeco*, loaded with kerosene and heating oil, ignited in a fireball that rose three hundred feet into the air and showered burning oil on the crew, killing twenty-four of the thirty-eight men—the fate the *E.M. Clark*'s crew had been so lucky to avoid. Mohr did not stop sinking tankers until he ran out of torpedoes. Before turning for home, he radioed Doenitz a poem he had composed to celebrate his success:

> *The new-moon night is black as ink.*
> *Off Hatteras the tankers sink,*
> *While sadly Roosevelt counts the score—*
> *Some fifty thousand tons*—by Mohr*

Mohr's departure did not slow the U-boats' assault. Throughout late March and early April 1942, tankers were being sunk at a rate of almost one a day—a litany of death for merchant mariners. Jobs on tankers grew harder to fill, as stories about the horrors of flaming tankers spread.

---

* The five tankers Mohr sank on the cruise actually displaced less than 40,000 tons combined, although his total for all his war cruises exceeded 100,000 tons.

Nathaniel "Nat" Foster Jr. was not dissuaded. Nat's ancestors had settled in Mathews along Mobjack Bay before the American Revolution, and had fought with a colonial militia against the British. Nat's grandfather had run a shipping company. Nat had quit high school to work on Bull Line freighters commanded by two of his neighbors, Captains Holly Bennett and Ellis Hudgins. Nat had married a girl from the seafaring community of Belfast, Maine, on Penobscot Bay, and settled there. Soon after Pearl Harbor, he had signed on to the *Muskogee*, which was part of the tanker fleet hauling Venezuelan crude oil to Britain. His first voyage had been tense from start to finish, and his wife, Ruth, asked him to stay ashore. But Nat signed on for another voyage.

As the *Muskogee* steamed south off Cape May, New Jersey, on February 1, her captain, William Betts, heard distress calls over the radio from torpedoed ships. He saw flares from their lifeboats, but did not dare stop for fear his ship would be torpedoed next. He wrote to his wife, "If I live to have grandchildren I will have plenty of exciting stories to tell them." Captain Betts guided the *Muskogee* safely to Venezuela, where the ship took on 67,000 barrels of heavy bunker C fuel oil, so viscous it had to be preheated to flow through the hoses. The tanker recrossed the Caribbean and stopped at Trinidad for routing instructions to New York. The Navy sent her alone and unarmed on a course roughly 600 miles offshore. On March 22—four days after Johann Mohr composed his poem off Hatteras—the *Muskogee* disappeared with all hands, including Third Officer Nat Foster.

The shipping company classified the tanker as missing. Nat's parents, Capt. and Mrs. Nathaniel Foster, drove from Mathews to the company's main office in New York, in the hope that their physical presence would pry loose information their phone calls had not. But the company had no information. The Fosters finally went home to Mathews, where their fears slowly crystallized into the certainty that Nat was dead. Nat's parents and his widow would go to their graves not knowing any more. It would be thirty-six years before the details of the *Muskogee's* end would be revealed in dramatic fashion.

Two days after the *Muskogee* vanished, the tanker *Dixie Arrow* burst into flames after being torpedoed off Hatteras and sank in a conflagration that evoked every tanker crewman's worst nightmares. Samuel Dow of Mathews, rowing for his life in a charred lifeboat, looked back at the dying ship and witnessed a sacrifice that was seared into the memory of every man who lived through that day.

The *Dixie Arrow* was an 8,046-ton tanker owned by the Socony-Vacuum Oil Co. of New York—later to become Mobil Oil Corp. Early on the morning of March 26, the *Dixie Arrow* approached Hatteras from the south, carrying 96,000 barrels of crude oil from Texas to a refinery in New Jersey. The *Dixie Arrow* was alone and unarmed, but her captain took every precaution, zigzagging and timing the voyage so that the tanker could round Hatteras while the sun was up. It was almost enough. The U-71—which had torpedoed Mellin Respess and the *Oakmar* the week before—was just preparing to dive after a night on the surface when a lookout spotted the tip of the *Dixie Arrow's* masts on the southern horizon. The U-boat submerged to periscope depth and waited.

The first torpedo tore into the *Dixie Arrow* amidships, wrecking the deckhouse and killing most of the ship's officers. The captain emerged from his cabin in full uniform—the first time the crew had ever seen him wearing it—and started up a ladder to the bridge. But a second torpedo jolted the ship and sent the captain hurtling through the air in a mass of flying debris. A third torpedo quickly followed, cracking the *Dixie Arrow* in half. Fire engulfed the fore half, and oil gushed from the cargo tanks onto the water's surface, where it too rippled into flame.

Dow, a thirty-six-year-old fireman, had just emerged from the engine room and sat down to eat breakfast in the mess hall near the stern. He jumped up and "ran like hell. Every man had to look out for himself, for there was no time to think about anything else." None of the officers were alive to give the order to abandon ship, "but it was plain there was nothing else to do." For the first time he could remember, Dow was scared.

The *Dixie Arrow* was only 15 miles offshore—close enough for onlookers to witness her destruction. The concussion of the torpedo explosions rattled windows in the Hatteras Island village of Buxton at the point of the cape. Children on the way to school stopped to see a pillar of black smoke boiling out of the sea. They forgot about their classes and ran toward the beach. Coast Guard rescue vessels raced for the sinking ship.

Two of the *Dixie Arrow*'s four lifeboats were on fire and a third hung over flaming oil. Dow and several shipmates hurried to lower the only remaining lifeboat before it too was cut off from the open water. The lifeboat swung wildly, crushing a man to death, and then splashed into the sea empty. Dow and the others dived after it, climbed in, and grabbed the oars, two of which were broken and useless. Other crew members threw a raft into a patch of open water, but it landed upside down. The men struggled onto the raft anyway, but they could not reach the paddles, and could not stop the raft from drifting toward burning oil. All of them jumped off except the *Dixie Arrow*'s old cook, who could not swim and was paralyzed with fright. The cook was beloved—"He was the only cook whose soup ever quite suited me," one seaman noted. His shipmates in the water pleaded with him to jump. One even tried to demonstrate how a nonswimmer could stay afloat by lying on his back and kicking. The cook could not budge. "He stayed on the raft and burned to death there right in front of our eyes," a crewman said. On the fore end of the *Dixie Arrow*, eight more crewmen were cornered by fire. The wind whipped the flames from the deckhouse toward them; the water below them shimmered with flaming oil. They agreed to share a last cigarette but nobody had a light. Only one man was in a position to save them. A skinny blond able seaman named Oscar Chappell, from the East Texas railroad town of Normangee, stood alone in the wreckage of the ship's wheelhouse. He had taken the helm just before the attack, working a shipmate's watch in exchange for a few extra hours of sleep. The men on the bow saw blood on Chappell's head and shoulders. They could not tell how badly he was injured or whether he could have saved himself. He did not try. "He stayed there at the wheel," a shipmate recalled. "He put the helm hard over into the wind to keep the flames from spreading to the bow where we were." Then Chappell swung the bow clear of the flaming oil so that the men could jump into open water. "When we jumped overboard, he was still at the wheel, with flames all around him," another seaman said. "All of us . . . owe our lives to Chappell."

Dow watched from his lifeboat and wondered what was going through Chappell's mind. Dow's lifeboat drifted on the fringe of the burning oil slick until a Navy destroyer rescued him and the boat's other occupants. Eleven men on the *Dixie Arrow* died, including the captain and Chappell, who was posthumously awarded the Merchant Marine Distinguished Service Medal. Dow returned to Mathews unscathed. A *Gazette-Journal* reporter described him as "calm and composed . . . One would not know to look at him that he had suffered such an experience." He went back to sea in time to satisfy Ms. Moody of the Mathews draft board, and sailed through the end of the war in the North Atlantic, the Caribbean, the Indian Ocean, and the Arabian Sea. But no records show him ever sailing on another tanker.

In March, oil company executives traveled to Washington, D.C., to plead with the Navy for better protection for their tankers. U-boats had sunk more than forty tankers in the Eastern Sea Frontier, the Caribbean, and the South Atlantic. Those were not bearable losses. Boston and other East Coast cities had barely enough oil for heat. Trains carrying oil in tanker cars were diverted from city to city to plug temporary gaps in the supply. The oil men said they were growing alarmed. If tankers kept being sunk at the current pace, one-third of the U.S. tanker fleet would lie on the seabed by the end of 1942, three thousand tanker crewmen would be dead, and the Allied war effort would stall.* The situation on the water was more

---

*When America entered World War II, the fleet of U.S-flagged tankers comprised roughly 350 vessels.

desperate than the Navy seemed to realize. The ship's carpenter of the tanker *Esso Baton Rouge* built fake guns out of wood and painted them gray to make it look as if the tanker could fight back, but the *Esso Baton Rouge* was torpedoed anyway.

The oil executives told Admiral King that if convoys still were not possible, the Navy should at least install real guns on the tankers and enlist the help of civilian pilots to patrol the shipping lanes. Shell Oil Co. offered to fly its own small planes from the decks of tankers to scout for U-boats. The oilmen also called for a blackout of U.S. coastal cities—an extraordinary request from an industry whose profits were tied to keeping the lights on.

King immediately agreed to start arming tankers and stationing Navy Armed Guard crews on them to operate the guns. The arming of merchant ships progressed throughout the war, although no Armed Guard crew on a merchant ship would ever sink a U-boat. King dismissed the idea of organizing civilian pilots to patrol the coast as "unworkable." He still did not order a blackout, instead asking on March 14 for a "dimout" of unnecessary lights. That half measure set off a debate over which lights were necessary, and while the debate went on, most shore lights continued to blaze. The night of King's call for a "dimout," an American freighter was torpedoed off Atlantic City, New Jersey, with the loss of twenty lives, and a survivor complained that shore lights had betrayed the ship to a U-boat: "It was lit up like daylight all along the beach."

King continued to withhold destroyers from the Eastern Sea Frontier, insisting he needed all of them to escort North Atlantic convoys and troopships to Britain. Admiral Andrews kept hustling. On March 12, he asked King and Roosevelt for blanket authority to requisition small craft of all kinds to help patrol the coast. Roosevelt pounced on the idea and warned the Navy not to impede it with red tape. The small craft were a meager line of defense. But Andrews also had Coast Guard vessels at his disposal, and he was starting to receive the first of two dozen armed fishing trawlers from the British. The 170-foot trawlers were coal-fired vessels armed with depth charges and deck guns for antisubmarine duty. They were manned by veteran British sailors. The fact that hard-pressed Britain was willing to lend twenty-four of them to the United States showed how worried the British were about the carnage along the U.S. coast.

The British were especially alarmed about the tanker sinkings. Britain needed an average of four tankers a day to fuel its tanks and planes and heat its homes. Churchill did not understand why the Americans allowed the losses to go on. In March, he wrote to his primary contact at the White House, Roosevelt aide Harry Hopkins: "I am most deeply concerned at the immense sinkings of tankers west of the 40th meridian and in the Caribbean Sea . . . The situation is so serious that drastic action of some kind is necessary."

Roosevelt relayed Churchill's message to Admiral King, who insisted he was doing all he could. He complained that the British needed to do their part by bombing the U-boat bases on the French coast. In fact, the British had missed a chance to bomb the concrete U-boat bunkers while they were still under construction and vulnerable. But by March they were finished, and impervious to British bombs.

Roosevelt remained confident in King, whose job as chief of the Navy encompassed much more than fighting U-boats offshore. But in a response to Churchill's message to Hopkins, Roosevelt distanced himself from King and the Navy. The president told Churchill the Navy had been preoccupied with building powerful warships, at the expense of humble escort ships that could have been protecting U.S. coastal waters from U-boats. "My navy has been definitely slack in preparing for this submarine war off our coast," Roosevelt wrote to Churchill. "You [British] learned the lesson two years ago . . . We still have to learn it."

The president also mentioned to Churchill King's advice that the British target the U-boat bunkers. A few weeks later, British commandos staged a nighttime raid on the bunker and other German naval facilities at Saint-Nazaire. The raid caused only temporary damage and the commandos suffered heavy losses. French partisans in the village mistook the raid for the long-awaited Allied invasion of France and joined in the attack with the commandos, only to be executed by the Germans after the commandos withdrew. The biggest impact of the raid on the Germans was that Hitler ordered Doenitz to move U-boat headquarters from the French coast to the safety of Berlin.

Hitler crowed in public over America's helplessness against his U-boats. He had once scoffed, "What is America but millionaires, beauty queens, stupid records and Hollywood?" Now he was more convinced than ever that America was soft. "The United States kept up the tall talk and left her coast unguarded," Hitler said. "Now I daresay that she is quite surprised."

Nothing the Americans tried seemed to work. At Britain's urging, the U.S. Navy armed three old freighters with hidden 4-inch guns, machine guns, depth charges, and sonar gear, and sent them into the shipping lanes to ambush U-boats. The Q-ships, as they were called, were loaded with pulp wood, which was buoyant enough to keep the ship afloat for a while even after being torpedoed and flooded. The hope was that U-boat captains would grow curious after the ships did not sink and venture close enough to be obliterated in a surprise attack. On March 27, Hardegan in the U-123 torpedoed the Q-ship *Atik*—formerly the freighter *Carolyn*, a favorite of Mathews men—300 miles off the Virginia coast. The *Atik* stopped as if crippled and dispatched men into lifeboats to further suggest a normal sinking. When the U-123 approached to finish off the ship with its deck cannon, the *Atik* opened fire, killing one of Hardegan's crew. The U-boat barely managed to retreat out of range. After dark, Hardegan returned to finish off the *Atik* with a torpedo. Hardegan made no attempt to aid the lifeboat survivors. All 141 men on the *Atik* died.

The attack by the *Atik* was the closest any Q-ship came to sinking a U-boat. But the idea of ambushing U-boats so fascinated Ernest Hemingway that he persuaded U.S. authorities in his adopted home of Cuba to arm his beloved 38-foot fishing boat *Pilar* with a light machine gun, hand grenades, and dynamite charges. The novelist envisioned luring a U-boat close enough to the *Pilar* to chase its crew down the hatch with machine-gun fire and then toss the grenades and dynamite down after them. Hemingway piloted the *Pilar* on several uneventful patrols along Cuba's northern coast. His estranged third wife, the war correspondent Martha Gellhorn, scoffed that his efforts were "nothing more than a fancy excuse to get gas rations" to fish for marlin. But Hemingway learned enough from the experience to help him write the novel *Islands in the Stream*, which was published after his death.

By the end of March 1942, the tide of the entire war was running in the Axis's favor. Invading German armies in Russia advanced toward Stalingrad and the precious oil fields of the Caucasus region. Panzer tanks rolled across the deserts of North Africa. Jews in Berlin were ordered to mark all homes they owned. In the Pacific, the Japanese drove ever closer to the trapped Allied troops on Bataan. Japanese troops landed on Guadalcanal in the Solomon Islands, which had a primitive airfield within bombing range of Australia. The entry of the United States had done little to change the war's immediate trajectory. Most of the good news on the front pages of American newspapers fell into the category of small victories in the shadows of disasters. But some of those small victories were so extraordinary, they seemed to pierce the gloom and foretell the war's outcome. First among them was the story of the *City of New York* and the lifeboat baby.

The *City of New York* was a combination freighter and passenger ship, owned by the American-South African Line, which ran between New York and Cape Town, South Africa. On the afternoon of March 29—two days after the *Atik* Q-ship disaster—the *City of New York* approached Hatteras on the last leg of a voyage covering more than 6,700 miles. The ship carried eighty-eight officers and crew, nine Navy armed guards, and forty-seven passengers, including a twenty-eight-year-old Yugoslav woman named Desanka Mohorovicic, who was eight months pregnant, and her two-year-old daughter, Vesna.

Desanka personified Europe at the mercy of the Nazis. She and her husband, Joseph, a diplomat from a prominent Yugoslav family,* had fled Europe for the safety of British-held Cape Town. No sooner had they arrived when Joseph was offered a post with Yugoslavia's government-in-exile in New York. Authorities in Cape Town refused to let Desanka sail because she was too far along in her pregnancy. So the family decided Joseph would travel to New York alone and Desanka would follow with Vesna and the new baby when possible. A few weeks after Joseph left, Desanka was told she could sail after all. She booked passage for herself and Vesna on the next passenger ship leaving Cape Town, the *City of New York.* "I did not have to think long on it, I decided to depart," she wrote. "I felt as a wife and mother I wanted to be alongside my husband. It is hard to live separated by continents and in constant uncertainty. I embarked on the voyage with great faith and confidence, and I was not afraid."

The ship was only a day out of New York when it approached Hatteras a little before 1 p.m. on March 29. A storm, which had been building all morning, darkened the sky to the southeast. Lunch was being served in the dining hall, but Desanka, who tired easily due to her pregnancy, had a waiter bring fruit to her cabin. She and Vesna were lying on their bunks when the first torpedo from the U-160 hit. Desanka heard people running outside their door. She looked for life vests, but they were buried under overturned pieces of furniture. The cabin door was stuck. Desanka threw her swollen body against it and forced it open. She and Vesna climbed a ladder to the main deck to find the crew already launching the lifeboats. They passed a young sailor with blond hair who saw they had no life vests and gave them his. Desanka never learned his name or whether he survived that day.

Mother and daughter struggled down a rope ladder into the ship's Lifeboat No. 4. The crew began lowering the boat, but the chain snagged

---

* Joseph's uncle was a world-famous geologist who was credited with discovering the layer between the earth's crust and mantle, the Mohorovicic Disconformity.

and the boat hung suspended over the sea, still tethered to the doomed ship. Then a second torpedo shook the *City of New York* and jarred the lifeboat free. It splashed into the water but did not capsize. Desanka was startled by how much rougher the ocean looked from the low-riding lifeboat than it had from the main deck. The *City of New York* sank right out from under the lifeboats. An outspread mast nearly snagged Desanka's boat on the way down. The U-boat also vanished.

The storm finally broke, drenching the castaways with cold rain. Desanka and Vesna huddled together for warmth on the lifeboat's port-side bench. Fifteen other people occupied the boat, including the ship's doctor, a bespectacled family physician from New York City named Leonard H. Conly. Conly had broken two of his ribs after losing his grip on a rope and falling hard into the boat, and was in considerable pain. The other survivors included a businessman, who wept inconsolably for his missing wife, and a woman who babbled in a voice too soft to hear over the shriek of the wind. A tough old second officer named Charles Van Gordon commanded Desanka's lifeboat. He kept the boat turned into the wind, but the storm roiled the ocean, and waves broke over the boat from all directions. The ocean was surprisingly warm because the boat was in the Gulf Stream, where water temperatures can reach 70 degrees in March. But despite its warmth, the Gulf Stream was not the castaways' friend. It veered northeast at Hatteras, and if they did not escape its grip, it would carry them into the middle of the Atlantic. Crew members and passengers argued over who should row. One passenger called the crew "a bunch of skunks." After dark, cold rain pelted the survivors. Few of them had warm clothes. Desanka wrote later of "bitter, bitter cold and bitter rain" and "dark mountains of water." Across her lap lay Vesna, drifting in and out of sleep.

At around 2:30 the next morning Desanka cried out, "Doctor, the baby is here." Conly was taking his turn at the oars despite his broken ribs. He crawled painfully across other castaways to her side. Van Gordon steadied the boat while other castaways laid the boat's sail over Desanka. "She was awfully courageous," able seaman Leroy Tate recalled. "She never whimpered or cried the whole time. She had her feet in water all the time. She was wet all over." The waves played with the boat while Conly worked. "It was like being on a scenic railway," he told *The New York Times*. "We were swooping up and down on these 15-to-20-foot waves." He delivered a healthy baby boy, and allowed the Gulf Stream to wash him clean. The baby bawled.

"I think it must have been a beautiful sound in that lifeboat," the baby's sister, Vesna, reflected many years later, "because how could you think you were going to die when a newborn baby was crying?" Desanka said some of her boat-mates were "superstitious" and saw the baby as a good omen. Others in the lifeboat were too frightened and preoccupied to care. "I felt sorry for the mother," one recalled, "but there was just so much going on that I really didn't give it much thought."

The doctor worried about the chill wind, and asked a woman if he could wrap the baby in a decorative turban she wore. She hesitated and he snatched the turban off her head, swaddled the baby in it, and presented him to Desanka. She tucked him inside her blue wool dress beneath her life vest, which made Conly think of a kangaroo's pouch. Desanka was exhausted. A seaman let her lean against him. Later, when the clouds briefly parted, the gruff Van Gordon turned grandfatherly and pointed out the stars to the lifeboat baby.

The storm abated by the next afternoon, but the Gulf Stream already had carried Desanka's lifeboat almost 75 miles farther out to sea. The destroyer USS *Roper*—the only destroyer Admiral Andrews had available— had already found another of the *City of New York*'s lifeboats and two of its rafts, rescuing a total of forty-eight people. Just before dawn on March 31—roughly forty hours after the sinking—the *Roper* found Desanka's lifeboat. The destroyer, which was longer than a football field, maneuvered close to the lifeboat and lowered a cargo net. The doctor handed the baby up to a young sailor, who thought he was receiving a bundle of documents and was flabbergasted to be clutching a baby instead. Conly had "never seen such an expression on anyone's face like that on the face of that seaman." The *Roper*'s crew cheered. Desanka would never forget the sight of the sailors in their white uniforms gently passing her son to safety. *Divini hrabni mornari*, she called them in Croatian—"divine, brave sailors." She named her son Jesse Roper Mohorovicic in honor of the destroyer, which itself bore the name of a Navy gunboat captain who died trying to save a member of his crew from a fire.

One of the *City of New York*'s lifeboats was still missing, but the *Roper* was ordered to break off the search and deliver the survivors to Norfolk. A man the *Roper* had picked up from another lifeboat had died in the ship's infirmary, shaking violently, in abject terror of another torpedo strike. As the *Roper* approached the dock, Dr. Conly and Van Gordon devised a birth certificate for the baby in the form of an entry in the *City of New York*'s logbook, listing the place of birth as "At sea in Life Boat." The Navy and the shipping line contacted the next of kin of the *City of New York*'s crew and passengers, including Joseph Mohorovicic, who had no idea his wife had even left Cape Town. Joseph too had had a hard voyage to America. His ship from Cape Town had gotten only as far as the Windward Islands before being torpedoed in the harbor at Port Castries. Joseph had spent three days in a hospital recuperating from cuts and bruises and a punctured eardrum, and then had ridden a Coast Guard vessel to New York City.

Joseph's duties at the Yugoslav embassy in New York included translating dispatches that came over the teletype machine in English. On the morning of April 1, he was shocked by a Navy bulletin that a Yugoslav woman had given birth in a lifeboat. Soon afterward, a telegram arrived for him from the general manager of the American-South African Line:

THE VESSEL ON WHICH MRS MOHOROVICIC AND
DAUGHTER WERE RETURNING TO THE UNITED STATES
IS A WAR CASUALTY STOP AND WERE LANDED AT ST
VINCENTS HOSPITAL NORFOLK VIRGINIA STOP IN
ADDITION A BABY WAS BORN TO MRS MOHOROVICIC
IN A LIFEBOAT AT SEA AND IT IS ALSO IN THE SAME

HOSPITAL WHERE THE DOCTORS REPORT THEY ARE IN
FINE CONDITION STOP OUR REPRESENTATIVES PRESENT
AND ASSISTING THEM

Joseph caught the first train to Norfolk. The next morning he was re-united with his family and then swarmed by reporters. Desanka praised her rescuers and played down her ordeal. "I [had] thought I would have my baby here, in free America," she said, struggling a little with her English. "But it wasn't so badly. He is here, we are well. *Grace de Dieu.*"

The story of the "Lifeboat Baby" appeared on the front page of *The New York Times* and dozens of other papers. "The war has yielded few stories as great as this," declared an editorial in the *International Herald Tribune*, "great in its eternal symbolism, great in its simple, almost accidental, statement of the deep mysteries of death and life with which we are all surrounded." Desanka's story was broadcast over shortwave radio to resistance fighters in Europe. The family moved into a predominantly Jewish neighborhood in upper Manhattan, where women called Jesse "the baby Hitler couldn't get." For twenty years afterward, New York tabloids would mark milestones in her son's life with stories such as "Lifeboat Baby Gains Two Pounds," "Lifeboat Baby, Now 11, Loves the Ocean and the Dodgers," and, on his wedding day, "Born in Lifeboat in WWII, He Pipes Life-Mate Aboard."

The press did not dwell on the final chapter of the *City of New York*'s story. Two weeks after the lifeboat birth, the ship's last lifeboat was spotted off the coast of Delaware, more than 300 miles northeast of Hatteras. Of the twenty people who had gotten into the boat, only two remained alive: a seaman and a three-year-old girl. The girl's mother, like Desanka, had sailed with her daughter out of Cape Town to join her husband in New York. The mother had been the last to die of thirst and exposure—only an hour before a plane spotted the boat. The child had begged the seaman not to cast her mother overboard as he had done with the other dead, and he had agreed.

If the story of the lifeboat baby had hinted at a brighter future, the story of the *City of New York*'s last lifeboat more truly reflected the state of the U-boat war in the spring of 1942.

The people of Mathews understood the vagaries of the U-boat war as well as anyone. The county was consumed by it. On April 2, a few days before Easter, the front page of the *Gazette-Journal* carried five separate stories about Mathews men confronted by U-boats. One story reported that Captain Walter Hudgins and First Mate Harold Davis were safe in Baltimore after being torpedoed on the *Barbara*. Other stories confirmed the safe returns of Allenby Grimstead and Robert Lee Brown to Gwynn's Island after the sinking of the *Mary*. Another mariner was quoted as saying his oil tanker had been chased three times by U-boats on a voyage across the Caribbean. And Captain Levy Morgan's brother wrote a letter to the paper saying the family had not given up hope for Levy. A sixth story on the front page reported that a Gwynn's Islander had been killed in a barge accident on the Bay—a reminder that the normal perils of the sea took no vacation in wartime.

Perhaps the most widely read story in the paper that day, however, was a one-paragraph note on a back page that the Ford Motor Co. freighter *East Indian* had returned safely to the Ford docks at Camden, New Jersey, "after a dangerous voyage." If any single vessel on the sea could be called a Mathews ship, the *East Indian* was the one.

The *East Indian* was the flagship of the Ford fleet. Unlike many Ford ships, she was not a tiny laker, small enough to squeeze through the canal between Lakes Erie and Ontario, but a true deep-ocean vessel, 445 feet long and displacing 8,159 tons. Ford had bought her from a Japanese company before the war to carry autos and auto parts from Ford manufacturing plants on the East Coast to customers in the Caribbean and South America.

Since 1930, Ford had entrusted the command of the *East Indian* to Captain Dewey Hodges. Everyone in Mathews knew the *East Indian* as Dewey's ship. Dozens of Mathews mariners had gone to sea for the first time aboard the *East Indian*, at Dewey's invitation. In 1936, Dewey had gotten

Ford's permission to take his wife, Edna, and his four children aboard the *East Indian* for a two-and-a-half-month run to South America, stopping to deliver auto parts at ports in Brazil, Argentina, Uruguay, and Paraguay. Dewey's son, George Dewey Jr., worked as a seaman. The two older girls, Doris and Jean, had their own stateroom and the run of the vessel. The Hodges's baby, Jan, spent her days in a playpen built by the ship's carpenter. The *East Indian* was a menagerie of friendly animals, including an elderly dachshund named Wimpy and more than a dozen canaries that sang in cages in a room designed to cheer up sick and injured seamen. At night, the crew invited the children into the wheelhouse and told them ghost stories under the glittering stars. At every port of call, people greeted Dewey as an old friend and took the family to see the local sights. Dewey's daughter Jean had never wanted the voyage to end. She loved seeing her father in his natural environment. It was the longest period she had ever spent with him.

Dewey had hoped to take his family on another South American cruise in 1940, but as the departure date neared, he decided to leave them at home for their safety. Even though the United States was still neutral at that point, the war already had bled into the South Atlantic. As the *East Indian* steamed past the mouth of the River Plate—the border between Argentina and Uruguay—Dewey had seen the wreck of the German pocket battleship *Graf Spee* lying just upriver. The ship had been crippled in a naval battle with British warships, and then scuttled by her crew. The German captain had shot himself in shame. The sight of the huge, dead warship had cast a pall over the voyage, and Dewey was glad Edna and the children had not been there to see it.

Dewey was normally healthy and robust, but while at home in the fall of 1941 he took severely ill with complications from an old appendectomy. He spent several weeks flat on his back in the hospital, looking so frail that his daughters feared for him. The doctors finally sent him home for a long recuperation, with orders to do as little as possible. He was in no shape to command the *East Indian*, so Ford found a substitute captain for what would be the ship's final voyage before America entered the war.

In November 1941, the *East Indian* set out from the Ford plant on the Delaware River on a 14,000-mile voyage to Calcutta, India. Even without Dewey, there were eight Mathews men aboard. The ship picked up a load of precious rubber in Calcutta, and then turned for home. She was working her way up the west coast of Africa, preparing to recross the Atlantic, when America entered the war. To the crew's chagrin, the *East Indian* was held in Africa all winter, shuttling between remote, barely developed harbors. She managed to avoid U-boats but not mosquitoes. Seventeen of the crew contracted malaria, including two of the Mathews men.

When the *East Indian* finally reached home in April 1942—the homecoming noted briefly by the *Gazette-Journal* on April 2, just before Easter— some of her crew had had enough and got off the ship for good. They included the chief engineer, who had sailed on the *East Indian* for eighteen years. He had been torpedoed twice in World War I and did not want to tempt fate again. Also departing was Walter Stillman of Mathews, who had sailed with Dewey since Spencer Hodges had recruited him from a life of plowing fields while "looking a mule in the butt" four years earlier. Stillman wanted to keep sailing, but he was superstitious and thought it might be bad luck to sail on the same vessel twice.

Seven other Mathews men stayed on the *East Indian*, however, including First Officer Clayton Hammond, whom Dewey had once threatened to fire if he did not quit putting off his first-officer's exam. Clayton and the other Mathews men assumed Dewey would be fully recovered and back on the bridge when the *East Indian* sailed again in a few weeks. Dewey had probably assumed that too.

But during the last week of April, a few nights before the *East Indian* was to depart, Dewey came to the docks to tell the crew he would not be going with them. He felt fine, but his doctors still would not clear him to command a ship on a voyage to the other side of the world. Dewey was disappointed, and so were his men. The ship's carpenter, Stanley MacLean, who had sailed with Dewey for eleven years, was particularly upset. He did not relish going back through dangerous waters without him. MacLean, however, stayed on the ship, and Ford chose a new substitute captain, Ovide St. Marie, to take the *East Indian* across the ocean.

Dewey went back to his home in Norfolk. He was not used to being idle, but he made the most of his time with his family. Dewey was as much of a doting husband and father as a mariner could possibly be. He bought his family a nice home in a leafy Norfolk subdivision, and employed a maid so that his wife, Edna, would not feel tied down at home. Despite the fact that Dewey had not finished grade school—or perhaps because of that fact—he stressed the importance of a wide-ranging education to his children. His son, George Jr., was the first Hodges to attend college. Dewey bought his daughters a piano and insisted they take music and dance lessons. Every night Dewey listened to the popular radio broadcaster Lowell Thomas, whom he considered erudite, and always kept a dictionary handy to look up any unfamiliar words Thomas spoke. Dewey had once brought home a beehive and a wide-brimmed hat with a protective wire screen, and invited the family to learn the science of beekeeping with him. That was more than Edna and the girls wanted to learn. After Dewey went back to sea, they never went near the hive again.

Dewey did not just sit at home after the *East Indian* sailed. Ford apparently found less strenuous work for him, such as overseeing repair work at local shipyards. When he was home, he never bossed his family around the way some captains did theirs. He seemed to enjoy a respite from the burden of command. He played with the children. He sat in the front yard, where he had made friends with a squirrel.

Even though the newspaper printed stories every day about merchant ships being sunk by U-boats, Dewey and his family never talked about it. "We tried to keep everything as normal as possible for my father when he was home," Jean Hodges said. But she and her sister felt their perspective changing. They had never worried about their father when he was at sea all the time. But now that he was spending more time at home, they worried. Sooner or later, he would have to go back out there.

CHAPTER SIX

Killing Ground to Battleground

Just after midnight on April 14, 1942, the radar operator on the destroyer USS *Roper* reported a blip on the screen, in the shallow ocean close to shore. No one on the *Roper*'s blacked-out bridge thought the blip was a U-boat. The *Roper*—the same ship that had rescued the lifeboat baby—had been patrolling the mid-Atlantic coast for weeks without seeing a U-boat. The sailors on the *Roper* had seen only the U-boats' victims. They had found dead bodies, empty lifeboats, and vast fields of floating debris. "Early this morning passed through a large patch of burnt paint where another tanker or supply ship sank last night," *Roper* sailor Robert Gillon wrote in his diary. "Paint about three inches deep on water. Lord only knows what this night will bring."

The *Roper* already had charged at several suspicious-looking radar blips, only to terrify the crews of fishing boats and Coast Guard vessels. A sense of futility was setting in. So the latest blip, only 14 miles from the shore of the Outer Banks of North Carolina, looked initially like yet another false alarm.

Instead, it was the start of a brutal encounter that would show not only how far the U.S. coastal defenses had come, but how far they still had to go.

A few seconds after the blip appeared on the radar screen, the *Roper*'s sonar operator reported a contact, as well as the sound of propellers turning fast—faster than any fishing boat's propellers. The blip and sonar contact came from the same place: two miles off to starboard, between the *Roper* and the darkened shore. The men on the *Roper*'s bridge exchanged glances. The officer of the watch, a young ensign named Kenneth Tebo, sent a sailor to wake his commanding officer.

The *Roper* had been diverted into these waters from its regular coastal patrol to follow up on a tip. The captain of a fishing trawler named the *Sea Roamer* had reported spotting a U-boat in the area. Such tips came over the radio with some regularity, and they never panned out. Even if the tipster had really seen a U-boat, as opposed to a whale or some floating debris, the submarine was likely to be long gone by the time the destroyer reached the spot. Still, pursuing a tip about a U-boat made at least as much sense as just patrolling back and forth along the coast in the hope of bumping into one. Such patrols were so ineffective that President Roosevelt, while a Navy undersecretary in World War I, had compared them to "hunting the hornets all over the farm."* And U-boats hunted back.

The *Roper* had replaced the USS *Jacob Jones*, which had been torpedoed by a U-boat off New Jersey on February 28, 1942, with the loss of 138 of her 149 officers and crew. Some of the men had jumped into the water only to be killed by the shock waves of the *Jones*'s own depth charges, detonating as the warship plunged into the depths. The *Roper*'s men had been warned not to let their ship become the next *Jacob Jones*, but the warning was hardly necessary. Many of them had lost friends on the *Jacob Jones*. They were eager to strike a blow.

---

* Doenitz wrote in his memoirs, "Single destroyers . . . sailed up and down the traffic lanes with such regularity that the U-boats were quickly able to work out the timetable being followed. They knew exactly when the destroyers would return, and the knowledge only added to their sense of security during the intervening period."

The *Roper* was a relic of World War I. She was called a "four-piper" because of her four distinctive slender smokestacks. She guzzled fuel and tended to leak and break down under the pounding of the winter seas. But she was much faster than a U-boat, and bristled with 3-inch guns, machine guns, torpedoes, and depth charges. She had microwave radar that could see farther than the Germans realized. The *Roper* was well equipped to sink a U-boat if she ever found one. And now maybe, at last, she had.

Ensign Tebo ordered the *Roper*'s helmsman to pursue the blip at an angle, as a precaution against torpedoes. His commanding officer, Lt. Cmdr. Hamilton Howe, made his way back to the bridge, half-asleep, still in his uniform. Howe was skeptical about the blip. He ordered the crew to prepare the *Roper*'s powerful 24-inch searchlight. The night was moonless. The only light in the sky was the stars and the rotating flash of the light-house on nearby Bodie Island. But the ocean was full of light. The water around the destroyer was bioluminescent—teeming with microscopic plankton that sparkled when stirred into motion.* Every wake and wave crest gave off a bright, bluish glow.

A glowing streak raced toward the *Roper* from the direction of the blip. Howe thought it was a dolphin. Tebo knew it was a torpedo. Its wake drew a bioluminescent line along the *Roper*'s port side. It shot past the destroyer's stern, a near miss. Sailors near the stern shouted. Howe called for the searchlight. The brilliant beam fell upon a gray submarine sitting on the water's surface, apparently recharging its batteries. One *Roper* sailor thought it looked too small to be a U-boat; another thought it "looked as big as the Empire State Building." The U-boat turned away from the *Roper*, and Germans began scrambling out of a hatch onto the deck. They were running toward the deck cannon. Howe "gave the word to fire anything,

---

*Bioluminescence is a common phenomenon in some parts of the ocean. Scientists think bioluminescent zooplankton release a glowing chemical in order to confuse predators and attract mates. Bioluminescence made it more difficult for U-boats to hide and attack, and some U-boat commanders took pains to avoid heavily biolumi-nescent stretches of ocean.

and we were all scared," a sailor recalled. One of the *Roper*'s guns jammed, and then another. The destroyer's torpedo officer screamed to back up and give him a firing angle. After what seemed like an eternity, the chief bo'sun's mate cleared a jammed .50-caliber machine gun and fired in a sweeping motion back and forth along the U-boat's deck. Every fifth shot was a bright tracer round. Some of the Germans were shot or jumped into the sea. Others took cover behind the conning tower. Still more Germans scrambled out of the hatch. The U-boat's tighter turning radius kept the *Roper* from closing the distance quickly. Finally, one of the *Roper*'s 3-inch guns opened fire. The first shell splashed into the ocean short of the U-boat. The second shell came closer. The third struck the U-boat with a flash and a clang, right at the base of the conning tower, exactly where gunners were taught to aim, where a breach in the U-boat's hull was a mortal wound.

The U-boat slowed and nosed down, still bathed in the searchlight glare. The *Roper*'s officers could not tell if the sub was diving, sinking, or being scuttled. The *Roper* ran straight at it. Tebo was afraid that ramming it would sink the old *Roper* too. But the U-boat submerged just as the destroyer reached it. The water all around was full of Germans, crying out in broken English. Some were treading water in a circle, holding hands. Word came down from the *Roper*'s bridge to release life rafts, but the destroyer was already past the swimmers, and word came down to wait. The sonar operator reported the U-boat was barely moving. Howe wondered if it was dead or playing possum. He had no time to mull it over. The *Roper* was alone in the middle of the night, facing an enemy that struck with no warning and left men to die. Howe ordered the *Roper* to circle back and prepare a barrage of depth charges.

The *Roper* raced to the spot where the U-boat had vanished, and bracketed the sonar target with eleven 500-pound depth charges. Tebo wrote in the ship's log that the nearest swimmers were 200 yards away, but other sailors recalled them being much closer. The *Roper* raced to get clear of the depth-charge blasts. In her wake, more than two and a half tons of TNT erupted in a thundering, bioluminescent plume. The old destroyer shook from stern to bow, rivets popping out of the seams in her hull. One sailor reported seeing some of the Germans blown out of the water.

The *Roper* sent a coded message to Norfolk that she had possibly sunk a U-boat, and was searching for others. Howe believed two U-boats might be working in tandem, but the sonar operator found no other targets. Twice more that night the *Roper* passed close to the spot of the attack, but there were no more cries for help, and no further orders to release the life rafts.

At dawn, an Army plane spotted an oil slick and some floating bodies. Howe sent out lifeboats. The dead Germans were mostly young men in gray and green clothing. Many wore breathing devices, which suggested they had swum out of the sub while it was underwater. The condition of the bodies made it clear they had been broken and battered by the depth charges.

Howe told some of his men that his uncertainty over the U-boat commander's intentions had left him no choice but to drop the depth charges. In the excitement of the moment, Tebo thought the captain had made the right decision. Tebo had not foreseen the result. "I should have known what would happen to those men in the water, but I didn't," he recalled sixty years later, his voice breaking.

The lifeboats delivered twenty-nine dead Germans to the *Roper*, where they were laid out on the main deck. The destroyer crew immediately descended on the bodies. "Our crew is like a pack of hungry animals in its desire for souvenirs," wrote a civilian who happened to be riding aboard the *Roper* that night. He reported that one sailor pulled a ring from a dead German's finger and found a lock of hair in a hidden compartment; another sailor grabbed a pair of boots, which eventually ended up on display in a bar on Michigan's Upper Peninsula. Howe angrily dispersed the souvenir hunters and posted an armed guard over the corpses. The *Roper* transferred the dead to a Navy tug, whose crew also looted the bodies for souvenirs as the tug made its way to the Norfolk naval base. The U-boat crewmen were the first enemy dead to reach American soil since the War of 1812, when a British officer, killed in a naval battle, was buried with honors on the coast of Maine.

After more than four months of false claims, the Navy finally had sunk a U-boat in American waters.* But instead of announcing the kill, the government set out to keep it secret; after all, it was not the first according to their claims. The crews of the *Roper* and the tug were ordered to keep quiet about it. An elite Navy dive team departed from Washington on a fruitless quest to salvage the sub for its Enigma machine and other secrets. FBI agents and Naval Intelligence officers searched the bodies and determined that the submarine was the U-85, under the command of twenty-seven-year-old Eberhard Greger. The U-85 had sunk three merchant ships, including a Norwegian freighter four nights earlier. The personal items recovered from the bodies included the diary of a young crewman named Erich Degenkolb. He had written mostly about girls back home and the unpleasantness of U-boat duty. His earliest entries included:

Seasick—Oh Neptune.

Severe vomiting.

It continues.

Slowly improving.

Frightful seas.

Food tastes good again.

But by the end, Degenkolb had grown accustomed to the hardships and was enjoying the experience.

---

* American planes based in Newfoundland had sunk two U-boats in Canadian waters in March.

Noon—magnificent sunshine just off America. Thoughts of home.

Abominable heat—all stripped bare.

Sighted a steamer and sank it.

Ready for attack—During the day heard three steamers.

We lie on the bottom all day. All is asleep off New York.

And Degenkolb's last entry:

American searchlights and beacons visible at night.

The U.S. Army Quartermaster General's Office in Washington contacted the nearest military cemetery, in Hampton, Virginia, and ordered twenty-nine graves dug quickly and quietly. At dusk the next day, a convoy of trucks delivered the bodies to the cemetery. The mid-April evening was unseasonably warm, and a curious crowd gathered from a neighborhood next to the cemetery. The Army said the bodies were those of American merchant seamen—an all-too-plausible lie. The crowd fell into respectful silence as an honor guard carried the dead from the trucks and laborers lowered the caskets by ropes into the graves. Catholic and Protestant chaplains offered prayers and a Navy bugler blew taps. The graves were left unmarked. The Navy promised to provide a chart later showing which Germans lay in which graves.

The sinking of the first U-boat in American waters hardly changed the course of the U-boat war. By mid-April, Doenitz had three hundred operational U-boats, including more than a dozen in U.S. and Caribbean waters. They sank thirteen Allied merchant ships within a week of the U-85's loss. Their victims included the tanker *Gulfamerica*, which Hardegan torpedoed only five miles off the beach at Jacksonville, Florida. The *Gulfamerica* was one of the first tankers to be armed, as the oil executives had suggested, but the Navy gun crew did not get off a shot. The U-123 surfaced and shelled the crippled tanker with its deck cannon in front of a crowd of tourists and sailors on leave from the nearby Navy base. "A rare show for the tourists," Hardegan wrote in his log. On April 18, four days after the U-85 sinking, the reeling Allies halted all tanker traffic north of Florida.

But if the *Roper's* victory was no turning point, it was at least a sign that the United States was learning to defend itself. Even the sardonic Hardegan, who had sneered at the Americans' weak defenses in January, acknowledged they had improved by the time he and the U-123 returned to U.S. coastal waters in April. "Some ships were beginning to sail without lights, and the coast was only brightly lit close to the big seaside resorts," Hardegan wrote. "When a ship was sunk, planes arrived quickly. They had woken up a bit." The waters off the U.S. coast were changing from a killing ground into a battleground.

By mid-April, Admiral Andrews had assembled an escort force in the Eastern Sea Frontier of about sixty vessels, including an increasing number of World War I–vintage destroyers, which Admiral King was releasing to the Eastern Sea Frontier for longer stretches. King even allowed Andrews to set up a partial convoy system along the coast known as the "bucket brigades." The name came from the firefighting method in which a line of people pass buckets of water hand to hand from a water source to the fire. In bucket brigade convoys, small groups of merchant ships steamed along the coast in a series of daylight-only voyages, spending nights in protected harbors or anchorages. The ships were protected on each leg of the journey by a group of escorts manning that stretch of coastline. The bucket brigade convoys forced the U-boats to operate more cautiously. But the convoy escorts were not formidable enough to deter the U-boats from attacking, or to fight them off when they did. The Eastern Sea Frontier remained a wild frontier, losing at least one merchant ship a day to U-boats.

On April 19, 1942, the Royal Navy sent Rodger Winn to Washington. Winn was the head of Britain's highly organized U-boat tracking center, which integrated daily intelligence reports, U-boat sightings in the field, and radio contacts. Winn's mission was to persuade Admiral King to re-organize the U.S. Navy's U-boat tracking center along similar lines. King was reported to view the British as know-it-alls. His deputy chief of staff, and gatekeeper, Rear Admiral Richard S. Edwards, tried to brush off Winn by telling him the U.S. Navy preferred to learn its own lessons about fighting U-boats. Winn replied, "The trouble is, Admiral, it's not only your bloody ships you're losing, a lot of them are ours. And we're not prepared to sacrifice men and ships to your bloody obstinacy." Edwards agreed Winn had a point, and set up a meeting with King. King agreed to start upgrading the Navy's U-boat tracking center immediately. He said he would set up a convoy system as soon as he had enough ships. The Navy had a plan for a fully interlocking convoy system to protect ships from Maine to the Caribbean to the Gulf, but so far it had received only a fraction of the new escort ships necessary to put it into effect. King's interlocking convoy system would eventually prove itself, but his timetable for implementing it was based on obtaining enough ships to run convoys his way, not on the urgency of the situation offshore.

America's production of new merchant ships was finally hitting its stride. By the spring of 1942, new vessels were joining the merchant fleet at a rate of one per day—about the same rate as the U-boats were torpedoing ships out of the fleet. Most of the new merchant ships were Liberty ships—slow, blocky freighters, 441.5 feet long, with two large boom cranes and five cavernous holds with room for 9,000 tons of cargo. The first Liberty ship had taken 217 days to build, but the shipyards constantly streamlined the construction process. In a publicity stunt, one yard completed the Liberty ship *Robert E. Peary* in 4 days, 15 hours, and 30 minutes. American shipyards would produce 746 Liberty ships by the end of 1942, and more than 2,700 before switching to faster Victory ships in 1944.*

---

* So many new ships were entering the merchant fleet that finding names for them became a challenge. Liberty ships would bear the names of a broad spectrum of people, including Big Foot Wallace, Sun Yat-sen, Frederick Douglass, Betsy Ross, Edgar

Liberty ships could be built quickly because they were built assembly-line style, like cars. Ships traditionally had been constructed by laying a keel and then building upward, riveting new sections onto the frame. But Liberty ships were built in prefabricated sections at factories outside the shipyards. Those sections then were hauled to the yard as needed and welded rather than riveted into place. Welding was much faster than riveting. The shipbuilders also saved time and money by powering the Liberty ships with old-fashioned three-cylinder steam engines. Those engines were easy to repair partly because they were interchangeable. An engineer who learned how to fix one could fix any.

Speed and ease of construction came at a cost to the men who sailed the Liberty ships. The vessels had one propeller rather than two, which increased the chance of a dead-in-the-water breakdown. Welding the hull together made it more rigid and susceptible to cracking in rough seas. The old-style steam engines could drive a Liberty ship at a maximum speed of only 11 knots—even slower than the old Ford and Bull Line freighters, and much slower than a U-boat on the surface. Liberty ships, however, were built to lumber along in protected convoys. The only speed that mattered with them was the speed at which they could be built.

The U.S. strategy for winning the Battle of the Atlantic was straightforward: Build more merchant ships than the U-boats could sink. Admiral Emory S. Land, the folksy, pipe-smoking chief of the Maritime Administration, would title his memoir, *Winning the War with Ships*. The United States also set out to produce more merchant mariners than the U-boats could kill. By the end of the war, a nationwide recruitment and training program for merchant mariners would expand their ranks from the prewar total of 55,000 to more than 250,000.

A strategy of overwhelming the enemy through sheer numbers made sense for a nation that could produce the ships at a pace no other nation

Allan Poe, Johnny Appleseed, Wyatt Earp, and Pocahontas, as well as Oscar Chappell, the helmsman who had died at the wheel of the tanker *Dixie Arrow*.

could approach. But pursuing that strategy while failing to protect the ships and mariners already on the water created the sense that they were expendable—easier to replace than to protect. The author Stephen Budiansky called America's approach to the Battle of the Atlantic "a brutal calculus, a naval war of attrition at its most elemental." The Mathews men and their shipmates bore the brunt of that strategy.

At the end of April, the German intelligence service reported that America was building ships at three times the anticipated rate. The U-boats would have to increase their sink rates accordingly. Doenitz, for the first time in the war, had the resources to answer such a challenge. He had enough U-boats to send a dozen to the Americas at the same time, the largest force to date. He also had the means to resupply those U-boats at sea. Big, lumbering supply submarines, which the Germans called "milch cows," or milk cows, rendezvoused with U-boats in remote stretches of the ocean to replenish their fuel and deliver food and spare parts. A visit from a milch cow could extend a U-boat's mission by two weeks. That extra time was especially precious in the Caribbean, where Doenitz sent most of the latest wave of U-boats.

The Caribbean was a plum assignment for U-boat crews. Targets were plentiful enough to make a U-boat commander's career, and Allied patrols were so rare that U-boat crews occasionally slipped ashore on remote islands to sunbathe, swim, fish, and even hunt. "It is a wonderful day today, and flying fish fall onto our deck," one U-boat crewman wrote in his diary of a Caribbean voyage. "At noon one of our pith helmets is blown into the water, and we jump in to get it and have a nice swim." U-boat commanders in the Caribbean—perhaps inspired by the laid-back lifestyle—tended to be more magnanimous toward lifeboat survivors in those waters than anywhere else.

William Hammond of Mathews would experience that phenomenon firsthand. William was the youngest of three brothers who had followed their friends the Hodgeses to sea. William's brother Clayton was Dewey Hodges's first officer on the *East Indian*; his brother Stacy served with

Leslie Hodges on the Ford freighter *Oneida*. William was an able seaman on the little freighter *Norlindo*, which shuttled around the Caribbean and the Gulf.

On May 4, 1942, the *Norlindo* was steaming through calm seas about 80 miles northwest of the Dry Tortuga islands, along the watery border between the Caribbean and the Gulf. The ship had sailed empty from Mobile to pick up cargo in Havana. Several men who normally would have been on lookout duty had been sent below to prepare the holds to receive cargo. Just before sunset, a torpedo from the U-507 struck the *Norlindo* with enough force to topple the mainmast into the sea. All five of the men working in the holds were killed. The *Norlindo* sank so fast that no lifeboats could be launched. The crew threw the ship's four life rafts into the ocean and jumped in after them. William had no sooner clambered onto a raft than the U-boat broke the surface about a mile distant and headed for the castaways. A face-to-face encounter with the Germans was surely the last thing William and his shipmates wanted, but they were in for a surprise.

The U-507 was freshly painted light gray and its conning tower bore an image of a laughing boar with flared pink nostrils. Several Germans emerged from the main hatch. The enlisted men wore nothing but blue swim trunks and the officers, khaki shorts and pith helmets. One German took photos of the castaways while another swept the horizon with binoculars. The U-boat crew did not bother to man the sub's deck cannon or machine gun. The U-507's commander, Harro Schacht, was a big man with sandy hair and a reddish beard. "Sorry we had to sink you, but this is war," he explained in English with only a slight German accent. He asked the men if they needed medical attention. They said they needed only cigarettes and drinking water. Schacht ordered his men to pull the raft alongside the sub with a boat hook. Then the Germans began handing out supplies: forty packs of German cigarettes, several boxes of French matches, a four-pound box of French cookies, and a ten-gallon water jug wrapped in a wicker apron like a Chianti wine bottle. Before handing over the water jug, one of the Germans squeezed fresh limes into it, apparently to fortify the castaways with vitamin C to prevent scurvy. "Be careful of the cigarettes and water as you are the same as ten thousand miles from home," Schacht cautioned. "Sorry we cannot give you a tow or send out a message for you, but we do not dare." As the U-507 pulled away from the rafts, Schacht called out, "Come over and see me sometime after the war is over."

William and twenty-three shipmates drifted on the rafts for three days, lacking nothing in the way of food and drink, but severely burned by the sun, whose rays were intensified by the spilled bunker oil coating the men's bodies. A passing freighter finally picked them up and took them to the port of Balboa on the Pacific side of the Panama Canal. Their account of Schacht's generosity drew keen interest from Navy intelligence officers, who speculated the U-boat had gotten the fresh limes from Nazi sympathizers in the Caribbean.* William made it back to the United States without a scratch. He went back to sea, where he soon would encounter another U-boat under circumstances far less cordial.

One day after the *Norlindo* sinking, Captain William Callis of Gwynn's Island was torpedoed off the coast of Florida in the old Bull Line freighter *Delisle*. The ship was only a few miles off Jupiter Inlet, north of Palm Beach, and Callis thought fast and ran the ship aground to keep her from sinking. The *Delisle* ended up being towed to Miami and repaired. But her days were numbered.

Less than twenty-four hours after the *Delisle* was torpedoed, the little Ford freighter *Green Island* was passing through the Gulf into the Caribbean en route from New Orleans to the oil-refinery island of Aruba. Third Officer Genious Hudgins Jr. of Mathews was worried. Genious was an

---

*In fact, the U-507 had brought the limes from France. But the U.S. Navy worried throughout the war that U-boats were being aided by sympathizers on the French island of Martinique, which was under the control of the German puppet Vichy government. No German records suggest U-boats ever received help on Martinique or any other island in the Caribbean, though U-boats sometimes raided passing boats to steal fresh food.

atypical Mathews mariner—trim, handsome, polite, and an impeccable dresser. His father, Genious Hudgins Sr., had been sheriff of Mathews and captain of a state oyster patrol boat. The family stressed honesty and duty. At age five, Genious Jr. had slipped a candy bar into his pocket at a general store. His grandmother found it when they got home and made him walk four miles back to the store by himself to return the candy bar and apologize. Genious and his wife, Salome, had been sweethearts since the fifth grade, breaking up only once for a couple of days. When Genious was twenty years old, his parents signed for him so that he could marry Salome. "To me, he was almost perfect," Salome would recall seventy years later. "He was truthful, and you could depend on him."

But the U-boat war was tearing at Genious and Salome's marriage. Genious disliked the long periods away from his family. He did not see his daughter, Vicki, until she was six months old. The problem was that no shore job in Mathews paid nearly as well as the Merchant Marine, and Genious needed money. He was supporting not only his wife and daughter, but also his parents. His father had quit working well before retirement age after contracting tuberculosis. But his father and mother were prominent in Mathews, and were accustomed to a certain way of life, including having nice things and hosting parties. They did not hesitate to ask Genious and his brother Russell for the money they needed to maintain their social position. When Russell moved out of Mathews, Genious wrote Salome of the "bad news"—the burden of supporting his parents was now his alone. Salome understood her husband's loyalty but thought Genious should rein in his parents' spending. As things stood, Genious could only support them by continuing to sail through war zones.

Genious wrote Salome every day he was at sea. "There is no man on earth who would rather be home with his wife and children than I do, darling," he declared, "but please don't ask me to quit." He felt a sense of duty to both his parents and his country. "Darling I believe and truly believe that I should do what I set out to do and help what little bit I can. It hurts me an awful lot when I say goodbye to you and all at home when I leave, but it would hurt me an awful lot worse if we had to live under Hitlerism or the Japanese."

Genious's ship the *Green Island* had narrowly escaped a U-boat in February off Florida by hiding in a blinding tropical rain squall. Then the freighter mistook a U.S. destroyer for the U-boat and rammed her. The *Green Island* was due for an overhaul in a dry dock in Norfolk, and Genious cherished the prospect of a long stay with Salome and Vicki. But the overhaul was postponed at the last minute, and the *Green Island* was dispatched to pick up a load of lumber in New Orleans and haul it across the Caribbean to Aruba.

Genious wrote reassuringly to Salome about the voyage, but he revealed his true feelings in a letter to his sister. "Don't say anything to mother or Salome about it, but this is about the worst place we can go," he wrote. He told his sister to make sure Salome received the insurance money due her if he did not come back. "Not that I think I won't," he added. "If I thought that, I wouldn't go at all, but you can never tell, you know." Genious promised to call his sister when he reached Aruba safely. At that point, she was to destroy his letter to make sure Salome never saw it.

Genious was dressing for breakfast in his room on the morning of May 6 as the *Green Island* steamed south through the Gulf, about 80 miles south of Grand Cayman Island. The ship was not zigzagging because she was low on drinking water and the captain wanted to reach port before it ran out. A torpedo exploded into the ship's hull, buckling the freighter amidships. Genious raced out onto the main deck with only the clothes he wore. Then he ran back inside to save a sextant his father had handed down to him. Waves were breaking over the main deck by the time he reemerged. He and the ship's twenty-one other officers and crew got away in two lifeboats. The U-125 surfaced to make sure the ship was done for, and a German officer waved farewell to the castaways before the submarine submerged. Genious and his shipmates spent a night in the lifeboats, firing flare guns every few hours, before the British freighter *Fort Qu'Appelle* picked them up and took them to Miami. The *Fort Qu'Appelle* then set out for Bermuda, where she was torpedoed with the loss of fourteen officers and crew.

Genious wrote to Salome from a hotel in Miami, downplaying the sinking and boasting playfully about some clothes that had been donated to him: "I have on an Irish linen suit and I look great." He went home to Mathews and obtained a new set of mariner's papers to replace the ones he had lost. To Salome's consternation, he began looking for a new ship.

If any waterway in America still seemed inviolable in May 1942, it was the Mississippi, the nation's main artery, the river of Tom Sawyer and Huckleberry Finn. But on May 10, Harro Schacht, who had treated the *Norlindo* survivors with such generosity, guided the U-507 to the mouth of the great American river. It was not shock value or symbolism he was after. It was oil. Huge tankers of 10,000 tons or more passed constantly in and out of the Mississippi. The river mouth was not a single, wide, bustling channel, but a spider's web of narrow passes through the dense marshlands of the Mississippi Delta. The passes were lonely places, inhabited chiefly by "bar pilots and millions of fiddler crabs," as the author Theodore Taylor put it. Before a tanker was allowed to head upriver, it had to anchor at a buoy just outside one of the passes and wait for a bar pilot, who would scramble up a ladder and guide the ship around the inevitable sandbar at the mouth of the river and then up a narrow channel into the main stem of the Mississippi.

On the morning of May 12, the 10,731-ton tanker *Virginia* sat at anchor at a buoy only 1.5 miles off the Southwest Pass, the westernmost of the Mississippi passes, waiting for a pilot. The *Virginia*'s holds were loaded with 180,000 barrels of high-octane gasoline. Thousands more barrels of gasoline sat in steel drums lashed to the ship's main deck, along with dozens of airplanes, tanks, and jeeps. The *Virginia* had been waiting for the pilot for more than two hours, due to a mix-up ashore, but there had seemed to be no hurry, because U-boats had never dared to venture so close to the river mouth.

The *Virginia*'s crew included Merritt Frank White of Mathews, whose life already had been shaped by fire. White's father had run a general store near Mathews courthouse until it burned down. He used the insurance money to build a new store, only to see it also burn down. White was still a boy when the family left Mathews in search of a better life, or at least better fire protection. They took everything they still owned, including a Holstein cow named Buttercup, and bought a dairy farm in Norfolk. Frank worked on the farm and in his brother's cigar store before deciding to follow two of his older brothers into the Merchant Marine. Whenever Frank or one of his brothers came home, the men in the family gathered in the barn to drink and sing along with the radio. The White brothers— like the Hodges, Callis, and Hammond brothers—rarely all came home from the sea at the same time. Frank came home least of all. He was the only brother who sailed the deep ocean. He wrote letters from foreign ports to a friend, Norfolk newspaper reporter Harry P. Moore, declaring, "When I come home, I'm going to stay." But he always ended up deciding, "I believe I will go back to sea for just one more voyage."

The *Virginia*'s pilot still had not shown up at 3:06 p.m. when a torpedo from Harro Schacht's U-507 exploded into the tanker's port side, igniting the gasoline in the holds. Two more torpedoes hit, and a fiery mass engulfed the ship. Any men who could still move leaped overboard without even looking, because it was obviously their only prayer. The men who jumped off the tanker's lee side landed in flaming oil and died in agony. Some who jumped off the windward side found a narrow path through the flames. "Great courage and bravery were exhibited by certain crew members who saved the lives of two or three men who were able to get off the ship but were so badly burned that they could not swim," the Coast Guard reported. The *Virginia* burned furiously and settled onto the shallow bottom, her blackened masts sticking up out of the Gulf to mark the mass grave she had become. Twenty-five of the *Virginia*'s forty officers and crew were lost, including Frank White, whose body was never found. A footstone on his empty grave in Mathews reads, "DIED AT SEA 1942."

More U-boats followed Schacht's U-507 into the Gulf and enjoyed similar success. A Louisiana man driving along the coast stopped to examine fresh wreckage on the beach and was aghast to discover an oil-smeared oar bearing the name of the oil tanker *William C. McTarnahan*—his son's ship. His son had survived the torpedoing of the *McTarnahan* hours earlier but had not had a chance to contact his family.

Eight days after the *Virginia* sinking, the U-506 torpedoed the tanker *Halo* less than 50 miles from the mouth of the Mississippi. Twenty-four men—exactly half the crew—made it into the water. But all the lifeboats and rafts had gone down with the ship, along with all the food and water. Some of the men had no life vests or life rings and had to tread water to stay afloat. The men held on to one another and vowed to stick together. They thought their nearness to land would lead to a quick rescue. They could not have been more wrong.

The first man to die had been suffering from severe burns on both legs. Without a word, he slipped out of his life preserver, pushed it to a man who did not have one, and swam off. On the second day, a seaman who had been helping the severely burned man drank salt water and lost his mind. He announced he was going to dive down to the wreck to bring up some canned pears. He dived three times and did not come up from the third. Two other men followed his mad example and dived in search of orange juice. They too vanished after a few attempts. Drinking salt water had swollen their tongues to the point where they no longer fit in their mouths. Late on the second day, the *Halo*'s fuel tanks ruptured under the crushing water pressure on the sea bottom, and a mass of heavy, black bunker oil burbled up from the wreck and engulfed the survivors in a vast slick. Pieces of the ship came up too. Two mariners from Gloucester County, Joseph "Pat" Shackelford and Jesse D. Hogge, pulled themselves onto a floating slab of wood. The Gulf sun bore down through a cloudless sky. Planes kept flying over the men in the water, low enough that the men could see the U.S. stars on their wings, but the pilots never spotted them. Several ships passed maddeningly close.

As night fell on the third day, the nineteen remaining men vowed to stay close and look out for one another. But by first light, only seven were left. Shackelford was too spent to move. He could not even raise his head to check on Hogge, who had fallen silent next to him. Shackelford promised himself not to drink salt water no matter how thirsty he got. But every time he lost consciousness, oily seawater splashed into his mouth and he woke up coughing. The oil had plastered his hair over his eyes. He left it there.

On the fifth day, the crew of a Mexican freighter spotted the oil slick from ten miles away. The Mexican seamen explored the floating wreckage and found Shackelford and Hogge still on the slab of wood. Hogge was dead. Shackelford was barely alive. There were only two other survivors, and one of them, John S. Gietek, died soon after being taken to a hospital. Doctors said he died from exposure and ingestion of toxic oil. Shackelford wrote Gietek's parents in Massachusetts that their son was buried "on a beautiful hill" in Tampico, Mexico, with full military honors, beneath a stone slab inscribed with his name and covered with flowers picked by local villagers. Shackelford and Gietek had pledged that if only one of them lived, he would visit the other's family and tell them as much as they cared to know. When Shackelford recovered enough to travel, he kept that vow. He eventually went back to sea and sailed through the end of the war. He wrote to his sister, "We get up to hot spots once in a while but I am OK."

"They can't hurt me."

The failure of the patrol planes and passing ships to find the *Halo* survivors prompted an official inquiry and some informal soul-searching. A Coast Guard report called it "strange that patrol planes which passed over the area daily made no effort to discover the source of the tremendous oil slick which came to the surface after this vessel was sunk . . ." The Coast Guard noted without comment that some sea captains steered away from any oil slick or lifeboats for fear a U-boat might still be in the vicinity. A Mexican oil company official wrote a letter to the U.S. Maritime Administration pointing out that if any of the *Halo* castaways had possessed a handheld mirror, they could easily have attracted the attention of passing pilots.

On the same day the *Halo* was torpedoed, Captain Walter Hudgins and First Officer Harold Davis, who had survived the sinking of the *Barbara* in the Windward Passage in March, approached the strait in a different ship, the Bull Line freighter *Elizabeth*, which Walter had commanded before the war.

The *Elizabeth* had set out from New York with forty trucks and various construction materials for the new U.S. Navy base at San Juan, Puerto Rico. The ship had enjoyed the protection of canals and bucket-brigade escorts for most of the voyage, but her last escort had put into port at Key West, leaving her to finish her voyage alone. The *Elizabeth* followed two other ships around the western tip of Cuba, only 100 miles from where the *Barbara* lay on the sea bottom. Just after 10:30 p.m., Harold was asleep in his bunk—he no longer slept on deck in his life vest, as he had for a week after the *Barbara* sinking—when a shipmate shook him awake. The ship in front of the *Elizabeth* had just been torpedoed.

Harold joined Walter on the bridge just as a U-boat fired a star shell with a flare that floated down on a fireproof parachute, illuminating the water around them as if it were daytime. From the darkness ahead, the U-boat opened fire with its deck cannon. Walter and Harold saw the muzzle flashes, which looked round because the cannon was aimed at them. One 88mm shell whistled over their heads and knocked down the ship's smokestack. Then a torpedo exploded into the *Elizabeth*'s engine room, killing every man inside and stopping the freighter dead in the water.

For the second time in two months, Walter gave the order to abandon ship and Harold oversaw the launching of the lifeboats. Once again, Walter and Harold were the last to leave the ship. The *Elizabeth* "settled just like a lady," as the Navy Armed Guard report put it, and the survivors rowed toward the coast of Cuba. After two days, the lifeboats crunched ashore on a remote beach near the Cape San Antonio lighthouse. The castaways bushwhacked twenty miles through a "desolate landscape" to a tiny settlement. The natives dressed the castaways' injuries and the owner of a "barkee"—a small fishing schooner—agreed to sail them to a larger village. There they were treated to "a big feed" and put on a bus to Havana. The Bull Line flew them home. Walter was given a few months of safe duty ashore, though he had not asked for it.

Harold sent his family in Mathews a telegram: "This is getting ridiculous."

The *Gazette-Journal* agreed. "The loss thus far suffered has been appalling," the paper editorialized, "not only because of the value of the ships and cargoes sunk and the precious lives sacrificed, but because of the humiliation of what amounts to a blockade of our shores and the injurious effect on our war effort."

The U.S. supplies of rubber and sugar had been cut off by the Japanese conquests in the Pacific. The rationing of rubber affected everyone in Mathews. Shipments of new tires to Mathews garages simply ceased, as all the available rubber was needed for tires for new warplanes, trucks, and other military vehicles. Gasoline was rationed initially to reduce wear on automobile tires and make them last longer. People were allowed to drive to work, to the grocery store, or to the doctor, but forbidden to drive for recreation or pleasure. Anyone caught "pleasure driving" had to forfeit some of their future gas rations. Every week, alleged violators were summoned to appear before a specially appointed panel at the Mathews courthouse to justify why they had been on the road.

The ban on pleasure driving virtually shut down Mathews's only regular public event, the traditional Saturday night gatherings on Main Street, because most participants came by car. On one Saturday night alone, Virginia State Police and federal investigators swooped into Mathews and cited more than two hundred motorists for defying the pleasure-driving ban. The number would have been much higher had the authorities not run out of tickets. The *Gazette-Journal* reported the busts, while noting somewhat defensively that other communities received their share of tickets and that "Mathews County was not exactly in a class alone with regard to pleasure driving."

Even the self-sufficient and resourceful cook faced problems—canning vegetables required sugar, which was rationed, and Henny Hodges cut way back on the hundreds of jars of vegetables she normally canned in preparation for the winter. As rationing expanded, the government urged Americans to start "victory gardens" to grow their own food. Most families in Mathews, of course, had been growing their own food in gardens long before the war.

Job opportunities in Mathews had never been so plentiful. Buses circled through the county several times a day to pick up and drop off shift workers for the shipyards in Newport News and Norfolk and the Navy Mine Depot in Yorktown, which produced mines to protect American rivers and harbors from U-boats. Mathews women who had never even considered taking jobs outside the home were being courted by the military, the defense plants, and even the crab-picking and oyster-shucking houses, whose male workers were gone. One of the Hodges daughters, Elizabeth, would join the Army Air Forces as a medical technician, and care for wounded soldiers in stateside hospitals.

Every week brought new reports of Mathews men being torpedoed, and for every ship actually sunk, two or three were falsely rumored to have gone down. Captain Stanley Hodges, Captain Jesse's distant cousin, survived the sinking of the tanker *Gulfpenn* near the mouth of the Mississippi. Floyd West escaped the torpedoed tanker *Harry F. Sinclair Jr.*, off Hatteras. The entire county was on edge. The Reverend Iris Belch of Gwynn's Island Baptist Church told his flock, "[W]e have been impressed by the anxiety in the hearts of the families of these brave men, that it requires courage on their part to endure, in keeping the home fires burning."

Amid all the gloom and uncertainty, the *Gazette-Journal* found cause for optimism in a report that a large Allied convoy had fought its way to the port of Murmansk in North Russia with arms and ammunition to help the beleaguered Red Army hold off the Nazis. That convoy, the paper explained, "had to not only evade the enemy forces in the Atlantic but elude a large naval force . . . in Northern waters." The Mathews mariners who had heard of the Murmansk Run at all knew it only by its evil reputation. But that was about to change.

CHAPTER SEVEN

"Avoid Polar Bear Liver"

Before setting out on the *Green Island*, Genious Hudgins Jr. had called the Caribbean the worst possible place for a merchant ship to sail in 1942. But that distinction belonged by general agreement to the Murmansk Run. The voyage to the bleak northern coast of Russia was a 5,000-mile gauntlet of diabolical weather, air raids, and U-boat attacks. And the Murmansk Run was as much about politics as it was about delivering supplies to the Russians.

Russia had joined the Allied cause only after Hitler broke his pact with Russian dictator Joseph Stalin and invaded the Soviet Union in 1941. By the spring of 1942, millions of Russians had died fighting on the eastern front—roughly 1 million at Kiev alone—and the Nazis were still advancing. Stalin complained to his new allies that Russia was doing most of the fighting against Germany, which at that point was true. The Russian dictator demanded that Britain and the United States relieve pressure on Russia by opening a second front with an amphibious invasion of France. Roosevelt and Churchill did not think their troops were ready. But they worried that if they ignored Stalin's complaints, he might negotiate a separate peace with Hitler.

Stalin's messages to Churchill left no doubt that he was absolutely ruthless. Stalin did not see why his allies balked at suffering heavy casualties. He reminded Churchill to send him fresh newsreel footage of a German city bombed to ruins. He accused his allies of standing by and allowing the Nazis and the Russians to destroy one another. It was true that Roosevelt and Churchill already saw Russia as a future threat. Churchill had called Bolshevism "foul baboonery and a plague-bearing infection," and said he did not think the Russians needed to be thanked for "fighting in their own country for their own lives." But he was willing to help anyone who stood against Hitler.

The best way to help Russia, short of invading France, was to ship weapons and supplies to the Red Army. The most direct route was through the Mediterranean, which was blocked by the Germans. The next best route was through the Arctic to Murmansk, a bleak port on the frigid Barents Sea. Murmansk was only a thousand miles from the North Pole, but its harbor stayed free of ice all year because the tail of the warm Gulf Stream ended there. The British had been sending convoys to Murmansk since 1941. In May 1942, Roosevelt, in an effort to keep Stalin in the Allied fold, added U.S. ships to the Murmansk convoys.

The route to Murmansk led north from Britain through the North Atlantic to Iceland, and then farther north into the Arctic Circle, east through the Strait of Norway, past Bear Island, and into the stormy Barents Sea. The trip subjected ships and men to some of the most extreme weather on the planet. Gales built mountainous waves. Sea spray froze so fast on ships' hulls and superstructures that men had to chip off the ice constantly to keep the ship from becoming top-heavy. The water was so cold that a man who fell in would be dead in minutes. Polar bears glared from caves in drifting icebergs. Collisions of cold and warm currents created dense fog, as well as thermal layers in the water that confused sonar. The nearness of the magnetic North Pole skewed compass readings. A ship could steam blindly for days before the navigator was able to fix her position by the stars. Ships had to be fortified for the Murmansk Run, their bows reinforced with cement and their bronze propellers replaced with steel ones less likely to shatter if they struck ice. *How to Abandon Ship* offered advice about life-boat survival in the Arctic, including a section on how to kill and eat polar bears. Among its key points: "Avoid polar bear liver."*

But the Germans posed greater hazards than the weather. U-boats painted white to blend in with the ice waited for the convoys in the fjords of Nazi-occupied Norway, as did the battleship *Tirpitz* and other German warships. But the worst threat by far to the Murmansk convoys was from German bombers. The North Cape of Norway was home to six Luftwaffe air bases, one of which was only thirty-five miles from Murmansk. The Arctic sun never set in spring or summer, which allowed the bombers to attack twenty-four hours a day.

The first Mathews man to set out on the Murmansk Run was Captain Guy Hudgins, a distant cousin of Genious Hudgins Jr. Guy Hudgins was a rugged mariner with a taste for the good life. Guy had been born in Portsmouth, Virginia, but moved to Mathews to live with relatives after his father vanished from a ferryboat in a storm. Guy always wondered if his father had faked his death and abandoned the family. Whatever the truth was, Guy quit school in the sixth grade to support his mother and sisters. He fished and crabbed and delivered newspapers on horseback. He became friends with Dewey and Leslie Hodges and worked on a tug and then on steamships. During a visit home to Mathews in 1926, he plunged into the Saturday night crowd on Main Street and locked eyes with Dorothy Powell, the pretty daughter of a Mathews sea captain. They married after Guy was promoted to captain by the American Export Lines, and bought a duplex in Jersey City, New Jersey, where the company docked its ships.

Guy commanded ships on voyages all over the world. He visited Beth-

---

* The booklet recommended shooting a polar bear in "a place just behind the shoulder, so that the bullet will pierce the heart. Do not shoot a polar bear while it is in the water. You will not be able to haul it out." The authors suggested eating bear meat raw, frozen, or half frozen because it becomes stringy when cooked. No records indicate a lifeboat crew ever ate a polar bear, or vice versa.

lehem and King Tut's tomb, and carried mail to Malta and Syria. Dorothy enjoyed life in Jersey City with plenty of free time and spending money. Friends from Mathews stopped in when their ships arrived in port, and Dorothy and Guy entertained them, though sometimes Guy could party too hard. Dorothy kept after him to cut back on his drinking, and he kept promising to. Guy's politics could seem conservative; he hated Franklin and Eleanor Roosevelt for championing social programs, which Guy had not needed to make his way. But Guy was open-minded toward the world at large. "My father did not care if you were a laborer or the Queen of England, he treated every person the same," his daughter Diana recalled. Guy became friends with two gay mariners in his crew and had a glossy photograph of one of them, an underwear model, oiled up and wearing leopardskin briefs. He liked to joke that all radio operators and second assistant engineers were gay. Guy attended church, mostly out of habit, but his faith had limits. He did not believe in life after death.

Guy began the war as captain of the Liberty ship *Zebulon B. Vance*. After several uneventful voyages, he was ordered to pick up military supplies in New York, including 400 tons of TNT, and join convoy PQ-15, bound for Murmansk. Convoys to North Russia in 1942 bore the designation PQ—the initials of a British convoy planner—followed by the sequential number of the convoy. PQ-15 was the fifteenth major convoy to Murmansk. Merchant ships bound for Murmansk always traveled in convoys, like those crossing the North Atlantic to Britain.

Guy sailed the *Zebulon B. Vance* across the Atlantic to Scotland to join convoy PQ-15. The convoy was about half the size of the big North Atlantic convoys, which could have as many as sixty ships. This one comprised twenty-five merchant ships, which formed a rectangle five miles wide and two miles deep. They were surrounded by antisubmarine vessels, mostly trawlers and minesweepers, which used sonar to screen the water around them for U-boats. An outer ring of destroyers and other warships kept watch for enemy ships and planes.

The convoy headed north into the Arctic Circle. The sea ice reached down into the shipping lanes, forcing the convoy even closer to Norway and the German bombers. The escorts spotted a cluster of German mines bobbing in the swells in front of the convoy and blew them up with shell fire. The convoy was 300 miles from Bear Island at the entrance to the Barents Sea when a German surveillance plane appeared overhead. The plane was a big, long-range Focke-Wulf Condor. Mariners called them the vultures. The plane kept pace with the convoy, flying just out of range of the ships' guns, as the pilot radioed the convoy's size, speed, and bearing to the bombers.

A few hours later, a faint bumblebee-like drone filled the air, and four black dots materialized in the sky astern. The *Zebulon B. Vance*'s dog, a black-and-white mongrel named Zebbie, barked a warning. The dots resolved themselves into German torpedo bombers, which launched small torpedoes from low altitude. The escort ships threw up a wall of antiaircraft fire. The planes broke formation and veered toward the convoy at different angles, flying so low that they seemed to skim the waves. All their torpedoes missed. Guy stepped out of the bridge to see the planes roar overhead, then watched as one plane crashed into the ocean. Some of the escorts began dropping depth charges, which meant they had found U-boats. Soon Zebbie resumed barking and five more dots raced toward them. This time, a torpedo bomber scored a direct hit on the British freighter *Cape Corso*, which was directly ahead of the *Vance*. The *Cape Corso* exploded. The *Vance* swerved to miss her. Guy saw men thrashing in the icy water, but the convoy could not stop without endangering everyone else on board the ships. Only nine men on the *Cape Corso* survived.

Next came Stuka dive-bombers, whose flared wings made them resemble birds of prey. They were equipped with sirens to emit piercing screams as they dived. The first Stukas hit no ships, but over the next few days, the planes attacked in waves that began to feel like one endless siege. "We did not take our clothes off during the entire trip through the Arctic region," Guy recalled. "We slept whenever and wherever we could. There were so many alarms I lost count. We were on the alert all the time." On the fourth day, the convoy was picking its way through a field of small chunks of floating ice known as growlers when a storm hit. The ships rode huge waves. Heavy snow piled up on their decks. The German air bases were socked in. The storm persisted until Russian destroyers emerged from the gloom to escort the convoy into Murmansk.

Guy had never been anywhere like Murmansk. It had an apocalyptic feel. Fires continuously burned throughout the city. German bombers attacked five or six times a day. Russian fighters rose to meet them, and engaged in dogfights with German fighters. Antiaircraft guns crackled from sandbagged bunkers in the rubble of buildings. A bomb hit the docks close enough to the *Vance* to rain debris onto her deck. The Russians quickly repaired any damage to the docks with lumber delivered daily by train. Salvage teams roamed the harbor, blowing up hulks of bombed ships to make way for new arrivals. Guy wrote that Murmansk "was almost deserted but for the soldiers, and only necessities are obtainable." He was impressed by the Russians' toughness, but when a friendly Russian asked him what he thought of Murmansk, he stood speechless.

The *Vance*'s cargo was unloaded by Russian women and Red Army soldiers on leave from the eastern front. The soldiers were hard-looking characters, and their presence so agitated Zebbie that she had to be shut up in the galley. The process took twelve days, during which Guy counted forty-five air raids. A plane crashed into the marshes a quarter mile away but Guy could not tell whose it was. Despite the hair-raising prospect of the return voyage, the scene in Murmansk was grimmer, and he was glad when the convoy re-formed to set out for home.

German bombers attacked the returning convoy almost immediately, but were driven off by a British fighter plane. The British pilot's mission was to take off from one of the merchant ships when the convoy needed air cover, fly for as long as his fuel lasted, and then ditch the plane in the ocean and be picked up from the water—the ship had no room for the plane to land again. The pilot ended up dying when his parachute failed to open. Months would pass before Guy would see his first escort carrier—a miniature aircraft carrier for convoys, with room for planes to take off *and* land.

Hardly one for military discipline, Guy stepped on a few toes during the voyage. He infuriated the convoy commodore by racing the *Vance* ahead of the rest of the ships, and he angered the Navy gun crew on the *Vance* by sticking them with the worst bunks and declining to order his crew to spell them in the gun tubs. But he got the ship home. Twenty-two of the twenty-five ships in PQ-15 delivered their cargo in Murmansk and got back safely. The convoy was considered a success, and the Allies decided to send even more ships in the next one, PQ-16. Four Mathews men would make that run, but only two would survive it.

PQ-16 formed off Halifax, Nova Scotia, in mid-May, crossed the Atlantic to England, and, like its predecessor, headed north into the Arctic Circle. On May 25, a Condor pilot spotted PQ-16 off Norway and called in the bombers. The first wave of bombers failed to hit a ship, but two bombs exploded in the water close enough to the old freighter *Syros* to cause damage in her engine room. The *Syros* straggled behind the convoy.

Her crew of thirty-nine included William Cecil Ripley Jr., an able seaman from the Mathews village of Susan. Cecil, as his family called him, was twenty-eight years old, tall and rail thin. He had quit fishing pound nets with his father in 1936 to join the Merchant Marine. Cecil had deep-set eyes that lent him a sorrowful aspect, but he had a wry sense of humor and plenty of girlfriends. A month before, he had written his family in Mathews that he had just been to India and thought his next stop was Russia. His family did not know the name of his ship.

Cecil had been at sea long enough to know that the bomb damage had placed the *Syros* in grave danger. The U-boats followed behind Arctic convoys just to pick off stragglers like her. Like many ships bound for Russia, the *Syros* was a floating bomb. Her holds were packed with explosives and ammunition. At around 1 a.m. on May 26, in hazy Arctic daylight, the U-703 crept to within a thousand yards of the *Syros* and launched a torpedo. Men on other ships saw the torpedo racing toward the *Syros* and fired machine guns at it to try to detonate it prematurely. But the torpedo struck the *Syros* just below the smokestack. Nothing happened for a second or two. Then a deafening explosion split the freighter in half. Both halves sank, leaving dozens of men thrashing or clinging to wreckage in 29-degree water. A rescue vessel picked up thirty of the crew, but ten others, including Cecil Ripley, were never seen again.

When Cecil's mother received her telegram from the government, she climbed the stairs to his old room and opened the door for the first time since his last visit. Cecil had left a coat and hat on the bed. She closed the door and told her daughter not to touch them because "they're all I have left of him."

Charles V. "Bud" Majette of Mathews watched the *Syros* explode from the deck of the freighter *Alamar*, which was sailing just ahead in the same column. Majette had left a $3-a-week job at an ice plant to join the Merchant Marine. He had just turned twenty-one and gotten his third-officer's license. He had known Cecil Ripley from grade school but had not known he was on the *Syros*. The explosion reminded Majette that the *Alamar* was carrying 350 tons of TNT in her holds. In addition, her main deck was crowded with planes, tanks, train locomotives, and drums of highly flammable aviation fuel. Majette did not like to think about what would happen if the ship got hit. He could stay calm only by working constantly, even when he was off watch. Some of his shipmates were so unnerved by the constant air attacks that they flailed their hands at the swooping planes as if swatting at wasps.

As the convoy approached Bear Island, Stukas attacked from several directions at once. Majette looked up to see a Junkers 88 light bomber dart through a gap in the wall of antiaircraft fire and drop a bomb squarely on the *Alamar*'s deck. The drums of aviation fuel burst into flames. The ship's deck cracked open. The crew coolly lowered two lifeboats and climbed down Jacob's ladders into them. Majette was on his way down the ladder when a new eruption of flames panicked the men in the lifeboat below him, and they pulled away too early. Majette splashed into water so cold it took his breath away. The lifeboat immediately picked him up. All thirty-six men on the *Alamar* got away safely and were picked up by other ships. The convoy struggled on to Murmansk. Majette thought he was lucky the bomb had found the aviation fuel rather than the TNT in the holds. But his voyage was far from over. The ships of PQ-16 still had to survive their stay in Murmansk, and then their trip home.

By June 1942, the war in the Pacific was starting to turn. The U.S. fleet had halted the Japanese advance across the Pacific at the Battle of the Coral Sea, in which the United States and Japan each lost an aircraft carrier. The U.S. and Japanese fleets collided on June 4 in the Battle of Midway. Dive bombers from U.S. carriers sank four huge Japanese carriers, reversing the balance of naval power in the Pacific. Admiral King distinguished himself in the Pacific as a strategist, halting the Japanese advance through skillful deployment of carrier task forces. He also disrupted the Japanese supply lines through aggressive submarine attacks on the Japanese merchant fleet, which was as poorly protected as America's.

But the war against Germany, which Roosevelt and Churchill had agreed to win first, was being lost. The Red Army continued to hemorrhage men and surrender Russian soil. In North Africa, German Field Marshall Erwin Rommel's Afrika Corps routed the British in a tank battle at Tobruk, Libya. In the Mediterranean, two Allied convoys trying to reach the strategic British-held island of Malta were pummeled by German bombers. Nazi storm troopers in a Czechoslovakian village responded to the killing of a German officer by executing every man and boy in the village and then torching it. Reports came from Eastern Europe that Jews were being killed with poison gas. The U-boat force was expanding by thirty submarines a month. Doenitz sent U-boats to attack Canadian vessels in the Saint Lawrence estuary, the river road to the Great Lakes.

U-boats had sunk forty-four merchant ships in U.S. waters in May 1942, the highest monthly total of the war to date. The U-701 added insult to injury on the night of June 9 by sneaking into the main channel at the mouth of the Chesapeake Bay and laying a string of mines. The mines went undetected for five days until an inbound Allied convoy blundered into them. William Coles Forrest Jr. of Mathews was sleeping in his bunk on the tanker *Robert C. Tuttle* when the ship triggered one of the mines. The impact knocked Forrest onto the deck. He grabbed a life vest and climbed down a ladder into a waiting lifeboat. Two other ships in the convoy also detonated mines. Black smoke from the damaged ships billowed into the sky. Wide-eyed tourists emerged from Virginia Beach hotels to watch. Firefighters saved the *Robert Tuttle*. Navy planes and ships raced back and forth in ferocious pursuit of a U-boat that was long gone.

Since the start of the war, jittery coastal residents had feared U-boats landing spies or saboteurs in their midst. Mysterious lights were reported on empty beaches. Dead Germans were rumored to have been found with ticket stubs from local movie theaters in their pockets. Now some of the fears would come true, as the U-boats grew bolder still.

On the night of June 13, the U-202 landed a team of four would-be saboteurs in dense fog on a beach at Amagansett, Long Island. Their mission, code-named Operation Pastorius, was to choose a vital industrial plant and wreck it, but their plans went wildly off track from the start. The Germans were spotted as soon as they arrived on the beach by a twenty-one-year-old Coast Guardsman named John C. Cullen, who was patrolling the beach on foot. The Germans first told Cullen they were clamming—in an area with no clams. Then the Germans' leader, George Dasch, abandoned the charade. He pointedly asked the unarmed Cullen if he had a mother and father, and added, "I wouldn't want to have to kill you." He offered Cullen $100 in cash to just go away and forget he had seen anything, then quickly upped the offer to $300. Cullen pretended to accept. Dasch told Cullen to look him in the eyes. Cullen did so, half afraid that Dasch intended to hypnotize him. Dasch asked, "Would you recognize me if you saw me again?" Cullen—no fool—said no, and Dasch let him walk away. Cullen ran to his station and reported the encounter to his superiors.

The Long Island saboteurs managed to reach Manhattan by train and melt into the crowds, but Dasch's confidence in the mission had evaporated. He gave himself up and provided the FBI with enough information to arrest the other members of his team, as well as a second four-man team of saboteurs who had landed on the beach near Jacksonville, Florida. Two of the Florida saboteurs made it to Cincinnati, and two others to Chicago, but no one got as far as picking a target. All eight of the Germans would be tried by a special military tribunal and convicted of espionage. Six would be executed; Dasch and another man who informed on his partners would receive long prison terms, commuted after the war by President Harry Truman. No U-boat would ever land a sabotage team on American soil again, although two spies were landed on a beach near Bar Harbor, Maine, in late 1944. Both were quickly apprehended.

Most U-boats stuck to torpedoing ships, and those in the Caribbean continued to find easy prey. A rising star among U-boat commanders, Hans-Ludwig Witt viewed his assignment to the Caribbean as a chance to rack up kills against weak defenses. He would in fact sink ten Allied ships in the Caribbean, including Dewey Hodges's *Onondaga*. Witt took command of the U-129 from Nicolai Clausen, who had used it to sink several American ships, including Captain Walter Hudgins's freighter the *Barbara*.

Witt guided the U-129 from the Atlantic into the Caribbean through the narrow Nicholas Channel between Cuba and the Grand Bahamas Bank. He probably did not expect to find his first victim right there in the channel, before he even reached the Caribbean. But when Witt spotted a heavily loaded freighter through his periscope, he knew what to do.

The U-129 drilled a torpedo into the freighter amidships, causing an explosion that blew men into the air. The ship plunged down by the stern. One lifeboat got free. Witt guided the U-129 alongside it. He pointed a machine gun at the castaways and demanded their ship's name, cargo, and destination. The men said their ship was the Bull Line freighter *Millinocket*. She had been hauling bauxite ore from the Virgin Islands to Mobile,

Alabama. Her captain, Lewis Callis of Gwynn's Island, was among the eleven men missing.

The castaways asked Witt for a first-aid kit, and the U-boat commander gave them one. Witt did not make small talk. He did not wish the survivors good luck. The U-129 submerged and headed into the Caribbean with one kill already to its credit. The castaways fired rockets until a Cuban fishing boat picked them up.

Lewis Callis's body was never found. He had sailed the Caribbean for the Bull Line for more than twenty years. His wife and children lived on Gwynn's Island, and he always took time at sea to write to them. One of his letters included a poem he had written about home:

There is an Island in Old Virginia,
Down on the Chesapeake,
It's my old home town,
And I'm going there this week
Yes, I'm going back tomorrow,
If I can steal, beg or borrow
I just want enough for fare
For you won't need money there.
Down on my old Gwynn's Island home

The *Millinocket* was the thirty-seventh merchant ship sunk in U.S.-patrolled waters that June, which was shaping up as yet another record month for ships lost. James Ashberry of Mathews survived the torpedoing of the freighter *City of Alma* in the deep ocean off Puerto Rico. Ashberry, a tough, hard-drinking seaman, came home to Mathews to rest up but feared dying of boredom. He said, "I had rather be in the Atlantic Ocean, for it is just as alive as Mathews." John Elmo Godsey Jr. of Mathews survived a U-boat assault on the Bull Line freighter *Manuela* off the Outer Banks of North Carolina. Godsey was knocked cold by the torpedo explosion but revived when cold seawater swirled over him on deck. He made his way into a lifeboat with a deep gash on his head and two black eyes. The ship stayed afloat and Godsey went back aboard to search for two shipmates who had been on watch in the engine room, but the door to the engine room was sealed shut in a misshapen way that ended all hope.

The sinkings prompted Army chief of staff George C. Marshall to write Admiral King: "The losses by submarines off our Atlantic seaboard and in the Caribbean now threaten our entire war effort . . . We are all aware of the limited number of escort craft available, but has every conceivable improvised means been brought to bear on this situation? I am fearful that another month or two of this will so cripple our means of transport that we will be unable to bring sufficient men and planes to bear against the enemy in critical theaters to exercise a determining influence on the war."

The pointed question from a respected colleague appeared to pierce King's detachment. He replied to Marshall that the Navy's resources were stretched thin with escort duty for the North Atlantic convoys and troop transports to Britain. As far as protecting coastal shipping, King wrote, "We had to improvise on a large scale . . . We took over all pleasure craft that could be used and sent them out with makeshift armament and untrained crews. We employed for patrol purposes aircraft that could not carry bombs, and planes flown from school fields by student pilots. We armed our merchant ships as rapidly as possible. We employed fishing boats as volunteer lookouts . . ."

King concluded his letter by professing a devotion to convoys. "I might say in this connection that escort is not just one way of handling the submarine menace; it is the only way that gives any promise of success."

In fact, King had shown little enthusiasm for any of the improvisational methods of protecting coastal shipping, such as pleasure craft and unarmed air patrols, for which he was now taking credit. And he had shown little interest in coastal convoys until he could accumulate enough new ships and planes to operate the kind of powerful convoys he favored. King did not acknowledge that to Marshall, but he apparently gave in to the latter's pressure. King began releasing more old destroyers to the bucket-brigade convoys for longer periods. Two weeks after Marshall's memo, the first convoy from Key West sailed for Panama. For the first time, a merchant ship could theoretically travel the length of the U.S. coast and into the Caribbean with an armed escort. Roosevelt wrote King that he was pleased, but added, "I think it has taken an unconscionable time to get things going." The convoy system still had a lot of holes for U-boats to exploit. It offered little or no protection in less traveled waters between small ports. But the open season on merchant ships in U.S. waters was finally over.

At the end of June, Captain Jesse came home to Gales Neck for the first time in months. He and his grandson J. W. Corbett had spent the last four months on a tug in the Caribbean, towing and pushing barges between ports. A torpedo whizzed past the tug's stern one day, but nothing further came of it, and Jesse said nothing to Henny about it. He had a reputation for fearlessness at sea. He once rescued two men from a leaking barge in a howling blizzard that blew off his tug's smokestack. He taunted men who cowered when seas swept the tugboat's deck, but when he came home, he just wanted to relax. He would sit for hours at a table in the stifling kitchen, cheating at solitaire in a blue haze of cigar smoke. Henny treated him like a king. He awoke every morning to a hot breakfast, a set of freshly cleaned and folded clothes, and a basin of warm water next to his razor. Nevertheless, he always found something to complain about, and Henny cried.

Captain Jesse's four-year-old grandson, Jesse Carroll Thornton, who lived at Gales Neck with Henny, reverted to his best behavior when his grandfather came home. He might get yelled at or even smacked by Henny if he acted up, but Jesse had a short fuse and meted out punishment with a belt. For all of that, Jesse Carroll was always glad to have his grandfather safely home. The boy saw a side of him that most people could never imagine. Jesse would comfort him when he woke up from a bad dream. He remembered being pulled in a wagon by Jesse as he and Henny walked the property at Gales Neck, talking about the farm, holding hands.

Henny celebrated Captain Jesse's visit home in June 1942 with a huge family gathering and feast, which she called a dining. The guest list for a Hodges dining included all members of the family, including every son who was in port. The list also included dozens of neighbors and friends. The turnouts always exceeded fifty and sometimes one hundred. Henny spent days cooking in a big woodstove with a firebox on one side and a tank for heating water on the other. She fixed fish, fried chicken, ham, spoon bread, and biscuits with fried hog parts. A Washington newspaper reporter who attended a dining described a meal "of such dimensions that the dessert course calls for three freezers of ice cream."

The Hodges dinner table seated only sixteen, so the guests at a dining ate in shifts. The men were served first, starting with Jesse, who sat at the head of the table facing east toward the sea. After the men ate, the women took their turn. The children went last. David, the youngest Hodges son, joked that he learned to drink coffee black because the milk never once got to him.

Though Henny loved to cook, her true pleasure in the dinings came from bringing her family together. They and the farm were her only interests. She loved to talk with her children, and soak up all the details of their families' lives. She liked it when her children stayed behind in the kitchen to sit with her after the commotion died down. These gatherings were the best times of her life. The dining in June 1942 stood out because four of her six seafaring sons happened to be home.

Captain Dewey Hodges brought his family from Norfolk. He was still recovering from his illness, but he never missed a dining if he was home. Dewey felt a responsibility to help keep the family together because he was the second oldest and Raymond rarely came home. The trip from Dewey's house in Norfolk to Gales Neck took five hours and included two ferry rides. On a hot summer day, it was nothing short of an ordeal. But Dewey piled Edna and the three girls into their Lincoln Zephyr and set out for Mathews. He sang all the way, as he always did, crooning "Mexicali Rose" and "You Are My Sunshine" until the girls started giggling and then singing along. Even Edna joined in.

At the dining, Dewey greeted his brother Leslie Hodges, and his wife, Cecile. Leslie was a licensed captain but did not have his own ship. He was serving as first officer on the Ford freighter *Oneida*, a laker running cargo between the Caribbean and the Gulf of Mexico. Leslie was something of an outlier in the Hodges family. He was the only son with dark hair, and wore a moustache that his brothers said made him look like Hitler. Leslie took the joking well but never joked back. He was also the only quiet Hodges son. Cecile was a slender, dark-haired firecracker from Mobile, Alabama, who had a sweet nature but swore like a stevedore. Leslie and Cecile lived in Norfolk and attended dinings when Leslie was in port, but they never seemed quite comfortable at them and hung at the edges. Leslie once told his sisters he never felt the same coming home after he caused the car crash that killed his two-year-old sister, Henrietta.

The guests at the dining included Willie Hodges, the captain of an oceangoing tug that guided ships and barges along the coast and into the Bay. Willie was a jolly man whose waistline was expanding as fast as Jesse's. His brothers joked that Willie had stayed at the table for the women's and children's shifts. Willie and his family lived only two houses away from Dewey in Norfolk, and the families often got together to share a bushel of steamed crabs or a bag of fresh oysters.

The three youngest Hodges brothers, Spencer, Coleman, and David, were so much younger than their older brothers, they were almost a separate generation. Spencer lived in Mathews with his wife and son and worked at the local creamery, making ice cream. He had started going to sea but injured his back while working for Dewey on the *East Indian*, and went ashore for good. Spencer became the only Hodges brother to graduate from high school. Though he stayed on land, he helped his seagoing brothers by recruiting Mathews men for their ships.

Coleman Hodges was tall and almost gangly, with a pronounced

Adam's apple and a grin like his brother Dewey's. He was a dedicated jokester. He could squirt milk from a cow's udder accurately for long distances. Only Coleman's wife and daughters saw his serious side. He was working his way up through the officer ranks at the Ford fleet and was determined to command a ship in time to serve his country in the war.

David Hodges, the youngest of the seven Hodges sons, lived with his family in Norfolk, where he worked in a shipyard as a rigger, securing heavy objects to be moved. David aspired to become a pilot in the Bay, guiding ships up the channels between Norfolk and Baltimore. He mentioned his goal to his father one day while working on the farm, and Captain Jesse replied, "Why don't you start by piloting that manure over here?" David and Coleman were best friends. David could make anybody laugh, and he sometimes used his wit to cut people he disliked.

The only Hodges boy absent from the dining that June was Raymond. He was ferrying American soldiers across the Atlantic on the *Mormacmoon*. Raymond's wife, Dolly, came to Gales Neck, however, along with her sons, Raymond Jr. and Bill. Fourteen-year-old Bill was impressed by the sight of many fine sea captains in one place. They included not only his grandfather and uncles but his cousin Will Hunley, who was about to be given command of a ship.

After the meal, the men strolled across the wide front yard to the point of Gales Neck, where several lawn chairs encircled a table near the water's edge. The men lit cigars and passed around a bottle of Jack Daniel's whiskey. The jokes flew and the captains told preposterous stories about one another and everything else. Dewey claimed to have grown a tomato so big that it had to be sliced with a crosscut saw. As David put it, "The only difference between a fairy tale and a sea story is that a fairy tale begins, 'Once upon a time,' and a sea story begins, 'Look, this ain't no bullshit.'" About the only subject that did not come up was the U-boat war. Nobody wanted to talk business. The brothers wanted to leave the war behind, and just enjoy their mother's cooking and the pleasures of an early summer evening on Gales Neck.

Inside the farmhouse, the four Hodges daughters directed the cleanup. Though overshadowed by their brothers, they were a formidable group. They answered only to Henny. The eldest daughter, Alice, was as tall and broad-shouldered as her brothers. She was a young widow with three children. She waited tables at a restaurant at the end of a fishing pier. The place got rowdy at night, and Alice was said to have picked up a man by his collar and belt loops and thrown him out the door. Alice was the most pious of the Hodges children, and frowned upon some of her sisters' activities, particularly those of Hilda Fourteen, who went to the dance halls.

Alice and her middle sisters, Elizabeth and Louise, had booming voices and argued all the time. They could go back and forth for hours over trivial points such as when it had rained last. They once got into a ferocious debate over what color sweater a woman had been wearing in her casket at her funeral. None of them ever conceded a point, and they held grudges for months. Their endless bickering made Henny cry, but Jesse sometimes egged them on for entertainment.

The men stayed out on the riverbank until the fireflies came out and the wives called that it was time to go. Each guest usually took home some freshly picked vegetables and sometimes a live chicken. Henny cried as each of her sons kissed her good-bye. One by one, they got into their cars and started down the driveway, back to their homes, and then to their ships. Dewey, Leslie, Willie, and Coleman would rejoin Raymond in the U-boat war. Jesse and J.W. would be close behind.

At Murmansk, the surviving ships of convoy PQ-16 finished unloading their cargo and were organized into a new convoy for the long trip home. Bud Majette and the others who had been pulled from the water after the *Alamar* sinking were given bunks on her sister ship, the *Massmar*. Naturally, Majette found a couple of Mathews men on the *Massmar*'s regular crew. The ship's first officer, Captain Sam Jones Diggs, who was named for the nineteenth-century evangelist Sam Jones, had left Mathews at age sixteen and sailed the world for almost three decades. Sam rarely returned to

Mathews, but he wrote to his family from every port. He addressed all his letters to his half sister Helen, the postmistress in the Mathews hamlet of Laban.

Sam's last letter from the *Massmar*, on April 26, had been cut to pieces by the censors. "Dear Sister," it began. "Arrived here today from _____. _____ just called for orders. Will go _____. _____ don't know how long we will be here." Sam told his sister not to write, "as we don't have any forwarding address. We don't know where we will go or be."

The other Mathews man on the *Massmar*, Charles Edwards, might have been the only mariner in the convoy excited about sailing to Murmansk. Edwards had been at sea for five years and was still intoxicated by travel. He kept a map of the world on his wall at home, and every time he got back from a voyage, he marked the route. The Murmansk Run would be an impressive addition to the map if he lived to add it.

The Germans ignored the *Massmar* and the other empty PQ-16 ships on their return trip from Russia. They threw all their U-boats and aircraft at the next Murmansk-bound convoy, PQ-17. Majette got a glimpse of PQ-17 when the two convoys passed at a great distance on the Fourth of July. PQ-17 was sailing beneath a fiery cloud of bombers and antiaircraft fire. Majette compared it to a Fourth of July fireworks display. He had no inkling that PQ-17 was about to turn into the worst convoy disaster of the war.

PQ-17 was the largest Arctic convoy yet, with thirty-eight merchant ships and forty-five escort ships, including thirteen British cruisers and destroyers. Soon after PQ-17 passed out of Majette's sight, the British Admiralty abruptly withdrew all of the escorts. The British believed, wrongly, that the German battleship *Tirpitz* was emerging from the Norwegian fjords to attack the convoy. The British escort ships could not match the *Tirpitz*'s firepower, and the British could not allow the *Tirpitz* to destroy them. So the Admiralty took the desperate step of ordering the escorts to abandon the convoy and save themselves. The merchant ships were ordered to "scatter" and run for Murmansk. The Germans could not catch them all.

But the Germans, as it turned out, came close. Over the next six days, the Condors tracked the scattered cargo ships into remote stretches of the Barents Sea, and then guided U-boats to sink them. One German Condor pilot radioed the captain of a merchant ship the exact time a U-boat would arrive to sink it. Men who had escaped their sinking ship in a lifeboat refused to be picked up by a second ship, reasoning that they would just have to get into another lifeboat when the second ship was torpedoed. They were right. The crews of the two ships met again later on the beach of a remote island. The *Tirpitz* never attacked the convoy, but the faulty intelligence and the decision to withdraw the escorts enabled the Germans to sink twenty-four of the thirty-eight merchant ships in PQ-17, killing 153 mariners. The Allies suspended all convoys to Murmansk.

After passing the ill-fated PQ-17, the *Massmar* and the other ships returning from the previous convoy encountered no threat except the weather. But the weather was enough. They were only a day out of the safety of the harbor at Reykjavik, Iceland, when a storm engulfed them. Two days of dense fog followed. Navigators could not take the stars and lost their bearings. A senior officer mistook an iceberg for land and, in his confusion, directed the convoy into the Allied minefield protecting Reykjavik. No one could see the mines bobbing in the rough seas.

Charles Edwards was oiling the steering gear on the *Massmar*'s main deck when a mine detonated against the hull with enough force to blow the ship's bow out of the water. The *Massmar* sank fast. Majette helped lower a lifeboat, but a huge wave caught it and threw it right back on the deck beside them, upside down. Majette, who could not swim, saw a hatch cover floating by and jumped toward it. The cold water hit him like a punch and quickly sapped his strength. A sailor on a Free French escort ship threw him a line but he was too weak to reach for it. "All I wanted to do was go to sleep," he recalled. The French sailor dove into the water and tied the line around him, and he was pulled to safety. Sam Diggs was not so lucky. He apparently was trapped in his stateroom and went to the bottom with the ship. His sister, the Laban postmistress, opened the government's official letter of regret. Forty men died on the *Massmar*, including twenty-three survivors of the *Alamar*.

Charles Edwards and Majette came home to Mathews. Edwards marked the route on his wall map but took no joy in it. He told a reporter that "[I] still can't get out of my mind the sight of so many men perishing." He had seen other men reduced to quivering wrecks by the constant air raids. "If I have my choice, I think I won't go back to Russia," he said. "The boys in the Caribbean have had it bad. But at least [the Germans] don't pound away at you there, and break up your rest for a couple of weeks before they finally get you."

Majette, who had survived two plunges into subfreezing water, agreed. He wanted to sail in southern waters, where at least "if I hit the water again, it would be warm."

Caribbean voyages were shorter, and the weather most of the year was perfect. Mathews men who had sailed before the war on Ford, Bull Line, or Moore-McCormack ships knew the Caribbean well and had friends in most of the ports. Everyone's favorite destination was Cuba, where the port authorities were laid back, the rum was cheap, and the women were lovely and prone to suggestion. Every mariner had a story about a magical night in Havana with a girl on his arm or a gang of shipmates at his side, raising hell. But those were peacetime memories. In 1942, Cuba had asked for U.S. help in ferreting out Axis spies, and outlawed the Nazi and Communist parties (Fidel Castro's revolution was more than a decade away). Cuban president Fulgencio Batista welcomed the construction of two American air bases and a seaplane base on Cuban soil to help patrol for U-boats, which had torpedoed merchant ships all around the island. The warm, turquoise waters off Cuba were no longer quite so inviting.

CHAPTER EIGHT

Catastrophe

D ewey Hodges had been back home in Norfolk for only two weeks after Henny's big June dining when the telephone rang. His boss at the Ford Motor Co. fleet wondered if Dewey felt well enough to serve as the substitute captain of a ship on a short run. The freighter *Onondaga*, a laker of just 2,309 tons, was being sent by the government from Mobile to Havana and back. The ship was to leave Mobile in late July.

Dewey felt fine. He had been surprised when his doctor had not cleared him three months before to command his own ship, the *East Indian*. But the *East Indian* was leaving on a six-month voyage halfway around the world, and the *Onondaga* would be gone for only a few weeks. His doctor had no objection, and Dewey called his boss and said he would go. Dewey followed the news enough to know that a run to Cuba was dangerous, but a lot of runs were dangerous in July 1942.

Dewey asked his brother Spencer in Mathews to help him fill out the *Onondaga*'s crew with Mathews men if possible. William Hammond signed on as bo'sun, returning to sea for the first time since being torpedoed on the *Norlindo*. Russell Dennis signed on as third officer. Genious Hudgins Jr. had been home only a week after being torpedoed on the *Green*

Island when he heard Dewey needed a second officer. Genious had just gotten his second-officer's license. Here was a chance to start his new job working for a captain he had known for years, and whom Genious trusted to bring them home. He gladly signed on.

Edna and the girls tried to make the days leading up to Dewey's departure feel normal, but they felt Dewey's anxiety. He was setting out on his first voyage in months—his first since America had entered the war. He was commanding an unfamiliar ship about one quarter the size of his *East Indian.* He did not say a word about it to his family. At the airport, he kissed Edna and the girls good-bye, bent down to the girls and smiled at them and said, "Be good for your mother." Then he got on a plane to Mobile.

The Navy destroyer USS *Corry* was approaching the eastern tip of Cuba near the Windward Passage on July 4 when a lookout spotted a raft bearing four oil-soaked men. They said they were the only survivors of the Bull Line freighter *Ruth,* torpedoed five nights earlier. The torpedo ignited she ship's magazine and blew off the entire stern of the ship. The *Ruth* sank so fast that thirty-four of her thirty-eight officers and crew never got out. Five were Mathews men.

The Navy sent word by telegraph to the Bull Line. That night at nine o'clock, the telephone rang at the home of Captain Robert Melville Callis on Gwynn's Island. The *Ruth* was—had been—Mel Callis's ship. He and four other Mathews men in his crew were among the missing. Mel was one of the best-known captains in Mathews, the brother of Captain Homer Callis and Captain Rodney Callis. Mel was the eldest of the three brothers, and the most carefree. It was he who had described seeing mermaids with "eyes as blue as the waters of old Milford Haven," who were "built like the steeple of Gwynn's Island Baptist Church." Mel had been a stalwart of the Bull Line for over twenty years. He lived with his wife, Lucy, whom everyone called Juna, in a house set back from the water in a patch of woods.

The Callis house stood literally within shouting distance of the homes of two of the other missing men.

Perry Collier, the *Ruth*'s carpenter, was one of the oldest mariners in Mathews at sixty years. He was tall and angular, with close-cropped gray hair. He was a devout man who sang like a songbird in the choir at Gwynn's Island Baptist Church. He gave all his spare change to children because no one had ever given him spare change when he was a child. "As long as I've got it," he told his wife, "I'm going to give it to them." Perry had known the Callis family most of his life. He fished pound nets and made runs on the *Ruth* when the fishing was poor. Perry's son Clarence had planned to ship out with him on the *Ruth* but was taken aback by the sight of new 3-inch guns installed on the old ship. "Dad, let's get off," Clarence said, but Perry replied, "No, I'm going to go ahead." In Perry's last letter, which arrived after the ship had sunk, he wrote he was excited about getting home to see a newborn grandchild.

The *Ruth*'s second officer, Howard Morris, had grown up with the Callises too. Only minutes before the torpedo struck, he had taken over the bridge from Mel, who was exhausted after several straight watches. Morris left behind a wife and a grown daughter. The *Ruth*'s bo'sun, Robert Belvin, grew up in the Mathews hamlet of Port Haywood, south of the courthouse, but the sea had been his home for the last nine of his twenty-eight years. He wrote regularly to his mother, who had just received a letter from him postmarked at Trinidad, the *Ruth*'s last port. His mother said she would not give up hope for Robert. "He was my only boy."

The fifth Mathews man killed on the *Ruth* was Ashley Clinton Williams, a black messman who had grown up in the village of Hallieford, just across Milford Haven from Gwynn's Island. Ashley was one of the few black Mathews men employed on a steamship. Blacks in 1942 were unwelcome in most of the sea unions—the National Maritime Union was an exception—and at many large U.S. shipping companies, including Moore-McCormack. The companies that did employ them relegated them to menial jobs such as steward and messman. Ashley served food to the officers and crew and did the dishes. He would have found no better opportunities in the Navy, where segregation still prevailed, and the few jobs open to black sailors were much like those open to black merchant mariners.

Ashley was the grandson of a Baptist preacher and the son of a fisherman. His family left Mathews for good in the 1930s and moved to Baltimore, where Ashley worked as a stevedore before obtaining a seaman's certificate and joining the Merchant Marine. His Mathews background may have helped him get the job on the *Ruth*. Mel Callis very likely knew that Ashley was from Mathews.

The families of Mel Callis and the other men missing from the *Ruth* were still awaiting official word from the government when the news reached Mathews that Captain Mellin Respess had been torpedoed a second time.

After his good-byes in the Mathews general store in March, Mellin had taken command of the Liberty ship *Thomas McKean*, operated for the government by Calmar Steamship Line of New York. The *Thomas McKean* spent much of June loading munitions to take to Russia. Convoys to Murmansk had been suspended since the PQ-17 debacle. Until they resumed, the only open sea route from the East Coast to the Russian front led 13,000 miles across the South Atlantic, around the Cape of Good Hope, north through the Indian Ocean, around the Horn of Africa, and through the Persian Gulf to Basra, Iraq. From Basra, trains carried the cargo thousands more miles to the front.

The *Thomas McKean* carried enough firepower to wage a small offensive. Her holds were packed with ammunition, small arms, and gasoline. Her main deck was crammed with tanks, trucks, and eleven medium-range bombers. The ship followed canals and convoys as far south as Norfolk. But from there, Mellin was directed to take her across the Atlantic alone. She was 245 miles north of Antigua on the morning of June 29 when a torpedo crashed into her hull. The explosion killed three members of the Navy Armed Guard crew who were assigned to the merchant vessel, and injured two other men.

Mellin stayed calm. He had been through the torpedoing of the *Oak-mar* only three months earlier. "How hard are we hit?" he asked the chief engineer. "It looks to me like the whole stern is gone," the chief replied. He took a closer look and declared the *Thomas McKean* "finished." Mellin gave the order to abandon ship. He disappeared into his cabin and emerged with a weighted bag containing secret Navy codes, which he threw into the sea, and a case of cigarettes, which he tossed to the chief engineer for the life-boat voyage.

Four lifeboats escaped the ship. The U-boat commander gave them time to get a safe distance away, and then finished off the *Thomas McKean* with the sub's deck cannon. Round after round smashed into the empty vessel. The men in the lifeboats counted fifty-seven shots. Finally, the am-munition in the cargo holds ignited, and flames engulfed the *Thomas Mc-Kean* as she sank by the bow. She was one of the first Liberty ships sunk.

Mellin commanded one of the four lifeboats. Another Mathews man, Roland Foster Jr., the second officer, also commanded a boat. Roland was short and wiry with enormous hands. As a boy in Mathews, he had strug-gled to stay in school, but at sea, Roland read every book he saw, including the Bible twice. He was thoughtful and opinionated, and never afraid to speak his mind.

The U-505 approached Roland's lifeboat. The sub's conning tower bore the painted images of a lioness and a swastika.* The U-boat commander, Peter Zschech, called through a megaphone in English, "Please come alongside," and then handed the megaphone to an officer with a bushy red beard and shorts. The officer asked about the *Thomas McKean*, and Roland said she was American. "Good," the officer said. He asked Roland if the castaways needed anything. Roland asked for medicine for a badly injured

---

* Mariners were instructed to pay attention to U-boats' markings and report them to Naval Intelligence agents as a way of tracking U-boats' movements. Foster obviously took that task seriously. He wrote in his report that the lioness figure on the conning tower "was standing on its hind foot, the left one I believe, and in its front paw it had a big hammer, and in its tail a torch."

mariner in his boat. The mariner had been found motionless on the deck by some Navy Armed Guard men, who risked their lives to carry him into the boat. Roland did not think he would live for long. The U-boat officer sent over a first-aid kit and apparently a sedative to ease the man's pain.

The German asked Roland and his boat-mates, "You are carrying munitions? Yes?" and, according to Roland, "looked at every one of us in the lifeboat with that wicked eye he had, as much as if to say that none of you had better say 'No' to that." Roland changed the subject, asking for the course to the nearest land. The German apparently thought Roland was asking for a tow, and replied, "We haven't got the time." Roland said he only wanted a course. "Steer with the wind," the German said, by way of ending the discussion. The U-505 pulled away and submerged, on its way to a dubious place in history.

The oarsmen had to work hard to keep the lifeboats from drifting apart. Roland called over to Mellin's lifeboat to ask his opinion about the severely injured man, who lay silent and still. Mellin told Roland to burn the man's foot with a cigarette to see if he reacted. He did not, so Roland tried burning his fingers. When he did not respond to that either, he was eased into the ocean. There was nothing more they could do for him. The survivors in all the boats had plenty of pemmican, chocolate, and malted milk tablets to eat. But the drinking-water casks in one boat had been built with green wood, which turned the water so dark that the men were afraid to drink it.

They made an effort to steer as a small convoy, heading south toward the Virgin Islands, but wind and current finally overpowered the oarsmen and separated the lifeboats. After five days, two of the four boats reached shore in the Virgin Islands. A week later, Roland's boat reached an uninhabited stretch of Anguilla Island in the Leeward Islands. Two more days later—fourteen days after the sinking—Mellin's boat finally landed on the coast of the Dominican Republic. Fifty-five of the sixty men on the *Thomas McKean* survived, but all the bombers, tanks, and ammunition lay on the sea bottom. Roland came home to Mathews and spoke his mind. "We're not getting anywhere like this," he told the *Gazette-Journal*. "We're simply throwing ships and valuable cargoes away, sending them over the southern route without convoys. The odds against us are too heavy." But he went right back to sea.

The *Thomas McKean* sinking prompted a Navy investigation into "possible leakage of information" about her route and cargo. The investigator concluded the U-boat had simply stumbled upon the ship. He added that a possible leak could not be ruled out, though, because the ship's schedule had been known to more than forty-five people in various offices from New York to London. In addition, the investigator noted, anyone walking along the pier while the *Thomas McKean* was loading had only to read the words on the cargo crates to determine their contents, or look up at a big sign reading, "*Thomas McKean*, Basra."

The day after the *Ruth* and *Thomas McKean* were sunk, Captain L. P. Borum of Gwynn's Island was torpedoed in his second world war. Borum, who was fifty-eight years old, had lost a freighter to a U-boat off the coast of Scotland in 1918, but had sailed a troopship across the Atlantic for the rest of that war. Once, while bringing the ship back empty from England, he had stopped in dangerous waters to pick up twenty-six lifeboat survivors from a torpedoed Belgian freighter, desperate after three weeks at sea. When World War II started, Borum picked up right where he'd left off, running his freight/passenger ship, the *City of Birmingham*, between the East Coast and Bermuda, hauling people and supplies to the new U.S. Navy base on the island. In May 1942, he stopped the *City of Birmingham* in mid-ocean to pick up twenty-five British seamen who had been adrift in a lifeboat for two weeks. Borum was not the kind of captain who left castaways in a lifeboat for someone else to save.

On the *City of Birmingham*'s final voyage, Borum's ship was escorted by the Navy destroyer USS *Stansbury*, steaming alongside at a distance of a mile. They were 250 miles short of Bermuda when the *Stansbury* received a radio report of a U-boat sighting well ahead of them. The *Stansbury* signaled in Morse code for the *City of Birmingham* to shift course. For some reason, no one on Borum's ship understood the signal, and the *City of Birmingham* had no signal light with which to reply; the vessels most likely had been communicating by whistles and, during daytime, by signal flags. Ten minutes later—too early for the change of course to have mattered— two torpedoes struck Borum's ship only seconds apart. A U-boat had fired a long-range shot and then fled while the torpedoes were still en route.

Borum knew as soon as the torpedoes hit that the *City of Birmingham* was doomed. For him, the stakes were much higher than they had been in World War I, when he lost an empty ship. The *City of Birmingham*'s cargo was 381 human beings, including the passengers, crew, and 261 men and women reporting to the base at Bermuda.

Borum made his way to the side of the ship and helped guide hundreds of people down cargo nets and into lifeboats. Each boat was filled and rowed to the *Stansbury*, which took the occupants aboard. The evacuation was fast and smooth. Borum and his officers were the last to leave. In all, 372 of the 381 people aboard the *City of Birmingham* survived and were landed at Bermuda. The Coast Guard afterward classified the sinking as a "noteworthy case" because of the unusually high survival rate. Borum was credited with helping to avert a catastrophe.

But another was coming.

Three days after Borum was torpedoed on the *City of Birmingham*, Captain Herbert Callis of Mathews, a cousin of Mel, Homer, and Rodney Callis's, was torpedoed near the Windward Passage. Herbert was a stout, taciturn man who expected everyone to do his or her duty. He did not have a fun side. He had sailed for thirty years and survived a sinking in the mid-1930s after his ship was hit by an ocean liner. More recently, in March 1942, he had stopped his ship, the freighter *Norlandia*, off Cape Lookout, North Carolina, to pick up lifeboat survivors of a torpedoed ship. Herbert had expected the *Norlandia* to be torpedoed eventually.

So when it happened, Herbert was calm. But he was also woozy from the torpedo blast, which had killed five men. He ran into his cabin to get his sextant but failed "because of his dazed condition." He missed both of the lifeboats pulling away from the ship, and had to jump off the bow and swim to one of them and be helped in. The U-575 surfaced and its commander, Gunther Heydemann, questioned the men in the boats. Heydemann was disappointed to learn the *Norlandia* had been small and empty. He apologized for having had to sink an American ship, and asked if the castaways needed anything. They said no, but Heydemann tossed them a bottle of German brandy. He had one of his men keep a flashlight trained on the bottle as it flew through the air so the men would be sure to catch it. He shined the light along the length of the U-boat so the survivors could see what it looked like. Heydemann obviously had no fear of antisubmarine patrols.

The *Norlandia* lifeboats reached the coast of the Dominican Republic two days later. The men in one of the lifeboats complained angrily about its unseaworthy condition. The mast had snapped at its base when the men tried to rig the sail. The matches in the survival kit were wet. The drinking water containers had not been replaced in so long that the water "smelled like putrefied rats." The lifeboat was certified to have passed a recent inspection, but that inspection obviously had not taken place. Unseaworthy, ill-equipped lifeboats were a common problem on merchant ships in World War II, and *How to Abandon Ship* advised crews to take it upon themselves to examine the lifeboats whenever they boarded a new ship, report any missing items to the captain, and buy the items themselves if necessary: "A few dollars from your pocket may mean all the difference between your becoming a 1943 casualty or a 1983 veteran."

Herbert complained about the way the *Norlandia* had been routed. He said confusion between two Navy commands delayed his departure needlessly for two days, and ended up delivering him straight to the U-boat. He also "stated emphatically" that the Navy should stop sending merchant ships east along the coast of Cuba, where they had to fight a strong westerly current. The current slowed ships down, Callis said, and they had to move fast around Cuba, because U-boats were prowling all around the island.

At that moment, both Dewey's and Leslie Hodges's ships were entering the same Cuban waters. Leslie's vessel, the *Oneida*, was on the sugar run, hauling raw sugar from the southern coast of Cuba to ports in the Gulf. Dewey's little *Onondaga* was hauling war supplies between ports in Florida, Cuba, and Hispaniola. Both ships made short, daylight runs to avoid U-boats.

When the *Onondaga* arrived in San Juan, Puerto Rico, the Mathews men on the ship—Dewey, Genious, William Hammond, and Russell Dennis—welcomed aboard a familiar passenger. Captain Mellin Respess of Gwynn's Island had arranged to ride aboard the *Onondaga* as a passenger back to Mobile. Mellin had spent twelve days in a hospital after being torpedoed on the *Thomas McKean* and drifting in a lifeboat for two weeks. He had earned a few weeks at home on Gwynn's Island with Eleanor. Mellin passed up a ride home on another ship in order to ride with Dewey on the *Onondaga*. Mellin would help out, of course, if an emergency arose.

The *Onondaga*'s radio brought warnings of U-boat sightings and attacks all around them. The weather was stormy and sultry. Genious wrote to his wife, Salome, from San Juan that he had been up all the previous night dealing with drunken seamen. He lamented that Russell Dennis had not returned to the ship from a night on the town, which left Genious to oversee cargo loading. Genious had not even had time for a haircut. But what seemed to eat at him the most was not getting letters from Salome. He and Salome were still at odds over Genious's sailing to support his parents. When Genious received no letters from her, he imagined the worst. "Do you love me, darling?" he wrote. "I love you with all my heart, soul and body and always shall. If sometime something should happen and I don't get back, remember I always loved you truly whether you think so or not. I am yours forever, Salome."

The *Onondaga* had sailed alone since its initial departure from Mobile. Genious had seen no convoys or patrol planes. He no longer pretended he was not worried. "You hear a lot about the protections they have, darling," he wrote Salome, "but it's a lie, every word of it so far as I can see." Later he wrote, "I had much rather be running to Russia or England, Salome, than [around the Caribbean] . . . I guess the censor will cut this part out, but this is suicide, Salome, and nothing else."

While Dewey Hodges waited in San Juan to learn the *Onondaga*'s next destination, his brother Leslie approached the Windward Passage on the *Oneida*. The *Oneida* was empty, en route south around Cuba's eastern tip to pick up a load of raw sugar at Punta Gorda. Leslie served as first officer under Captain Walter Deal, a veteran captain from Gloucester County, next to Mathews. Leslie had written to his wife, Cecile, that he planned to stay home from a voyage soon and spend time with her. The *Oneida*'s second officer was Stacy Hammond, another of blacksmith Harry Hammond's sons. Unlike some of his shipmates, Stacy had yet to be torpedoed, but he counted himself lucky to be alive. He was one of several Mathews men who had gotten off the *Lake Osweya* before she vanished in the North Atlantic in February.

In the early morning hours of July 13, the *Oneida* was approaching Cape Maysi, Cuba, when one of the lookouts shouted. The feathering plume of a torpedo was heading straight for the ship. The helmsman swung the wheel, but it was too late. The torpedo slammed into the *Oneida* just below the water line, blowing a gaping hole in the hull. The sea barreled in, and the *Oneida*'s boilers exploded.

Leslie Hodges had stopped in the galley for a cup of coffee on his way to the bridge when the torpedo hit. Stacy Hammond caught a glimpse of Leslie struggling to launch a lifeboat in a cloud of steam. Captain Deal remembered Leslie running up to him to say he was going into the crew's quarters to search for the cook. Deal told him there was no time. Leslie went anyway. He was never seen again.

The *Oneida* sank by the stern, its bow rising high out of the water. Stacy dived off the bow from a height he estimated at sixty feet. He forgot to remove his glasses, and they smashed when he hit the water, leaving him with a bloody gash above his eyes. He swam with all his strength to get away from the suction of the sinking ship. He spotted an empty raft, climbed on, and picked up two other men. They rowed to a coral island only two miles away. Two other rafts arrived with more of their shipmates, and the men hiked for about five miles to a village. Stacy, who had lost his shoes, lacerated his feet on the jagged coral. The castaways eventually caught a ride to a larger village aboard a sailing schooner, and then traveled to Havana by bus. Most of the *Oneida*'s twenty-three survivors suffered severe sunburns. Leslie and five other men were missing.

Afterward, Captain Deal and Stacy Hammond vented their frustration to the Coast Guard, which routinely interviewed survivors of sinkings about how to improve safety measures. Deal complained that the fledgling coastal convoy system was full of holes. "Put the ships in convoy and stop sending them around without protection," he said. "Since this war has started . . . all the airplanes I have seen protecting ships you could put on one hand and all the destroyers could be put on one hand and you would have a whole lot of fingers left." Stacy agreed. "We saw no planes or nothing until about probably an hour after [the torpedoing], then I saw three or four different planes," he said. "We should be convoyed. Have no business running alone like that."

Stacy wired his wife in Mathews that he was safe. Leslie's wife, Cecile, apparently learned of her husband's death in a call or telegram from Ford. The next person who would have to be told about Leslie was Henny Hodges. And the person to tell her was her son Spencer.

Spencer had always been the one to whom the family turned to calm tempers and resolve disputes. He had a gift for reasoning with people. The family respected Spencer for having finished high school. He was the only one who could mend hard feelings between the quarreling Hodges daughters. His job got him out and about in the community. Spencer not only made ice cream at the creamery but drove a truck to deliver it to homes and general stores in a fifty-mile radius. He often took along his four-year-old son, Spencer Jr., in order to expose him to a wide variety of people and situations. The boy seemed to enjoy it, and always handled himself well.

At suppertime on Thursday, July 16, the telephone rang at Spencer's house. It was one of the few telephones in that part of Mathews, installed years before when Spencer's father-in-law was sheriff of Mathews. Spencer picked up the phone and his son could tell by his expression that something was wrong. Spencer thanked the caller and hung up. He told the family his brother Leslie was lost. He said he had to go to Gales Neck and tell Henny. He got to his feet and looked at Spencer Jr., and the boy got up too. "My father used to carry me to a lot of places that I wouldn't take my kids," Spencer Jr. said years later.

Father and son got into the family's black Chevrolet sedan. Neither spoke. Spencer drove out to the main highway and then turned onto the long driveway to Gales Neck. The car bobbed slowly through the holes and ruts. It was hot in the late afternoon and the car windows were down. Spencer parked on the left side of the house near the kitchen door. He told Spencer Jr. to wait in the car while he got out and walked to the door, tapped, and let himself in.

A cry came from inside the house and built into a wail. The sound of a second female voice told Spencer that Alice or one of his other aunts was home. The wailing continued for what seemed to the boy like an impossibly long time. It finally subsided, and a few minutes later his father came out of the house and started the car. He did not speak all the way home. Neither did Spencer Jr., who still heard the wailing in his head.

Leslie was the thirteenth Mathews man killed by U-boats since January. At least one man from the county seemed to die every week. "It was happening so much that you wondered it if was ever going to end," said the Hodgeses' cousin and neighbor Edwin Jarvis. "You were tired of it all. You expected more bad news every day. You were just numb." For the most part, families dealt with their sorrow privately. Every Sunday, Mathews pastors led prayers for the lost.

The losses of so many Mathews men on the *Ruth* in June prompted the Reverend Belch of Gwynn's Island Baptist Church to organize a memorial service for Mathews County. He may have assumed the *Ruth* disaster was the worst the war could inflict on Mathews. The service was held on

July 19, the hottest day of the summer, with the temperature rising into the nineties by nine o'clock in the morning. People from all over Mathews overflowed the church an hour before the service. The crowd sang hymns with images of the sea:

> *I've anchored my soul*
> *In the Haven of Rest,*
> *I'll sail the wide seas no more;*
> *The tempest may sweep*
> *O'er the wild storms deep*
> *In Jesus I'm safe evermore.*

Pastors of several Mathews churches took turns at the pulpit. Belch called merchant mariners "the unsung heroes of this war." He said he constantly heard of brave deeds by military men, who deserved all honors, but no less honors were due to the men on merchant ships. "Perhaps [I] feel more strongly because of the fact that so many of our Mathews men have helped man those ships, and many have made the supreme sacrifice."

From the church, the families of Mel Callis, Howard Morris, Perry Collier, and Robert Belvin Jr. led a procession down Old Ferry Road, the island's main thoroughfare, past the Gwynn's Island cemetery to the steel drawbridge over Milford Haven. The sheriff closed off traffic, and the crowd lined both sides of the 728-foot span. The next of kin tossed flowers from the center of the drawbridge into Milford Haven, where a falling tide carried them toward the Bay.

Robert Belvin's sisters wrote later:

> Brother it was so hard to scatter your flowers here on the sea
> And knowing your sweet form lies way out on the deep

None of the Hodges family attended the ceremony. Eleanor Respess did. She had known Mel Callis and most of the other men lost on the *Ruth*.

But her thoughts must have strayed to her husband, Mellin. She had almost lost him twice, but now he was headed home on the *Onondaga* with Dewey Hodges. He was to be at her side in a matter of days.

After Mellin came aboard the *Onondaga* in San Juan, Dewey was ordered to sail the ship to Nuevitas, the industrial port on Cuba's northern coast, to pick up a load of magnesium ore. The ship headed west along the coast of Hispaniola, across the northern end of the Windward Passage, and along the coast of Cuba to Nuevitas. The *Onondaga* docked, and began using her boom cranes to lift the heavy ore on wooden pallets and lower them into the cargo holds.

It's possible Dewey learned about his brother Leslie's death at Nuevitas. Loading the magnesium took three days, and Leslie's ship was sunk only 200 miles away. But Dewey did not mention Leslie in a letter to his family, dated July 23, 1942.

"My darling and babys," Dewey wrote. "Well, here I am all ready to go, but now they won't let me, as the port is closed until further notice . . . Gee is it hot here and am I working. I thought my Bees were busy but they haven't a thing on me, from 5 a.m. yesterday until midnite last night, and all day today, and the mosquitoes just eat you up at night." He wrote he was enclosing all his cash in the letter because "I do not want to carry any money to sea with me in these times."

"Darling, I am not expecting anything to happen to me," he continued, "but if it does, you should have enough with my insurance property to take care of you for a long time, and above all I want [our son] George to finish college unless the army takes him. What you do with whatever I leave is all right with me as long as you take care of yourself and the children. I leave all of that to your judgment."

Dewey reviewed the family's savings accounts and described how Edna could gain access to them without him. He suggested that if he did not return, his boss at Ford might feel an obligation to give George Jr. a job on a ship.

Dewey suggested Edna take the girls to Gales Neck, which he called "the country," and stay with Henny. "Hope you go up the country for a month, think you should if Mama wants you," he wrote. "Think the change will do you good, also the children." Dewey wrote that he might not be able to contact them for a while, "but if you don't hear from me, don't worry as no news will be good news . . . Kiss the children for me and tell them to be good girls. With all my love & kisses for my sweetheart & babys, from your true & loving husband, from daddy."

The *Onondaga* finally was allowed to leave Nuevitas on July 23. Dewey headed west with the current along the northern coast of Cuba, steering along the 100-fathom line, where the shallow continental shelf drops off into the depths. The ship stayed within 5 miles of a string of barrier islands lining a remote stretch of the coast.

Had Dewey waited at Nuevitas for a few hours, the *Onondaga* could have joined a convoy with armed escort ships and even air cover, passing Nuevitas en route to Havana. But Dewey had had no way of knowing the convoy was coming. Those convoys on that route were the latest link in the expanding U.S. Navy convoy system, which extended all the way up the East Coast. But the system still had flaws. It was not yet set up, for example, to notify merchant captains in Nuevitas of approaching convoys.

Dewey kept the *Onondaga* running at top speed, which in her case was barely 8.5 knots. He did not zigzag. His only concern was reaching the safety of Havana before dark. The *Onondaga* passed through the Old Bahama Channel and into the Nicholas Channel, approaching the Straits of Florida. Dewey posted lookouts on the bridge and the "monkey island" above it. He did not need to remind Mellin, Genious, and William Hammond to stay alert. The *Onondaga* chugged into the glare of the late afternoon sun. The weather was fair and the sea was calm, and dotted with small fishing boats. Dewey had the time to beat the sunset to Havana, but not the luck.

Heading straight at the *Onondaga* from the opposite direction was Hans-Ludwig Witt in his U-129. The sub was passing through the Nicholas Channel on its way out of the Caribbean after sinking eight merchant ships in four weeks—a performance that would earn Witt an Iron Cross. The U-129's voyage had been productive from the start, when Witt had stumbled upon the freighter *Millinocket* in the channel on his way *into* the Caribbean and torpedoed the ship, killing Captain Lewis Callis of Gwynn's Island. Now, as the U-129 departed the Caribbean, Witt had saved a torpedo in case he got lucky in the channel again. At 4:30 p.m., the *Onondaga* appeared in the U-129's periscope. It was almost too easy. Witt maneuvered the sub into position for a torpedo strike and waited for the little freighter to come closer.

Dewey was on the bridge and apparently saw the torpedo coming. He looked astern and shouted, "Everybody aft stand clear!" and "Here she comes!" A seaman turned to look but "a white flash and sharp explosion" knocked him unconscious into the ocean. Another seaman recalled a geyser of seawater and "things shooting up into the air. Everything went sky-high." Third Officer Russell Dennis of Mathews was in his room when he heard the shouts and felt the jolt of the torpedo. He ran out onto the main deck to see Dewey descending a ladder from the bridge. Captain Respess was "sawing at a rope that held one of the life rafts." The *Onondaga*'s main deck already was awash. Genious shouted, "Everybody jump overboard." Dennis dove. When he came up, the *Onondaga* was gone. The heavy ore had pulled her under in less than one minute.

The U-129 was gone too, resuming its trip home. Dennis swam to a raft and then moved to a different raft occupied by eight of his shipmates. They said they had been looking for survivors but had almost lost hope. They had not seen Dewey, Mellin, Genious, or William Hammond. The men rowed to a barrier island and lay on the beach. At daybreak, an American search plane spotted the *Onondaga*'s oil slick and then the men on the beach. The pilot found another raft with six more survivors. Eighteen of the thirty-three men on the *Onondaga* were missing, including Genious, William Hammond, Dewey, and Mellin. "Both captains went down with the ship," Dennis said.

The American vice consul in Nuevitas wrongly blamed the sinking on the *Onondaga's* crew, who supposedly talked so loosely that "practically everyone in Nuevitas knew the ship's destination and time of departure."

Dennis, as the sole surviving Mathews man on the ship, was bound by Mathews tradition to get word about the sinking and the casualties to the county at once. He sent a telegram from the Exchange Hotel in Miami to the telegraph office across from the Mathews courthouse saying: "Arrived in Miami OK. Capt. Hodges Respess Hudgins and Hammond failed to return."

It's unclear who telephoned Dewey's family. Telegraph operators in Mathews usually passed bad news to family members, if they could be reached, or consulted the courthouse crowd of lawyers and businessmen to choose a suitable messenger. The system was efficient but not always compassionate. The phone rang at Dewey's house in Norfolk and Edna answered. A man whose voice she did not recognize said the *Onondaga* had been lost and that Dewey "was not one of the survivors." Then the caller hung up.

Edna, characteristically, showed little emotion. She repeated the caller's statement to the girls, and told them she would try to determine if it was true. They could tell she believed it was. Edna telephoned Ford, the Navy, and the Coast Guard, but it was late and she could not reach anyone. She was furious at the caller for delivering such news and hanging up before she could ask questions. She and the girls wondered if the call had been a malicious prank.

The phone also rang in Spencer Hodges's home, and he took the call as he had taken the call eleven days before. He hung up and told his family that now Dewey had been lost. He got up and looked at Spencer Jr., and the boy got up too.

To four-year-old Spencer Jr., everything about the second trip to Gales Neck seemed exactly like the first one, eleven days earlier: the silent ride in the black Chevrolet, the long crawl up the driveway, his father parking by the kitchen door and stepping inside. The only change was that, this time, the wailing began the moment his father stepped in the door. More than seventy years later, Spencer Jr. would feel a chill at a TV news broadcast of Filipino mothers wailing after a ferryboat disaster. "It was exactly the same sound," he said.

The night after the *Onondaga* sinking, the Cuban fishermen named Carillo set out in their boat, the *Donatella*, to fish for shark in the Nicholas Channel. Most of the Cubans on the water were poor, subsistence fishermen, catching shark to eat or barter. Their boats generally had sails but no motors, and their shark-fishing rigs were floating oil drums dangling heavy lines with fist-sized hooks, baited with bloody fish. The bait hung just above the bottom, where the big sharks hunted.

The Carillos caught a big tiger or bull shark, at least six feet long. They killed it and gutted it right on deck, and found human remains—and two rings. They apparently set out directly for Havana, about a day's sail away, to turn in their discovery.

Authorities in Havana took custody of the remains and the rings. They inspected the rings and discovered that one of them, a heavy gold signet ring, was engraved with the initials "G.D.H." Word of the discovery spread along the docks. It reached R. M. Jenkins, who managed an office in Havana. Little is known about Jenkins. He knew Dewey well enough to know his full name was George Dewey Hodges. Jenkins took the trouble to get the story from the Carillos personally and to examine the ring. He was convinced it was Dewey's, but was not sure whom to tell. He wrote letters to U.S. government offices in Havana and to steamship companies. He mistakenly thought the *Onondaga* was owned by the Lykes Brothers Steamship Company.

Months would pass before one of Jenkins's letters would find its way to Dewey's family. But news of Dewey's death spread quickly among mariners whose careers and lives he had influenced. His longtime crewman M. Stanley MacLean wrote of Dewey, "To me, George Hodges, the seagoing diplomat and my friend, is not dead, only away."

In Mathews, anger at the federal government festered. The *Gazette-*

Journal's account of the *Onondaga* sinking included the observation that "the people [of Mathews] are becoming more and more critical of the seeming lack of effective effort to protect the Merchant Marine . . . against the submarine force. The sending of merchant ships through submarine-infested waters, alone and entirely unprotected, is being bitterly decried in this county, which supplies the Merchant Marine with more men, perhaps, than any other area of comparable population."

In August 1942, the *Gazette-Journal*'s complaints drew a reply from the region's congressman, Rep. Schuyler Otis Bland, who was chairman of the House Merchant Marine and Fisheries Committee. Bland wrote to the paper that he had spoken personally with Navy leaders and believed they were doing everything possible. He said he wished the Navy were more forthcoming about its successes against U-boats because "I think the Navy has done a much better job than they have been given credit for." The editors replied that while they believed Bland was sincere, they stood by their view that the nation "had failed . . . to give the most effective aid possible to our merchant marine and the men who operate it."

In the same issue of the paper, a Mathews fisherman who had just returned from a trawler off the mid-Atlantic coast said the trawler crew had been accosted and questioned by two U-boat captains and had seen two merchant ships torpedoed.

Captain Jesse Hodges came home to Gales Neck in late August from another long voyage on his tug in the Caribbean. Henny broke the news to him that two of his sons had been lost, only eleven days apart. Jesse's immediate reaction to the news was not recorded. But a few days later, he curtly told a reporter, "There's been a whole lot of slack in this business, mister." He was home only a few days when Ford sent him a telegram summoning him to sail a freighter. He showed the telegram to a photographer, who arranged a photo of him sitting on the couch and displaying the telegram to Henny. She looks as though she is about to cry.

Jesse returned to sea. For the first time in the war, however, he and his ship could expect to be protected from U-boats. After seven months of horrific losses, Admiral King finally had enough ships and planes to establish a strong, interlocking convoy system, extending from along the U.S. East Coast and through the Gulf of Mexico and Caribbean. Convoys moved along feeder routes in the Gulf and Caribbean to the main routes, which ran from Trinidad to Cuba to New York. New York replaced Maritime Canada as the departure point for North Atlantic convoys to Britain. All the convoys moved on a tight schedule, arriving at intervals to avoid clogging up ports. The convoys were guarded by destroyers and smaller escorts, as well as Army and Navy aircraft, and few ships were left to make their solo voyages alone and unguarded.

Even coastal lights at East Coast ports finally had been extinguished, after much wrangling, long after the time of greatest need had passed. Admiral Andrews called those who had fought the blackout "selfish, greedy and unpatriotic." Morison, the Navy historian, concluded, "Ships were sunk and seamen drowned in order that the citizenry might enjoy business and pleasure as usual."

By midsummer, American planes and escort ships were no longer easy foils for U-boats. Many pilots had radar, as well as training in how to bomb U-boats. Navy crews on escort ships had learned that killing U-boats took patience and strategy. It was a chess game with depth charges.

In the Gulf of Mexico, a Navy patrol vessel depth-charged and sank the U-166, which had torpedoed the *Oneida* and killed Leslie Hodges. The U-boat's entire crew was killed, as was often the case when a U-boat was sunk. The U-153, which had torpedoed the *Ruth* and killed five Mathews men, was depth-charged by a destroyer off Panama, with no survivors. The U-701, which had embarrassed the Navy in June by laying mines at the mouth of the Chesapeake Bay, was depth-charged by an Army plane off Hatteras. The U-boat commander and three other survivors were rescued from the ocean and taken prisoner.

Just like that, Admiral King's interlocking convoy system put an end to the U-boat successes in U.S. waters. Sinkings of merchant ships along the East Coast plummeted from twenty-three in April to four in May. They

rose to thirteen in June, but dropped back to four again in July. Admiral
Andrews, who had suffered through a miserable winter and spring, noted
in his war diary for July: "This month is the most significant in operations
in the history of this Frontier, since it demonstrates that the increasing
success of past weeks rests upon a solid basis of strong forces properly
used."

Doenitz tracked the numbers too. The time had come to pull back his
subs from the U.S. Atlantic coast. He was not wistful. He had expected the
Americans to chase him off long ago. For seven months the U-boats had
had their way in American waters, sinking more than three hundred merchant ships and killing thousands of merchant seamen. They had sunk
millions of tons of Allied food, supplies, munitions, and fuel into the sea,
playing havoc with the enemy's supply line. Doenitz already knew where
he wanted to shift the U-boats. He kept a few in the Caribbean, the Gulf,
and the South Atlantic, but sent most to the North Atlantic air gap, beyond
the range of Allied planes. Doenitz thought an all-out attack in the air gap
could win the Battle of the Atlantic for Germany. Ending the assault on
America's coast did not end the U-boats' assault on merchant shipping.

Nor did it end the U-boats' war-within-a-war against the Mathews men.

CHAPTER NINE

"Please Don't Tell Me"

C aptain Homer Callis of Gwynn's Island, who proved that a sea captain could also be a gentleman, quit the bridge of the old Bull Line freighter *Mae* in August 1942 to become assistant port captain for the Bull Line in Baltimore. The job was a promotion, and Homer had earned it. He had commanded Bull Line ships for twenty years, and he enjoyed a sterling reputation among mariners, fellow captains, his bosses, the Navy, and even the unions.

The port job in Baltimore kept Homer from having to face U-boats, which had killed his brother Mel and had almost gotten Homer on his last trip on the *Mae*. On a stormy night in the Windward Passage, several U-boats had attacked the *Mae*'s convoy and sunk ships all around her, five in all. One had been so close to the *Mae* that Homer had to turn sharply to avoid hitting the sinking vessel. Another ship exploded with such force that pieces of it clattered against the *Mae*.

Homer's new job allowed him, for the first time at age forty-five, to live full time with his wife, Nancy. Nancy commanded the Callis home at Dunrovin' the way Henny Hodges commanded the Hodges farm at Gales Neck. Nancy was tall and slender, with shoulder-length brown hair. She drank her coffee black and her whiskey neat, and told friends, "I hate old people." She was a Diggs, a family known on Gwynn's Island for producing women who were outspoken, even brassy. She and the deliberative Homer seemed to be polar opposites, but they were close. The U-boat war weighed on Nancy. She had one of the few telephones on Gwynn's Island, and knew everyone. She often received the first phone call from a survivor of a sunken ship or a representative of a shipping company that a man from the island had been lost. Nancy had begun to feel that neighbors shrank from her approach "as if I was the angel of death."

Homer and Nancy's two sons were nearly grown. The elder, twenty-one-year-old Homer Jr., was a quartermaster on a Navy destroyer in the Pacific. He took after his father, with a quiet, thoughtful attitude. The younger son, Bill, had a rowdy Diggs demeanor. Bill was seventeen and bursting to get out of Mathews. His brother warned him to stay out of the Navy, which had more regulations than Bill could possibly follow. Homer Jr. suggested Bill try the Merchant Marine.

When Homer Sr. left the *Mae*, the Bull Line followed its longstanding tradition and replaced him with another captain from Mathews. Their choice, Captain Willard Hudgins, was a veteran captain from a seafaring family. He had commanded military transport ships in World War I and merchant ships ever since. He was an officer in the U.S. Naval Reserve, but was needed more as a merchant captain than as a naval officer. Though no one could replace Homer, Willard was a solid successor. He had the approval of the only other Mathews man on the *Mae*, the irrepressible Thomas Lester Smith.

Lester, as he was called, was a compact pile driver of a man. He was good company, although he sometimes drank and fought. Bill Callis once saw him whipping a man twice his size. Lester was a fisherman's son who joined the Merchant Marine for the adventure and the money. By the time he turned eighteen, he had saved enough to buy a red Buick convertible, which he drove around Mathews High School with the top down, flirting with all the girls. Then he met Lottie Mise, who knew at age sixteen that

Lester was the one. He knew it too. "When he came home, the first thing he made for was me," Lottie said, "and I was waiting for him."

Lester had sailed on the *Mae* with Homer since before Pearl Harbor. Even though he had been on the last trip, with ships blowing up all around them, Lester stayed on the ship for its first voyage under Captain Hudgins. He and Jack Rowe of Gwynn's Island had talked about taking that trip off. Jack decided he could afford to sit out one voyage, but Lester had blown all his pay from his last voyage and decided to stay on the ship. The *Mae* was being sent to the port of Georgetown, British Guiana— today, simply Guyana—to pick up a load of bauxite ore. As the *Mae* prepared to leave Mobile, she was armed for the first time with a 3-inch gun and a .50-caliber antiaircraft gun, operated by a Navy Armed Guard crew.

The *Mae* sailed from Mobile empty, in ballast, and alone. She encountered no U-boats en route to Cuba and then to Trinidad. After she turned south for the final leg of the voyage, the captain ordered a zigzag course and assigned men extra watches as lookouts. Lester was too excited to close his eyes. Finally he flopped down exhausted on his bunk, with his feet at the end where he normally laid his head. That deviation from normal saved his life. Just after midnight on September 17, one of the *Mae*'s lookouts saw a blinking light ahead of them. He was turning to report it when a torpedo bore into the freighter's starboard side, blowing up the magazine holding the shells for the new guns. The magazine was located directly beneath Lester's bunk. The explosion mangled his legs and hurled him against a bulkhead, unconscious.

The *Mae* was sinking. The U-boat approached the ship and trained a spotlight on the Armed Guard crew, which was trying to fire the 3-inch gun. Captain Hudgins warned them to stop or get shot, then gave the order to abandon ship. The cook was rushing to the main deck when he saw Lester motionless in the wreckage of his bunk. The cook called for Captain Hudgins and another man to help pull Lester free. Lester's legs were a gruesome mess, but there was no time even to examine them. The captain tied some lines into a makeshift cradle, and Lester was lowered into one of the three lifeboats.

On closer inspection, Lester's left leg appeared to be shattered at the knee, and his right leg was broken or worse. His shipmates used a tourniquet to cinch off the bleeding in his left leg, but not before Lester's blood had pooled at their feet. Lester faded in and out of consciousness. The U-boat broke the surface and drilled several rounds from its deck cannon into the *Mae* to finish her off. The U-boat captain asked the men in the lifeboats the usual questions, then left them alone on a rough, windy sea.

Lester's blood attracted sharks, which shot past the lifeboat and sometimes tested it with their snouts. A frightened seaman said Lester would get them all eaten, and that he was going to die anyway. He wanted to throw Lester overboard. Captain Hudgins said they were going to do all they could for Lester. It was clear, though, that Lester would not survive for long in the lifeboat.

Only three hours after the sinking, a Norwegian freighter on its way out of Georgetown spotted the lifeboats and began taking the survivors aboard. As soon as Captain Hudgins found the Norwegian captain, he asked him to turn the ship around. He pointed out Lester and said his only chance was to get to a hospital, and Georgetown had a small one. The captain changed course and ran full-speed back to Georgetown. A Navy teletype about the *Mae* sinking mentioned Lester by name and summed up his status as "severely injured, hospitalized, recovery doubtful."

Lester awoke on a stretcher on the beach at Georgetown and began talking rapidly and smoking cigarettes "like they were going out of style." He kept passing out and waking up. Once he awoke to find a sheet had been pulled over his head. Later, at Mercy Hospital, he heard one nurse whisper to another that they must at least comfort him because "he is some mother's son."

To some in Mathews, the loss of the *Mae* felt almost like the loss of a family member. Like the *Ruth* and the *East Indian*, the *Mae* had never sailed without several Mathews men in the crew. Homer had taken dozens of young men from Mathews to sea for the first time on the ship. When Homer heard about the *Mae* and about Lester, he went to his boss in Baltimore and told him he no longer wanted to work on shore. He wanted a new ship.

The latest man to join the brotherhood of Mathews sea captains was Will Hunley, a Hodges cousin who was practically a brother. Childhood friends with David Hodges, Will never thought about going to sea until one afternoon in 1930 when David announced he was going to work on his brother Raymond's ship. Will, who was seventeen, decided to go along. He sold his bicycle to Henny Hodges for $10 for bus fare to New York Harbor. He was so homesick that David had to beg him not to jump ship in every port, but Will ended up staying with it long after David left. He idolized Raymond Hodges and kept his photograph on his desk. Will had a booming voice, a feel for ships, and a fine eye for a vessel's finances. Moore-McCormack promoted him up through the ranks and in August 1942 named him captain of the freighter *Commercial Trader*. At age twenty-eight, Will was probably the youngest captain in Mathews. He had been a captain for three months. Now came his trial by fire.

On the morning of September 16, 1942, the *Commercial Trader* was about 75 miles from Trinidad when a torpedo exploded into the hull, throwing up a geyser of water that knocked Will off the bridge onto the deck below. He got to his feet and realized his pants were gone. He gave the order to abandon ship and plunged into his cabin for the secret codes. The water was three feet deep in the cabin and he was struck by floating furniture, but he got the codes and threw them overboard in their weighted bag. The *Commercial Trader*'s cargo had been magnesium ore, with large bags of castor beans piled on top. Will called out to his men to be careful not to swallow seawater, because the beans released castor oil that could make them sick. Castor oil contains a deadly poison, ricin.

Will got into the last lifeboat. A line from the sinking ship snagged on the lifeboat and flipped it, throwing Will and the other occupants into the water. Will, who could not swim, clung to the side of the overturned boat with a few others. They saw a man on a raft in the distance. He was trying to paddle to them but was being swept away. A Norwegian seaman named Nils Antonsen volunteered to swim to the raft and help the man. His shipmates warned he would be eaten by sharks or carried away by the current, but Antonsen set out through a heavy swell. He reached the raft and helped the man paddle back to Will and the others; on their way, they picked up two other men from the water. All the men heaved together to right the lifeboat, and then climbed in. They also rescued the ship's dog, a mongrel named Hendrick Wilhelm Berg Johanson that was floating past on a bag of castor beans.

Will ordered the lifeboat's sail rigged, and used a compass to guide the boat to the island of Tobago in only four hours. The boat landed on the beach estate of a British oil executive, who met the castaways "with a bottle of rum in each hand and several servants to help them ashore," Will said. The injured, including a man with mild castor oil poisoning, were taken to a hospital. Will and the others spent a comfortable night at the executive's estate. Twenty-eight of the *Commercial Trader*'s thirty-eight officers and crew survived the sinking. Moore-McCormack commended Will for showing such presence of mind at his young age. Like Homer Callis, Will immediately asked for a new ship.

On Gwynn's Island, Lester Smith's parents and his fiancée, Lottie, prayed constantly. They knew only that Lester was fighting for his life at Mercy Hospital in Georgetown, British Guiana, a place they had not known existed until a few weeks before. Traveling to Georgetown was too dangerous. They could only wait. Then letters from Georgetown began arriving in the mailbox, with reports on Lester from nurses and representatives of the Salvation Army. At first the letters were bleak. Lester had lost so much blood that doctors and nurses at the hospital had to donate their own blood to keep him alive. Both his legs were crushed and his left foot had been blown off. A surgeon had amputated his left leg at the knee. "He is very brave and although suffering, never murmurs," a Salvation Army officer wrote of Lester. "I feel very distressed for him, but he is taking it all like a man. I know that this will be a terrible blow to you, but you must try to be as brave as your Lester is."

But weeks passed and Lester stayed alive. One day, a letter noted his "wonderful improvement." A young Filipina nurse who tended to Lester wrote, "I am with him all the time and try to keep him at rest. One night, asleep, he called to his mates. I think he dreamed he was at sea. He is not changed but still carries the heart of gold. Today we sat him up in the bed and he had the smile of a conqueror and said he would soon be coming back home to Gwynn's Island."

The *Gazette-Journal* printed updates on Lester's recovery for all of Mathews to read. Captain Willard Hudgins surprised Lester's family by bringing three of his shipmates from the *Mae* to Gwynn's Island. They said Lester was brave even in his times of great suffering. Lester's mother was overwhelmed: "I think it is so wonderful that with all the fighting and killing going on that there is still so much kindness and sympathy," she said. "I think it wonderful that far away in a strange land, my boy should receive so much attention . . ."

News of a different kind arrived for the families of the men lost on the *Onondaga*. Salome Hudgins's telegram about Genious read:

THE NAVY DEPARTMENT DEEPLY REGRETS TO INFORM
YOU THAT YOUR HUSBAND GENIIS [*SIC*] THOMAS HUDGINS
IS MISSING FOLLOWING ACTION IN THE PERFORMANCE OF
HIS DUTY AND IN SERVICE OF HIS COUNTRY. THE COAST
GUARD APPRECIATES YOUR GREAT ANXIETY AND WILL
FURNISH INFORMATION PROMPTLY WHEN RECEIVED. TO
PREVENT POSSIBLE AID TO OUR ENEMIES PLEASE DO NOT
DIVULGE THE NAME OF HIS SHIP.

Salome, however, refused to believe Genious was dead. She told neighbors he was marooned on an island or hospitalized in a foreign country,
like Lester Smith. Salome insisted Genious would walk in their front door
any day. When two men from the government came to the door with Genious's $5,000 life insurance payout, she refused to take the envelope. A
friend persuaded her to hold on to it, "just in case," for her daughter, Vicki.

Unlike Salome, Dewey's widow, Edna Hodges, harbored no false
hope that he was alive. Edna, in fact, was trying to prove Dewey was dead.
Much of the family's savings was in bank accounts under only Dewey's
name. Edna and the children could not access it unless a judge declared
Dewey legally dead. Edna filed a petition in Norfolk Circuit Court, and
offered the official government letters of regret as evidence. But the case
dragged on for lack of witnesses. All of the *Onondaga* survivors had gone
back to sea. Edna's lawyers finally tracked down Russell Dennis and two
other crew members. None of them had seen the U-boat or the torpedo.
But they had seen Dewey on the ship during her last moments afloat, and
they had searched for survivors afterward in the wreckage. They knew
Dewey could not swim. That was enough evidence for Judge Alan R.
Hanckel, who declared Dewey dead on October 15, 1942. The judge ruled
that since Dewey had left no will, his last letter to his family—the one
that began, "My darling and babys"—would serve as his last will and
testament.

Dewey's story was not quite over, though. His old ship, the *East Indian*,
was nearing the end of the odyssey his illness had forced him to miss. The
ship had sailed across the South Atlantic, around the Cape of Good Hope,
and north through the wild Mozambique Channel to avoid *Japanese* subs.
She rounded the Horn of Africa and transited the Persian Gulf to Basra,
where her cargo of ammunition was transferred to trains for the rest of the
trip to the Russian front. The men endured fifty-five days in the Persian
Gulf, cursing the heat, the sand fleas, and the dust storms that rolled up
like rogue waves and blotted out the horizon. Some men were so desperate

for relief that they jumped into the bathtub-warm Gulf, only to be chased from the water by a swarm of yellow-banded sea snakes, which the locals warned were venomous.

The *East Indian* sailed to Colombo, Ceylon (now Sri Lanka), whose harbor was full of charred shipwrecks from a Japanese bombing raid. The ship steamed up the Ganges River, the sacred river of the Hindus, where clusters of worshippers waded in the shallows. The *East Indian* took on a load of rubber and burlap in Calcutta, where the tension was palpable. India's British governors had just jailed the Indian spiritual leader Mohandas Gandhi, and protests had degenerated into bombings, arson, and other violence that left more than a thousand people dead. The mariners were happy to leave India and even happier to reach Cape Town, which they assumed was their last stop before crossing the Atlantic to New York.

Instead, the men were crestfallen to learn at Cape Town that the *East Indian* was to take a long roundabout route home. To avoid U-boats, she was to cross the South Atlantic to Chile, pass through the Strait of Magellan into the Pacific, then pass back through the Panama Canal into the Caribbean, and then sail up the East Coast to New York. Captain St. Marie could hardly believe it. He thought the U-boats had abandoned the South Atlantic. But the Navy and the War Shipping Administration made the decisions. At noon on November 3, 1942, the *East Indian* sailed out of Cape Town's picture-book harbor, heading southwest toward Tierra del Fuego. She carried a total of seventy-three people, including forty-five officers and crew, twelve Navy gunners, and twelve passengers.

Cape Town was a meeting point for Allied convoys heading around the Cape of Good Hope for the Persian Gulf. Doenitz dispatched U-boats to the waters off Cape Town when the convoy traffic surged, and he had just sent four subs, including the U-181, commanded by Wolfgang Luth. Luth was a U-boat ace, with twenty-seven Allied ships to his credit. He was also an ardent promoter of Nazism. He gave weekly talks to his men on such topics as "racial and population problems" and "the struggle for the realization of the Reich." On Hitler's birthday, Luth told the crew stories about the Führer's life.

The U-181 was sitting on the surface off Cape Town, and Luth spotted the *East Indian* almost as soon as she cleared the breakwater. He ordered the U-181 to periscope depth and watched. The *East Indian* was zigzagging. Luth timed her changes of course with a stopwatch, and when he thought he had figured out her path, he fired two torpedoes from long range. The ship changed course unexpectedly, and the torpedoes missed by such a wide margin that no one on the freighter noticed them. The *East Indian* continued on its way, oblivious to Luth. He gave chase. The U-181 pursued its quarry for nine hours and more than 200 miles to get into position for a second attack. Luth made this one count. Two torpedoes struck the *East Indian* on the starboard side only seconds apart.

Vernon Davis, an able seaman from Mathews, had just gotten up from breakfast and headed out to the stern to smoke a cigarette. He was never seen again. Captain St. Marie was eating with Clayton Hammond, Dewey's hand-picked first officer, when the ship shook and ceiling tiles crashed down on the table between them. They ran out to the main deck. The ship already was listing so steeply they could barely stand up. Noxious smoke filled the air and made it hard to breathe. The captain climbed a ladder to the bridge, possibly to get the secret codes. Clayton ran to his cabin, grabbed a life vest, and jumped. The sinking vessel tugged him toward the bottom but he broke free and swam to an empty raft.

Marion Capers of Mathews, the *East Indian*'s bo'sun, managed to launch a single lifeboat. He and about a dozen other men got in. They looked up to see the U-181 coming to the surface nearby. Luth and four other Germans emerged from the hatch on the conning tower. Luth and every other U-boat commander had just received fresh orders from Doenitz to stop helping survivors of torpedoed ships. "Rescue contradicts the most fundamental demands of war for the annihilation of enemy ships and crews,"

Doenitz ordered. "Be harsh, having in mind that the enemy takes no regard of women and children in his bombing attacks on German cities."*

Luth was a big man with reddish hair and a thick beard. He glared down at the men in the *East Indian*'s only lifeboat.

"Are you Limeys?" Luth asked.

"Americans," a mariner replied.

"Why are you helping the Limeys and the black Russians?" Luth asked. "We have nothing against you."

Luth added a disparaging crack about Roosevelt, and some of the other Germans chimed in. The Americans said nothing. Luth said if the *East Indian* had not been zigzagging, they would have been sunk hours before and within sight of land. "As it is, you are now 300 miles from Cape Town, and there is nothing for you to do but row," Luth said. "I'm sorry, for you had a beautiful ship. But this is war." Luth asked to speak to the captain, first officer, or chief engineer. Clayton was the only one of those three still alive, but he lay silently on his raft, worried that if he identified himself he would be taken prisoner. His shipmates protected him by claiming all three of the ship's top officers were dead. Luth asked if the castaways needed food, water, or medical treatment. They said no, afraid if they got close to the sub they would be taken aboard. In fact, Luth, the most ardent Nazi in the U-boat force, was disobeying a direct order by trying to help them.

Luth questioned the castaways about their ship and cargo. He seemed to mark their answers on some kind of checklist. His questions prompted the *East Indian*'s third officer to ask Luth if he had known their ship was about to leave Cape Town. Luth said he came upon the *East Indian* purely

---

*Doenitz's message was prompted by the bombing of a U-boat that had been towing lifeboats to shore. The U-boat had torpedoed the armed British troopship *Laconia* only to discover she was carrying 1,800 Italian prisoners of war. The U-boat crew was trying to save as many of them as possible when an Allied bomber spotted the sub and damaged it with depth charges. Doenitz's order to offer no aid to castaways would later become one of the prosecution's chief pieces of evidence at his war-crimes trial at Nuremberg.

by accident.* He wished the castaways "Godspeed," and clasped his hands above his head in a gesture of farewell. The other Germans on the conning tower gave the castaways a "Heil Hitler" salute as the U-181 prepared to submerge. Luth later claimed an *East Indian* crewman returned the Hitler salute and wished the Germans, "Good luck and good hunting." This seems to have been his fantasy, though; none of the survivors' accounts mention an American making any such response.

The men in the lifeboat rowed to Clayton's raft and took him aboard. As the highest-ranking officer alive, he was in command. Clayton was the personification of self-control. As a boy, he awoke one night and looked out the window to see his school on fire down the street. He went back to bed and said nothing until his mother called for him to get up for school. "There won't be any school today," Clayton told her. "It burned down." On another occasion, Clayton walked calmly into the living room and told his parents his grandfather was trying to hang himself from the apple tree in their back yard. They leaped to their feet but Clayton said there was no hurry. None of the limbs was strong enough to support his grandfather.

Now Clayton faced the challenge of his life. A head count showed twenty-three men from the *East Indian* dead or missing, including Vernon Davis and Second Officer Lemuel Marchant of Mathews. The survivors numbered fifty-one, including seventeen in the only lifeboat and thirty-four scattered among four rafts. One of the men in the lifeboat was Bernard Pierson of Gwynn's Island, a husky able seaman known for his temper. He would be remembered instead for an act of sacrifice. Pierson saw that one of the men on the rafts was badly injured, and gave up his seat in the boat to the man and took his place on the raft. He must have known the exchange could cost him his life.

---

* Luth's denial did not convince Navy intelligence officers, who always looked for more complicated explanations for sinkings than the simple fact that the ships had been sent into harm's way unescorted. In this case, the Navy suggested a "Nazi-controlled vice ring" in Cape Town had pried information about the *East Indian*'s schedule from crewmen "under the influence of passion and intoxicants."

Clayton had no charts and only a compass with which to navigate. Based on the ship's position before the sinking, he estimated the castaways were 317 miles southwest of Cape Town. The lifeboat had oars and a sail and enough provisions for two weeks. If the weather was favorable, it might reach Cape Town within a week. The rafts, on the other hand, could do little but stay afloat. Clayton decided the survivors' best chance was for the lifeboat to run for Cape Town and send help.

The thirty-four men on the rafts understood the decision, and its ramifications for them. They would be left alone in the deep ocean to hope for a miracle. None of them flinched. "I remember that not any of the boys left on the four rafts acted panicky," wrote M. Stanley MacLean, who was in the lifeboat. The men on the rafts included Bernard Pierson; Andrew Dennis, an orphan living with relatives in Mathews, who had found a home at sea; and Wilson Forrest, whose brother Coles's ship had been mined at the mouth of the Chesapeake Bay.

Clayton's hopes for favorable weather were obliterated on the second day by a howling storm that blew the lifeboat all the way around the Cape of Good Hope into the Indian Ocean. A week passed. A pod of whales surrounded the lifeboat one night and MacLean worried they would capsize it: "Whenever one surfaced and made its mournful sound, a chill went up my spine." Clayton rationed the food and water. Each man received a small quantity of pemmican and five ounces of water per day. The men were perpetually thirsty. They regretted not having collected rainwater during a recent downpour. Every time a rain squall approached, they prepared to catch the rain in a sail and with "our mouths open like young birds," as MacLean put it. But the squalls bypassed the boat. Tempers grew short, and two men stood up in the boat to throw punches, but Clayton got them to sit down. Clayton announced he had a .45-caliber pistol on his hip, and would use it if anyone endangered the boat. The men could see a holster under his shirt, but Clayton never displayed the gun, if, in fact, he really had one.

On the second day, the radioman became delusional. He was wracked with guilt for not having gotten off an SOS call. He called the lifeboat a prison ship. Men held him down to keep him from jumping overboard. They finally had to tie him up. He passed out and never woke up. The drinking water ran out, and the men regretted having refused the water Luth had offered from the U-181.

On the lifeboat's thirteenth day adrift, a British merchant ship spotted it and took the survivors to Cape Town. Clayton reported the last known position of the rafts, but after two weeks of rough weather, they might be anywhere, or nowhere. Search planes flew grid patterns for three days but found nothing. Six months later, in June 1943, one of the *East Indian*'s rafts would turn up off the coast of Brazil, more than 2,500 miles from the sinking, bearing an unidentified set of remains.

Five Mathews men had died on the *East Indian*—the same number killed on the *Ruth* five months earlier. This time, there was no memorial service, no symbolic tossing of flowers in the water. Mathews was in shock. In the nine months since the United States entered the war, twenty-two Mathews mariners had been killed. At least twice that many had been torpedoed. Seven Mathews men had been torpedoed at least twice. Mellin Respess was torpedoed three times on three different ships in a little over three months before he finally was killed. And the war was only starting.

Just days after the *East Indian* sinking, Edna Hodges received a call from her lawyer. He had finally received a copy of one of R. M. Jenkins's letters from Havana about the ring in the shark's belly. On October 22, 1942, Jenkins had written:

> I have come in touch with a matter which might be of great sentimental value to some person, and I will explain the matter to you thinking you might care to and be able to contact who might be the interested party. In the vicinity of where the *SS Onondaga* was torpedoed and several of the crew lost is a great shark fishing ground. Around there for years, a family by the name of Carillo has fished commercially for sharks.

A short time after the sinking of the ship, according to them and as told to me by the one I think the most reliable, they caught a shark that had in its belly the flesh and bones of a human being. They say they took out and saved the bones from the hip to the ankle. Also at the same time they found with the rest two rings. They have shown me the rings and I have carefully examined them.

I thought they would be of interest mainly because the outside initials on the heavy gold signet ring are G.D.H. As it was my understanding that the captain who went down with the ship was G.D. Hodges, it has occurred to me that it might be his ring. On the inside of this same ring it [is] engraved as follows: "E.R.G. '17." The bottom of the ring is broken.

The other ring seems to be made of some such material as bone and is of light yellow color with a large dark top imitating a stone of some kind.

If the widow of this good old man who went down with his ship knows this ring, I imagine it would be of great sentimental value to her. I am giving you this information for you to do with as you think best.

Edna knew instantly that the ring with the initials G.D.H. was Dewey's. She had given it to him as an engagement present in 1917. Her initials and the date were engraved inside the band. Her head surely spun. "Since it all had to be, I'm glad to know about the rings because they relieve a lot of anxiety and wondering," Edna told a British magazine. But the discovery raised the question of whether Dewey had been killed by a shark— unanswerable but hard to let go. The discovery also raised a practical question: Did Dewey's family want the remains shipped to Norfolk? Edna called her daughters together. She told the girls she had never seen the second ring before. She assumed it was not Dewey's. That meant the remains might not be all Dewey's. They might not be his at all. She did not want to bury a stranger. Dewey had wanted to be buried at sea anyway. "I think we have been through enough," Edna told her daughters, and they agreed. The family asked for the return of only the ring with Dewey's initials.

The Norfolk newspapers got wind of the story, and soon it made headlines all over the state and around the country. Two days later, on November 7, Henny Hodges's young cousin Edwin Jarvis, who lived across a creek from Gales Neck, rowed over to visit. He walked into the kitchen and found Henny sitting back in a chair sobbing, with a newspaper laid on a table in front of her. For a second the boy wondered if a third Hodges son had been torpedoed. Henny's daughter Alice showed him the headline: "Death of Captain Hodges Confirmed by Ring Found in Shark's Belly." Edwin thought Henny had just learned the news from the paper. It seems more likely that she already had been told, but was upset all over again by the headline.

Henny could not stop crying. She could not even work. She told her daughters, "If anything else happens, please don't tell me. I couldn't stand to hear it." Her daughters for once agreed: Their mother could not take another blow. Alice, Elizabeth, Louise, and Hilda Fourteen decided to act. They went to Captain Jesse and their brothers Willie and Coleman and asked them to stop sailing in war zones, if not for their own sake, then for Henny's.

The Hodges men were not used to taking orders on seafaring matters from their sisters, and the request was complicated. The idea of retreating from danger in wartime was hard to swallow. No one in Mathews would think ill of the Hodges family for thinking they had sacrificed enough after the deaths of Leslie and Dewey. But small communities had long memories. Almost seventy years after World War II, Clarence Collier Jr. of Gwynn's Island, who was eleven years old when his grandfather Perry Collier was lost on the *Ruth*, rattled off the names of five islanders who quit sailing steamships when the U-boats attacked. "Those sons of bitches," Clarence Collier Jr. said. "They were draft dodgers and they died draft dodgers."

The Hodges daughters could not have known what to expect when they asked their father to find safer work. Captain Jesse could find work on the water anywhere he wanted, and he agreed at once to work on tugs that stayed in the Bay.

Captain Willie Hodges discussed his sisters' request with his wife over the dinner table. Willie and his family lived only two houses from Dewey's family in Norfolk. Willie had yet to encounter a U-boat while working offshore on his tug, but he knew it could happen. Willie too decided to honor his sisters' request. Like Captain Jesse, he could easily find work on tugs inside the Bay.

David Hodges already was ashore, working in the shipyard. Spencer was ashore too. That left Raymond and Coleman Hodges still sailing the deep ocean.

The only way for the sisters to reach Raymond would be to send him a letter and hope it found him halfway around the world in a war zone. Raymond had taken the *Mormacmoon* to Suez, Egypt, with tanks, planes, and ammunition for the Russians. Off the Cape of Good Hope, the *Mormacmoon* was swept by huge seas known as cape rollers, which opened a three-inch crack in the hull. The crew patched it with cement, wire, and caulk. After the *Mormacmoon* finished unloading its cargo, the ship was placed under temporary command of the British Admiralty, for a special mission. Raymond was not told what it was.

Coleman Hodges simply refused his sisters' request. Coleman was driven to command a ship in the war, and he was almost there. He had a reputation as a light-hearted jokester, but at home, when he got angry, his eyes flashed. His wife, Ethel, and daughters froze until he relaxed. Coleman never laid a hand on his family. In fact, he left all discipline to Ethel. But "you got this feeling that he was running and couldn't run fast enough," his daughter Betty said of him.

Coleman was a dutiful son to Henny. He and his family lived in Norfolk, but he came home to Gales Neck often. He fetched wood for Henny's stove and found other ways to help her without being asked. When he stayed at the farm, he sat up with her for an hour every night before she went to bed, telling her about his family and hearing her complaints about

Jesse's slights. Coleman "was a mama's boy," his daughter Betty said. But he was not going to stop sailing offshore. His brothers' deaths would only have hardened his resolve. Coleman was stubborn enough to do the opposite of whatever his sisters or anyone else wanted him to do.

Coleman and Raymond would join a new phase of the U-boat war. For ten months after Pearl Harbor the U.S. Merchant Marine had kept the war from being lost. They had kept Britain supplied with the oil, munitions, and food it needed to continue fighting the Nazis. They had delivered enough oil and raw materials such as manganese and bauxite to keep American factories churning out ships, planes, tanks, and other weapons. They had carried tens of thousands of American troops to England for future invasions. They had endured the cold of the Murmansk Run and the heat of the Persian Gulf to deliver supplies to the Red Army and keep Stalin in the Allied camp.*

By the fall of 1942, the number of merchant mariners had almost tripled, to 150,000. The rate of new Liberty ships being launched had nearly doubled to two per day. The Merchant Marine was still "America's cross-eyed stepchild," as Admiral Land of the Maritime Commission said, but it was growing into a juggernaut. Its role in the war, like America's role, was about to shift from defense to offense. The Merchant Marine would sustain the great Allied amphibious invasions to liberate Europe from the Nazis.

The first of those invasions was Operation Torch, the Allied invasion of North Africa, set for the first week of November 1942. The strategic objectives were to capture Tunisia, trapping German armies in Libya, and to reopen part of the Mediterranean to Allied shipping. Roosevelt and Churchill had chosen North Africa largely because it was a softer target for their untested troops than France, or any territory defended by the

---

* Fifty years after the end of World War II, in the spirit of *Glasnost*, Soviet president Mikhail Gorbachev decided to award medals to U.S. merchant mariners who took part in the Murmansk Run. The medals would end up being awarded under the presidency of Boris Yeltsin, who replaced Gorbachev after a coup removed him from power. Some Mathews families still have the Russian medals.

Germans. The defenders of North Africa were mostly Vichy French. They officially served the German puppet government in France, but might not follow its orders. They might even lay down their arms and welcome the invaders ashore. If not, the invasion force was strong enough to overrun them.

Operation Torch would employ nearly four hundred merchant vessels and troop transports, in addition to three hundred warships, to deliver more than 100,000 troops to the beaches of North Africa. Three-quarters of those troops would be American—the first American armies to join the European war. Once those men started pouring into North Africa, the United States was committed to supporting them for months, even years. They would need not only guns, ammunition, tanks, planes, artillery, trucks, jeeps, and ambulances, but food, clothing, shelter, medicine, blankets, and insect repellent. Each American soldier serving overseas in World War II would need between seven and eight tons of supplies. They would also need reinforcements. Cargo ships were the only way to move everything.

The invading Allied troops were most vulnerable on the beaches, where a moment's interruption in the flow of supplies could bring disaster. But even when the troops were far inland, they would depend on a long skein of freighters, tankers, and Liberty ships, plowing across the ocean in giant rectangles, hunted by an increasingly desperate enemy.

CHAPTER TEN

Counterattack

C aptain Guy Hudgins had returned from the Murmansk Run with a big, fur-lined hat with long ear flaps. He modeled it for his wife and daughter, and for guests who dropped by for a drink at their duplex in Jersey City. Guy was enjoying catching up on the good life when he and his Liberty ship, the *Zebulon B. Vance*, were temporarily assigned to the British Admiralty in August 1942 for a special mission. He would be told the details later.

Guy was ordered to sail the ship to Liverpool, England, where her holds were filled with U.S. Army tanks and trucks, guns, and ammunition. Two big landing barges were lashed to the main deck. The barges were so heavy that special cranes had to be brought to the wharf to lift them onto the ship. A British gun crew came aboard, followed by fifty American soldiers. No one was allowed to leave the ship. The *Vance* sailed to a rendezvous point at sea, where ships stretched in all directions, farther than Guy could see. Sixty merchant ships were protected by a ring of warships, including the British escort carrier HMS *Avenger*. Guy had never seen an escort carrier before. The carrier was a floating airfield with enough planes to maintain air cover for the convoy all across the ocean. The *Avenger* sent a boat to collect Guy and the other merchant captains for a conference. It was there that Guy learned the *Vance* was part of Operation Torch.

The invasion force to North Africa was divided into three prongs. One, Task Force 34, commanded by General George S. Patton, was sailing from Norfolk across the Atlantic to land troops on the ocean coast of Morocco. The two other prongs of the invasion force were sailing from the British Isles through the Strait of Gibraltar to the Mediterranean coast of Oran and Algeria. All three prongs followed their plans perfectly, and the invasion took place on the night of November 8.

The invaders were welcomed with artillery fire, not open arms. Hutson Hudgins of Mathews, an eighteen-year-old Navy sailor, drove landing craft full of soldiers to the beach at Morocco, and compared the scene to "Christmas at home, with plenty of Roman candles and pop crackers . . . With the ships blazing away at the planes and shore batteries, the planes bombing, dropping flares and firing at each other, the shore batteries firing as fast as they could be handled, the sky afire with tracer bullets and bursting shells and bombs—boy it was some show!"

Guy Hudgins's prong of the invasion force landed near the Algerian port of Arzeu. He saw Allied warships exchange long-range volleys with shore batteries. No one shot at the *Vance*, so Guy brought her to her assigned anchorage and started unloading cargo. The crew rigged one of the heavy landing barges to the *Vance*'s largest boom crane and prepared to lift it. The British crew climbed into the barge, saying they wanted to get under way as soon as it hit the water. The crane lifted the barge and swung it out over the sea. Then the crane bent and broke. The barge splashed into the water from a height of fifteen feet. It stayed upright but a crewman was injured. The falling end of the broken crane just missed two men on the pier.

Later that day, another of the *Vance*'s cranes broke and dropped a five-ton Army truck into a cargo hold. The falling truck knocked a young American soldier into the hold, killing him. The truck tumbled into the hold after him, killing a second man and injuring two others. The *Vance* had suffered two deaths and three injuries in Operation Torch without encountering the enemy.

After those accidents, the *Vance* was moved to a newly captured dock, where unloading was easier. Guy had sailed in these waters before the war and had Arab friends and business associates in Oran. He caught a ride on a jeep to pay them a visit. The roadside was littered with dead livestock and charred Vichy French vehicles. Many of the buildings were pockmarked with bullet holes. Guy's friends welcomed him, and the invasion. His favorite ship chandler in Oran told him, "Get this war over with, captain! Come back and see us, the sooner the better!" Other residents were more hostile; the Vichy French fought for two days in North Africa, killing more than 800 Allied soldiers, before signing an armistice.

Operation Torch caught the Germans by surprise. They had not thought the United States was ready to launch a large-scale invasion. Doenitz fumed that the German intelligence apparatus "had failed completely." His U-boats had made no contact with the invasion force. After the Allies had landed in North Africa, Doenitz belatedly sent out his U-boats. They torpedoed four troop transports returning from the beaches off Morocco, killing 111 Americans. But the U-boats had failed to prevent the buildup for the invasion, or stop it. Guy took the *Vance* back to the United States, picked up another load of supplies for the troops, and joined another convoy to North Africa. Once again, he encountered no U-boats.

While the Germans were reeling from Operation Torch, Captain Raymond Hodges was dispatched on a different special mission for the British. The *Mormacmoon* was ordered from Suez, Egypt, where it had dropped off supplies for the Russians, to Port Sudan, where it was loaded with food, coal, ammunition, and gasoline. The gas was stored in scores of small five-gallon containers. A seaman asked the ship's agent in Suez where they were going, but he "refused to tell us our destination, but said he did not think we would return."

Raymond, ever a stickler for routine and detail, insisted the crew practice launching the lifeboats every day, even when the wind blowing off the desert made rowing an ordeal. He was a consummate professional who would never think of questioning his orders, but he was accustomed to being in control of events, and could not have liked not knowing where he and his ship were headed next. Finally, on the night of November 16, the *Mormacmoon* was ordered to sail out through the northern end of the Suez Canal into the eastern Mediterranean. Three freighters that had been taking on cargo near the *Mormacmoon* followed. The four ships entered the Mediterranean at dawn and were quickly encircled by British warships. At that point, Raymond was told he and the *Mormacmoon* were part of Operation Stoneage, a convoy to Malta.

Malta is a tiny limestone island in the Mediterranean 50 miles south of Sicily. It is famous for its stone towers and medieval knights, but in 1942 it was better known as one of the most bombed places on earth. Malta was a base for British planes and submarines that attacked the Germans' supply lines to Africa, frustrating the Germans' attempts to capture Egypt and the Allied oil fields in the Mideast. The Germans were desperate to drive the British from Malta, and bombed the island daily from air bases in Sicily and North Africa. They reduced entire villages on Malta to rubble. Malta's 250,000 citizens and 20,000 British defenders lived in caves and tunnels carved into the limestone hills. Their greatest danger was not bombs but starvation. Malta produced little food. Any Allied ship trying to deliver supplies to the island was attacked by German bombers and U-boats. Shortages of food and aviation fuel became critical. The most recent convoy to Malta, Operation Pedestal, had delivered enough supplies in August to save the islanders from having to surrender. But Malta remained isolated and vulnerable, and any ship approaching the island was sure to be attacked.

Raymond's four-ship convoy was escorted by four cruisers and seven destroyers—nearly three times as many warships as cargo ships. That reversal of the normal balance of warships to merchant ships in a convoy showed how much trouble the British anticipated, and how vital the cargo was to Malta. British fighters flew overhead. The *Mormacmoon* led the other merchant ships west through a calm sea at a speed of 15 knots. Malta was four long days away. The only question was when the first attack would come.

Less than four hours after the escorts had joined the convoy, five German light bombers flew directly overhead and dropped bombs. One bomb exploded in the water close enough to the *Mormacmoon* to make the whole ship rattle. Other German planes passed ahead of the convoy, and the British planes pursued them. At dusk, a German torpedo bomber severely damaged a British cruiser in the escort force, killing 129 men. The convoy kept going.

After dark, the greatest danger was accidentally colliding with another ship. Every ship was blacked out, and commands to zigzag were transmitted by signal light or whistle. If a ship missed one of those commands, it might smash into a ship in the next column. Raymond stayed on the bridge with his binoculars. On the third day, gales swept across the Mediterranean and grounded the German bombers. The storms blew until the next day, when the convoy was close enough to Malta for British Spitfire fighters based on the island to fly out and provide air cover.

That night, the *Mormacmoon* led the three other merchant ships into Grand Harbor at the Maltese port of Valetta. Submarine nets opened to admit the convoy, and depth charges were dropped behind it to make sure no U-boats followed it in. Amphitheater-like Grand Harbor was blacked out, but people lined the stone walls under a full moon and cheered the convoy in. Malta's governor, General Sir William Dobbie, went aboard the *Mormacmoon* to welcome Raymond. The confident, debonair Raymond was perfectly comfortable in the presence of high-ranking officials.

British soldiers started unloading the *Mormacmoon* and discovered gasoline had leaked from the little containers and pooled two feet deep in the holds. A spark could blow up the ship. Raymond set the whole crew to work. They hauled out the leaky gas containers and pumped out the spilled gasoline. The fumes in the hold were overpowering. Men held their breath, scrambled down a ladder for a few seconds of work, and then scrambled back up to breathe. An air-raid alarm sounded every few hours, as if to remind the men to hurry. Neither Raymond nor any of his officers took a break until the job was finished.

Once the crisis was over, Raymond accepted an invitation to dine with Governor Dobbie. The view from the governor's home was impressive, but daylight had revealed the bombed hulks of several ships in Grand Harbor, and the meal was little more than "a dish of beans and a glass of wine." Raymond felt guilty eating any of the islanders' scarce food. Unloading took a little over two weeks. On December 7, one year after Pearl Harbor, the *Mormacmoon* led the convoy out of Grand Harbor through the submarine nets.

The Germans were waiting. Torpedo bombers damaged a British escort ship and killed three seamen. Their funeral services had just begun the next morning when two waves of Junkers 88 bombers attacked. A British fighter chased them off, but more attacked at dusk. Bombs exploded in the water all around the *Mormacmoon*. One bomber roared right over the ship, barely higher than the masts, and dropped a bomb just astern. Later in the day, four planes headed straight for the *Mormacmoon*. The first officer saw Raymond drop to his knees, apparently in prayer. The planes passed directly over the ship and kept going. They were unarmed transport planes, probably evacuating German troops from North Africa to Italy.

The *Mormacmoon* and the other ships got back to Suez unscathed, and Raymond set out on the long trip home. The bombers did not follow. On Christmas Day, the *Mormacmoon* was steaming south through the Indian Ocean. One of the lookouts spotted two submarines in the distance off Tanzania, but the subs showed no interest in their ship.* The *Mormacmoon* stopped in Portuguese East Africa to take on a load of chrome ore. Ray-

---

* The submarines may have been Japanese. Japanese subs patrolled the waters off Tanzania, but did not pursue merchant ships as aggressively as the U-boats did, mainly because Japanese subs were constantly being diverted to other missions by Japanese admirals. German submariners sometimes exhorted their Japanese counterparts to attack more merchant ships.

mond decided to wait for a high tide to take the ship through the tricky Mozambique Channel. Some of the crew took the opportunity to go on safaris, hunting predators in the African bush—a surreal end to the first full year of the U-boat war on America.

The year had treated merchant mariners cruelly. A preliminary Navy summary of losses in the western Atlantic in 1942 included 548 Allied and neutral ships sunk, and more than 3,000 American mariners killed. The Allies had lost 2.2 million tons of cargo, more than half of it in the Caribbean.

The war had treated Mathews cruelly too. Some mariners' families were bitter. "We had some animosity toward the government for leaving my father unprotected," Dewey Hodges's daughter Jean said. The U.S. government seemed to consider merchant ships and mariners expendable. Would Admiral King spend the lives of his Navy men so freely?

Christmas was always a subdued time in Mathews. Families of mariners at sea hung special ornaments on the tree, set symbolic plates before empty dinner chairs, and wrapped Christmas presents to sit unopened for weeks or even months. The melancholy penetrated even deeper than usual in 1942. "Those of us who live in small towns are able to see more clearly the suffering caused by war," the *Gazette-Journal* said. "We have a friendly, personal interest in each other. The spirit of neighborly love and devotion has eased many a saddened heart . . ." Captain Jesse's new job on a tug in the Bay allowed him to come home on Christmas, which was also his and Henny's wedding anniversary. Coleman happened to be in port and brought his family to Gales Neck for a few days. Most of his brothers were on the water.

Captains of ships at sea on Christmas tried to boost the crews' spirits. The benevolent Captain Robert Gayle of the collier *Achilles* set up a Christmas tree in the ship's dining room and canceled all routine duties. The cook outdid himself with a huge turkey dinner with gravy. The crew of the *Achilles* was lucky to be alive to enjoy the meal. In dense fog off the coast of

Rhode Island, the *Achilles* had nearly collided with a U-boat. Gayle could hear the Germans shout and smell their cigarettes. The fog swallowed the vessels again before either could react. Gayle ordered the *Achilles* to steam at full speed the rest of the night despite the fog.

The new year of 1943 began promisingly for the Allies. In the Pacific, the U.S. Marines were driving the Japanese off Guadalcanal after months of bloody fighting over a strategic jungle airstrip. In Europe, the German Sixth Army was bogged down in the freezing ruins of Stalingrad, and American and British bombers were pummeling German cities night and day. The Allied campaign in North Africa was progressing so well that Roosevelt and Churchill traveled to Casablanca in January for a meeting to decide their next step. They declared the Allies would accept nothing less than "unconditional surrender" from the Axis nations. Stalin once again was demanding that the United States and Britain launch an amphibious invasion of France to siphon German troops away from the Russian front. But Roosevelt and Churchill still were not ready to hurl their troops across the English Channel at the fortifications Hitler called the "Atlantic wall." The Allied armies needed a new target to maintain their momentum. Churchill persuaded Roosevelt it should be Sicily, the island at the end of the Italian boot.

Sicily was not so important strategically as it was there for the taking. It was only a day's voyage from North Africa. Its defenders were mostly Italians, who might not fight any harder than the Vichy French in North Africa had. Where the Allies would go after capturing Sicily was left open, but the most obvious choice was invading mainland Italy. Sending thousands of Allied troops to Sicily, and then possibly to mainland Italy, would require a larger and more complex supply chain. It would take thousands of ships steaming up and down the U.S. coast, through the Gulf and Caribbean, back and forth across the Atlantic between New York and Britain, Italy and North Africa, and between North America and Italy. No supply operation on that scale had ever been attempted.

U-boats continued to pick off ships from the fringes of convoys. Johnie Hall, a twenty-eight-year-old mariner from Gwynn's Island, survived a sinking after his ship, the *Steel Navigator*, straggled behind a convoy in the fog. Roland Howard Garrett of Mathews lived through the sinking of the Liberty ship *Benjamin Harrison*, torpedoed in a convoy en route to North Africa. In January, Alton Hudgins of Mathews survived the torpedoing of the little freighter *Collingsworth* in a convoy off Dutch Guiana.

But ships sailing alone were always in the greatest danger, as Alton Hudgins's cousin Allen Hudgins discovered. Late on the night of February 3, 1943, his vessel, the Liberty ship *Roger B. Taney*, was steaming alone through the middle of the South Atlantic. The ship was empty, en route to Brazil to pick up a load of bauxite ore. The lookouts shouted that a torpedo was coming. It missed the ship's bow by 10 feet. The *Taney* ran, but a Liberty ship's maximum speed was 11.5 knots; a U-boat on the surface could make 17. The U-160 quickly overtook the *Taney*. An hour after missing with its first torpedo, the submarine fired a second torpedo straight into the *Taney*'s engine room, killing all three men on watch there, and buckling the ship's deck. The rest of the crew got away in two lifeboats.

The U-boat surfaced and the commander asked the men in the boats about their ship. No one responded and he barked, "It doesn't matter, we know all about your ship." He offered to tow the lifeboats closer to land, but the mariners were suspicious and declined. The U-boat left them alone. Both lifeboats were nearly full, with twenty-eight men in one and twenty-six in the other. The *Taney*'s captain, Thomas J. Potter, decided they should rig the sails and ride the southeast trade winds to Brazil. The lifeboats became separated in rough weather the first night. The breeze kept dying and the castaways cursed the calm. They had plenty of water because rain squalls kept drenching the boat. Days passed, and then weeks. The men in Allen's lifeboat kept each other's spirits up by talking constantly about thick steaks and ice cream. In the absence of those choices, they speared a fish, drank its blood, and cooked it over a fire in a metal bucket in the boat, smashing up a spare oar for firewood. After three weeks adrift, the twenty-eight men in Allen's lifeboat were picked up by a British ship on March 1.

Captain Potter's lifeboat drifted for another week. Finally, the captain saw birds and knew they were nearing land. Frigate birds and storm petrels nested on land but ranged far out to sea, so the sight of them meant land was only a few days away. Then Potter "saw one dragon fly and one butter fly [sic] and I was definitely sure that land was near." He could tell from the small fish in the water that they had reached the shallow banks south of Trinidad. Potter may even have been able to smell the coast. Land gave off distinctive smells that carried long distances across the sea. The Cape Verde Islands off Africa smelled like oranges, and some tropical isles, like coconuts. All land gave off a sweet smell after a rain.

Three nights after spotting the birds, the men in the lifeboat saw the glow of a city against the clouds in the western sky just before dawn. The captain said it was Rio de Janeiro. Sunrise revealed a mountaintop in the distance. The breeze quit again. The captain worried the current would sweep them south, away from land. He handed out extra rations of water and crackers and urged everyone to take a turn at the oars and row with all their strength. The lifeboat drew close to a wild shore. The captain thought the exhausted men might have to row to the beach through thundering surf. But a half mile from the Brazilian coast near the city of Santos, a steamship picked them up. In the 42 days since the *Taney* sinking, their lifeboat had traveled more than 2,600 miles.

The U-boat attacks in the South Atlantic in the first months of 1943 were only a prelude to the main event. Despite the Allied victories and the new defenses mounted for convoys, the decisive clash of the Battle of the Atlantic was about to begin. Doenitz could hardly wait.

Doenitz believed U-boats could still win the war if they sank enough Allied merchant ships, and for the first time, he had enough influence in Berlin to put that theory to the test. Doenitz had been promoted to Grand Admiral of the German Navy, replacing his old boss Erich Raeder, who was tired of Hitler's red-faced tirades. Unlike Raeder, Doenitz had Hitler's ear, and money and resources for U-boat construction flowed. By early 1943, Doenitz had 430 U-boats in service, of which roughly a hundred were always on active patrol. The U-boat force had never been larger.

Doenitz believed he could stagger the Allies by launching his wolf packs in an all-out assault on the North Atlantic convoy routes, the regular supply runs to Britain that the Royal Navy called "the heartbeat of the war." The main point of attack would be the air gap, the 600-mile stretch of ocean south of Greenland where Allied planes could not reach. When the weather finally cleared at the start of March, Doenitz sent forty-eight U-boats into the air gap and surrounding waters—too many for Allied convoys to avoid. Convoy after convoy plunged into the submarine gauntlet. What had been a contest of hit-and-run, hide-and-seek had turned into a brawl.

Clashes between the U-boats and the convoy escort ships were ferocious. One British escort rammed a surfacing U-boat, only to be sunk by a second U-boat, which in turn was sunk by a French escort ship. In mid-March, wolf packs attacked two convoys passing in opposite directions through the air gap and sank nineteen ships, killing 740 mariners and sending 82,049 tons of cargo to the sea bottom. The ebullient Doenitz called the attack "the greatest success that we had so far scored against a convoy." He did not see disaster approaching, as the Allies began for the first time to seize the initiative against the wolf packs.

The counteroffensive against the U-boats did not erupt suddenly from a single event or invention. It had been building slowly for years, as improvements in Allied strategy, technology, and weaponry coalesced into a critical mass.

Almost from the start of the war, the British had engaged some of their most brilliant scientists to analyze U-boats' vulnerabilities. Physicists such as Patrick Blackett advised pilots and seamen on topics ranging from the most productive settings for depth charges—30 feet—to the best routes and times of day for aerial patrols. British engineers developed microwave radar that could spot U-boats on the surface at a distance of 10 miles, even at night or in thick clouds and fog. That radar, which could be installed in planes and escort ships, robbed the U-boats of the only sanctuary they enjoyed at sea. A U-boat commander could no longer relax on the water's surface at night, enjoying a glimpse of the sky and a few gulps of fresh air while the sub's batteries were recharging. Now, he might look up to see an Allied bomber racing at him out of the darkness, shining a blinding spotlight in his eyes. The searchlights, named Leigh Lights after Humphrey de Verd Leigh, the British squadron commander who invented them, were designed to pick up where radar left off. A bomber approaching a U-boat at night would lose the submarine's image on radar about three-quarters of a mile from the drop point—not close enough for the pilot to see his target in the dark. At that point, he would switch on the Leigh Light, whose brilliant beam guided him the rest of the way. U-boats were equipped with rudimentary radar detectors, but they were clumsy to set up and dismantle, prone to buzzing constant false alarms, and incapable of detecting microwave radar.

Night or day, planes enjoyed a clear advantage over U-boats. A sharp-eyed U-boat lookout might be able to spot an approaching plane from a distance of three miles. But the plane could cover that distance in less than fifteen seconds, while the U-boat needed at least twenty-five seconds to crash dive. Doenitz, who once had boasted that a plane "can no more kill a U-boat than a crow can kill a mole," had come to recognize the plane as the U-boat's nemesis. U-boats rarely received air cover from German planes, partly because Doenitz and the chief of the Luftwaffe, Field Marshal Hermann Goering, loathed each other.

Radar combined with sonar enabled convoys to detect U-boats approaching on the surface or underwater. New technology combined with new escort ships and planes meant that large, well-protected convoys, like those crossing the North Atlantic, no longer had to be content with fending off U-boats. Once they found them, they could hunt them down and destroy them.

Convoys increasingly were accompanied by new, American-built

Navy destroyer escorts (DEs), inexpensive versions of destroyers, which were fast enough to outrun U-boats, built to withstand winter seas, and armed with new Mark 9 and Mark 10 depth charges, which sank fast and could be set to explode at 600 to 800 feet—the depth to which a desperate U-boat captain might take his sub as a last resort.

The DE was designed by Rear Admiral Edward L. Cochrane, a naval architect and the future chief of the Navy's Bureau of Ships. Cochrane had failed to persuade Admiral King and others in the U.S. Navy hierarchy to build DEs, so he pitched the design to the British, who ordered some of them built at American shipyards through the Lend-Lease program. When Roosevelt learned about the British orders, he diverted the DEs to the U.S. Navy, and then ordered more DEs. Later, Roosevelt and Admiral King would each blame the other for not building DEs sooner.

American shipyards also produced escort carriers like the one that had impressed Captain Guy Hudgins in Operation Torch. The "baby flattops," as they were called, were miniature versions of the aircraft carriers anchoring the U.S. fleet in the Pacific. Escort carriers operated 28 planes compared to a big aircraft carrier's 103. Some escort carriers were embedded in convoys to provide a moving umbrella of protection wherever the convoys went. Their planes patrolled the convoys' paths and flanks, searching for U-boats on the surface. When they found one, they either attacked it or forced it underwater and radioed its location to the escort ships.

The U.S. Navy pioneered the use of escort carriers as the nuclei of "hunter-killer groups," designed to destroy U-boats. A typical hunter-killer group consisted of an escort carrier and four destroyers. The group prowled the convoy routes, beaming radar and sonar in search of submarines. It also chased down leads from the Allied radio direction-finding network, which used Doenitz's daily radio communications with his U-boats to find his subs for the hunter-killers. What made hunter-killer groups so lethal was that they never had to break off from attacks in order to keep up with a convoy, as escort ships did. When a hunter-killer group found a U-boat, it could take all the time necessary to destroy it. The group's sole purpose was hunting down one U-boat after another. From early 1943 to the end of the war, they would be the most prolific destroyers of U-boats.

By late March 1943, the counteroffensive against the U-boats had tilted the convoy battles in the North Atlantic in the Allies' favor. Captain Raymond Hodges saw the change firsthand when the *Mormacmoon* was assigned to the first big North Atlantic convoy of April. Raymond had returned only a few days earlier from his voyage to Malta. On the way home from Malta, he had first learned of his brothers' deaths from a six-month-old newspaper clipping. He wrote to Captain Jesse and Henny:

> I heard about Dewey and Leslie after we left Cape Town. One of my mates gave me a Norfolk paper to read, and I happened upon the sad news while we were at sea. You know how shocked I was. I suppose one must expect such things when the whole crazy world is fighting, like, as you used to say, 'a passel of Arabs.' We shall have to bear our losses until it is all over. If I am not mistaken, very few of us will come out of this war free from some sort of damage. It has not really started yet. Day in and day out, our people are losing their lives on every sea, even more so than on the land. As I see it, no one stands to gain much from this everlasting fighting. I hope it will end before we suffer more losses. I am about to go on another trip and this time think I shall go to England.

The *Mormacmoon* left New York Harbor on April 2 in Convoy HX-232,* the latest in the long series of huge North Atlantic convoys, and typical of them: thirty-nine merchant ships carrying oil, aviation fuel, steam locomotives, landing barges, sugar, grain, and lumber, along with 200 U.S. Army soldiers. Several ships in the convoy carried passengers, including the *Mormacmoon*, which also carried thirty-eight precious bags

---

* The HX designation referred to Halifax, Nova Scotia, where many transatlantic convoys to Britain originated.

of mail for American soldiers in Britain. The escort force included three destroyers and four corvettes, but no escort carrier and therefore no air cover.

The Germans tracked the formation of Raymond's convoy by reading coded Allied messages, and assembled wolf packs to intercept it. The Allies, who had broken back into the German Navy's Enigma code in December, tracked the U-boats tracking the convoy. Allied code breakers would continue to read secret German messages through Enigma, with few interruptions, through the end of the war. As HX-232 made its way across the Atlantic, neither side suspected the other had tapped into its secrets and knew most of its moves in advance. This didn't necessarily mean either side was in a better position to attack or defend its vessels.

The first vessel in convoy HX-232 to be sunk was a Liberty ship that had straggled far behind the convoy, alone. The U-615 fired four torpedoes in a fan pattern. Only one torpedo hit the ship, and it was a dud. The U-boat chased the ship down and sank her with two more torpedoes. All sixty-nine of the Liberty ship's passengers and crew were killed.

Halfway across the Atlantic, the main body of Convoy HX-232 ran into a storm. The *Mormacmoon* scaled mountainous waves. She hung momentarily on the wave crests, and then slid down into the troughs. That kind of roller-coaster motion placed a strain on ships' hulls. One of the escort ships developed cracks in her deck plates and had to turn back. The commodore in charge of the convoy received a radio warning of a wolf pack dead ahead. He briefly changed course, but decided there was no avoiding the U-boats. Convoy HX-232 would have to run through them.

On April 11, the wolf pack code-named *Lerche*—"Lark"—attacked the convoy. A destroyer spotted a U-boat on the surface but did not bother to fire because the destroyer was rolling violently, and any shell aimed at the U-boat from the warship's guns might end up flying wildly into the air or straight into the sea. The escorts detected other U-boats by radar and sonar. Some escorts darted out from the convoy to drop depth charges on sonar targets. Every such foray by an escort left a temporary gap in the screen around the merchant ships. Early the next morning, an Australian destroyer left her position in the screen to investigate a radar contact, which turned out to be nothing. The destroyer was hurrying back into place in the screen when the U-563 sneaked into the gap she had left and fired a spread of torpedoes into the heart of the convoy.

Explosions shook three freighters. The first two sank quickly, leaving dozens of survivors adrift in lifeboats, including a group of women. Raymond was horrified that he could not stop for the survivors, but a rescue ship trailing the convoy picked up most of them. A fourth ship was torpedoed, bringing the toll to five, including the straggler. The *Mormacmoon* and the rest of the convoy kept going.

First light brought the convoy air cover in the form of Very Long Range (VLR) B-24 Liberator bombers based in Newfoundland. Liberators could fly at 290 mph, with a range of 3,000 miles—long enough to reach the air gap and essentially close it. Admiral King had not assigned the VLRs to convoy duty until March, when Roosevelt, alarmed by the surge in convoy losses, asked where the VLRs had been. The Liberators provided air cover for HX-232, scouring the ocean ahead of the convoy and forcing any U-boats in its path underwater. The planes thoroughly disrupted the wolf pack attack. One U-boat commander in the *Lerche* group complained, "Am continually being harassed by aircraft." Another U-boat was forced to crash-dive three times in the course of a few hours. By night, when the planes had to return to Newfoundland, the U-boats had fallen far behind the convoy. Doenitz urged them over the radio to race ahead and strike the convoy again before the planes returned at first light. But the U-boats did not catch the convoy that night, or ever. The *Mormacmoon* and thirty-three other merchant ships of HX-232 unloaded their cargo safely at Loch Ewe, Scotland.

The Allied antisubmarine forces built on their successes. The next major North Atlantic convoy, HX-233, lost only one ship. The convoy after that, HX-234, did not lose any.

The U-boats' losses, however, were soaring. Fifty-five U-boats were sunk in the first three months of 1943—the worst losses since the start of the war. Doenitz recalled many of his subs to their bunkers in April to repair the damage from a winter of pounding seas and near-miss depth-charge explosions. He sent the U-boats back out in May, hoping for a fresh start and a return to glory. But the Allied defenses had simply grown too strong. Another forty-one U-boats were sunk in May—"Black May" as U-boat men afterward called May 1943. The Germans were losing a U-boat for almost every ship they sank.

Part of the reason was that U-boat men were no longer Germany's warrior elite. The mounting casualties had reduced the number of top-flight volunteers, forcing Doenitz to increasingly fill his submarines with inexperienced men who did not want to serve in submarines. Studies after the war would show that a core of twenty U-boat commanders accounted for nearly a fourth of all the Allied tonnage sunk, and that many command-ers accomplished little or nothing. Not every U-boat commander had what it took to charge into a convoy, wreak havoc, and slip away in the confusion.

Because U-boats often suffered their death blows deep underwater, their entire crews often died with them and were entombed in them. The growing list of U-boats lost with all hands included the U-124, whose young commander, Johann Mohr, had written a poem about sinking tankers off Hatteras. The list also included the U-507 and commander Harro Schacht, who had squeezed fresh limes into a jug of drinking water for the *Norlindo* survivors and told them to "come see me after the war." Lost as well were the U-125, which had torpedoed Genious Hudgins Jr. on the *Green Island*, and the U-563, which had slipped through the gap in the screen of convoy HX-232 and torpedoed three ships. And sunk too was the U-954, whose crew included Doenitz's twenty-one-year-old son, Peter.*

---

* Doenitz's older son, Klaus, was allowed to withdraw from the German military as a result of his brother's death, and was studying to become a doctor. A year after his brother, Peter, was killed on the U-954, Klaus Doenitz tagged along with some old friends from the military on a mission across the English Channel on a torpedo boat, and died when the torpedo boat was sunk.

Doenitz took each U-boat loss hard. When one was reported, he "would sort of go into his private room and sort of cry about it," his former chief of operations recalled. At month's end, shaken and most likely heart-sick, Doenitz withdrew all his U-boats from the North Atlantic convoy routes. The Battle of the Atlantic, far from his defining victory, seemed to be lost, or at least slipping away from him. Black May had demonstrated how far behind the U-boats had fallen in tactics and technology. U-boats urgently needed technological upgrades, especially a defense against air-borne radar. Without them, they were so vulnerable that Doenitz consid-ered whether he should send them back out at all.

He ultimately decided he owed it to the Third Reich to keep going. Even though U-boats were no longer effective—even though they had become death traps—they still posed a threat that tied up hundreds of Allied escort ships and planes. If those ships and planes no longer had to worry about U-boats, they surely could be diverted to other missions against Germany. "I finally came to the conclusion that we had no option but to fight on," Doenitz wrote. Hitler agreed. "There can be no talk of let-up in submarine warfare," he declared. "The enemy forces tied up by our submarine warfare are tremendous, even though the actual losses inflicted by us are no longer great." The U-boats had become bearable losses.

Doenitz tried to rally the U-boat force with a message promising bet-ter days ahead. He said new radar-jamming equipment was coming. U-boats would be equipped with snorkels, long retractable tubes through which subs could draw fresh air while submerged. Conning towers would be better armored. Torpedoes would finally stay on course and blow up when they were supposed to. A new generation of U-boats would run faster and stay submerged all day. "The time will come," Doenitz promised his men, "in which you will be superior to the enemy with new and stronger weapons, and will be able to triumph over your worst enemy—the aircraft and the destroyer." But promises did not help the U-boat crews setting out on patrols in the spring of 1943. The predators were becoming prey.

CHAPTER ELEVEN

The Conveyor Belt

Eighteen-year-old Navy sailor Bernard Stansbury squinted up into the bright afternoon sun over the island of Sicily and saw two dozen planes approaching in a V formation. Bernard was a spotter for a Navy Armed Guard gun crew on the Liberty ship *Robert Rowan*. It was July 11, 1943, and the *Robert Rowan* was one of the first cargo ships to unload supplies after the Allied invasion of Sicily.

The ship sat at anchor in the harbor at Gela, on Sicily's southern coast, amid dozens of other vessels of the invasion fleet. Bernard's job was to watch for enemy planes. Normally, the sight of a large V formation would have spurred him and his gun crew into action. But they had been warned that Allied planes would fly over in a V formation en route to drop paratroopers farther inland. They were to hold their fire. One Allied parachute drop in Sicily already had turned disastrous when Allied ships mistakenly shot down 23 of their own planes, killing or wounding 229 men. So Bernard did nothing but watch the planes through his binoculars. They were passing at about 12,000 feet, like bombers. They were nearly overhead when Bernard saw swastikas on their tails.

"Those are German planes. Shoot!" he shouted to his gun crew. The gunners on other ships also recognized the truth. A wall of antiaircraft fire took shape, but it was too late. The men on the *Rowan* saw bombs tumble from the planes directly above them.

The Allied invasion of Sicily, code-named Operation Husky, had begun two days before. The invasion armada sailed from North Africa. It comprised seven Allied divisions and 3,300 ships—a larger force than even the one that would land at Normandy on D-Day. "There is no way of [describing] the size of that fleet," the war correspondent Ernie Pyle wrote of the Sicily armada. "On the horizon it resembled a distant city. It covered half the skyline and the dull-colored, camouflaged ships stood indistinctly against the curve of the dark water, like a solid formation of uncountable structures blending together. Even to be part of it was frightening. I hope no American ever has to see its counterpart sailing against us."

U-boats did not confront the invasion force on the 90-mile voyage from North Africa to Sicily, but German bombers from the Italian mainland took aim at Allied ships. German and Italian soldiers fought hard at Gela and at other pockets in the landing zone, but the invaders moved inland. The *Rowan* carried mostly artillery shells, with crates of small-arms ammunition piled on top, on the theory that an invading army would need bullets before artillery shells. The captain ran the *Rowan* right onto shore to get as close as possible for the Army DUKW vehicles. The "Ducks" were two-and-a-half-ton Army trucks balanced on flotation tanks and powered by propellers. They operated as floating shuttle barges, receiving cargo from the ships' cranes and then carrying it to the docks and up onto land.

Soon after the *Rowan* arrived at Gela, German tanks in the brown hills three miles above the harbor began shooting at the ship. Every minute or so a tank round fell into the water around the *Robert Rowan*. The shells arrived with a rush of air and a splash but did not explode when they hit the water. A few landed close to the ship. A tugboat towed the *Rowan* into deeper water, out of the tanks' range. The unloading had just resumed when Bernard Stansbury spotted the planes in the V formation.

Bernard was not a Mathews native but a "come-here," a vaguely dis-missive term for anyone not born in the county.* He had grown up in Richmond but spent his boyhood summers and weekends at his family's cottage on Gwynn's Island. He sailed and sculled with some of the Callis boys, but joined the Navy instead of the Merchant Marine. He envisioned himself on a warship charging across the Pacific to trade volleys with the Japanese. But he was assigned instead to the Navy Armed Guard, a branch of the sea service established in 1942 to operate the guns being installed on merchant ships. Among Navy men, an assignment to the Armed Guard was widely considered undesirable, partly because of the danger of serving on merchant ships. Navy nicknames for Armed Guard units were "Sitting Ducks" and "Clay Pigeons." Armed Guard men recited a facetious motto, "Sighted sub, glub, glub"—a parody of "Sighted sub, sank same," the widely quoted comment of an Army pilot hunting U-boats. Bernard kept an open mind about the Armed Guard. He wanted to stay positive.

The delay in shooting at the German bombers proved disastrous for the *Robert Rowan*. Three bombs fell directly on the ship. They were falling too fast for Bernard to see them, but he heard a faint whistle and felt a rush of air. One of the bombs was a dud. It flew in through a cargo hold and was going so fast, it poked a hole in the hull on its way back out of the ship, into the water. The other two bombs fell directly into the sixteen-foot-square opening of the No. 3 cargo hold. The *Rowan* gave a slight jolt, and black smoke began streaming from the No. 3 hold. The bombs were incendiaries and had started a fire. Crew members wrestled two thick fire hoses across the deck, lowered the nozzles into the hold, and turned on the water. The fire was detonating the small-arms ammunition on top of the artillery shells. Live rounds ricocheted around the hold and flew out of the hatch in bursts. The men were afraid to get close enough to the edge of the hold

---

*Even a person brought to Mathews as an infant was regarded by the natives as a "come-here," although after long years of residence, he or she might jokingly be pro-moted to a "been-here."

to direct the hoses. The black smoke thickened and formed a smudge in the sky over the harbor. Every man on the ship was thinking about the artillery shells under the small-arms ammunition. Bernard and his gun crew stayed at their posts, watching an empty sky and stealing glances at the No. 3 hold.

After thirty anxious minutes, the captain gave the order to abandon ship, and men scrambled down cargo nets into Ducks, which ferried them to ships a safe distance away. The abandoned *Rowan* simmered for another hour and then exploded in a sheet of flame and a boiling cloud, with pieces of the ship pinwheeling thousands of feet in the air. The roar was audible for miles. The Liberty ship split in half and settled onto the shallow bottom with much of her superstructure still above water. The wreck burned furiously all night, lighting the harbor for enemy pilots. Bernard came away from the experience energized and feeling lucky. But the crew of Liberty ship *Timothy Pickering*, moored on another side of Sicily, was unlucky. A bomb landed directly in one of the ship's cargo holds and detonated tons of ammunition in one sudden, devastating blast, killing twenty-two crew members, eight Navy gunners, and one hundred British soldiers traveling on the ship. Flaming pieces of the *Timothy Pickering* flew across the harbor and hit other ships, killing three men on one vessel and starting a fire that blew up an oil tanker.

On July 27, 1943, the Hodges family suffered another blow with the death of Captain Jesse's father, John Thomas Hodges, at the age of ninety-three. John, who had grown up in Mathews, listed his profession in Census forms as farming. But like many in Mathews, he had eked out a living from farm work, carpentry, boatbuilding, and whatever other work he could find. He had lived through the Civil War in Mathews. He had founded the Macedonia Baptist Church there. Since the death of his wife, Sarah, years before, he had lived alone in a small brick house across the creek from Gales Neck. He was a frail man with a long white beard who sat on his porch with his chin perched on the tip of his cane. He liked to tell stories, and he credited his longevity to "hard work, good food, and abstinence from hard liquors." He was a gentler sort than his son Jesse, but not a man of means. In his will, he left six children and three of his grandchildren $10 apiece.

The Allies took Sicily by the end of July after losing 25,000 men, including nearly 10,000 Americans. They carelessly allowed three retreating German divisions to escape Sicily by crossing the narrow Strait of Messina to the mainland. Roosevelt reluctantly agreed with Churchill that the Allies should invade mainland Italy next, while building up another invasion force for France.* The Allied armies would land in far southern Italy and fight their way up the 750-mile-long Italian boot to liberate Rome.

The focus of the war in Europe had shifted to the Mediterranean. The clear, shallow, crowded Mediterranean was a nightmare for U-boats. Doenitz called it a "mousetrap." Just entering the Mediterranean through the Strait of Gibraltar was so challenging for U-boats that it was called "breaking in." Staying alive in the sea was almost as difficult. Allied planes were so numerous that U-boats had to stay submerged, blind to much of what was happening above them. But with the Allied victory in Sicily and eyes clearly turning toward Italy, Doenitz had no choice but to send U-boats into the Mediterranean. His men recognized what he was asking of them. Herbert Werner of the U-203 was crestfallen at first to be ordered to break into the Mediterranean. "But what difference did it make where we sailed?" he concluded. "It was all the same everywhere—furious attempts to destroy [the enemy] combined with desperate attempts to avoid being bombed, mutilated and sunk. It was like committing slow-motion suicide. The end was the same, only the name of the sea would change."

Captain Homer Callis of Gwynn's Island arrived in the Mediterranean in August. He had quit his desk job with the Bull Line in Baltimore after his old ship, the *Mae*, was torpedoed on its first voyage without him, leav-

---

* The Army chief of staff, General George C. Marshall, disagreed with the Allies' entire Mediterranean strategy and pressed for an immediate invasion of France.

ing Lester Smith maimed. He had taken the job ashore because it was a promotion, and to reduce the family's risk after his brother Mel was killed on the *Ruth*. But the *Mae* sinking had changed his thinking. He could not sit at a desk when the country needed sea captains. When he asked for a new ship, the Bull Line gave him the freighter *Cape Mohican*. His schedule was busy. The stops included Panama and Cape Town. He sailed up the Red Sea, briefly running aground on a sandbar not on the maps. The *Cape Mohican* hauled everything from ammunition to soldiers' mail.

Homer was unaccustomed to such long voyages and missed talking with his wife, Nancy. He and Nancy worried about their older son, Homer Jr. He never complained but they could tell from his letters that he did not like serving on a Navy destroyer in the Pacific. When his ship docked in San Francisco, Nancy flew all the way out to see him. Homer wrote to Nancy:

My Darling,

There never was anything as pleasant to me as that which happened last night when I was told your letter was waiting for me. It was such a swell thing for you to do, Darling, for it has seemed so many eternities since I left and not a word from you or anyone in that time. That has been the toughest part of my journey, and now I'm happy to know that you and my boys are alright and soon I shall have that greatest of all joys of seeing you again. I wish I knew how to say how badly I've missed you. I'll try to tell you when I come back and say all the other things that I've penned up in my heart to wait that happy hour. I know how long and hard these days are for you, but please God may you enjoy many more happy years with Homer Jr. and Bill. I'm so glad that he could [get leave from his ship and] come to see you. I wondered about that and I'm so anxious to hear about him. We've made out alright and are feeling swell with the knowledge that we will be home before very long. I wish I could notify you, Darling, but I can't send any messages so I'll have to wait until I reach a phone. I'll save all the other things I have to tell you until then too. All of my love to you and to Bill. Always.

Homer commanded the *Cape Mohican* through the Mediterranean with the same careful attention to detail he'd shown throughout his career. He took every precaution against U-boats and enemy bombers. But he was not expecting an attack by his own side. On the night of August 21, 1943, the *Cape Mohican* was sailing in a convoy between Sicily and Malta. One of the escorts picked up a U-boat on sonar and sounded a general alarm. The warships maneuvered, looking for the enemy. A torpedo exploded into the *Cape Mohican*, breaking the rudder and the main propeller shaft, and flooding the engine room. A Navy gunner was seriously injured. The ship stayed afloat but sat dead in the water. Homer assumed a U-boat had torpedoed them, but an inquiry later determined that a British destroyer had fired the torpedo after mistaking the *Cape Mohican* for a U-boat. The torpedoing was the fourth for the *Cape Mohican*'s radio operator, Jay Lopez, who had been sunk on the *Barbara* with Captain Walter Hudgins.*

The *Cape Mohican* was declared repairable, and towed to Malta and then through the Strait of Gibraltar toward a shipyard in Scotland. The tugboat's tow line snapped in a gale and the fully manned but crippled *Cape Mohican* drifted for fifty-two hours in heavy seas before the tug could retrieve the ship and finish the voyage. The ship needed major repairs, and the Scottish yard was already overburdened. Overseeing the work would take months. Homer's hopes of a quick family reunion were gone. He sent a telegram to Nancy saying, "Am OK All Love."

---

* Lopez was quoted in a magazine as saying, "I've sat in a lifeboat and made a vow that if I ever put my foot on dry land again I'd stay there. But when I get home, most of my friends are at sea, and I remember the friends who didn't get back. I guess it's a sort of personal fight with me."

Homer's headstrong sixteen-year-old son, Bill, reacted to his father's torpedoing by promptly joining the Merchant Marine. "I wasn't doing so good in school, and my father and brother were in the war, and I just figured I might as well be with them," he recalled. Nancy had seen it coming. She drove Bill to Norfolk to sign for him because he was underage. Bill filled out forms at the union hall, and someone at the Bull Line arranged for him to receive an able-seaman's license. He set out on a freighter hauling supplies to U.S. troops in North Africa, while Homer made the daily rounds at the shipyard in Scotland.

In Russia, the Red Army had finally stopped the German invasion and was driving Hitler's armies west, out of Russia, along a thousand-mile front. The Russians had revived some of their bombed-out defense plants but still needed weapons and munitions from their allies. Mathews men continued to make the dangerous, unpredictable run to Murmansk. None of them saw more of Russia than Captain Herbert Callis, a distant cousin of Captain Homer Callis.

Herbert, who had survived the sinking of the freighter *Norlandia* off Puerto Rico in July 1942, had set out in a convoy for North Russia in January 1943, in command of the Liberty ship *Thomas Hartley*. The voyage to Murmansk was rough. A bomb hit close enough to the ship to crack steam pipes in the *Hartley*'s engine room. Nonstop air raids reduced one crew member to a "mental case." After they reached Murmansk, the *Hartley* and the other ships in the convoy were held in port for months awaiting a convoy back home.

Herbert got so tired of sitting around Murmansk that he hitchhiked almost a thousand miles to Moscow just to have a look around. The fact that he could not speak a word of Russian did not trouble him in the least. While strolling through the streets of Moscow in August 1943, he happened to bump into the famous Russian correspondent for *Collier's* magazine, Quentin Reynolds. Reynolds was amazed to find a Virginia sea captain wandering the streets of Stalin's capital. He gave Callis a tour of the city and then quoted him in an upbeat article about how Russians coped with the rigors of war:

> Recently, Captain Herbert Callis, skipper of an American merchant ship temporarily anchored in a Russian port, came to Moscow for a week's vacation. I showed him around town. Captain Callis, whose home is in [Mathews], Virginia, made a rather profound observation on Russia's capital. "Friendliest town I ever did see," he declared enthusiastically in his Southern drawl. "And it's the truth that anyone in this town big enough to walk is wearing a uniform."

Reynolds concluded that Moscow "is a strange town, but it's a town of friendly people. No foreigner, and very few Russians, understand this country of paradox where the unusual is typical." The city "has not allowed the scanty food, the lack of fuel and the horror of a battlefront only an hour away by air to dampen its spirit or to shake its faith in its eventual destiny."

When the *Collier's* story ran, Herbert's family in Mathews was deluged with copies of the magazine from friends, relatives, and total strangers. The magazines were still arriving in September, when the Allies finally organized a homebound convoy. Herbert brought the ship into New York Harbor eleven months and twenty-six days after having set out for Murmansk. They became known as the "forgotten convoy." He and each of the others who took part were given hand-drawn certificates by the U.S. naval attaché in Murmansk saying they "did suffer 8 months confinement in North Russia and did undergo all privations connected therewith, that he did shiver through the Arctic winter and bask in the rays of the Midnight sun and by virtue of these facts is herewith declared to be a member of the forgotten convoy." When Herbert got home, he told his family he had rarely accepted food from the perpetually hungry Russians, and had subsisted for the entire eight months mostly on Spam, the canned meat "product" with a gelatinous glaze. Herbert told the family he "never wanted to see Spam again."

The Allies invaded the Italian mainland in the first week of September 1943. Italy's government quickly surrendered. Many Italians were weary of war and realized their leaders had picked the wrong side. The German occupation was harsh and unforgiving. The Allied invasion force came ashore at Salerno, just south of the great port of Naples, and raced to seize the port. No other port in Italy could handle the flow of cargo necessary to support the invasion. A U.S. soldier in Italy required at least half a ton of supplies every month, and more than 750,000 American soldiers would fight in Italy.

The Germans understood the importance of Naples. German field marshal Albert Kesselring, assigned to defend Italy, dispatched demolition teams to render the port unusable. They wrecked 130 vessels in the harbor, blew up 73 cranes, and toppled piers and dockside buildings into the water. They wrecked virtually everything in the waterfront area except churches, and planted booby traps. They set bombs with delayed-action fuses in undamaged buildings, to explode after the Allies moved in. One such bomb detonated forty-two days after the Germans abandoned Naples.

The Allies went to work clearing the wreckage. Liberty ships unloaded their cargo into Ducks until docks were uncovered or rebuilt. After two weeks, 3,500 tons of cargo a day was flowing through Naples. After two more weeks, that number doubled.

Benny Fitchett of Mathews arrived in Naples in November 1943 on a Liberty ship to find the harbor still crowded with wrecks. German planes bombed the docks every night and sometimes strafed them during the day. Benny and his shipmates pulled on their gas masks in case the Germans dropped poison gas. The Allies thought Hitler might resort to poison gas, and shipped mustard gas to Italy so they would be able to retaliate in kind. Hitler, it turned out, used poison gas on the helpless in concentration camps but never on enemy troops. The Germans nonetheless unleashed the Allies' mustard gas against them by accident. On December 2, 1943, the gas was stored in the cargo holds of the Liberty ship *John Harvey*, docked at the port of Bari on Italy's Adriatic coast. The port was attacked by German bombers, and the *John Harvey* exploded, releasing the mustard gas over the waterfront. The gas contributed to the casualties, which exceeded 2,000 merchant mariners and military personnel. Secrecy by the U.S. and British governments prevented an accurate accounting of how many died from the gas.

As horrific as the losses at Bari were, they did not interrupt the flow of Allied cargo. America's war machine was running at full speed. New Liberty ships were entering the U.S. fleet at a rate of 140 per month. The average construction time for a ship had shrunk to 42 days. A total of 1,896 new Liberty ships would be launched in 1943, more than twice as many as in 1942. The Merchant Marine had evolved into an enormous conveyor belt of ships hauling supplies to every theater of the European war. Convoys crisscrossed the Atlantic and shuttled across the Mediterranean between North Africa and Italy. The belt kept running despite the German bombers and U-boats. During the fourth week of October alone, 363 Liberty ships unloaded their cargo in eastern Mediterranean ports. A new loop of the conveyor belt began delivering U.S. troops and supplies to Britain for the invasion of France, which was scheduled for the late spring of 1944. The final outcome of the war seemed less in doubt every day. But winning the war was no guarantee that your loved ones would come home alive. The war and the sea were too unpredictable.

On a chill night in October 1943, off the coast of Newfoundland, Paul Grubb of Mathews took part in a rescue that skirted the edges of myth. Grubb was first officer on the Bull Line freighter *Delisle*, which had been repaired and returned to service after Captain William Callis of Gwynn's Island ran her aground in May 1942 to keep her from sinking. Now the *Delisle* was in a small convoy heading south along the coast of Newfoundland when two ships near her were rattled by explosions. Grubb turned to the captain, William Clendaniel of Baltimore, Maryland, and said, "I guess we will be the next." The men assumed a wolf pack had found the convoy, but, in fact, they had stumbled into a string of mines released by a U-boat.

As the last ship in her column, the *Delisle* drew the perilous duty of picking up the survivors of any ships sunk ahead of her. Captain Clendaniel and Grubb saw the red flashes of men's life vests in the water. The captain called down to stop engines. Before a lifeboat could be lowered, the *Delisle* struck a mine. The force of the explosion blew the little freighter's bow out of the water. The foremast crashed down on the bridge, knocking the captain unconscious and pinning him in the wreckage. While the rest of the crew abandoned ship, Grubb and Third Officer Alberto Galza struggled to free Captain Clendaniel, whose leg was trapped. They could see by match-light that his trapped leg was a wooden leg. Grubb said he grabbed a fire axe and cut off the leg to free the captain, but Galza said he was able to unstrap the wooden leg. The men carried the captain to the main deck and lowered him by rope onto a raft. Galza said he then returned to the bridge, where the wreckage had shifted and released the wooden leg. He grabbed the leg and two puppies in training to become the ship's dogs, and brought them to the lifeboat. But a wave tore the leg and the puppies out of his hands and carried them overboard. Clendaniel's surviving family members believe the government's version of the rescue, that Galza alone saved the captain.

Captain Clendaniel spent several weeks in the hospital in St. John's, Newfoundland, recuperating from broken bones and pneumonia. He faced a long wait for a new wooden leg, the war having consumed the inventory. But a few days before he was to be sent home, his old leg was delivered to his hospital bed, "done up like a Christmas present, wrapped up in a fancy paper with a ribbon around it." Exactly how the leg got there was in dispute. The captain's hometown newspaper, the *Brooklyn* (New York) *Eagle*, reported that the leg had been picked up at sea by commercial fishermen, who passed it to the crew of a Canadian escort vessel. But a press release from the Maritime Commission said the leg washed up on shore near St. John's and was taken to the hospital by a beachcomber. The Maritime Commission awarded Galza the Distinguished Service Medal for saving the captain, and also noted that Galza had rescued a different shipmate with a wooden leg when the *Delisle* was damaged by a torpedo five months earlier.

After the mine sank the *Delisle* in October 1943, Paul Grubb went home to Mathews to recuperate. While he was there, an accidental explosion leveled a warehouse at the Navy Mine Depot in nearby Yorktown, killing six men. The sound of the blast carried across the lower Bay to Mathews, and Grubb threw himself on the floor of his living room. He would go back to sea, but for years afterward, any loud noise made him jump.

On the same day the *Delisle* sank, the tanker *Esso Providence* was unloading gasoline at Malta when a fire broke out in the ship's magazine. The magazine held .50-caliber antiaircraft rounds, artillery shells, and powder. The steel door blew open and flames and .50-caliber rounds flew out of the opening, setting fire to an abandoned hulk the *Esso Providence* was using as an anchor. The tanker's first officer, Leslie Winder, of the Mathews village of Hudgins, ignored the bullets and the fire and ran for the valve that would flood the magazine. The valve was in a padlocked box that was too red-hot from the fire to touch. Winder grabbed an ax from a lifeboat station and smashed the padlock. He pried open the hot box and turned the valve, burning his hands. He very likely saved the ship and many of the crew. "Windy" Winder was a big, florid man who liked to tell outlandish stories, but when a war correspondent interviewed him, he said, "Nothing interesting happened on the voyage. There was a fire and it was put out." He changed the subject. "I'm going on my vacation down home in Hudgins, Virginia. My father is going to kill a hog for me."

By October 1943, some of the gloom had begun to lift from Mathews. No Mathews mariner had been killed in almost a year. The convoy system had sharply reduced sinkings and deaths on ships that were sunk. A mariner whose ship was bombed or torpedoed in a convoy in Allied-controlled waters stood a good chance of being quickly picked up. The war stories on the front page of the paper were finally about Mathews soldiers, sailors, and airmen earning medals, and only sometimes dying in combat.

The danger of Mathews itself being bombed was declared officially over, and the volunteer plane spotters who had shivered in the Mathews fire tower were thanked for their "useful and worthwhile service" and sent back home.

Eleanor Respess was invited to the Bethlehem-Fairfield shipyard in Baltimore to christen the Liberty ship *John Russell Pope* as a tribute to her late, thrice-torpedoed husband, Mellin. She broke the bottle of champagne with one swing, and the *Pope* slid down the shipyard's ways and into the war. The sheer number of ship christenings forced the events to be shortened from lavish formal affairs to a few perfunctory speeches and the crash of a bottle on the hull. But the tradition ran too deep in the superstitious ranks of shipbuilders and mariners to be abandoned altogether in the name of efficiency. It was said that a ship denied her drink at christening would drink her crew's blood instead.

The Germans and the winter mud halted the Allies midway up the Italian boot, creating a bloody stalemate that dragged on for months, consuming thousands of lives and tons of supplies. Merchant mariners with free time in Naples caught rides inland and saw sides of the conflict others missed. Seventeen-year-old Jack White, who had never left Mathews before the war, rode a Liberty ship full of ammunition to Sicily and explored the ancient ruins of Syracuse and Augusta. In Naples, White borrowed a jeep and drove to the front lines. He was shocked to see how many Italians had been reduced to begging.

Another Mathews mariner, Jack Ward, hitched rides to the Italian front and spent time with American soldiers. They thanked him for bringing them food and ammunition, and always asked how people in America felt about the war. Jack said the public was fully behind it. He was impressed by how resolute the soldiers seemed, even after months of fighting. On one of Jack's forays inland, two officers in a jeep picked him up just ahead of a German counterattack. He spent the night with an artillery team and slept in a haystack. On his way back to Naples, he passed a house where an Italian family insisted on feeding him dinner. They had little to eat, and apologized for the poor quality of their wine. On the docks, Jack saw two beggars who collected rubbish together beat each other bloody over an empty coffee tin. One hot night when the ship was in port, Jack dragged his mattress up on deck in search of a breeze, and awakened to an air raid. Hot shrapnel from flak exploding above him as Allied guns fired at German planes whistled down in the dark and rattled onto the deck around him. He pulled the mattress over him and went back to sleep.

The Allies tried to break the stalemate in Italy in January 1944, by landing an invasion force on the beach at Anzio, the birthplace of the Roman emperor Nero. Anzio was behind the German lines and only thirty-five miles south of Rome. The strategy was to land troops behind the German lines and spread the lines so thin that they broke. The Allies poured 36,000 troops and 3,200 vehicles into Anzio the first day. But the Germans reacted quickly and pinned the invaders in a crescent-shaped expanse of beach. The Germans could not throw them into the ocean despite repeated attempts, but the Allied troops could not break out of the beachhead. Weeks passed. Churchill later wrote about Anzio, "I had hoped that we were hurling a wildcat onto the shore, but all we got was a stranded whale."

The survival of the Allied troops on the beach at Anzio depended on a stream of Liberty ships. They anchored a few miles offshore and sent the cargo to the beach in Ducks. For the crews of the merchant ships, being anchored off Anzio was a white-knuckle experience. Several times every day, the Germans fired at them with huge railroad guns hidden in tunnels in the hills above the beach. The guns, which the Americans nicknamed "Anzio Annie" and "the Anzio Express," flung six-hundred-pound shells at the Liberty ships. No ship had been hit, but every shot sent a spectacular geyser of water two hundred feet into the air. Nervous merchant captains demanded the freedom to move their ships if the shots got any closer. A high-ranking Navy admiral replied, "The chances of being hit by a shell from a shore battery are negligible . . . If shells are falling near you, there is no objection to your moving a few hundred yards, but remember that you are just as likely to move into as you are out of the path of the next shell."

Every night German planes attacked the anchorage off Anzio. They began each attack by dropping parachute flares. John Frederick Livesay of Mathews admitted he would "tremble with fear" when the flares illuminated his Liberty ship. The drone of bombers always followed. Livesay was relieved when his ship finished unloading at Anzio and sailed back to the relative safety of Naples.

The Allied invasion of Italy had forced the Germans to concentrate their aircraft in the Mediterranean, leaving few to attack convoys to Murmansk. But a ship on the Murmansk Run could still count on being attacked by the U-boats based in the Norwegian fjords, as Bernard Stansbury, returning to sea with the Navy Armed Guard, would see.

After escaping the fireball of the *Robert Rowan* off Sicily, Bernard was given command of a Navy Armed Guard unit on the Liberty ship *Penelope Barker*. In New York Harbor, the entire crew was issued heavy winter coats, boots, and mittens. His shipmates whispered they were going to Murmansk. Bernard had never heard of it. The *Penelope Barker* carried tanks, locomotives, steel, food, and containers of acid. The ship crossed the Atlantic to Scotland, joined a convoy, and headed north into the worst storm Bernard had ever seen. The *Barker* would climb to the top of a huge wave, then tilt down the back side of the wave, her propeller spinning crazily in the air, shaking the ship as if to pull it apart. Other ships in the convoy turned back to Scotland, but the *Barker*'s captain was afraid to turn. He thought the *Barker* might turn too slowly and be broadsided by the next huge wave. He rode out the storm, keeping the bow turned into the seas and wincing every time the propeller vibrated. The storm abated on the third day, and the convoy reassembled and set out for the Arctic. The convoy entered the Barents Sea on January 24, 1944. The ocean was relatively calm but the air temperature was below freezing, and the ship passed through snow squalls. Bernard finished his watch in the starboard gun tub and stopped to warm himself against the smokestack, which funneled hot exhaust from the ship's engines into the air. He leaned on the stack for about a minute, trying to decide whether to go for some coffee in the galley.

The ship was rocked by two torpedoes exploding only seconds apart. Bernard hit his head and lost consciousness. He awoke on his back with the heavy steel rim of the smokestack lying across his legs. He struggled out from under it and looked around. The gun tub he had just left was gone, blown to pieces. The ship was sinking. Bernard decided to check the crew's quarters to make sure everyone was out. He was going through the door when a merchant mariner shouted to him that everyone was out and the lifeboats were leaving. Bernard hurried to one of the boats. Two other men ignored the mariner and went into the crew's quarters, never to come out. The ship sank suddenly. Some men had no time to find life vests and jumped into the subfreezing water with only the clothes they wore.

The U-boat did not show itself. Sailors in an escort ship called to the men in the lifeboats to switch off the blinking red lights on their life vests. They said a rescue ship would return to the lifeboats after dark to pick them up. The rescue ship indeed arrived, and fifty-four of the sixty-nine men on the *Barker* survived. Bernard was one. It was his second sinking in six months, but this one affected him. Men had been killed. He had narrowly missed dying three times in only five minutes: being relieved from the gun tub just before the torpedo destroyed it, being struck with the smokestack rim, and then almost joining the two doomed men for a last search of the crew's quarters. Seventy years later, the memory would bring tears to his eyes.

The Allied troops at Anzio clung to the beachhead all winter, fighting off German attempts to push them into the sea. The Liberty ships not only kept them supplied, but continually delivered artillery shells to be stockpiled for an all-out attack to break out of Anzio. One of the Liberty ships helping to build the stockpile was the *Paul Hamilton*, which set out for Anzio from North Africa in April 1944, carrying 7,000 tons of ammunition and 504 American soldiers. Most of the soldiers were to be handed the task of clearing land mines the Germans had planted around the beachhead. The *Paul Hamilton*'s convoy was sailing along the coast of Algeria on April

20 when the convoy commander warned that an attack by German torpedo bombers was likely that evening.

The *Paul Hamilton*'s third assistant engineer was Charles Ogletree Billups Jr. of Mathews. Billups was thirty-two years old and came from an old Mathews family living on land granted to them by the King of England. Charles Billups had sailed on merchant ships in his twenties, but had gone ashore to work in a shipyard. When America entered the war, he obtained his engineer's license and went back to sea. The *Paul Hamilton* was his first ship in wartime.

Just after sunset, three German torpedo bombers flew toward the convoy at wave-top height. The Naval Armed Guard gunners threw up a wall of antiaircraft fire, but a light bomber slipped through a hole in the wall and released a torpedo at the *Paul Hamilton* at point-blank range. The ship exploded in a cloud of fire and black smoke that boiled 1,000 feet into the air, looming over an empty spot on the ocean where the ship had been. Nothing was left of the *Paul Hamilton* or the 580 passengers and crew. "The ship was observed to explode with such violence," a Navy report said, "it is now concluded there were no survivors." Charles's family received a telegram declaring him "missing and presumed lost in the performance of his duty and in the service of his country," but no other details.

On May 25, 1944, the Allied troops at Anzio pulverized the German lines with their stockpiled artillery shells, and broke out of the beachhead. They ran through the retreating Germans toward Rome. British and American troops broke the German lines farther inland. American and British armies literally raced to be first to liberate Rome. The world's attention, however, was about to shift to the Normandy coast.

On the eve of the D-Day invasion of France, tens of thousands of Allied soldiers, sailors, and merchant mariners sat on ships at anchor in the British Isles, waiting for the order to cross the English Channel. The invasion fleet comprised more than 5,300 vessels, including 1,213 warships and 4,100 cargo ships, troopships, and landing craft. The Allies originally had planned to invade southern France at the same time as Normandy, but had to postpone that part of the invasion because all the available vessels were needed at Normandy. The D-Day armada was the second-largest amphibious invasion in history—the one that had landed at Sicily was actually larger—but it was the invasion that all the others had been building toward, and the one that could fail. Among those waiting for the order to cross the Channel to France was Homer Callis's younger son, Bill.

Bill Callis had just returned to Gwynn's Island in May from his first deep-ocean voyage as an able seaman when Virgil Respess at the Bull Line office called. A job was waiting for Bill on a freighter that was preparing to sail from Norfolk. "I can't tell you where she's going," Virgil said, "but you might get a chance to see your father." Homer was in Scotland, still overseeing repairs on the *Cape Mohican*. Bill could guess that the ship was heading to a Scottish port, and he also guessed it would take part in the long-anticipated invasion of France. Bill packed a bag and his mother, Nancy, drove him to Norfolk.

The ship took on a full load of C rations in Norfolk and then sailed to Nova Scotia in a small convoy, which was then folded into a much larger convoy. Warships appeared at the far edges, barely visible. Bill had never seen so many ships. They telescoped out beyond the horizon in every direction. Bill's ship was near the center, as best he could tell. He heard reports of U-boat alarms on the convoy's perimeter, but never saw or heard anything. He was impressed by the choreography of the convoy. "It was amazing to me to see that many ships all sailing in formation," he said. "They would communicate changes of course by signal flags. The flags would go up, and all the ships would make the change at the same time. It was like a dance. Planes were flying overhead of us. We had more escort ships than I had ever seen before, even a teeny little escort carrier." For the rest of Bill's life, he would shake his head at the memory of the sheer size of the convoy. It was a pure expression of America's power, no longer restrained by the U-boats.

Two days before the Normandy invasion, on June 4, 1944, an American hunter-killer group off South Africa captured the U-505, which had torpedoed Captain Mellin Respess on the *Thomas McKean*. The Americans forced the U-boat to the surface with depth charges and sent a boarding party to secure the sub before the Germans could scuttle it. The commander of the hunter-killer group, Admiral Daniel Gallery, thought he had achieved a great feat by seizing the sub. But Admiral King was furious that Gallery had not just sunk it. King worried that if the Germans learned the U-505 had been captured, along with its Enigma machine, they might change the Enigma system again and cut off the Allies' access to their secret messages on the eve of the Normandy invasion. That did not happen. The Germans suspected from time to time that Enigma had been compromised, but always managed to reassure themselves that it was secure.

On D-Day, June 6, the narrow Channel was jammed with the Allied invasion fleet. Thousands of landing craft churned back and forth between troopships and the beaches. Allied warships pressed close enough to shore to shell the German coastal fortifications. Tugboats towed 75 old merchant ships into the shallow waters off the invasion beaches, and volunteer mariners scuttled the vessels to create breakwaters to absorb the Channel waves: The volunteers rigged the old merchant ships to sink, and then jumped onto tugs for a ride back to England. More than 5,800 Allied planes flew over the invasion fleet in the Channel.

"Every ship in the world seemed to be there," the captain of the Liberty ship *Cyrus McCormick* recalled. "There wouldn't be enough room to squeeze in another ship. You have to be constantly alert to avoid hitting somebody, or being hit . . . Constantly overhead are hundreds of our own bombers and fighters . . . Air power is overwhelming."

The overcrowded Channel was no place for U-boats, whose survival depended on their ability to hide. But Doenitz sent them anyway. He had expected for months that an Allied invasion force would one day fill the Channel, and had decided that when that day came, the stakes would be so high that "the U-boats must be there," no matter the cost. When the attack came, he quickly assembled thirty U-boats that were equipped with snorkels, which allowed them to draw fresh air while submerged, and sent them into a meat grinder. His orders made the mission sound like a suicide attack, which was not far from the truth: "Every vessel taking part in the landing . . . must be attacked regardless of risk. Every boat that inflicts losses on the enemy while he is landing has fulfilled its primary function even though it perishes in so doing." During the assault, the Allies sank twenty of the thirty U-boats in the invasion zone, killing 750 German submariners. The U-boats sank twelve Allied merchant ships, five escorts, and four landing craft—boats filled with men, but far too few of them to have any impact on the D-Day invasion. Morison, the naval historian, concluded, "The Allies were able to pull off the greatest invasion in modern history . . . and to sustain it by sea, with insignificant interference by U-boats. No more striking evidence of the collapse of Hitler's policy and Doenitz's strategy could be adduced."

Several days into the invasion, Randolph Payne of Mathews, a young messman on a Liberty ship, got a chance to go ashore at Omaha Beach. Young and perhaps naïve, he was excited, but he had not expected to see the bodies of scores of American soldiers, wrapped in white, awaiting burial, and he wished afterward that he had stayed on the ship. He told his family, "No one should ever have to see that."

Bill Callis's ship ended up being held in reserve off the coast of Scotland, in a lovely harbor beneath green hills dotted with sheep. The pastoral scenery was wasted on Bill, who wanted to be at D-Day. He learned about the invasion by reading a notice posted on the ship by the captain, who had received the news during a trip ashore. Three weeks later, Bill's ship finally unloaded its C rations at the great French port of Cherbourg. The Allies had just captured Cherbourg, which the Germans had left in the same ruined, booby-trapped condition as they had left Naples the year before. Bill's ship had to weave among sunken hulks to reach the dock. The ship was directed to a spot where Allied demolition teams had blasted away just enough wreckage for a ship to squeeze in. Bill walked out on the dock and picked up a German gas mask for a souvenir, but got right back on the ship. He was worried about mines in the rubble.

The Ducks unloaded Bill's ship at such breakneck speed that they kept sinking from overloading or careless handling. The men who drove them did not seem to care. They all wore life vests, and whenever a Duck sank, its crew climbed aboard the next Duck and got back in the rotation. Their lack of concern about the tons of cargo piling up on the floor of the harbor gave Bill a sense of how vast the D-Day supply operation was. By the end of June, the Allies had landed 200,000 troops on Omaha Beach alone, along with 68,799 tons of supplies and 27,340 vehicles.

Rome had been liberated in D-Day's shadow. In early July, the streets of the Eternal City were full of soldiers on leave, and full of rubble from bombed buildings. Jack Ward and a friend caught a ride from a port into Rome and wandered through the city to the Vatican, which had been spared from the bombs. The Liberty ships brought food not just for Allied troops but for starving Italians whose homes had been plucked clean by the retreating Nazis.

German armies were in retreat all across Europe, beaten down by a never-ending flow of American troops and supplies. The Germans would keep fighting for another year, but the U-boats were growing less and less relevant. The D-Day invasion troops forced the U-boats out of their bomb-proof bunkers in France and back to Norway, and they were being sunk everywhere. By the final months of 1944, three out of every ten U-boats that went out on patrol never came back.

Off the coast of France, a plane depth-charged the U-107, which had killed Ernest Thompson on the *Major Wheeler.* Off Africa, near the Azores, a bomber from an American escort carrier sank the U-575, which had torpedoed Captain Herbert Callis on the *Norlandia.* In the South Atlantic, a hunter-killer group sank the U-515, which had torpedoed the *Mae* and ruined Lester Smith's legs.

Lester, for his part, was back at home on Gwynn's Island. He had been re-leased from the hospital in British Guiana in June, and flown home. His fiancée, Lottie, had prepared herself to see his mutilated legs for the first time, but they were worse than she had expected. His left leg was artificial below the knee, and his right leg was heavily wrapped and still painful. A surgeon in British Guiana had grafted silver plating into the leg, but infection kept developing around the plating. Lester nonetheless was in excellent spirits. He was excited to be back in Mathews. He wanted to get married immediately. Lester had learned to drive with his artificial leg, and he and Lottie took rides in his red convertible just like before. He was already talking about going back to sea. Lottie couldn't believe he was serious.

Captain Walter Hudgins. Denied an officer's commission in the Navy for being too old, he commanded merchant ships and survived two sinkings.

This wartime poster, produced by the War Shipping Administration, dramatized the fact that thousands of merchant mariners chose to keep sailing despite the dangers.

"YOU BET I'M GOING BACK TO SEA!"

Register at your nearest U.S. Employment Service Office

U.S. MERCHANT MARINE

War Shipping Administration

MAN THE VICTORY FLEET

Dead crewmen of the U-85—the first U-boat sunk in American waters—piled unceremoniously on the deck of the American destroyer USS *Roper*.

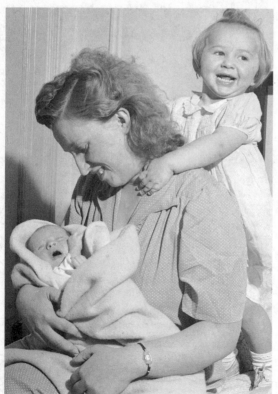

The "lifeboat baby," Jesse Roper Mohorovicic, with his mother, Desanka, and four-year-old sister, Vesna, after his birth in a lifeboat off Cape Hatteras, North Carolina.

UNITED STATES COAST GUARD
42 BROADWAY
NEW YORK 4, N. Y.

ADDRESS REPLY TO
~~XXXXXXXXXXXXXXXXXXXXX~~
REFER TO FILE

5 April 1944

M/V CITY OF NEW YORK - of UNITED STATES REGISTRY

The following is a copy of the entry made in the Official Log Book
of the M/V CITY OF NEW YORK, under date of 30 March 1942:

"March 30, 1942:
2:30 AM - At Sea
In Life Boat:

"This is to certify on this date and hour
set forth a male child was born to Mrs Desarka
Mohorovicic, a passenger aboard the vessel.
The Birth occurred in lifeboat after the
vessel was destroyed by enemy action. At
approximately 4 AM March 31,1942, the U. S.
Navy Destroyer "JESSE ROPER" picked up all
survivors in said lifeboat. The mother and
child were placed in care of Lieut. Johnson,
Surgeon aboard the "JESSE ROPER. All sur-
vivors of this lifeboat were landed at Norfolk,
Virginia. Upon arrival at Hospital, Norfolk,
Va. the mother of the child named him Jesse
Roper Mohorovicic."

(SGD) Leonard H. Conly, MD   (Sgd) G. T. Sullivan
Ship's Surgeon   Master

Witnesses:

(SGD) Charles O. Van Gorden - 2d Officer

"   Miguel P. Davila - Oiler

(Signed) John J. Daly
U. S. Shipping Commissioner."

The above is a true and correct copy of entry
as shown in the Official Log Book of the M/V
CITY OF NEW YORK.

Raymond A. Shea
Acting Shipping Commissioner.

The birth certificate of the lifeboat baby, copied from an entry in the *City of New York*'s log book after the ship was torpedoed.

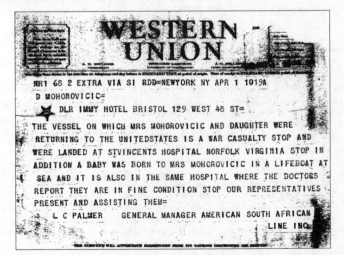

WESTERN UNION

NR1 68 2 EXTRA VIA SI RDD=NEWYORK NY APR 1 1019A

D MOHOROVICIC=

DLR IMMY HOTEL BRISTOL 129 WEST 48 ST=

THE VESSEL ON WHICH MRS MOHOROVICIC AND DAUGHTER WERE
RETURNING TO THE UNITEDSTATES IS A WAR CASUALTY STOP AND
WERE LANDED AT STVINCENTS HOSPITAL NORFOLK VIRGINIA STOP IN
ADDITION A BABY WAS BORN TO MRS MOHOROVICIC IN A LIFEBOAT AT
SEA AND IT IS ALSO IN THE SAME HOSPITAL WHERE THE DOCTORS
REPORT THEY ARE IN FINE CONDITION STOP OUR REPRESENTATIVES
PRESENT AND ASSISTING THEM=
L C PALMER   GENERAL MANAGER AMERICAN SOUTH AFRICAN
LINE INC

A copy of the telegram that informed a shocked Joseph Mohorovicic that his wife had given birth to his son in a lifeboat at sea.

The destroyer USS *Greer* contends with ice while on convoy escort duty in the North Atlantic.

This U.S. Navy report describes the rigors of the Murmansk Run, the notorious 5,000-mile voyage from the U.S. East Coast to North Russia.

A ship taking part in the disastrous Allied convoy PQ-17 to Murmansk is struck by an aerial torpedo from a German torpedo bomber.

CREDIT: NATIONAL ARCHIVES

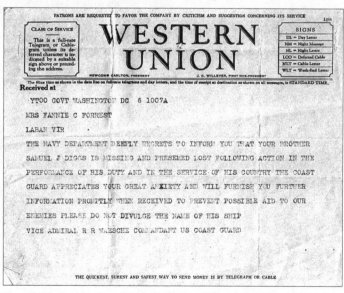

The official telegram from the Navy to the parents of Captain Sam Diggs expressing regret at his death on a convoy run to Murmansk.

CREDIT: COURTESY OF GARY W. BROWNLEE

Captain Sam Jones Diggs, who was killed when his ship struck a "friendly" mine in dense fog on a return trip from Murmansk.

The freewheeling Captain Guy Hudgins, with his daughter Diana. He sailed in the invasion of North Africa and on the Murmansk Run.

Captain Mellin Respess's ship *Thomas McKean* under attack by the U-505 in the Atlantic. The U-505, later captured, is displayed today in a Chicago museum.

Captain Herbert Callis. He survived a torpedoing, rescued castaways at sea, and endured eight months in Murmansk with the Forgotten Convoy.

Captain Lewis Callis, who was killed when his ship was torpedoed off Cuba. He left behind a poetic tribute to Gwynn's Island, his lifelong home.

The *Zebulon B. Vance*—Guy Hudgins's future ship—is prepared for launch in Baltimore. American shipyards built more than 2,700 Liberty ships during the war.

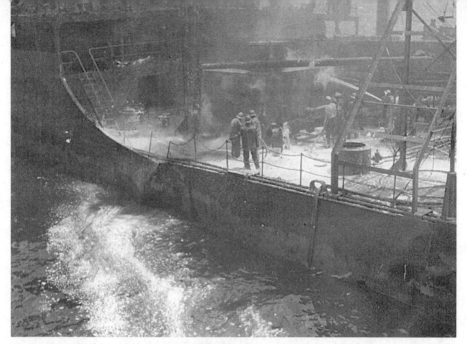

Firefighters work to save the tanker *Robert C. Tuttle* after it struck a mine laid by a U-boat at the mouth of the Chesapeake Bay (above and below).

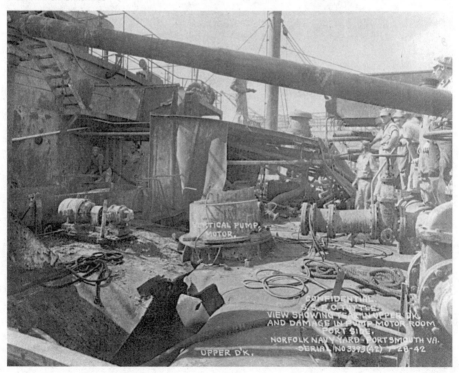

Stacy Hammond, one of three seafaring sons of a Mathews blacksmith. All three were torpedoed, on separate ships, over a four-month span in 1942.

CREDIT: COURTESY OF STACY L. HAMMOND

William Hammond, the youngest Hammond brother. He survived one sinking, with help from a generous U-boat captain, only to die aboard the *Onondaga*.

CREDIT: COURTESY OF STACY L. HAMMOND

Genious Hudgins Jr. at home in Mathews with his wife, Salome, and daughter, Vicki, a few months prior to his death aboard the *Onondaga*.

CREDIT: COURTESY OF VICKI HUDGINS PRITCHETT

Genious Hudgins Jr. with his daughter, Vicki, and a neighbor, Jerome Hudgins.

CREDIT: COURTESY OF VICKI HUDGINS PRITCHETT

The unstoppable Lester Smith, who returned to sea after nearly being given up for dead when both of his legs were mangled in a torpedo explosion.

CREDIT: COURTESY OF LOTTIE MITCHEM

Russell Dennis, the only Mathews man to survive the sinking of the *Onondaga*. He later testified in two court cases about the sinking.

CREDIT: COURTESY OF THE DENNIS FAMILY

Homer's elder son, Homer Verdayne Callis Jr., who served in the Pacific on a U.S. Navy destroyer and was killed in a kamikaze attack.

CREDIT: COURTESY OF LISA CALLIS AND MAVA MILES

Captain Homer Callis, the "gentleman captain," aboard the Bull Line freighter *Mae*. He was one of three Callis brothers commanding merchant ships during the war.

CREDIT: COURTESY OF LISA CALLIS AND MAVA MILES

Homer's younger son, Willie "Bill" Callis (right), at a waterfront bar. He joined the Merchant Marine to follow his father and brother into the war.

CREDIT: COURTESY OF LISA CALLIS AND MAVA MILES

Crewmen from the U.S. Coast Guard cutter USS *Spencer*, hunting a submerged U-boat while on convoy escort duty, watch as the ship's depth charges explode astern.

Captain Robert Melville "Mel" Callis, Homer's brother, who was killed along with four other Mathews men when the freighter *Ruth* was torpedoed off Cuba.

The freighter *Commercial Trader*. She was torpedoed off Trinidad only four months after Will Hunley was promoted to serve as her captain.

Captain James Wilber "Will" Hunley. A cousin of the Hodges brothers, he sold his bicycle to get enough money to follow David Hodges to sea.

Charles Ogletree Billups Jr. left a safe shoreside job to go to sea in the midst of the war and died aboard the *Paul Hamilton*.

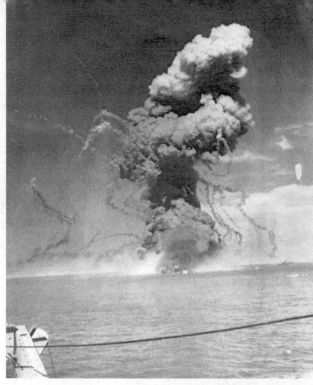

The Liberty ship *Robert Rowan* erupts in a spectacular explosion off Sicily after being bombed by a German plane. Bernard Stansbury escaped the blast.

CREDIT: NATIONAL ARCHIVES

A Navy memo describes the atomizing of the Liberty ship *Paul Hamilton* by a German bomb. The ship carried explosives and hundreds of U.S. soldiers.

CREDIT: NATIONAL ARCHIVES

An unidentified U-boat under attack by an Allied plane. After Allied pilots acquired radar and proper training, planes became the U-boats' nemeses.

CREDIT: NATIONAL ARCHIVES

An Allied convoy moves across the Atlantic escorted by warships and a blimp. As the war progressed, U-boats became increasingly helpless to stop convoys.

CREDIT: FROM THE COLLECTIONS OF THE MARINERS' MUSEUM AND PARK, NEWPORT NEWS, VA

Captain Jesse and Henny Hodges in retirement.

CREDIT: COURTESY OF THE HODGES FAMILY, VIA JESSE CARROLL THORNTON

CHAPTER TWELVE

War's End

C oleman Hodges, who had refused his sisters' pleas to quit sailing in war zones, had finally achieved his goal and was promoted to captain of the Liberty ship *Edward A. Savoy* in late 1943, at the age of thirty. He took the *Savoy* on a couple of short runs along the East Coast, and then was ordered to sail her to New York to take on cargo for a deep-ocean voyage. He was surprised to find that his new second officer was his nephew J. W. Corbett.

J.W., the son of Coleman's sister Elizabeth, was a quiet, slightly built young man. He had grown up on Gales Neck with Henny, and gone to work as a teenager on Captain Jesse's tugs. J.W. regarded his grandfather Jesse and his uncle Raymond as consummate mariners. He used one of Jesse's old sextants to take the ship's position by the stars, which was his favorite activity. J.W. had grown up watching his uncle Coleman running around Gales Neck with his brother David, playing pranks, raising hell. J.W. considered Coleman "a good, jolly fellow." But Coleman was all business on the bridge of the *Savoy*, and he would need to be. The crew was issued heavy winter clothing, which told the story: They were going to Murmansk.

Murmansk convoys had been suspended for most of the summer because of the pressing need for ships for the Normandy invasion and its immediate aftermath. The Russians were driving the Germans back, but the Red Army needed arms and food as badly as ever. The *Savoy*'s holds were filled with guns, ammunition, and food. Two narrow-gauge locomotives were lashed with steel cables to the ship's main deck.

The Murmansk run had grown less lethal for mariners since the first years of the war. The rate of sinkings of merchant ships fell from 12 percent in 1943 to 1 percent in 1944. But those were statistics. Murmansk was still the last place most men wanted to go. The Arctic weather and the U-boats, which were plentiful in the Norwegian fjords, still made for an anxious voyage.

On the eve of the convoy's departure from New York, Coleman and the other merchant captains were summoned to port headquarters on Battery Place in Manhattan to meet the port captain and the convoy's commodore. The merchant captains all affirmed their ships could maintain the convoy's planned speed of 10 knots for the entire Atlantic crossing. A large blackboard showed each ship in its assigned column and row. The *Savoy* was near the front, in the middle. The port captain handed out folders with sealed orders, codes, and other documents and the captains returned to their ships.

The next morning, September 7, 1944, the *Savoy* and seventy-one other merchant ships streamed out of the harbor at intervals of one ship per minute. They formed a line 19 miles long that took three hours and twenty minutes to clear the last channel buoy. Offshore, the convoy was joined by Canadian and British escort ships, as well as several merchant ships that had been delayed by a storm. The convoy formed into a rectangle nearly 7 miles wide and 1.5 miles deep, covering more than 10 square miles of ocean.* The convoy encountered no U-boats on its eight-day crossing until, almost within sight of the Irish coast, a British tanker was torpe-

---

* The convoy was not close to being the largest HX convoy; an earlier convoy had included 168 ships and 7 escorts and presented a front 9 miles wide.

doed, as was a rescue ship searching for survivors of the tanker. One hundred and twenty-five British seamen died.

The convoy split at the British Isles, as planned, with the *Savoy* and eleven other ships joining a larger group of ships at Loch Ewe, Scotland. Together, they formed a new convoy of thirty-one merchant ships, bound for Murmansk. They were surrounded by an unusually large escort force, including twelve destroyers, two escort carriers, a cruiser, and even the British battleship HMS *Rodney*. The *Rodney* was insurance against another PQ-17 debacle. If the *Tirpitz* or another German warship emerged from the fjords to attack the convoy, the *Rodney* had enough firepower to fight her. The escorts would not be told to withdraw. The merchant ships would not be told to scatter.

From Scotland, Coleman's convoy set out through heavy weather into the Arctic Circle. No German planes appeared, but nineteen U-boats in the *Panther* group waited for the convoy in the Barents Sea just east of Bear Island. The escort ships surprised the U-boats by racing out ahead of the convoy, forcing the U-boats to submerge. The escorts held the U-boats down with depth-charge attacks while the merchant ships steamed past the ambush. Five U-boats managed to fire torpedoes at the escorts, with no success. The convoy reached Murmansk intact.

As soon as they'd landed and J.W. was free to come ashore, he hiked up a hillside in the wrecked city to the only place that sold alcohol. All they had was cheap vodka. "It was rough stuff, barely drinkable, but they weren't stingy with it," said J.W., who choked down two glasses and then quit. Unloading the ships went quickly. As the date neared for the convoy to set out for home, the Nazi propagandist Axis Sally addressed the mariners over the radio. "We missed you on the way in," she purred, "but we'll be waiting for you to return." The *Panther* U-boats waited just outside the narrow Kola Inlet, the passage to Murmansk. The escorts tried the same tactic, racing out of the inlet ahead of the convoy and forcing the U-boats to dive. This time, one U-boat torpedoed the British frigate *Mounsey*, forcing her to quit the convoy and struggle back into Murmansk. But once again, the merchant ships escaped the U-boats' ambush. They plowed west through the Barents Sea in the direction of home. One gale after another swept down on them from the Arctic. No German plane could fly. J.W. had never been so glad to see bad weather. The skies did not clear until the convoy was approaching Scotland. From there, the *Savoy* returned to the United States. Coleman brought the ship into New York Harbor on December 17. He felt satisfied finally that he had done his duty to the country and his brothers.

Coleman did not make it from New York to Gales Neck in time for a festive dining on Christmas Day, 1944, to celebrate Captain Jesse and Henny's fiftieth wedding anniversary. The guests included 125 family, neighbors, and friends. Henny and her daughters cooked for days, preparing four turkeys, two hams, and platter after platter of fish and crackling biscuits. Henny enjoyed getting dressed up for parties, and the *Gazette-Journal* reported that she was in "a two-piece afternoon dress of grey crepe, with which she wore black accessories and a corsage of orchids." She and Captain Jesse cut a three-tiered wedding cake and exchanged rings a second time. Five of their nine surviving children were present—David, Alice, Elizabeth, Louise, and Hilda Fourteen—along with most of their twenty-four grandchildren.

After the guests had finished their shifts at the kitchen table, Henny gave the order to clear the living room for a square dance. The ice truck driver and his cousins played fiddle tunes. The dancers formed a circle and people took turns in the middle showing off. Hilda Fourteen "trucked"—a dance that included strutting while waggling the index finger. Sheriff W. E. Aldrich, a friend of the Hodges family, danced an old-fashioned jig.

No one at any point raised a glass to the Allied cause, or even brought up the war. No one mentioned Leslie or Dewey, whose framed photographs had been placed on the mantel above the fireplace. No one had told their seven-year-old niece, Stormy Heart, that they had been killed by U-boats. She assumed they were alive on ships at sea.

Raymond also was absent, though he really was on a ship at sea. Afterward, he wrote his sister Louise that he had just docked the *Mormac-moon* in New York on Christmas Eve after his latest trip to Europe, and was forced to remain on the ship to await orders. He wrote:

> Have just returned from a trip to France where things are not so very nice. We are in the habit of taking many of our boys over, so I see lots of our fighting men. Leaving in a few days for England or perhaps the north part of France and hope we have good luck again.

Captain Homer Callis spent the holidays at home on Gwynn's Island after eighteen months overseas. He had sailed the *Cape Mohican* halfway around the world only to be torpedoed by mistake and then stuck in a shipyard in Scotland. The *Cape Mohican* was finally back in service, and being loaded for her next voyage. Homer's wife, Nancy, picked him up at the docks in New York and they drove home to Dunrovin'. Nancy took Homer to see a new stained-glass window in the Gwynn's Island Baptist Church dedicated to his brother Mel. Mel's wife, Luna, had chosen an image of Christ praying for strength in the garden of Gethsemane as storm clouds swirl overhead. Nancy had contributed money on behalf of their side of the Callis family.

The couple talked about their sons. Bill seemed to be thriving in the Merchant Marine, but Homer and Nancy were not sure about Homer Jr., who was still on the destroyer USS *Hazelwood* in the Pacific. One of Homer's old crew members on the *Mae*, Jack Rowe of Gwynn's Island, had seen Homer Jr. at a supply pier in the Marshall Islands. Homer Jr. looked thin. He told Jack the Navy chow did not agree with him. Jack took him aboard his supply vessel and got him a huge meal. Homer Jr. protested but cleaned his plate. As he was leaving, he told Jack he was worried. The *Hazelwood* had experienced several close calls and he confided, "I feel like we are going to run out of chances." Jack was caught off guard by the comment and said they would all just have to hope for the best. He suggested Homer Jr. put in for a transfer to a different ship. But Homer Jr. smiled and said,

"No, I don't think I'll mess with it." Jack could not get over how much he looked like his father, whom Jack called Big Homer. When Jack got back to Mathews from the Pacific on leave, he told Nancy her son seemed fine. He did not see what good the truth would do her.

After his Murmansk run, in January 1945, Coleman Hodges set out in the *Edward A. Savoy* for Antwerp, Belgium. His nephew J. W. Corbett stayed on as second mate. Antwerp was the newest link in the conveyor belt carrying Allied supplies to Europe. The Belgian port on the North Sea was one of the largest in Europe, crowding the mouth of the Scheldt River with more than six hundred cranes, dock space for hundreds of ships, and rail connections to any part of Western Europe. Antwerp's cargo facilities and location made it the ideal supply port for the drive into Nazi-occupied Belgium and Holland, and then into Germany itself. The Allies had captured Antwerp largely undamaged, thanks to Belgian resistance fighters who harassed the German demolition teams trying to wreck the port. Hitler understood the importance of Antwerp. He had made Antwerp the final objective of the German counteroffensive in December 1944 that became famous as the Battle of the Bulge. After the Germans were stopped short of Antwerp, Hitler rained a special kind of destruction on the city, and it was still coming as the *Savoy* came into port

J.W. was standing watch on the *Savoy*'s gangway in Antwerp when he heard a growling noise behind him. Over his head flew a black object resembling a torpedo with wings. It was a German V-1 flying bomb, more commonly called a buzz bomb. Hitler, who called them "cherry stones," ordered dozens of them launched at Antwerp every day. The V-1 was not accurate enough to aim at specific targets, but its randomness magnified its power to frighten. The "V" in V-1 stood for *Vergeltungswaffen*, or "weapons of revenge." A buzz bomb flew until it ran out of fuel, and then dropped onto whatever was under it. The V-1 that flew over the *Savoy* stopped growling and fell onto a building a block away. The blast's concussion knocked J.W. off his feet. He got up, checked himself for injuries, and resumed standing watch. Black smoke rose from the building the buzz bomb had hit. A few days later, J.W. was in a hotel in another part of Antwerp when he saw a buzz bomb fly past the window.

The Germans also fired V-2 rockets, which carried more powerful payloads. V-2s were too fast to shoot down and made no sound as they were about to hit. A V-2 struck a movie theater in Antwerp and killed 567 people, including many merchant mariners and American military personnel, who were watching Gary Cooper star in the western film *The Plainsman*. The Germans continued pouring V-1s and V-2s into Antwerp even after they had been pushed back onto their home soil. The only city hit by more V-1 and V-2 rockets than Antwerp was London.

Captain Raymond Hodges finally came home to Mathews in the first week of March 1945. He had not been to Gales Neck for three years. Although the war was still going on, and he would soon return to it, Raymond's visit felt like a harbinger, a sign the war was nearing its end. There were other signs. The *Gazette-Journal* devoted most of the front page to the danger of forest fires rather than the war. A story described Representative Bland's effort in Congress to develop a postwar plan to sell off some of the nation's surplus war vessels without hurting the shipping industry. The front page even had a sports story about the Mathews High School baseball team sweeping a doubleheader.

Raymond invited the entire family to dinner at his farm in Gloucester. Captain Jesse, Henny, and about a dozen children and grandchildren put on their best clothes. Dolly had decorated the house in a style the Hodges had seen only in movies; to young Stormy Heart, visiting her aunt and uncle was "like going to the White House." The dining room had a big picture window overlooking green, rolling hills, where Raymond's cattle roamed. Raymond had taken an interest in raising beef cattle, though his sons did all the work.

Raymond greeted his guests in a coat and tie, of course. He was as confident and self-assured as ever. But the family could not help but stare at his hair, which had turned from brown to snowy white. Raymond told his sisters his hair had changed color overnight after a scare on one of his convoy runs. A ship ahead of him had been torpedoed, and he nearly ran over a lifeboat full of women and children. Raymond gave no further details. Navy records show that a ship with female passengers was torpedoed in convoy HX-232, in which Raymond's *Mormacmoon* sailed. The records do not mention a near miss between a ship and a lifeboat. All the women in the lifeboat were rescued.

Raymond assured Henny he would come through the rest of the war unharmed, and this time, it was easier to believe him. Henny acted like her old self most of the time, but since Dewey's and Leslie's deaths, her crying spells came more frequently. "When times were hard, she would cry a lot," said her grandson Jesse Carroll Thornton.

Captain Jesse still commanded tugboats, as did his son Willie, both of them staying in inland waters as the Hodges daughters had asked. Willie, in fact, would never sail offshore again. David Hodges had been promoted to head rigger at the shipyard. Spencer Hodges had quit the creamery to become a Mathews deputy sheriff. He would carry Spencer Jr. on his patrols as he had carried him on his ice-cream deliveries. Spencer would go on to become sheriff of Mathews, and Spencer Jr. would succeed him. Raymond and Coleman were still the only Hodges brothers at sea, Raymond ferrying U.S. soldiers across the Atlantic in the *Mormacmoon*, and Coleman hauling cargo on the *Edward A. Savoy* with J. W. Corbett as second officer.

Two more of the next generation of Hodges men had gone to sea, and to war—the sons of Willie and Raymond. Willie's son Horace, who was known as Brother, told his mother on the day he turned seventeen that he was joining the Merchant Marine. Brother was a serious young man who had driven a dump truck in Norfolk since he was fifteen without a driver's license. He told his mother he would be safe at sea. The U-boats "were pretty well whipped," and he would avoid getting drafted into the Army. His mother agreed. His father was on his tug and unreachable.

Raymond's younger son, Bill, also joined the Merchant Marine when he turned seventeen. Raymond suggested it. He did not challenge Bill to become a captain by age twenty-one, the way Jesse had challenged Raymond a half century before. Raymond told Bill only that the Merchant Marine needed men who knew how to handle ships. Bill had little interest in school and seized on the idea of following in the Hodges seafaring tradition. By the spring of 1945, just as many Hodges men served on merchant ships as on the day the United States entered World War II.

In February 1945, Bill Callis, Big Homer's younger son, signed on with a Liberty ship in Norfolk and was astonished to see Lester Smith employed as an able seaman. Lester had hounded the Bull Line and the union to let him go back to sea almost since the day he came out of the hospital in British Guiana. The Bull Line finally agreed to give him a chance to show he could still perform the physical work. Bill did not think Lester looked ready to come back. Lester's one whole leg hurt and sometimes bled. It did not slow Lester down, however. Bill noted that the new Lester, much like the old Lester, "would fight a tomcat after a few drinks." The ship sailed for the Pacific.

After the *Rowan* and then the *Penelope Barker* were sunk out from under him, Bernard Stansbury was offered a shore job, but he told his superiors in the Navy Armed Guard he would rather go back to sea. He ended up on another Liberty ship, carrying pack mules to India, where they would haul supplies across the Himalayas for General Joseph "Vinegar Joe" Stilwell's forces, descending into China to fight the Japanese. Several mules died on the voyage. The crew watched to make sure the carcasses were thrown to the sharks and not smuggled into the galley.

On April 12, 1945, President Roosevelt died at his retreat in Warm Springs, Georgia. His death shocked a nation he had led through the Depression and to the brink of victory in World War II. Part of the shock was due to the fact that he never allowed the public to see how ill he was. His death had special meaning for merchant seamen and sailors, who considered

Roosevelt a mariner at heart. "To the men of the sea Franklin Delano Roosevelt was a blood brother," the Masters, Mates & Pilots (MMP) maritime union declared. "His love of the sea, his pride in our Navy, his concern for our Merchant Marine and the welfare of 'the men who go down to the sea in ships' were part of his very life."

But the union's regret cut deeper. The unions had counted on Roosevelt to see that the government rewarded mariners for their service in the war. Congress had excluded merchant mariners from the G.I. Bill of Rights, passed in 1944 to provide military veterans with free college tuition and low-interest loans for homes and businesses. Some Navy and some veterans' groups opposed including the Merchant Marine. Roosevelt had signed the G.I. Bill despite its exclusion of mariners, but he had been pushing legislators to produce a new bill giving mariners at least some postwar benefits. "I trust Congress will soon provide similar opportunities to members of the Merchant Marine who have risked their lives time and time again for the welfare of our country," Roosevelt said. But Congress had not acted quickly, and Roosevelt's successor in the White House, his vice president, Harry S. Truman, was a midwesterner with no ties to the Merchant Marine, and different priorities. The sea unions now saw trouble coming. The MMP predicted that at war's end, "the scramble for land, jobs, new businesses, new merchandising methods will obscure and dim the heroism of the Merchant Marine. The public has a short memory." The MMP encouraged mariners to look out for their interests by steadfastly supporting the union. Unfortunately for the mariners, that would not be nearly enough.

Roosevelt's death did not change the course of the war. The Axis powers were collapsing. Allied troops crossed the Rhine River into Germany. The Red Army pressed toward Berlin from the east. In the Pacific, the Navy sank three Japanese carriers in the Battle of the Philippine Sea. U.S. forces recaptured the Mariana Islands and forced the Japanese back ever closer to their home islands. The news reaching Mathews from the Pacific was not all good. Shortly after Christmas, 1944, the parents of Wendell Hudgins, a young Navy sailor on the destroyer USS *Monaghan*, received a telegram saying his ship had been sunk in the South Pacific—by a typhoon. The *Monaghan* and two other ships in a Navy task force had been capsized by enormous waves in Typhoon Cobra after Admiral William S. "Bull" Halsey refused to allow the ships in the task force to break out of a refueling formation and maneuver to save themselves. Halsey had brushed aside warnings about the typhoon's growing intensity. On the three capsized ships, 756 men lost their lives.

The Japanese grew more desperate as the war turned more lopsidedly against them. On the island of Saipan, thousands of Japanese soldiers died in suicidal assaults on heavily defended Allied lines. As the Allies closed in on the Philippines, the Japanese turned to the suicide plane, the kamikaze.

Kamikazes flew directly into ships. They often carried bombs and extra fuel for added explosive power. The planes were mostly the fast and nimble Japanese Zero fighters. The pilots ranged from fanatical veterans to wide-eyed teenagers. Kamikaze attacks were well organized and used diversions. A decoy formation of planes would draw the attention of the targeted ships. Then three or four kamikazes—the designated killers— would race at the ships from a different direction. They would skim the ocean to avoid radar and bear down on their targets with machine guns hammering. The pilots were taught to aim at a ship's bridge, to kill as many officers as possible. Kamikaze attacks grew more and more frequent as U.S. warships approached Okinawa, which was just 350 miles from Japan.

Homer Callis Jr.'s destroyer, the USS *Hazelwood*, was off Okinawa on April 29, 1945, protecting the flank of an aircraft carrier, when a radio message warned of a possible kamikaze attack. Homer Jr. was on the bridge, possibly steering the ship. Three planes came into sight but banked away. Navy Hellcat fighters from the carrier rose to pursue them. The radio said two more enemy planes were inbound. A kamikaze roared low along the side of a second destroyer, the USS *Haggard*, and exploded into the hull near the water line. The *Hazelwood* was untouched, but was ordered to stand by the damaged ship to offer help as needed. She was still standing by an hour later when a kamikaze appeared without warning and raced straight at her. The *Hazelwood*'s gunners knocked the plane into the sea. Another kamikaze came at the ship from astern, almost brushing the wave-tops, strafing. The plane's right wing clipped the destroyer's aft smokestack, and the plane spun into the bridge. It exploded in a fireball, killing forty-six men, including Homer Callis Jr. His remains, like most of those in the blackened hulk of the bridge, were never identified. The crew put out the fire and saved the ship.

Nancy Callis received word of Homer Jr.'s death while she was alone at Dunrovin'. Her close friend Eleanor Respess was with her when her younger son, Bill, happened to telephone from San Francisco, where his and Lester Smith's ship was preparing to sail for the Philippines. Nancy broke the news to Bill with no emotion in her voice. Bill asked if she wanted him to come home, and she said, "No, I'll be all right." She contacted the Bull Line to get word to her husband, Homer, who was at sea. Homer wrote to her from the middle of the North Atlantic:

My Darling,

I am going to try to write a few lines to you every once in a while until I reach my next port and perhaps my effort might lessen the endlessness of these days and if possible bring to you a semblance of comfort insofar as may be possible for us to get comfort from the thoughts that are in our minds and hearts.

I've hoped and prayed for some word each day that would give back to us the joy of living again and with each message that comes to me from our Radio Room there is a silent prayer that it may be the one that we most want from life. What earthly joy it would be for me to have the happiness of telling you that all is well with our wonderful Son. The greatest day of life would be so small to compare with such a glorious event. We must hope even against hope, My Darling, until we know that there is none left.

Forgive me if the words I write are causing you a greater grief, but I can't seem to think of anything but that fate has turned its eye away from us and I hate the knowledge that it has hurt so much you, who have been such a wonderful mother. We love you, Darling, but I know that a mother's love is so great that no other love can erase or minimize the pain of the loss of her son. But if our love and devotion to you can help to salvage anything that is left to bring you peace and comfort I know that the rest of my life is justified. You have always been a wonderful wife and mother and it has been with gratitude always that we have been privileged to belong to you. For us there couldn't have been a greater glory and we know that you will always be wonderful even in your sorrow. Good night, Darling.

The Navy confirmed Homer Jr.'s death a few days later.

The day after the kamikaze killed Homer Jr., Hitler committed suicide in his bunker in Berlin. In his will, he designated Doenitz as his successor as leader of the Third Reich. Hitler at the end seemed to see Doenitz as a loyal professional on a staff of traitors and cowards. Doenitz told the German people in a speech that Hitler "has fallen," and exhorted them to fight on. He knew Germany had lost the war, but wanted to give retreating German troops time to escape a massacre by the Russians. Sixty-two U-boats remained at sea, and they continued to sink ships and be sunk. On May 4, 1945, Doenitz finally ended the U-boat war with a terse message to his commanders: "All U-boats cease fire at once. Stop all hostile action against allied shipping."

One U-boat did not receive his message immediately. The U-853 was at periscope depth off the coast of Rhode Island, lining up a torpedo strike, when Doenitz broadcast his cease-fire message. A submarine could not receive radio transmissions while submerged. The U-boat commander fired a torpedo into the starboard side of the collier *Black Point* as she passed Point Judith, Rhode Island, with a load of coal. The ship sank quickly, taking twelve crewmen with her. The *Black Point* got off a distress call that brought two destroyer escorts and a Coast Guard vessel. The three ships located the U-boat with sonar and depth-charged it until its insides burst to the surface in a mass of debris, including a U-boat officer's cap. There were no survivors.

Four days later, on May 8, the Bull Line's main office in New York sent a radiogram to all the company's ships at sea:

> GERMANY HAS SURRENDERED UNCONDITIONALLY.
>
> CEASE FIRE HAS BEEN ORDERED FROM 10 P.M. EIGHT
> MAY.
>
> PENDING FURTHER ORDERS ALL EXISTING
> INSTRUCTIONS REGULATING THE DEFENSE SECURITY AND
> CONTROL OF MERCHANT SHIPPING ARE TO REMAIN IN
> FORCE.
>
> MERCHANT SHIPS AT SEA WHETHER IN CONVOY OR
> SAILING INDEPENDENTLY ARE TO CONTINUE THEIR
> VOYAGES AS PREVIOUSLY ORDERED.

Doenitz had hoped the U-boat force would be allowed to destroy its submarines in a symbolic ceremony. The Allies, however, insisted that all U-boats be surrendered intact. Doenitz told his commanders to hoist black flags of surrender and sail to the nearest Allied or neutral port. U-boats surrendered at the docks of Cape May, New Jersey, and Portsmouth, New Hampshire. One defiant U-boat commander committed suicide in a Boston prison by smashing his eyeglasses and cutting his wrists with the shards of glass. U-boats surrendered at Halifax, Nova Scotia; St. John's, Newfoundland; Bergen and Narvik, Norway; Gibraltar, Spain; Loch Foyle, Scotland; and Liverpool, England. Two U-boat commanders let their crews vote on whether to surrender. They voted to run for Argentina to try to escape capture. Argentine authorities turned over the rogue U-boats and crews to the U.S. Navy.

Numerous damaged and mothballed U-boats were discovered by Free

French troops entering the abandoned concrete U-boat bunkers on the French coast. Among those U-boats were Hardegan's U-123, which had killed Ernest Thompson on the *Norvana* and Frank White on the *Muskogee*, and the U-129, which had sunk the *Mary*, *Millinocket*, and *Onondaga*, killing Dewey Hodges, Mellin Respess, Genious Hudgins, William Hammond, and Lewis Callis.

Months after the war ended, the British destroyed most of the surrendered U-boats in a naval gunnery exercise. But as after World War I, a few U-boats were given to other Allied nations for testing and publicity. One was secretly towed up the Chesapeake Bay, right past Mathews. The U-505, which had torpedoed Mellin Respess on the *Thomas McKean* and then had been captured just before D-Day, was sailed up and down the U.S. East Coast by American sailors, docking at coastal cities to serve as an attraction for War Bond rallies. The U-505 drew 13,200 people during a five-day visit to Norfolk.

Germany's surrender ended only the Atlantic war, of course, and much of the Merchant Marine's work simply shifted to the Pacific. "The end of organized resistance in Germany brings no lessening of any of the tasks of the United States Merchant Marine," the Maritime Commission told mariners in a radiogram. "Closing of hostilities in the European theater means . . . a situation unchanged basically except for a shift in emphasis in time and places. There will be no lesser demand for ships or for men to sail them." The Maritime Commission estimated that 70 percent of the surplus war equipment in Europe would be shipped 13,000 miles to the Pacific.

But the end of the Pacific war was near as well. In April 1945, Captain T. O. Rainier of Mathews docked his troopship *Cape Victory* at Seattle, Washington, and took aboard 1,400 Army Air Forces personnel in an atmosphere of great secrecy. The *Cape Victory*'s crew was confined to the ship, and Rainier was allowed ashore only in the company of an Army Intelligence officer, who listened to his phone calls. Rainier had to use a private phone because all the pay phones on the pier had been disconnected. Finally, he was ordered to take the airmen to the remote island of Tinian in the Marianas chain. The elaborate secrecy puzzled Rainier. He had been ferrying troops across the Pacific for three years. He saw from the airmen's uniforms that they were B-29 bomber personnel with specialized ratings. He finally asked a colonel from the squadron what was up. The colonel deflected his question and told Rainier, "Give us four and a half months, and if Tokyo isn't flat, then turn your guns on us." Rainier had no idea what the colonel meant. He would not realize for years that he had delivered most of the crew and support personnel of the B-29 Superfortress *Enola Gay*, which would fly from Tinian to drop the first atomic bomb on Hiroshima, Japan, on August 6, 1945.

Another Mathews man helped deliver the uranium-235 for the atomic bomb to Tinian. William Franklin Hale, a Navy seaman 2nd Class, served aboard the heavy cruiser USS *Indianapolis*, which stopped at Tinian to drop off a vial of the subcritical uranium. Then Hale and the *Indianapolis* were sent across the Philippine Sea alone, with no equipment for detecting submarines. A Japanese sub torpedoed the cruiser, casting approximately 900 American sailors into the North Pacific. Many had only life preservers to keep them afloat. The Navy inexcusably lost track of the *Indianapolis* and did not know she was missing until four days later, when a patrol plane spotted the oil slick. In the meantime, the men in the water died of thirst, exposure, drowning, and ferocious attacks by oceanic whitetip sharks, which pulled men screaming from the cluster of swimmers. As many as 80 men may have been killed by the sharks. Only 316 of the 900 *Indianapolis* sailors who went into the water survived. William Hale was among the lost.

The Navy withheld news of the sinking until after Japan surrendered. Hale's daughter Betsy was only two years old at the time. She would know nothing about the circumstances of the *Indianapolis* sinking until decades later, when she started attending reunions for *Indianapolis* survivors and their families. She met a close friend of her father's. He showed her a snapshot of the two of them in a photo booth. Betsy asked him if he knew how

her father died. She wanted to hear he had died in the ship and not in the
water. The man said he did not know how her father died, but his expression made Betsy wonder.

The second atomic bomb was dropped three days after the first, on
August 9, 1945, on Nagasaki. Japan surrendered on August 15. The war's
end set off wild celebrations in New York, Norfolk, and other cities across
the United States. Mathews did not celebrate. A few drivers tooted their
horns as they passed the courthouse on Highway 14. The stores on Main
Street closed at 7 p.m. when President Truman announced Japan's surrender, and stayed closed the next day, even though it was Wednesday. The
Gazette-Journal soberly welcomed the end of anxiety "which shadowed
practically every home." The paper observed:

> With so many local boys still far away from home, the general
> attitude seemed to be one of quiet, thoughtful thanksgiving, that
> with the war's end they are no longer in great danger. Many remem-
> bered, too, those fine fellows who, having given their lives in the
> war, will not return. And so, it was not difficult to restrain any urge
> there might have been to blow off in any extremely hilarious cele-
> bration at this time.

The Merchant Marine losses in the war were staggering. The official
mariner death toll announced by the Maritime Commission at the war's
end was 5,662, but government records on mariners' deaths were spotty
and did not include deaths of American mariners on foreign ships. Subsequent tallies by merchant mariners' support organizations turned up more
than 3,500 additional deaths, for a total of roughly 9,300. The exact number of American merchant mariners killed in World War II may never be
known.

Mathews County—population 7,500—lost 23 mariners to torpedoes,
bombs, fires, explosions, shark attacks, drowning, exposure, hunger and
thirst, and other violent ends as their ships plunged into the depths. None

of their families learned exactly how they died, or had the opportunity to bury them. The deaths touched every corner of Mathews. Every family in the county lost a member, relative, or friend.

The U.S. Merchant Marine's fatality rate in World War II was approximately 3.9 percent—one of every 26 mariners who sailed on a merchant ship. The only branch of the U.S. military with a comparably high fatality rate was the U.S. Marines. The casualty rate for the U.S. Navy was 1.49 percent—less than half the casualty rate of the Merchant Marine. British seaman had borne the brunt of the U-boat war for two years before America entered. The British lost 32,000 merchant seamen in World War II, almost a quarter of Britain's total war deaths.

The most staggering losses, however, belonged to the German U-boat force. Of the roughly 39,000 men who served in U-boats during the war, more than 27,000 were killed. That fatality rate of nearly 70 percent was, and is, the highest for any fighting force in modern warfare. Of the 830 U-boats commissioned to serve in World War II, 717 were sunk.

American merchant ships delivered more than 300 million tons of war cargo, including ammunition, explosives, aircraft, aviation fuel, tanks, trucks, landing craft, jeeps, ambulances, locomotives, food, clothing, and medicine. No Allied invasion force was ever thrown back for want of arms, food, supplies, or munitions. "Our merchant seamen displayed their highest qualities," Churchill wrote, "and the brotherhood of the sea was never more strikingly shown than in their determination to defeat the U-boat." Even Admiral King had praise for the Merchant Marine: "During the past three and a half years, the Navy has been dependent upon the Merchant Marine to supply our far-flung fleet and bases. Without this support, the Navy could not have accomplished its mission. Consequently, it is fitting that the Merchant Marine share in our success as it shared in our trials."

King prepared to retire and reap praise for his role in winning the war. In September 1945, he rode at the head of a two-and-a-half-mile-long victory parade through the streets of his hometown of Lorain, Ohio. An estimated one hundred thousand people lined the parade route, and confetti swirled through the streets. Warplanes flew in formation overhead. Ohio governor Frank J. Lausche praised King as "Ohio's most illustrious son, one of the leaders who helped pave the way" to victory. King had indeed done just that, but historians on both sides of the Atlantic would call his failure to protect merchant ships and mariners in coastal waters in 1942 a terrible error. The German naval historian Jürgen Rohwer called King's slowness in setting up coastal convoys "one of the greatest mistakes in the Allied conduct of the Battle of the Atlantic." The British historian Martin Middlebrook called it "almost criminal." American historian and author Michael Gannon compared the sinkings in the first half of 1942 to "an Atlantic Pearl Harbor" that dragged on for six months. A few historians have defended King, including the late Clay Blair, who said King did all he could and that suggesting otherwise was "absurd."

In the midst of the victory celebrations, the United States set out to dismantle the huge fleet of merchant ships it had built to win the war. The nation could not afford to sustain that fleet. America had finished World War II with more than five thousand merchant ships—five times as many as at the start of the war, and 54 percent of all the merchant ships in the postwar world. Most of those ships were owned by the government. So in 1945, the Maritime Commission began selling off the Liberty ships and other vessels for as little as one-third the construction price. The ships were sold not just to American companies and investors, but to buyers in Britain, Norway, and other Allied nations whose merchant fleets had been decimated by the U-boats. Among the beneficiaries of the sell-off was the Greek businessman Aristotle Onassis, Jacqueline Kennedy's future husband, who bought tankers from the United States. Helping rebuild the Allies' merchant fleets was a worthy goal, but dumping almost two thousand new ships on the global market was a gamble. The new owners would use the ships to compete directly with established American shipping companies. The sell-off would be the first step in the U.S. Merchant Marine's long decline.

At the war's end, however, merchant ships and mariners were busy, busier in fact than they had been at any point *during* the war. The nation's first priority was bringing home more than 1 million soldiers from overseas. Raymond Hodges carried six loads of troops from Liverpool to New York on the *Mormacmoon* in late 1945 and early 1946 without stopping on either side of the ocean for more than a few days. Captain Frank G. Boyer of Mathews brought home 5,000 soldiers on three consecutive trips to the Pacific on a troopship, stopping in Mathews only to spend New Year's Day in 1945 with his family. The soldiers came home to brass bands and red-white-and-blue bunting. The mariners who delivered them receded into the background. When they arrived in port, they got a couple of days off and then a call to return to the ship to pick up another load of troops.*

On their return trips to Europe, merchant ships hauled food and supplies to the European nations devastated by the war. They carried grain, steel, chemicals, tools, construction equipment to repair bombed cities, and explosives to level what could not be saved. Cargo would continue to surge in 1948 when Secretary of State George C. Marshall announced the Marshall Plan to ship an additional $17 billion worth of supplies to help rebuild Europe and forestall the spread of Communism. Norfolk became an export center for American livestock to Eastern European countries whose native animals were eaten or slaughtered by passing armies.

Brother Hodges made several trips to Poland on Liberty ships hauling chickens, cows, and horses. On one voyage, the horses began suffocating due to poor ventilation in the holds, and the captain abandoned caution and steamed full speed through the fog all the way to port. On another trip, Brother arrived at the docks in Odessa, Russia, on a ship carrying mostly horses. The horses were kept on deck in wooden stalls. A company of cowboys from Pennsylvania fed them and shoveled their shit overboard. Brother got off the ship and saw his uncle Raymond's *Mormacmoon* docked

---

* Two years later, merchant ships would bring home the bodies of many of the 150,000 Americans who were killed overseas but whose families wanted to bury them in American soil.

a few berths away. Raymond went to the gangplank and spoke to a black messman he recognized as a Mathews man. Raymond was dealing with an oil spill but the messman promised to get word to him. Later, Raymond sent a seaman to invite Brother to dinner. Raymond and his officers all dined in uniforms and jackets; Brother's best clothes were dungarees and a sweater. Brother was surprised to be served a steak and fresh milk; most of the food he ate was canned. After dinner, Raymond and Brother smoked cigars while looking out over the Black Sea.

CHAPTER THIRTEEN

Legacy

No sooner had the war ended than Captain Jesse and Henny Hodges sold their farm on Gales Neck. The Hodges children were surprised but they understood. Henny was seventy-one years old. She simply could no longer handle the work. Jesse was seventy-four. His legs were no longer strong enough to carry him up and down ships' ladders. He tried working on tugs and even fish steamers in the Bay, but it was no use. After more than six decades at sea, he had to stay ashore. "I'm dying," he complained to his niece Stormy Heart.

Jesse and Henny bought a large, wood-framed house in the village of Hudgins. The new house was only a few miles from Gales Neck, but it was dramatically different. It had four acres to farm instead of forty. It stood right on State Route 14, the main road through Mathews, and was only a five-minute walk from a country store. The new house had no indoor plumbing, but it had electricity, oil heat, and a well much closer to the kitchen than the well at Gales Neck.

As soon as they were set up in their new home, Captain Jesse and Henny held a dining. Henny did what she had always done at Gales Neck: prepared a huge meal, orchestrated all the activity in the house, and withdrew from time to time to cry. Her sons Willie, Coleman, and David brought their families, as did her daughters Alice and Louise. Leslie's widow, Cecile, did not attend. Although she remained in close touch with Henny, Cecile had never felt comfortable at the boisterous dinings. Dewey's family did not come either. The long trip from Norfolk to Mathews by car and ferry was too arduous without Dewey behind the wheel of the Lincoln Zephyr, cracking jokes and crooning "Mexicali Rose."

Other Mathews families felt the war's aftershocks as well. The father of Bernard Pierson, who had died on the *East Indian*, looked up one day from the counter of a store he ran on Gwynn's Island to see an unfamiliar young man standing in front of him, struggling to speak. The man finally said, "Your son gave his life to save me." He was the seaman who had been badly injured and lying on a raft when Bernard insisted on giving him his spot in the *East Indian*'s only lifeboat, hundreds of miles off Cape Town. Only the men in the lifeboat had survived; Bernard and the others on the rafts were never seen again. The young man had traveled down from New York to tell the story to Bernard's father.

In October 1945, the family of a young Navy machinist's mate named William Burton Gay, who had been missing since the fall of Bataan, learned in an official telegram that he had died two years earlier, in the brutal Japanese prison camp at Cabanatuan in the Philippines.

A month later, Captain Otis Levering Callis of Gwynn's Island, who had spent the war sailing the Liberty ship *Benjamin Chew* back and forth across the Atlantic without incident, was killed in a car accident thirty minutes from Mathews. His ship had just returned a few days earlier from India.

After more than a year, Salome Hudgins finally abandoned hope that her husband, Genious, had survived the sinking of the *Onondaga* in July 1942, and would return to her from a foreign hospital or deserted island. Salome had kept every letter Genious ever wrote. As a last farewell to him, and perhaps a symbolic new start for herself, she carried most of his letters into the backyard and burned them.

The official verdict on the U-boats' conduct of the war against merchant shipping came in 1946 near the end of the Nuremberg trials, in which twenty-two former Nazi leaders, including Karl Doenitz, were tried for war crimes by a military tribunal. Doenitz maintained a rigid dignity throughout the proceedings. He resented his jailers for taking his razor away. "I wouldn't commit suicide," he said. "That would be cowardly."* Doenitz and his lawyers convinced the judges that he had been promoted late into Hitler's inner circle and knew nothing about the death camps and other atrocities the Nazis perpetrated on land. But for Doenitz's conduct of the U-boat war, he was charged with "murder and ill-treatment of persons on the high seas"—specifically, with ordering his men to kill the survivors of torpedoed ships and to leave other survivors to die without hope of rescue. Doenitz testified in his own defense. He expressed no regrets. He pointed out that he had insisted in the final days of the war that all the U-boat force's records be kept intact, while other branches of the German military were destroying theirs. He argued that Allied merchant ships had forfeited all claim to noncombatant status by carrying guns and depth charges, and by radioing the locations of U-boats to Allied antisubmarine forces. Doenitz's lawyers introduced evidence showing that British warships had sunk German ships they could easily have seized and brought into port under the so-called prize rules. The defense's most powerful evidence was a sworn affidavit from Admiral Chester Nimitz, commander in chief of the U.S. Pacific Fleet during the war, acknowledging that American submarines had routinely sunk Japanese merchant ships without trying to aid survivors. One of the American judges on the Nuremberg tribunal, Attorney General Francis Biddle, favored acquitting Doenitz because his U-boats had "waged

---

* Doenitz may have been referring to Heinrich Himmler, who oversaw the Nazi death camps. While Doenitz and other leaders of the German government were being arrested, Himmler was caught trying to slip out of Germany on a phony passport. When a doctor tried to examine his teeth, Himmler committed suicide by swallowing a cyanide pill hidden in his mouth.

a cleaner war than we did." But a majority of the judges convicted Doenitz and sentenced him to ten years in Spandau prison—the lightest sentence for any of the nineteen defendants convicted at Nuremberg.* The judges added somewhat ambiguously that Doenitz's sentence was "not assessed on the grounds of his breaches of the international law of submarine warfare," given the Allies' conduct of the sea war. Admiral Gallery, who had scoffed at the idea of trying to hold U-boats to the prize rules, would later accuse the Nuremberg tribunal of "barefaced hypocrisy" in convicting Doenitz. Gallery said Doenitz's only offense was "almost beating us in a bloody, but fair, fight."

Doenitz would live in Germany until his death on Christmas Eve, 1980. A long line of old U-boat men filed past his casket.

The real verdict on unrestricted submarine warfare, however, was handed down in the corridors of power in Washington, D.C., and Moscow even before World War II ended. Submarines already were evolving into a role in the Cold War more significant than anything Doenitz had ever imagined. By 1946, Travers Thompson of Mathews, who had joined the American submarine force after a U-boat killed his father, was in a sub patrolling the North Pacific for Soviet subs. His next submarine would carry long-range ballistic missiles, preprogrammed to strike Russian cities in the event of a nuclear war with the Soviet Union.

Mathews men felt the first chill of the Cold War on the docks in Eastern Europe. Benny Fitchett of Mathews got his introduction on a wintry afternoon in the Baltic Sea port of Gdynia, Poland. The Russians had seized Poland from the Germans during the war, and made it clear they intended to keep Poland. Benny arrived in Gdynia on a Liberty ship delivering horses. While the ship was being unloaded, he noticed a huge warship at

---

* Three of the twenty-two Nuremberg defendants were acquitted of all charges. Twelve other defendants, including Field Marshal Hermann Goering, the head of the *Luftwaffe*, were sentenced to hang.

the end of a long stretch of empty wharves. He and a friend had time to kill, and hiked to the vessel for a closer look. The warship was the old German battleship *Schleswig-Holstein*, scuttled by her crew on the shallow bottom before the Russians took the port. The warship looked deserted. Benny noticed a red flag on the stern, which caused him to pause but not stop. He and his shipmate walked across a gangplank onto the vessel and then down a passageway with a low overhang, which gave the passageway the feel of a long tunnel. Within seconds, Benny realized they had made a dangerous error. A man's silhouette crossed the opening at the far end of the passageway, followed by a second silhouette. Benny whispered to his friend to keep walking and hand him all his cigarettes. When the mariners reached the opening at the end of the passageway, two uniformed guards carrying rifles stepped in front of them. One of the guards held out his hand for the mariners' identification documents. Benny tried to explain that he and his friend meant no harm and just wanted to get back off the ship. He felt his heart banging in his chest. If he was taken prisoner on this derelict vessel, no one would ever know what had happened to him. Benny handed over all of his and his friend's cigarettes to the guards, who accepted them without a word or a change of expression. The guards spoke to one another in Russian. Then they returned the men's documents, and gestured toward the gangplank. Benny had to fight the urge to run across it to safety.

Mathews slowly regained its prewar rhythms as the restrictions imposed by the war fell away one by one. The end of rationing of gas and rubber revived the Saturday-night gatherings on Main Street. The Mathews County Fair resumed, as did the Mathews High School graduation ceremonies. The first postwar commencement ceremony in 1946 attracted more than one thousand people, the largest turnout anyone in Mathews could remember. The county held a four-day series of sailboat races that drew large crowds. Plans were laid to establish a Mathews yacht club, of which Lester Smith eventually would become president.

Scores of military veterans returned to Mathews, giving the county less of a ghost-town feel. Many of those veterans signed up for college and other educational opportunities under the G.I. Bill. Veterans returning to the farm were given the inside track in buying new farm equipment. None of the merchant mariners were eligible for those benefits.

Nor were merchant mariners included in the "Gold Star Honor Roll" compiled by the Commonwealth of Virginia to honor men who had given their lives for their country. The citizens of Mathews created their own Gold Star Honor Roll to include mariners, who accounted for roughly half of the county's war dead. Henny Hodges was chosen to unveil a small monument in front of a Mathews school bearing the names of all the Mathews men killed in the war—with the exception of the black mariner Ashley Clinton Williams, who had been lost on the *Ruth*. Although it's impossible to be certain, every indication is that those who designed the monument were unaware of Williams's roots in Mathews.

More than a dozen new businesses sprouted in Mathews, including some run by former mariners. Roland Foster Jr., who had survived the sinking of the *Thomas McKean*, opened an auto dealership with his brother. Boyd Dixon, who had survived the torpedoing of the tanker *E.M. Clark* in a lightning storm off Hatteras, opened a service station not far from the Hodgeses' new home. Captain Will Hunley, who had survived the sinking of the *Commercial Trader* and its cargo of castor beans, took a job sailing steamships on the Bay between Norfolk and Baltimore. Will bought a house on the Bay near the tip of New Point, where only ten miles of water separates Mathews from Virginia's Eastern Shore. Will's ship passed within sight of his home every night at the same time, and Will always blinked the lights on the ship's bridge to say goodnight to his children. They blinked the lights in their bedrooms in reply.

Commercial fishing in the Bay rebounded, as if rejuvenated by the war's end. The catch of blue crabs in 1946 was the best in more than a decade. The market for Virginia oysters expanded with a new air freight service that could deliver them fresh to Chicago and other midwestern cities. Striped bass, which the locals called rockfish, were plentiful. Even a few shad showed up in fishermen's nets. The good fishing, of course, would not last.

World War II had been over for more than a year by the time Mathews felt like celebrating. In September 1946, the county held a two-day festival to welcome the return of peace to Mathews. The assault transport ship USS *Mathews*, which had been named to honor the county's war losses, anchored just off Gwynn's Island as a centerpiece. The festivities included a seafood feast, a baseball game, and water sports. Eleanor Respess won one of the motorboat races, and more than five hundred people gathered on the riverbank to listen to a speech by Congressman Bland, who was still trying to persuade Congress to offer postwar benefits to merchant mariners. Bland evoked Mathews's seafaring history and pointed out that Mathews mariners had refused to let U-boats chase them from the sea. "Wherever you go, the world over, in far distant ports, there you will find men at sea from Mathews," Bland said. He recalled that on a voyage he had taken to Brazil, he discovered that the ship's captain was from Mathews. The celebration attracted the attention of the *Richmond Times-Dispatch*, which declared in an editorial: "Mathews mourns its losses, but it has long been reconciled to the furies and hazards of the sea. It is a certainty that a good proportion of its sons will continue to make their living from it, just as did their fathers and grandfathers before them."

A month after the ceremony, Captain A. G. Gaden of the USS *Mathews* wrote a letter to the *Gazette-Journal* from the Pacific. Gaden reported that the *Mathews* was encountering Mathews mariners everywhere the ship went. He confessed being "dumbfounded" when a Panama Canal pilot who came aboard to guide the warship through the canal introduced himself as a Mathews man. At least six other Mathews men worked on the canal as pilots or tug operators. Gaden concluded, "[I]t is impossible to get away from Mathews County people if one is in the seafaring business!"

One final act remained in the saga of the ring found in the belly of the shark. In 1948, Dewey Hodges's widow, Edna, petitioned the New York Life

Insurance Co. to double a $10,000 payout the family had received after Dewey's death. (Dewey apparently bought more life insurance than the government's basic coverage for mariners.) Edna contended the *Onondaga* had been sunk not by a U-boat but by accident. She asked the company to honor a double-indemnity clause in the insurance policy that doubled the payout if the death was accidental.

New York Life rejected her claim, and Edna filed a lawsuit and took her case before a jury in Norfolk's federal court. Her lawyers argued that the cause of the *Onondaga*'s sinking was unclear, since none of the survivors actually had seen a sub or a torpedo. Russell Dennis of Mathews, the ship's former third officer, returned to the witness stand to reiterate he had seen nothing. The insurance company responded that all available evidence pointed to the ship having been torpedoed, and that Edna had argued as much in 1942 when she had persuaded a judge to declare Dewey legally dead. How, then, could the jury allow Edna to claim six years later that the sinking was accidental? The jury sympathized with the widow, however, and ordered New York Life to pay Edna an additional $10,000.

Immediately after the jury's verdict was read, the insurance company's lawyers asked U.S. District Judge John Paul to reject it as "plainly contrary to the evidence." Such requests were standard for the losing side in a jury trial, and judges usually let the verdict stand. Judge Paul, however, agreed to consider the request. A month later, in a written ruling, he threw out the jury's verdict and made it clear in his ruling that he had found Edna's case entirely unpersuasive. Edna did not dwell on the defeat. She made use of the money Dewey had left to buy a beauty shop in Norfolk, then sold it and ran a Norfolk hotel, and then bought a motel and restaurant in what is now Virginia Beach. She remarried, and died in 1960 at age sixty-three. Her pallbearers included Dewey's brothers Willie, Coleman, and David Hodges.

Edna and Dewey's son, George Dewey Jr., finished college as Dewey had wished, though the Navy interrupted his studies and deployed him on a warship to China, where he contracted malaria. He served his stint in the Navy and then came home and got his degree, becoming the first member of the Hodges family to graduate from college. Edna never asked Dewey's old boss at Ford to give her son a job. Dewey Jr. had no interest in the Merchant Marine. He built a successful insurance business. He inherited his father's initialed ring, and then passed it on to his son George Dewey Hodges III. None of Dewey's descendants ever went to sea.

Captain Homer Callis sailed merchant ships until the end of his life. He never again considered working ashore. He stayed with the Bull Line, which kept him busy hauling freight around the Caribbean. Homer took every opportunity to come home to Gwynn's Island. His wife, Nancy, was never the same after Homer Jr. was killed by the kamikaze. She made a shrine of sorts to her son in the house, using photographs and some of his letters. Nancy, who had always loved the Christmas holidays, never celebrated them again after the war. She and Homer installed a marble bench in Homer Jr.'s memory in the Callis section of the Gwynn's Island cemetery. It says, "To live in our hearts is not to die."

Homer's visits home to Dunrovin' sometimes came when younger son Bill was also home from the sea. Bill was moving up through the ranks toward captain. On one of Bill's visits home to Gwynn's Island, he saw young Kathryn Hudgins on the beach in a blue bathing suit, and that was that. They married and had a baby girl named Lisa. She was Homer's first grandchild. He proudly showed her picture to his crew and his passengers, and wrote letters to the infant on Bull Line stationery. One of Homer's letters to Lisa, early in 1955, read:

> Granddaddy surely feels bad because he could not come home from New York to see you last week. He is just counting the days until someone comes to relieve him of this job so he can come home to play with you. . . . I hope you can dance for me when I come home again, and I know that Mommy and Grandmother will let you stay up and watch the television with me when you are not real sleepy. You make them let you do the things you want to do, or Granddaddy will fuss up a storm when he comes home . . .

In May 1955, Homer experienced chest pains while sailing the Bull Line ship *Jean* up the East Coast to Philadelphia. He had suffered a heart attack. The ship stopped in Baltimore so that Homer could be rushed to a hospital. He spent a week there before he felt better and was allowed to go home. Being at Dunrovin' always seemed to reenergize Homer, and his family assumed he soon would return to sea. But on the afternoon of May 19, he lay down on the couch for a nap and never woke up. He was sixty-two years old. Homer was buried in the Callis family plot in the Gwynn's Island cemetery, next to the marble bench dedicated to Homer Jr. The inscription on Big Homer's headstone reads: "We know that the waters he sails on now will be peaceful, as he was a pilot and our God needs good pilots."

Nancy Callis would live on the island well into her eighties. She drove a pickup truck with a bumper sticker saying "To Hell with Japan." Her close friend Eleanor Respess—Mellin's widow—also would live well into her eighties. Eleanor would become something of a Renaissance woman, serving on various civic boards, and becoming a gourmet cook and a master gardener. She would wage a long, lighthearted, and ultimately successful campaign to persuade state and federal mapmakers to add an apostrophe to "Gwynn's" in Gwynn's Island. Guy Hudgins sailed merchant ships for years after the war. He had always wanted to command a cruise ship but never was chosen for one of those jobs. He came to believe it was because the steamship companies thought he had too many rough edges, and maybe he did. Guy would retire from the Merchant Marine at age sixty-two and move to Ormond Beach, Florida, where he drowned in the surf while on a morning swim at the age of eighty-two.

Lester Smith ended up walking on two artificial legs, but he never stopped working. He bought a fishing boat and hauled seine nets in the Bay, often working alone on his boat at night with his artificial legs jammed into hip boots. At least Lester knew how to swim. Lester also opened an ice plant and seafood store. He was a relentless boss but an affectionate husband and father. In the last year of his life, he spent summer mornings crabbing in a skiff in the creeks near Gwynn's Island with his daughter Ellen and granddaughter Kim. Ellen said catching crabs was secondary to spending "quiet time with my daddy."

Captain Jesse Hodges had settled into a landsman's life at his new home in Hudgins. He and Henny worked their four acres as a small farm, raising vegetables, corn, chickens, and hogs, much as they had on Gales Neck, but on a smaller scale. Jesse mostly spent his time tending his prized watermelon patch and visiting with other sea captains who dropped by to ask his advice or just to reminisce.

One day in August 1957, Jesse felt strange and checked into the Marine Hospital in Norfolk. The U.S. Marine Hospitals were a network of hospitals operated by the federal government to provide free care for sick or injured merchant mariners. Mariners helped pay the cost of operating them with deductions from their wages. Until the Marine Hospitals were closed in the 1980s by President Ronald Reagan, they were the merchant mariners' equivalent of the Veterans Administration hospitals, which were open to veterans of the armed forces but not to veterans of the Merchant Marine. Most of the Marine Hospitals were large, imposing buildings with an institutional feel.

The Marine Hospital in Norfolk was a long trip from Mathews, but the distance did not deter Henny. She got up before dawn several days a week, cooked Captain Jesse a big breakfast of fried fish or whatever he wanted, and brought it to his hospital bed. He always complained it was too cold, or too bland, and made Henny cry.

Jesse died in the hospital on August 22, 1957, with his daughter Hilda Fourteen at his side. His funeral service was held in Mathews Baptist Church, less than three hundred yards from the Hodges house in Hudgins. Henny would not leave the house to attend the funeral, because she could not stop crying. The rest of the Hodges family turned out in force. Captain Jesse's grandchildren lined the walkway to the church, carrying armloads of flowers. The pallbearers included Spencer; Dewey's son George Jr.; Raymond's oldest son, Raymond Jr.; and Elizabeth's son J. W. Corbett. More than a hundred people came to say good-bye to Jesse, including dozens of Mathews mariners who had learned to sail from him.

His star pupil, the oldest Hodges son, Raymond, was promoted by Moore-McCormack after the war to captain of the cruise ship *Brazil*, which carried tourists from New York to Rio de Janeiro and Buenos Aires, Argentina. Commanding a cruise ship required not just fine seamanship but a knack for charming the wealthy passengers, with whom the captain dined each night. Raymond took dancing lessons before starting the job. Photos taken aboard the *Brazil* show him dancing in conga lines with bejeweled matrons, and posing with his arms around their lovely daughters.

The *Brazil*'s passengers typically included diplomats, captains of industry, and celebrities. Raymond dined with the actor Cesar Romero, and with the Catholic archbishop of New York, Francis Cardinal Spellman, who in 1955 rode the *Brazil* with hundreds of other Catholics to the 36th International Eucharistic Congress in Rio de Janeiro. On the way to Rio, Raymond steered the *Brazil* out of the path of Hurricane Diane. "That's one lady I really wanted to get away from," he joked.

Raymond seemed to have been born to command a cruise ship. He especially loved visiting Argentina, where he had good friends dating back to before the war. His son Bill said Raymond bought a small cattle ranch in Argentina and hired a woman to oversee it for him. He continued to pay his sons to raise his cattle in Gloucester.

The *Brazil* was retired in 1957 and Raymond was offered the job of captain of her replacement vessel, which was under construction in a shipyard in Pascagoula, Mississippi. Raymond was sent to Pascagoula to supervise the work. He stayed in a hotel and took a taxi to the shipyard every morning to deal with the contractors. One morning on his way up the gangplank, he lost his balance and nearly fell. It was the first sign that Raymond suffered from Parkinson's disease. His condition rapidly worsened. On December 23, 1960, three years after his diagnosis, Raymond died peacefully at his farm in Gloucester. His last wish was that he be buried at sea, off the coast of Argentina. After a memorial service in

Mathews, his body was released to Moore-McCormack, which loaded it on the first cruise ship heading for South America. The ship stopped its engines off the coast of Argentina, and the crew slid Raymond's casket into the South Atlantic.

Coleman Hodges quit sailing the deep ocean as soon as the war ended. He felt he had done his duty, and wanted to go home to Mathews. He bought a house in the woods near the drawbridge to Gwynn's Island, and piloted tugs for a lumber company, which allowed him to come home most nights. He kept five beagle-mix hounds in a kennel, and spent every Saturday fox hunting with his brother David. His daughters asked how Coleman could stand the dogs' howling. "Have you ever heard the birds sing?" he said. "Well, this is music to my ears." Coleman bought a small boat and fished in the lower Piankatank River and the Bay. He loved the outdoors and especially the stars. He showed his daughters how to use his sextant. "This'll always get you home," he told them.

Coleman continued to entertain his family and friends with his jokes, but he occasionally made comments that revealed a gloomy view of life in general. He did not understand how a just God could have allowed U-boats to kill his brothers Dewey and Leslie. He never forgave the Germans or the Japanese. He once smashed a knickknack against a wall because it had been made in Japan. He shouted at his wife, Ethel, "Don't you know that they attacked us?"

In 1964, Coleman was diagnosed with renal cancer. He clung to life for months in the Marine Hospital on Staten Island, which specialized in cancer treatment, but which his daughter Betty recalled as being "like an asylum, a big, brick, drafty place with steel beds, ice everywhere. It was a very poor picture." Coleman died on February 13, 1965, at the age of fifty-one, with his wife and his sister Elizabeth at his side. His brother David was vacationing in Hawaii, and felt guilty for not having been with Coleman at the end. On the first Christmas Eve after Coleman's death, David left his home on Gwynn's Island without telling his family where he was going. Hours passed. David's children found him standing before Coleman's grave.

Henny Hodges did not attend Raymond's or Coleman's funeral services. She moved in with her daughter Louise, who set up a bed for her in the living room. Her children and grandchildren were always coming in and out, and her friends dropped by to see her every day. She died at Louise's house on March 19, 1965, at the age of eighty-six, having outlived seven of her fourteen children as well as her husband. Members of her extended family filled the funeral home. They included seven children, twenty-six grandchildren, forty-eight great-grandchildren, and two great-great-grandchildren. She was buried in the cemetery of the Episcopal Church, next to Captain Jesse. Henny left $134 to each of her surviving children.

The grandson Henny reared at Gales Neck, Jesse Carroll Thornton, saw a basic difference between his grandparents, whom he called Mama and Papa: "I loved both of them," he said. "If there is a heaven, I know Mama is there. Papa, maybe not."

The physical remains of the U-boat war on America are scattered along the coast for those who know where to look.

A periscope salvaged from the U-190 is installed in the Crow's Nest Officers Club in the old section of St. John's, Newfoundland. Patrons at the bar can peer through the periscope at the city's magnificent harbor, from which convoys set out across the North Atlantic to Britain.

An anchor from the destroyer USS *Roper*—which rescued the lifeboat baby and then sank the first U-boat in U.S. waters—is displayed at the entrance to the Pratt School of Naval Architecture and Marine Engineering at the Massachusetts Institute of Technology in Cambridge, Massachusetts. MIT had no particular connection with the *Roper* but requested an anchor at a time when the destroyer was about to be scrapped.

Two Liberty ships that sailed in World War II still operate today as floating museums that take visitors on harbor cruises out of Baltimore and San Francisco. The Baltimore-based *John W. Brown* offers lunch and tours, with flyovers by World War II–vintage warplanes. Other surviving Liberty ships sit in mothballs in the U.S. government's reserve fleets, collecting dust and seagull droppings, waiting their turns in the scrap yard.

The U-505, which torpedoed Mellin Respess on the *Thomas McKean* and then was captured by a hunter-killer group two days before D-Day, is a marquee attraction at the Museum of Science and Industry in Chicago.* Every year, approximately 2 million museum visitors squeeze through the narrow, dimly lit U-505 for a sense of what life was like on the devil's shovel.

The U-85's main hatch and the Enigma machine it carried are on display in the Graveyard of the Atlantic Museum in Hatteras Village, on the southern tip of Hatteras Island on the North Carolina Outer Banks. A few elderly residents of the island still remember waking up at night to the rattling of their windows from torpedo strikes on ships offshore.

The sea continues to reveal secrets of the U-boat war.

Off the Outer Banks in 1965, the scallop boat *Snoopy* hauled up a live torpedo in its nets. When the crew attempted to disentangle it, the torpedo exploded, killing eight of the twelve men on board. A decade later, another fishing boat pulled up a torpedo in its nets off Rhode Island. A U.S. Navy ordnance disposal team blew it up at a safe distance from the boat. Other live ordnance from the U-boat war surely waits on the ocean bottom for the unlucky.

In September 1992, a group of elite divers discovered the wreck of a U-boat about 60 miles off the coast of Point Pleasant, New Jersey. How it ended up there was not clear from either the Allied or German war records. The wreck lay in 230 feet of water, and diving it was especially dangerous because of strong, shifting currents and blinding silt, but the divers were determined to identify it. Two divers lost their lives over the course

---

* Admiral Gallery, the commander of the hunter-killer group that captured the U-505 off South Africa two days before D-Day in 1944, was a Chicago native who pulled strings with the Navy to have the sub spared from destruction and made available to the museum. An American crew sailed the U-boat up the St. Lawrence River and across four of the five Great Lakes to the shore of Lake Michigan, where it was hauled a short distance overland to the museum.

of a five-year search before an artifact from the sub identified it as the U-869, which had vanished in December 1944. The sub may have been sunk by one of its own malfunctioning acoustic torpedoes, a "circle runner" that circled back to its source after being launched.

In 2014, oceanographer and shipwreck archaeologist Robert Ballard explored the wreck of the U-166 in the Gulf of Mexico off the Louisiana coast and changed the Navy's conclusions about who sank the sub. Ballard and his team of explorers used unmanned, remotely operated vehicles (ROVs) to dive down to the wreck, 5,000 feet deep, and send up high-resolution images. The images showed devastating damage to the U-166's bow, which suggested a depth charge had exploded against it, as the commander of a Navy patrol vessel had claimed in 1942.

The Navy had originally discounted the patrol vessel's claim of sinking the sub, and further criticized the vessel's commander, Herbert G. Claudius, for errors in conducting the depth charge attack. The Navy had credited the sinking to a Coast Guard bomber. The wreck of the U-166 sat undiscovered until 2001, when an oil company stumbled upon it while exploring the gulf bottom for a route for a natural gas pipeline. No one closely examined the U-166 wreckage until Ballard in 2014. After he presented his findings, the Navy shifted credit for the sinking of the U-166 to Claudius and posthumously awarded him a medal for heroism in battle. His son accepted it on his behalf.

Also in 2014, a research team with the U.S. National Oceanic and Atmospheric Administration (NOAA) found the wreck of the U-576 about 30 miles off the North Carolina Outer Banks. The U-576 was bombed by a U.S. plane after sinking the Nicaraguan freighter *Bluefields*, whose wreckage lies only 240 yards from the sub's.

The U-576 and the *Bluefields* are only two of hundreds of World War II shipwrecks resting on the seabed of America's shallow continental shelf. More than eighty such wrecks lie off the Outer Banks of North Carolina, which is sometimes called the Graveyard of the Atlantic. For thirty years those wrecks were ignored by everyone except fishermen, who took note of them because they attracted fish. Recreational divers discovered the World War II wrecks in the 1970s, creating a cottage industry of dive shops, charter boats, and historical guidebooks. Divers had gradually stripped the U-boats and other wrecks of all recognizable artifacts by the beginning of the twenty-first century, when NOAA began discouraging the practice.

Jim Bunch, a veteran diver from North Carolina, said divers had long assumed they could keep whatever they found in the old wrecks. He had gone on dive trips with off-duty FBI agents and North Carolina state investigators. Bunch took pictures, mostly, but brought up several artifacts, including the U-85's Enigma machine. "We did it for the thrill, crawling into narrow spaces, fighting the current and the low visibility, and then the fun of showing pieces to our friends," said Bunch, who is now in his seventies. "No one was in it for the money."

Then, in 2004, President George W. Bush signed the Sunken Military Craft Act, which made it clear that any sunken military vessel belonged to its nation's government, and that disturbing the dead or removing artifacts was illegal. Jim Bunch donated the Enigma machine to the Graveyard of the Atlantic Museum in Hatteras, which obtained permission from the German government to display it.

NOAA is considering adding the U-boats and some of the sunken merchant ships to its marine sanctuary program, which protects historic wrecks such as the Civil War ironclad *Monitor* off Cape Hatteras. Some divers are angry over what they consider government overreaching, but Bunch said the issue is moot: All the World War II wrecks that remain undisturbed are either too deep or too hazardous for divers, and chemicals in the seawater are breaking down the old ships into unrecognizable piles of metal.

The U-boat war has continued to stir emotions.

In the late 1960s, George Betts of Milo, Maine, was reading a German book about the U-boat war and found a clue to the fate of his father's ship, the Marine Transport Lines oil tanker *Muskogee*, which had vanished in 1942 with all hands, including Nat Foster of Mathews. According to the book, Reinhard Hardegan and the U-123 had sunk a tanker named the *"Muscogee"* on March 22, 1942. Betts contacted a U.S. Navy archivist who examined newly declassified records, including the captured logbook of the U-123. The records showed Hardegan's sub had indeed sunk Betts's father's tanker, the *Muskogee*. Betts tracked down Hardegan, a retired businessman in Bremen, West Germany, and the two exchanged cordial letters.

"I'm glad that you are not angry at me," Hardegan wrote, "and you have the right idea, that all soldiers did their duty. The single persons were not our enemies and when we sunk a ship, the sailors etc. were comrades and we tried to help them as much as we could. In the case of *Muskogee* I was not able to [take] the crew on board, because we were westbound and had no place for so many people." Hardegan told Betts the *Muskogee* sank so fast that her crew only had time to launch two rafts. The U-123 approached the rafts and offered the men food, water, and cigarettes. But the castaways were hundreds of miles from land, Hardegan wrote, "and it was bad for us all to let them alone with the wind and sea . . . This personal contact with men probably condemned to death was one of the moments which shows me that this must be the last war . . ."

Hardegan gave Betts copies of photos the U-123's propaganda photographer had taken of the *Muskogee* sinking, as well as a series of photos of the U-boat approaching the rafts. The last photo in the series is one of the most haunting images of the U-boat war. It shows seven doomed castaways facing the U-boat. Two of them appear to be shouting, but others stare hollow-eyed, knowing they can expect no salvation from the Germans, or from anyone.

Betts was relieved to know at last what had happened to his father, and he figured that family members of the thirty-three other men killed on the *Muskogee* would feel the same. He set out in the late 1980s to share his knowledge with them, including the relatives of Nat Foster. Betts tracked down children, grandchildren, nephews, cousins, and great-nieces. The NBC TV show *Unsolved Mysteries* publicized his quest. Most of the family members he contacted thanked him. "After all these years, due to your perseverance, we now know what happened," one wrote. But not all the families wanted to revisit the past. Betts identified two of the seven men on the raft in the photograph, and suspected Nat Foster was one of the others. He mailed a copy of the photo to Foster's sister, Lucy Marchant. She thanked him but concluded, "I do not need further information. I am unable to identify my brother in this picture."

German relatives of the crew of the U-85 gather occasionally on April 14 in the Hampton National Cemetery in Virginia, where the twenty-nine bodies recovered in 1942 were buried in unmarked graves. Today the U-boat men's graves are marked in the same style as the American graves, though they are kept separate from them. A cousin of the U-85's captain called the killing of the sub's crew in the water by the *Roper*'s depth charges "murder." But the families of other U-85 crewmen apologized for Germany's actions in the war.

Farther south, on Ocracoke Island, North Carolina, a memorial service is held every May for four British sailors from the armed trawler HMT *Bedfordshire*, who are buried on the island. The *Bedfordshire*, one of the twenty-four antisubmarine trawlers lent to the United States by the British to help protect the East Coast, was torpedoed by a U-boat off the Outer Banks on May 14, 1942, with the loss of all hands. The bodies of two of the trawler's Royal Navy crew washed up in the surf at Ocracoke—one of very few cases in which the bodies of U-boat victims washed up on American beaches. Two more bodies of the *Bedfordshire* crew were found in the shallow water just offshore. All four of the Brits were buried with military honors in Ocracoke's cemetery. Today, the sailors' graves are enclosed by a wooden picket fence and shaded by live oaks. Two more of the *Bedfordshire* sailors are buried in a rural part of Virginia Beach.

Two British merchant mariners from the British freighter *San Delfino*, whose bodies washed up on Hatteras Island, are buried a short distance from the iconic, candy-striped Cape Hatteras Lighthouse. The men's graves are adorned with flowers and seashells.

The lifeboat baby, Jesse Roper Mohorovicic, who was born after the

City of New York was torpedoed in 1942, gradually escaped the scrutiny of the tabloid press and became a shipping company executive. He shortened his last name to Mohorovic, shaving off the last "ic" for easier pronunciation in the business world. Jesse never mentioned the circumstances of his birth unless someone asked him directly where he was born. "It's really my mother's story," he would tell people. "I didn't do anything." In fact, he felt like "the football at the Rose Bowl." His mother never talked about how hard it had been for her in the lifeboat. She never lost sight of the fact that she had been one of the lucky ones. Jesse felt a lifelong attachment to the U.S. Merchant Marine. He had been born in the midst of its finest hour. Before he died of lung cancer in 2009, he would witness firsthand its steep decline.

The U.S. merchant fleet shrank steadily after the sell-off of vessels after World War II, despite temporary revivals during the wars in Korea, Vietnam, and the Persian Gulf. One by one, the Bull Line, Moore-McCormack, and other American companies went bankrupt or were swallowed up by competitors. By the 1980s, U.S. flag ships had become so costly to operate that they could no longer compete for international trade. Unionized U.S. mariners were paid three and four times as much as their counterparts from Eastern Europe and the Philippines. U.S. flag ships were subject to U.S. taxes and U.S. Coast Guard safety regulations, which added still more overhead costs. A shipowner who wanted to avoid paying the high wages, taxes, and costs of complying with U.S. safety regulations could simply switch the flag of his vessel to that of a country with no such requirements. Nations such as Liberia, Panama, and the Marshall Islands offered "flags of convenience" under which merchant ships, in exchange for registration fees, could sail with low-paid, foreign crews and avoid taxes and many safety requirements.

The U.S. government did not allow the U.S. Merchant Marine to disappear, as most private businesses would after pricing themselves out of the market. The federal Jones Act restricts the shipment of cargo between U.S. ports to U.S. flag vessels built in American shipyards, giving American mariners and shipyard workers a near monopoly on coastal shipping. The

U.S. government also continues to use subsidies to sustain a fleet of U.S. flag vessels capable of hauling supplies overseas for America's next war. The current subsidies include longstanding Cargo Preference laws, which require a percentage of America's food aid to foreign countries to be shipped on U.S. flag ships, even though the cost is higher than hauling those supplies on foreign-flagged vessels. In addition, the government's Maritime Security Program pays yearly stipends to the private owners of sixty U.S.-flagged cargo ships to keep those vessels flying the U.S. flag and available immediately to the government if needed. The vessels in the Maritime Security Program comprise the bulk of the eighty-one privately owned U.S.-flagged commercial ships that are still engaged in international trade.

The number of U.S. merchant mariners actively sailing internationally has plummeted from a high of about 250,000 at the end of World War II to roughly 11,000 today. Those 11,000 mariners compete for only about 5,000 jobs. The number of mariners and jobs has been shrinking fast for almost a decade, with little apparent prospect of a reversal. But more than 200,000 American merchant mariners are licensed or certified to sail along the coast or in inland waters on smaller vessels, ranging from tugboats to fishing boats, dive charter boats, and water taxis. Most Mathews men still working on the water are fishermen and tugboat operators. One of Captain Jesse and Henny's great-grandsons, David Callis, is captain of a tug in the Gulf of Mexico and returns to Mathews when he has time ashore. David revels in the Hodges family seafaring history and tells salty tales about Captain Jesse and his boys. Jimmy Hunley, son of Captain Will Hunley and a cousin of the Hodges brothers, is captain of a tug in New York Harbor. He said well over a dozen Mathews men work on tugs. "I can't go anywhere in the tugboat crowd without people asking me if I know other tugboat men from Mathews."

It took Congress forty-three years after Roosevelt's request to extend veterans' benefits to World War II merchant mariners, which lawmakers finally voted on in 1988. Most of the mariners who faced the U-boats were dead by then, but some of those still alive were grateful for access to Veterans Administration hospitals after the old Marine Hospitals were shuttered.

Joseph Elliott of Mathews, who had seen action on a Liberty ship during the war, sought treatment at VA hospitals for post-traumatic stress disorder. When he was eighty years old, he would awaken his wife and daughter in the middle of the night, believing he was back in the engine room with U-boats and bombers closing in. At those moments, Joseph seemed to move about in a claustrophobic trance. He would usher his wife and daughter out of the house into the yard, even in the dead of winter. They would stay out with him until he regained his senses and led them back into the house.

One national veterans' organization, the Veterans of Foreign Wars, prohibits merchant marine veterans of World War II from joining, although some individual chapters ignore the rule.

For the past twenty years, a nonprofit advocacy group for World War II merchant mariners has tried to persuade Congress to distribute cash payouts to them. For years the group argued that each mariner who served in the war should receive $1,000 per month for the rest of his life. But in 2015 the group changed its request to a one-time $25,000 payout for each mariner. There are approximately 5,000 World War II mariners still alive, which means the payout would cost U.S. taxpayers roughly $125 million. Other Allied nations, including Britain and Canada, have made similar one-time payouts to their World War II–era merchant mariners. But the bill's chances of going anywhere in the gridlocked U.S. Congress appear low.

Mathews is still not on the way to anywhere. It remains one of Virginia's smallest and least populous counties. It is still a place young people leave in search of opportunities. Instead of jumping onto merchant ships, they move to Hampton or Newport News for jobs at medical offices and technology companies. Mathews still has no stoplights, four-lane highways, or motels. "If you come to Mathews, you are either lost or visiting somebody," said Sonny Richardson, a realtor who grew up in Mathews. Mathews still feels like the country. On Main Street, farmers leave pickup trucks full of fresh produce, for sale by the honor system. Drivers wave to one another on the back roads. Most of those back roads still narrow into country lanes, and end at the water's edge.

The story of the Mathews mariners in the U-boat war lives mostly in two small museums with irregular hours, the Gwynn's Island Museum and the Mathews Maritime Foundation's museum. The old mariners themselves are almost gone. One of the last, Bill Callis, died in December 2014.

Bill had sailed the world's oceans for forty years. He had been to the Arctic and the Antarctic, and to every country except China. When Bill came home from the sea to visit Gwynn's Island, he was unpredictable. He once tumbled drunk down the steps of his plane and landed in a heap on the tarmac. His angry wife spun around on her heels and got into the car, leaving Bill's daughters to help him up. Bill lost track of his daughters' ages while he was at sea, and sometimes brought home gifts that were ten years out of date—a giant stuffed animal, a tiny child's kimono. But Bill just as often was funny and charming on his visits. He was never dull. He loved Dunrovin' and left it to his daughters. He found it incomprehensible that anyone who owned property on the island would sell it to outsiders for vacation homes, although many of his neighbors did just that.

Louise Hodges Leigh, the last surviving child of Captain Jesse and Henny's fourteen children, died in 2011, but the Hodges family still gathers periodically in Mathews for dinings that recall Henny's celebrations at Gales Neck. A reunion of Hodges family and friends in an American Legion hall in the fall of 2014 attracted more than a hundred guests, including descendants of Raymond, Dewey, Willie, Spencer, Coleman, David, Alice, Elizabeth, Louise, and Hilda Fourteen Hodges.

Some of the Hodges grandchildren have revisited Gales Neck, which is now owned by a historic trust. The farmhouse is long empty, but well maintained. Despite a number of additions and alterations, the property looks much as it did in 1942. Willie's son, Brother Hodges, and Hilda Fourteen's son Jesse Carroll Thornton had no trouble remembering the locations of the well pump, the barn, the hog pen, the smokehouse, and the chicken house. The years seemed to fall away as they stood in the kitchen, which still had a big iron cook stove like Henny's; and in the dining room, where the furniture had been shoved aside to clear the way for square dancing. The most striking change at Gales Neck was that the farmhouse no longer commanded the headwaters of the East River. It was hidden behind a wall of marshes and foliage that had grown up along the river-bank.

The visit to Gales Neck took Brother Hodges, now in his late eighties, back. He had lost two uncles to U-boats, but he had joined the Merchant Marine in 1944 as soon as he turned seventeen. He had gone to sea not out of duty or a desire for revenge, but because the Merchant Marine offered opportunities for a young man comfortable on the water—the same reason Mathews men had always gone to sea. He said the U-boats took a toll on his family but never cowed or deterred them.

"The Hodges kept going to sea like they always had. Men all over Mathews County kept going to sea like they always had. They didn't do anything different during the war. The torpedoes just got in the way."

Hidden History, Living History

Two weeks after *The Mathews Men* was originally published, I was signing copies at the Jimmy Carter Presidential Library in Atlanta when a man came up to the table and held out a smartphone displaying an old photograph, in black and white. It showed a young German U-boat officer, with a wispy beard and his cap cocked at an angle, posing on the foredeck of his submarine. The man with the phone said, "This is my father."

He went on to tell me that his father had joined the German U-boat force late in World War II and was imprisoned by the British after Germany surrendered. When he was released, he married a young woman he had met while his U-boat was docked in Nazi-occupied Holland. Her mother was slow to warm to the idea of a U-boat officer's son for a son-in-law. She had been a nurse in England during the war, and her father had been captain of a British merchant ship. The family would always wonder if one of the old men had ever hunted the other in the North Atlantic. The couple emigrated from Germany to New York, where their son—the man with the smartphone—grew up to become a U.S. Navy aviator and then a commercial airline pilot. "It's certainly an unusual family story," he said.

"Unusual" family stories have now become a usual part of my experience of talking about *The Mathews Men*. I had always thought of the book as a work of history, helping to illuminate an overlooked chapter of World War II. But everywhere I go I am reminded that the U-boat war on the United States is living history, with power to touch people's lives. I think it is especially true because the stories in my book are all about the U.S. Merchant Marine, whose heroics and sacrifices in the war have been forgotten, except by family members, and sometimes even by them.

A woman in Atlanta introduced herself to me as the niece of a Mathews County sea captain whose unlucky life and loss at sea I had described in the book. Capt. Mellin Respess was torpedoed three times on three different ships over only a few months in 1942, suffering worse injuries each time, until he was finally killed in the third sinking. His contribution, and his death, rank as the highest kind of patriotic devotion and sacrifice. She was simply grateful that I had taken an interest in his efforts. I could not think of anything fitting to write in her book.

In Raleigh, North Carolina, I was telling the story of the sinking of the oil tanker *Muskogee* and showing a photograph, taken by a German U-boat crew, of seven crewmen from the torpedoed ship clinging to a raft in rough seas, doomed (see page 15 in the first photo insert). Some of the men in the photo had eventually been identified by friends and families, and I mentioned them by name. I noticed a woman in the audience fighting back emotion. She told me later that one of the men believed to be on the raft, Nat Foster of Mathews, was her uncle. She had never known how he died, or seen the photo of the men on the raft. She had been astonished to hear me speak his name. She quickly contacted her sister in New Mexico and they agreed to study the photo together, to try to determine, after 74 years, whether it was really her uncle Nat. Either way, she said, the photo "is priceless to us." By the time our conversation ended, I was as shaken as she was.

Not all the family secrets are sad, of course. After an appearance in Arlington, Virginia, I went out to dinner with Joe Mohorovic, the son of the "Lifeboat Baby," Jesse Roper Mohorovic, whose story is told in chapter five. Jesse was born in a lifeboat off Cape Hatteras, North Carolina, after his mother's ship was torpedoed by a U-boat in a storm. I had interviewed Jesse before his death and told his story in the book. The unusual circumstances of his birth had shaped his life. He was named for the U.S. Navy destroyer that rescued him, his mother, and his sister from the lifeboat. The ship owner paid his way through college, and he went on to become a shipping company executive and a vice president at CSX Corp. He never mentioned his lifeboat birth unless someone asked where he was born. Jesse's family has quietly cherished the story but has followed his advice to look ahead, not behind, said his son Joe, who is a commissioner with the U.S. Product Safety Commission in Washington, D.C.

Almost everywhere I spoke about the book I met relatives of the main characters—members of the Hodges, Callis, Hudgins and Respess families. They and others told me stories I wished I had known when I was writing the book. I particularly liked the story of a man who volunteered to help defend America's coastline and had been given command of a large sailboat that had been jury-rigged to drop depth charges from the stern. The sailboat was assigned to protect convoys off the coast but to stay far enough away from them that men in the convoys would not realize the sailboat was all the protection they had.

I met lots of mariners, and their widows and children. Some just thanked me for writing the book. Others asked my advice in researching their loved ones' records. They brought new meaning to what my publisher called "non-traditional" readers: an old mariner's daughter said *The Mathews Men* was the first book he had read in fifty years. I met military families who saw their own lives in the book's depiction of mariners risking their lives far away while their families waited helplessly. I was not surprised to encounter people with close connections to the sea in Baltimore, New Orleans, Falmouth on Cape Cod, and of course Mathews, where seafaring families filled the high school auditorium for my book talk. But I also met merchant marine veterans in Columbus, Ohio, Southern Pines, North Carolina, and Nashville, Tennessee. After a while, I would walk into every venue scanning the people in attendance and wondering who would emerge to tell me an unexpected story that day.

Unfortunately, too many of the stories were tinged with sadness. As I explain in the book, after World War II, merchant mariners were left out of the GI Bill and most other government benefits, despite having suffered a higher casualty rate than any branch of the U.S. military. Petitions for help from Congress have so far failed, but Congress is not the only avenue to put something right. Most of the Mathews men I met would be pleased if the Merchant Marine merely found a place in the American narrative of "How We Won the War." "Maybe when your book comes out, my grandkids will finally believe I did something useful in the war," one Mathews man told me.

There is no time to lose. When I started work on *The Mathews Men* in earnest in 2011, there were about fifteen old World War II mariners living in and around Mathews. Today there are about four or five. One of my favorite Mathews men, Bill Callis, told me in our last conversation, "If you want me to read this book, you better hurry up and write it." Three weeks later I went to his funeral. We are almost at the point where we will have to reconstruct World War II stories entirely from documents rather than from talking with people who were there. I hope this book can help encourage people to preserve the stories of all the men and women who sacrificed so much to win that war, through families and friends telling and sharing. The time to start is right now.

LOCATIONS OF THE MATHEWS MEN'S SHIPS

ARCTIC CIRCLE

Jan Mayen Island

Iceland

Norway

United Kingdom

Ireland

German Axis Controlled, 1942

Atlantic Ocean

Canada

Newfoundland

Azores Is.

USA

Chesapeake Bay
Mathews County, VA

Bermuda

Gulf of Mexico

Canary Is.

Caribbean Sea

Cape Verde Is.

Area of Detail

EQUATOR

Atlantic Ocean

0 Miles 1000 2000
0 Kilometers 2000
Scale at Equator

USA

Bermuda

Atlantic Ocean

Gulf of Mexico

Bahamas

MEXICO

CUBA

Jamaica

HAITI

DOM. REP.

Puerto Rico

Caribbean Sea

PANAMA

Trinidad

Pacific Ocean

COLOMBIA

VENEZUELA

© 2016 Jeffrey L. Ward

SUNK OR DAMAGED IN WORLD WAR II

1. **NORVANA**, General location: off coast of North Carolina
   Position: unknown
   Sunk – January 22, 1942

2. **MAJOR WHEELER**, General location: East Coast of United States
   Position: unknown
   Sunk – February 6, 1942

3. **LAKE OSWEYA**, General location: North Atlantic
   Position: 43.14 N/64.45 W
   Sunk – February 20, 1942

4. **MARY**, General location: 250 mi. NE of Paramaribo, Dutch Guiana
   Position: 8.25 N/52.50 W
   Sunk – March 3, 1942

5. **BARBARA**, General location: 9 mi. NNW of Tortuga Island
   (Dominican Republic)
   Position: 20.10 N/73.05 W
   Sunk – March 7, 1942

6. **COLABEE**, General location: 10 mi. off Cape Verde, Cuba
   Position: 22.14 N/77.35 W
   Damaged – March 12, 1942

7. **E.M. CLARK**, General location: 22 mi. SE of Cape Hatteras, NC
   Postion: 34.50 N/73.35 W
   Sunk – March 18, 1942

8. **OAKMAR**, General location: 300 mi. E of Cape Hatteras, NC
   Position: 36.22 N/68.50 W
   Sunk – March 20, 1942

9. **MUSKOGEE**, General location: 450 mi. SE of Bermuda
   Position: 28 N/58 W
   Sunk – March 22, 1942

10. **DIXIE ARROW**, General location: 12 mi. off Cape Hatteras, NC
    lighted buoy
    Position: 35 N/75.33 W
    Sunk – March 26, 1942

11. **HARRY F. SINCLAIR JR.**, General location: 7 mi. S of Cape Lookout, NC
    Position: 34.25 N/76.30 W
    Damaged – April 11, 1942

12. **NORLINDO**, General location: 200 mi. NE of Havana, Cuba
    Position: 24.57 N/84 W
    Sunk – May 4, 1942

13. **DELISLE**, General location: 15 mi. outside of Jupiter Inlet, FL
    Position: 27.05 N/80.05 W
    Damaged – May 4, 1942 (the same ship appears later in this list,
    sunk this time, on October 19, 1943)

14. **GREEN ISLAND**, General location: 80 mi. SW of Grand Cayman Island
    Position: 18.25 N/81.30 W
    Sunk – May 6, 1942

15. **VIRGINIA**, General location: 1.5 mi. from the mouth of
    the Mississippi River
    Position: 28.53 N/89.29 W
    Sunk – May 12, 1942

16. **GULFPENN**, General location: 30 mi. from the entrance to
    the Mississippi River
    Position: 28.29 N/89.12 W
    Sunk – May 13, 1942

17. **ELIZABETH**, General location: 30 mi. S of Cape Corrientes, Cuba
    Position: 21.36 N/84.48 W
    Sunk – May 20, 1942

18. **SYROS**, General location: Barents Sea, 200 mi. SW of Bear Island
    Position: 72.35 N/5.30 E
    Sunk – May 26, 1942

19. **ALAMAR**, General location: 100 mi. SE of Bear Island,
    Position: 74 N/20 E
    Sunk – May 27, 1942

20. **CITY OF ALMA**, General location: 400 mi. NE of San Juan, Puerto Rico
    Position: 23 N/62.30 W
    Sunk – June 2, 1942

21. **ROBERT C. TUTTLE**, General location: within 5 mi. of Virginia Beach, VA
    Position: 36.51 N/75.51 W
    Damaged – June 15, 1942

22. **MILLINOCKET**, General location: off La Isabella Island, Cuba
    Position: 23.12 N/79.58 W
    Sunk – June 17, 1942

23. **MANUELA**, General location: 75 mi. E of Cape Lookout, NC
    Position: 34.30 N/75.40 W
    Sunk – June 24, 1942

24. **RUTH**, General location: 100 mi. N of Cape Maysi, Cuba
    Position: 21.44 N/74.05 W
    Sunk – June 29, 1942

25. **THOMAS MCKEAN**, General location: 350 mi. NE of Puerto Rico
    Position: 22 N/60 W
    Sunk – June 29, 1942

26. **CITY OF BIRMINGHAM**, General location: 250 mi. E of Cape Hatteras, NC
    Position: 35.16 N/74.25 W
    Sunk – June 30, 1942

27. **NORLANDIA**, General location: 25 mi. NE of Cape Samana,
    Dominican Republic
    Position: 19.33 N/68.39 W
    Sunk – July 3, 1942

28. **MASSMAR**, General location: NW coast of Iceland; Allied minefield
    Position: 66.39 N/22.33 W
    Sunk – July 5, 1942

29. **ONEIDA**, General location: 2 mi. N of Cape Maysi, Cuba
    Position: 20.17 N/74.06 W
    Sunk – July 13, 1942

30. **ONONDAGA**, General location: 5 mi. N of Cayo Guillermo, Cuba
    Position: 22.40 N/78.44 W
    Sunk – July 23, 1942

31. **COMMERCIAL TRADER**, General location: 75 mi. E of Trinidad
    Position: 10.30 N/60.15 W
    Sunk – September 16, 1942

32. **MAE**, General location: 100 mi. N of Georgetown, British Guiana
    Position: 8.03 N/58.13 W
    Sunk – September 17, 1942

33. **STEEL NAVIGATOR**, General location: North Atlantic
    Position: 49.45 N/31.20 W
    Sunk – October 19, 1942

34. **EAST INDIAN**, General location: 275 mi. SW of Cape Town, South Africa
    Position: 37.23 S/13.34 E
    Sunk – November 3, 1942

35. **COLLINGSWORTH**, General location: 100 mi. NE of Paramaribo,
    Dutch Guiana
    Position: 7.12 N/55.37 W
    Sunk – January 9, 1943

36. **ROGER B. TANEY**, General location: South Atlantic
    Position: 22 S/7.45 W
    Sunk – February 3, 1943

37. **BENJAMIN HARRISON**, General location: 150 mi. ENE of Terceira, Azores
    Position: 39.09 N/24.15 W
    Sunk – March 16, 1943

38. **ROBERT ROWAN**, General location: Harbor of Gela, Sicily, 5 mi. from shore
    Position: unknown
    Sunk – July 11, 1943

39. **CAPE MOHICAN**, General location: off the coast of Libya
    Position: 33.42 N/16.43 E
    Damaged – August 21, 1943

40. **DELISLE (AGAIN)**, General location: off the coast of Newfoundland
    Position: 47.19 N/52.27 W
    Sunk – October 19, 1943

42. **PENELOPE BARKER**, General location: 115 mi. from North Cape, Norway
    Position: 73.22 N/22.30 E
    Sunk – January 24, 1944

43. **PAUL HAMILTON**, General location: off the Algerian coast
    Position: 37.02 N/3.41 E
    Sunk – April 20, 1944

THE MATHEWS MEN AND WOMEN

The Hodges Family

Capt. Jesse Hodges

Tugboat and steamboat captain, and patriarch of the Hodges clan. He survived the war. Six of his sons would become merchant sea captains.

Capt. Raymond Hodges

The eldest of the fourteen Hodges children. Captain of the Moore-McCormack deep-water freighter *Mormacmoon*, crossing the North Atlantic in numerous large convoys under attack by U-boat wolf packs. He lived to become captain of a luxury cruise ship.

Capt. Dewey Hodges

Second oldest of the Hodges children, he was captain of the Ford Motor Co. flagship *East Indian.* Temporary captain of Ford freighter *Onondaga* on July 23, 1942, when it was torpedoed by the U-129 off Cuba. Dewey and three other Mathews men were killed.

Capt. Willie Hodges

The jolly and highly skilled captain of oceangoing tugboats, he sailed in dangerous waters until his sisters asked him to stay ashore after two of his brothers had been killed. He survived the war.

Capt. Coleman Hodges

The fourth son, driven by ambition and a sense of duty to become captain of a ship during the war. Commanding the Liberty ship *Edward A. Savoy*, he sailed on the notorious Murmansk Run through the Arctic Circle to North Russia, and to Antwerp, Belgium, where German V-1 buzz bombs rained down. He survived the war but died of illness at age fifty-one.

Capt. Leslie Hodges

An outlier among the seven Hodges brothers, dark and quiet, he became a captain but was serving as first officer aboard the freighter *Oneida* on July 13, 1942, when it was torpedoed by the U-166 off Cuba. Leslie died, apparently while trying to rescue another man.

Spencer Hodges

The only Hodges son to choose a career ashore, after he severely injured his back as a teenager while working on his brother Dewey's ship. Served as a recruiter in Mathews for crewmen for his brothers' ships. Became sheriff of Mathews.

Capt. David Hodges

The youngest of the Hodges brothers, he quit going to sea before the war and spent World War II working in one of the scores of U.S. shipyards racing to build new ships. After the war he became a captain and worked as a federal pilot guiding ships up and down the channels and into the ports of the Chesapeake Bay.

Horace "Brother" Hodges

The son of Willie Hodges, he went to sea toward the end of the war, as soon as he reached the qualifying age of seventeen. He sailed on Liberty ships in war zones but none of his ships were hit. He survived the war.

Herman "Bill" Hodges

The younger son of Captain Raymond Hodges, Bill joined the Merchant Marine toward the end of the war, when he turned seventeen, and sailed on Liberty ships to the Mediterranean and the coast of France. He survived the war.

James Wilber "Will" Hunley

A Hodges cousin, he followed his cousin and boyhood friend David Hodges to sea on Raymond Hodges's ship. Will went on to become captain of the freighter *Commercial Trader*. On September 16, 1942, the ship was torpedoed off Trinidad by the U-558. He survived and went back to sea, sailing through the war's end and long afterward.

Henrietta "Henny" Hodges

The matriarch of the Hodges family of Gales Neck, she reared fourteen children and ran the family's forty-acre farm, with little help from her husband, Captain Jesse Hodges, who was always on a tugboat.

The Hodges daughters

Alice, Elizabeth, Louise, and Hilda Fourteen Hodges rarely agreed on anything, but after two of their brothers were killed by U-boats, they took the unusual step of asking their father and brothers to stop sailing in war zones.

Edna Hodges

Dewey Hodges's wife, she received word of his death in a jarring manner, and afterward struggled with the court system to get the money to support her family. She received Dewey's ring.

The Callis Family

Capt. Homer R. Callis

One of three sea-captain sons of Willie and Lucy Callis of Gwynn's Island, Homer guided the freighter *Mae* through a ferocious U-boat attack in the Caribbean in 1942, but his new ship, the *Cape Mohican*, was torpedoed by accident by a British warship in the Mediterranean in 1943. He survived the war but lost a son and a brother.

Homer Callis Jr.

The twenty-one-year-old son of Captain Homer Callis, he served as a U.S. Navy quartermaster in the Pacific and was killed when the bridge of his ship, the destroyer USS *Hazelwood*, was struck by a kamikaze off Iwo Jima on April 28, 1945.

Willie "Bill" Callis

The younger son of Captain Homer Callis and little brother of Homer Callis Jr., he went to sea after his father's ship was torpedoed, and sailed throughout the war and long afterward.

Capt. Robert Melville "Mel" Callis

Brother of Captains Homer and Rodney Callis, he was killed when his ship, the *Ruth*, was torpedoed by the U-153 off Cuba on June 29, 1942. Four other Mathews men also were killed on the *Ruth*.

Capt. Rodney Callis

Brother of Captains Homer and Mel Callis, he sailed throughout the war and served as captain of two Liberty ships. He survived the war without serious incident and sailed for years afterward.

Capt. Lewis Callis

A distant cousin of the three Callis brothers, who also lived on Gwynn's Island, he was killed when his freighter, the *Millinocket*, was torpedoed by the U-129 off Cuba on June 17, 1942.

Capt. Herbert Callis

Another Callis cousin, he survived the torpedoing of the freighter *Norlandia* on July 3, 1942, and also a trip to Murmansk in the so-called Forgotten Convoy, which was stranded for eight months in Murmansk.

Capt. William W. Callis

A Callis cousin from Gwynn's Island, he saved his freighter, the *Delisle*, from sinking by running it aground after it was torpedoed off Florida on May 4, 1942, by the U-564. He survived the war and sailed on different ships for years afterward.

Capt. Otis Levering Callis

Brother of William Callis, he sailed between the United States and Britain throughout the war on the Liberty ship *Benjamin Chew* without serious incident. Only days after he returned to Gwynn's Island from the war, he was killed in a car accident.

Nancy Callis

The wife of Captain Homer Callis of Gwynn's Island, she managed the family home and often served as the reluctant bearer of bad news when islanders were killed in the war. She lost a son to a kamikaze attack in the Pacific.

The Hudgins Family

Capt. Guy Hudgins

He commanded the Liberty ship *Zebulon B. Vance* on the Murmansk Run and during Operation Torch, the invasion of North Africa, in November 1942. He survived the war and sailed for years afterward. At age eighty-one he drowned during a morning swim in the Atlantic Ocean off Florida.

Genious Hudgins Jr.

A member of the large network of Hudgins cousins in Mathews, he survived the torpedoing of the freighter *Green Island* on May 6, 1942, by the U-125, but was killed when the *Onondaga*, under the command of Captain Dewey Hodges, was torpedoed off Cuba on July 23, 1942.

Capt. Walter Hudgins

A Gwynn's Islander, he survived the torpedoing of the *Barbara* in the Windward Passage on March 7, 1942, by the U-103, and also the torpedoing of the *Elizabeth* in nearby waters on May 20, 1942. He survived the war and sailed for years afterward.

Capt. Willard Hudgins

Another Gwynn's Islander, he took over the freighter *Mae* from Captain Homer Callis, only to have it torpedoed on his first voyage, on September 17, 1942, off British Guiana. He helped rescue Lester Smith of Mathews, whose legs were severely injured by the torpedo explosion.

Alton Hudgins

He survived the torpedoing of his freighter, the *Collingsworth*, off South America on January 9, 1943.

Allen Hudgins

He survived a sinking and a 2,400-mile lifeboat odyssey after the Liberty ship *Roger B. Taney* was torpedoed in the middle of the South Atlantic on February 3, 1943, by the U-160.

Wendell Hudgins

A Navy enlisted sailor, he died when the destroyer USS *Monaghan* was sunk by Typhoon Cobra off the Philippines on September 18, 1944.

Salome Hudgins

The wife of Genious Hudgins Jr., she tried to persuade him to stop sailing in war zones, and refused to accept his death.

The Hammond Family

William Hammond

One of three seafaring sons of a Mathews blacksmith, William survived the torpedoing of the *Norlindo* in the Gulf of Mexico on May 4, 1942, by the U-507, but was killed in the torpedoing of the *Onondaga* off Cuba on July 23, 1942, along with three other Mathews men.

Stacy Hammond

The brother of William and Clayton Hammond, he survived the torpedoing of the freighter *Oneida* off Cuba on July 13, 1942, by the U-166. Captain Leslie Hodges was killed in the sinking.

Clayton Hammond

The oldest of the three seafaring Hammond brothers, he survived the sinking of the freighter *East Indian* off South Africa on November 3, 1942, by the U-181, and was forced into a terrible choice to try to save his shipmates' lives.

The Respess Family

Capt. Mellin Respess
He was torpedoed three times on three different ships in 1942. He survived the sinking of the freighter *Oakmar* off Cape Hatteras, North Carolina, on March 20, 1942, as well as the sinking of the Liberty ship *Thomas McKean* off the British West Indies on June 29, 1942. But he was killed along with three other Mathews men when the *Onondaga* was torpedoed off Cuba on July 23, 1942, by the U-129.

Capt. Virgil Respess
Retired from the sea, he did most of the hiring for the Bull Line steamship line in Baltimore during World War II, and went out of his way to employ as many men from Mathews as possible.

Eleanor Respess
The wife of Captain Mellin Respess, she suffered as death came closer and closer to him before she finally lost him when he was torpedoed a third time in six months.

Other Mathews Men and Women

Wallace M. Albertson
A Navy electrician's mate 2nd class, he was killed after Japanese bombers sank the airplane tender USS *Langley* off Java on February 7, 1942.

James Ashberry
He survived the torpedoing of the freighter *City of Alma* in the mid-Atlantic on June 2, 1942, by the U-159.

Robert Lee Belvin Jr.

A seaman, he was killed when the *Ruth* was torpedoed by the U-153 off Cuba on June 29, 1942.

Charles Ogletree Billups Jr.

He quit a safe job in a shipyard to go to sea and was killed on his first voyage when the Liberty ship *Paul Hamilton* exploded after being torpedoed by a bomber in the Mediterranean on April 20, 1944.

Capt. Lewis P. Borum

A Gwynn's Island native, he survived a torpedoing in each world war—first in the freighter *City of Memphis* off Ireland in 1917, and then in the troopship *City of Birmingham* off the Outer Banks of North Carolina on June 30, 1942, by the U-202. Borum also rescued men in lifeboats in both wars. He survived the wars and sailed for years afterward.

Robert Lee Brown

A twenty-one-year-old seaman, he survived the torpedoing of the freighter *Mary* off South America on March 3, 1942, by the U-129. Immediately afterward, he joined the Navy.

Marion Capers

He survived the torpedoing of the freighter *East Indian* off South Africa on November 3, 1942, which killed five Mathews men. He sailed throughout the war and afterward, but was killed in 1951 when his ship sank in a hurricane.

Perry Collier

He was killed along with four other Mathews men when the freighter *Ruth* was torpedoed off Cuba on June 29, 1942, by the U-153.

Harold Davis

Along with Captain Walter Hudgins, he survived the torpedoing of both the *Barbara* in March 1842 and the *Elizabeth* three months later. Like Hudgins, he went back to sea and served throughout the war and afterward.

Vernon Davis

A seaman, he was killed when the freighter *East Indian* was torpedoed off South Africa on November 3, 1942, by the U-181.

Reginald Deagle

A young engineer, he sailed on several Liberty ships during the war. He survived without serious incident and continued sailing after the war.

Russell Dennis

He was the only survivor among the five Mathews men on the *Onondaga*, torpedoed off Cuba on July 23, 1942, by the U-129. He survived the war and sailed for years afterward.

Capt. Sam Jones Diggs

The veteran mariner was killed when the freighter *Massmar* struck a mine en route home from Murmansk on July 5, 1942.

Boyd Dixon

He survived the torpedoing of the oil tanker *E.M. Clark* off Cape Hatteras, North Carolina, on March 18, 1942, by the U-124, and apparently survived another sinking in the Gulf of Mexico and a bombing attack on the docks of southern France.

Samuel Dow

This seaman survived the torpedoing of the tanker *Dixie Arrow* off Cape Hatteras, North Carolina, on March 26, 1942, by the U-71, and witnessed an ultimate sacrifice by one of his shipmates.

Charles Edwards

A young Mathews seaman, he survived the sinking of the *Massmar* by a mine off Iceland on July 5, 1942. He continued sailing throughout the war and afterward.

Joseph Elliott

He joined the Merchant Marine to help feed his family and served on several Liberty ships. He survived the war and continued sailing afterward.

Benny Fitchett

This young mariner joined the Merchant Marine in the middle of the war and sailed on Liberty ships to the Mediterranean and the Pacific. He survived the war and continued sailing long afterward.

William Coles Forrest Jr.

A seaman, he survived the mining of the tanker *Robert C. Tuttle* at the mouth of the Chesapeake Bay on June 15, 1942. He survived the war but lost a brother, Wilson, on the *East Indian* on November 3, 1942.

Wilson Forrest

A seaman, he was killed after the torpedoing of the freighter *East Indian* off South Africa on November 3, 1942, by the U-181.

Nat D. Foster

A Mathews native living in Maine, he was killed when the oil tanker *Muskogee* was torpedoed off the mid-Atlantic coast on March 22, 1942, by the U-123.

Roland Foster Jr.

He survived the sinking of the freighter *Thomas McKean* in mid-ocean on June 29, 1942, by the U-505, and apparently survived the bombing of another ship in the Pacific later in the war. He sailed for years afterward.

Roland Harold Garrett

He survived the torpedoing of the Liberty ship *Benjamin Harrison* in the Mediterranean off Algeria on March 16, 1943, by the U-172.

William Burton Gay

A Navy machinist mate 1st class, he was reported missing early in the war after the fall of the Philippines, and was later discovered to have died in the Japanese prison camp Cabanatuan on July 16, 1942.

Capt. Robert Gayle

The captain of the collier *Achilles*, he survived a close encounter with a U-boat in dense fog off Rhode Island in 1942. He sailed throughout the rest of the war without serious incident.

John Elmo Godsey Jr.

He survived the torpedoing of the freighter *Manuela* off the Outer Banks of North Carolina on June 24, 1942, by the U-404, and later survived a collision between his ship and another vessel near the mouth of the Chesapeake Bay.

Allenby Grimstead

A shipmate of Robert Brown's, he also survived the sinking of the *Mary* off South America on March 3, 1942, by the U-129. He kept sailing merchant ships throughout the war and afterward.

Paul Grubb

He survived the mining of the freighter *Delisle* off Newfoundland on October 19, 1943, and helped to rescue the ship's captain by separating him from his trapped wooden leg.

William Franklin Hale

A Navy seaman 2nd class, he was killed after the cruiser USS *Indianapolis* was torpedoed off the Philippines by a Japanese submarine on July 30, 1945, after delivering the uranium-235 for the first atomic bomb to the island of Tinian.

George Ernest Harrison

He was killed when the freighter *Major Wheeler* was torpedoed off the mid-Atlantic coast on February 6, 1942, by the U-107.

Capt. Stanley Hodges

A distant relative of Captain Jesse Hodges, he survived the torpedoing of the tanker *Gulfpenn* near the mouth of the Mississippi River on May 13, 1941, by the U-506. He went back to sea.

Capt. Elvin "Bubba" Lewis

He got a head start on World War II when he tried to drive the oil tanker *Nantucket Chief* through a Fascist blockade during the Spanish Civil War, and was captured and whipped with rubber hoses. He survived that experience and sailed tankers throughout World War II and afterward.

Victor "Bud" Majette

A young seaman, he survived the bombing of the freighter *Alamar* on the Murmansk Run on May 27, 1942, and then the mining of *Alamar*'s sister ship, the *Massmar*, on the way home from Murmansk, off Iceland, on July 5, 1942. He sailed for the rest of the war and afterward.

Lemuel Marchant

Second officer of the *East Indian*, he was killed after the ship was torpedoed off South Africa on November 3, 1942, by the U-181.

Capt. Levy Morgan

The Gwynn's Island captain was killed when the freighter *Colabee* was torpedoed off Cuba on March 13, 1942, by the U-126.

Howard Dale Morris

The second officer of the *Ruth*, he was killed when the ship was torpedoed by the U-153 off Cuba on June 29, 1942.

Bernard Pierson

He died after the torpedoing of the freighter *East Indian* in the deep ocean off South Africa on November 3, 1942. He gave up a safe seat in the ship's only lifeboat to an injured man, and took the man's place on a raft.

Capt. T. O. Rainier

The commander of the troopship *Cape Victory*, he delivered the crew and support staff of the B-29 Superfortress *Enola Gay* to the island of Tinian in 1945 for the mission of dropping the first atomic bomb on Hiroshima, Japan.

William Cecil Ripley Jr.

A seaman, he was killed when his freighter, the *Syros*, was torpedoed on the Murmansk Run on May 26, 1942.

Lottie Smith

The fiancée and then wife of mariner Lester Smith, she worried constantly about him while he was at sea and helped him recover from devastating injuries.

Thomas Lester Smith

He suffered severe injuries to his legs when the freighter *Mae* was torpedoed off British Guiana on September 17, 1942, by the U-515. He went back to sea and sailed for the rest of the war and afterward.

Bernard Stansbury

A gun captain in the Naval Armed Guard, he survived the bombing and explosion of the Liberty ship *Robert Rowan* off Sicily on July 11, 1943, and, on his very next voyage, the torpedoing of the Liberty ship *Penelope Barker* on the Murmansk Run on January 24, 1944, by the U-278.

Walter Stillman

He went to sea before the war to escape farm work, and sailed throughout the war and for years afterward.

Capt. Ernest Thompson

He was the first Mathews man killed by a U-boat in World War II when the freighter *Norvana* was torpedoed off the Outer Banks of North Carolina on January 22, 1942, by the U-123.

Capt. Jack Ward

He served on several Liberty ships and often caught rides inland to visit soldiers on the battlefields of Italy. He sailed throughout the war without serious incident, and became a tanker captain afterward.

Floyd West

A young seaman, he survived the torpedoing of the tanker *Harry F. Sinclair Jr.* off Cape Hatteras on April 11, 1942, by the U-203.

Charles "Pete" White

A young seaman who joined the Merchant Marine during the war, he sailed on Liberty ships to ports in Europe. He survived the war without serious incident, and continued to sail afterward.

Merritt Franklin White

A Mathews native, he died in the inferno caused by the torpedoing of the gasoline tanker *Virginia* near the mouth of the Mississippi River on May 12, 1942, by the U-507.

Ashley Clinton Williams

One of the few black Mathews mariners, he was killed when the *Ruth* was torpedoed by the U-153 off Cuba on June 29, 1942.

Leslie Winder

He served on tankers throughout the war and distinguished himself on October 19, 1943, when he risked his life to extinguish a fire on the oil tanker *Esso Providence* at the docks in Valetta, Malta.

This list does not include all the Mathews men who sailed against the U-boats in World War II. Merchant Marine records are scattered, and some Mathews men moved to distant cities, where their connections to Mathews faded. Others left no descendants to tell their stories. Still other descendants chose to keep their stories to themselves.

AUTHOR'S NOTE

The idea for this book dates back to 1991, when as a reporter I covered a forum at which old men recalled watching merchant ships explode into flames right off the beach in my home city of Virginia Beach. I was astonished, and began reading all I could find about the U-boat war on America. A few good books told parts of the story, but they left me wanting to know more, particularly about the men on the sinking ships. They had exhibited a different type of courage than what I was used to reading about in war stories.

In 2005, I wrote two historical pieces about the U-boat war for my newspaper, the *Richmond Times-Dispatch*. But I still hadn't gotten enough of the topic, and I began to wonder if I could write the book I had not been able to find in the stacks. Six years later, while working for Maersk Line, Limited, a shipping company based in downtown Norfolk, Virginia, I was wandering around the Kirn Memorial Library (since demolished and replaced by the Slover Library) on my lunch break and ended up in a section devoted to old books on local history. I started thumbing through a dusty, forty-three-year-old edition of a yachtsmen's guide titled *A Cruising Guide to the Chesapeake*, and noticed a section about Mathews County, Virginia, where I once had lived, a short distance from tiny Gwynn's Island. One paragraph stood out from all the descriptions of the channels and shoals: "According to a local authority on the [Mathews] fish wharf who talked convincingly, 5 of the first 61 merchant marine captains whose ships were torpedoed in World War II came from Gwynn's Island—out of a population of 700 . . . [I]n 1942, 57 men from the Island were serving the Nation in some capacity, including 19 sea captains."

I wondered if that was true (it was close). And I wondered if it would be possible, seventy years after World War II, to recover enough information to tell the story of the Mathews men's experiences in the U-boat war. I called the little museum in Gwynn's Island and got a few names and phone numbers.

At that point, no one in Mathews had any reason to believe anything would come of my inquiries, but everywhere I went, old mariners took the time to tell me their stories, and their children and grandchildren dug through trunks and closets for old letters, photos, and documents. They had long ago accepted the idea that the mariners and their sacrifices had been forgotten. But they were not angry or indignant. They just seemed to enjoy the opportunity to tell the stories. I'm not sure any of them truly expected to see them in print.

Every person who spoke with me gave me a few more names and numbers. Several also told me, "Hurry." Most of the Mathews mariners from World War II were dead, and the surviving ones were in their late eighties and early nineties. Parts of the story would not be there for the telling much longer. But most of the old mariners were razor-sharp and crudely funny. They were unfailingly modest and self-effacing. Their children, grandchildren, and other family members were much the same way. They said they hoped the stories would help show what the mariners went through, how they helped to win the war. If this book does that, most of the credit belongs to them.

I am particularly indebted to the members of the Hodges family: Dewey's daughter Jean McFarlane and her husband, Mac; Coleman's daughter

Betty Fernald; Bill Hodges, the keeper of his father Raymond's memory; Louise Hodges's daughter, Stormy Heart Romaniello; Jesse Carroll Thornton, who provided great insight into the characters of his beloved grandparents, Captain Jesse and Henny; and Horace "Brother" Hodges, Willie Hodges's son, who opened doors for me with members of his family and others in Mathews.

Bill Callis informed me and entertained me with tales of his family over the course of numerous interviews. I only wish he were alive to see the result. After his death, his daughter, Lisa, picked up where Bill left off.

I am grateful to Elsa Verbyla, the longtime editor of the *Gloucester-Mathews Gazette-Journal*, who shared the paper's files and photos with me, and frequently used her encyclopedic knowledge of Mathews to put me in touch with relatives of long-lost mariners. I received valuable help from Jean Tanner at the Gwynn's Island Museum, Toni Horodysky at usmm.org, and Nathaniel Patch at National Archives II in College Park, Maryland.

This book is the product of years of support and inspiration from a long list of friends and former colleagues. The names at the top include Paul Tyler and Bill Graves, as well as Tom Kapsidelis, Bill Tangney, Rex Bowman, and Carlos Santos. Those at the *Times-Dispatch* who indulged my interest in the U-boat war include Bill Milsaps, Louise Seals, Dave Burton, Tom Silvestri, and John Dillon. Colleagues at Maersk Line, Limited, in Norfolk, including David Sloane and Bob Bowers, taught me a lot about merchant shipping.

My agent, Farley Chase, took the time to show me how to turn a concept into a book proposal. My editor at Viking, Wendy Wolf, then showed me how to turn a draft into a book. Between them, they made writing *The Mathews Men* more enjoyable than I had imagined it could be. Others at Viking I'd like to thank include Jason Ramirez, Daniel Lagin, Jeannette Williams, Ted Gilley, Melanie Tortoroli, Carolyn Coleburn, Shannon Twomey, Kate Stark, and Georgia Bodnar. Thanks also to Jeff Ward for the fine maps.

I could not have written this book without the love and support of my family. My wife, Kema, has read every sentence a half-dozen times. My son Cody plowed through early drafts with care and good humor. My son Nick and daughter, Sarah, also offered suggestions, while never letting me take myself too seriously.

NOTES ON SOURCES

I use the following abbreviations of frequently mentioned sources:

The National Archives and Records Administration (NARA) Record Group 38, kept at the Archives II branch in College Park, Maryland, contains the files of the Chief of Naval Operations and the Tenth Fleet antisubmarine command, and thus many of the documents relating to merchant ship sinkings in World War II. NARA's Record Group 26 in the main Archives building in Washington, D.C., holds Coast Guard records, including interviews with the survivors of torpedoed ships. In these notes, those two sources will be described as NARA Record Groups 38 and 26.

I use *GJ* for the *Gloucester-Mathews Gazette-Journal*, and *GJ* notes for the reporters' drafts and notes, which often contained details and comments edited out of the published articles.

Prologue: A Gift from the Predators

The description of the shark fishermen finding the ring comes primarily from a letter written by a businessman in Havana harbor on October 22, 1942, as part of his efforts to find the owner of the ring. The letter finally found its way to Dewey Hodges's family in Norfolk, Virginia, and was to be entered into court. The story was so unusual that both Norfolk news-papers, the *Virginian-Pilot* and the *Ledger-Dispatch*, printed the letter in its entirety in their November 7–8 editions. Dewey Hodges's daughter Jean also provided details of the discovery of the ring.

The description of the fishermen's experience with U-boats and their attitude toward them is based on numerous accounts of sinkings in the National Archives. As a rule, U-boats attacked fishing boats only when the fishermen radioed warnings about them. U-boats in the Caribbean also raided fishing boats for fresh food.

Dr. Jack Musick, a biologist and expert in sharks and shark fishing, provided details about the shark fishermen's operations. Musick, a profes-sor emeritus at the Virginia Institute of Marine Science (VIMS) in Glouces-ter Point, Virginia, said the Carillos most likely were poor and living hand to mouth on shark and whatever they could get in trade for them. He said the *Donatella* most likely had no motor and a single sail.

Details about the rescue of some of the *Onondaga*'s crew came from NARA Record Group 38. The file for each sunken ship typically contains a summary of the statements by survivors describing the sinking and their rescue; a two-sided card with the official Navy summary of the sinking; and any number of other documents, including investigations by Naval Intelligence, crew lists, and charts.

I found the detail about Dewey Hodges replacing the wires holding the life rafts on the Onondaga with ropes for faster launching, in NARA Rec-ord Group 26, which contains Coast Guard interviews with survivors of sunken ships about how to improve lifesaving equipment.

The descriptions of Captain Dewey Hodges were drawn from inter-views with his daughter Jean and several other people in Mathews who knew him, including Horace C. "Brother" Hodges, Bill Hodges, and Edwin Jarvis. The quote beginning, "How he loved life!" came from the book *13 Days Adrift*, self-published in 1943 by M. Stanley MacLean, Dewey's long-time ship's carpenter aboard the *East Indian*.

Dewey's last letter to his family is contained in the Chancery section of Norfolk Circuit Court, where the letter is filed as Dewey's last will and testament.

Details of the *Onondaga*'s voyage came from the vessel's Ship Movement Card in NARA Record Group 38. Such cards document each ship's port calls, including the dates of arrival and departure. Genious Hudgins's letters to his wife, Salome, provided other details. Genious's daughter, Vicki, shared her father's letters.

The information about U-129 commander Hans-Ludwig Witt came from Kenneth Wynn's *U-boat Operations of the Second World War, Vol. I* (1998). Wynn's book, in two volumes, is an extraordinary piece of work, offering encapsulated histories of individual U-boats during World War II.

The firefight between Hemingway's protagonist Thomas Hudson and a stranded U-boat crew takes place at the climax of Ernest Hemingway's novel *Islands in the Stream* (1970), which was published after his death.

Russell Dennis's descriptions of the sinking came from *GJ* articles after he returned to Mathews, and from reporters' drafts of the articles, which frequently contain more details. Dennis also is quoted in a Navy account of the sinking, and in a federal judge's ruling in the case in 1948.

Chapter One: Born to the Water

I first got to know Mathews in 1985, while I was working as a newspaper reporter for the *Newport News Daily Press* in Gloucester, Virginia. I rented the upper floor of a house on Stutts Creek in Mathews, where I could see through a gap in the barrier islands—the Hole in the Wall—out to the Chesapeake Bay. The owner, a retired Navy rear admiral, had crab pots in the creek and a dock where I would sit on warm evenings and gaze into the water at a scrum of tiny fish, crabs, jellyfish, oysters, and other creatures. I lived in Mathews for only about a year before I got a better job, but I liked the place so much that afterward I often went out of my way to visit (you always had to go out of your way to reach Mathews). The opportunity to write a book about Mathews was a special treat.

Descriptions of the poor roads in early Mathews are from articles in the *GJ.* Many of the newspaper's stories are collected in *History and Progress: Mathews County, Virginia,* published by the Mathews County Historical Society in 1982. Mathews roads remained poor well into the twentieth century. A newspaper headline in 1954 read: "Mathews County Marooned When Three-Day Rain Turns Main Roads into Quagmire."

Several people who grew up in Mathews during the 1940s described the community's way of sharing labor at harvest and hog-killing time. Benny Fitchett of Mathews told me his parents regularly sent him around to the homes of elderly and needy neighbors to lend a hand, especially when winter was approaching. His efforts on behalf of one elderly neighbor paid off when she turned out to be the beloved aunt of a girl Benny wanted to ask out. The aunt spoke glowingly of Benny, and the girl not only went out with him but ended up becoming his wife.

Descriptions of "downtown" Mathews came from interviews with people who lived in the county during the 1940s. A feature story in the *Richmond Times-Dispatch* on December 21, 1941, described the Mathews courthouse area in detail, and as "straggling." The *Times-Dispatch* published a story on the Saturday night gatherings on Mathews's Main Street on July 17, 1938.

A photo of hooded and robed Klansmen at a Mathews Fourth of July parade in 1925 appears in *Mathews County Panorama* (2000). The description of the Hodgeses' views on race relations comes from interviews with several members of the family, including Brother Hodges, Stormy Heart Romaniello, and Jesse Carroll Thornton.

The circumstances of Captain Jesse's first going to sea were described by numerous members of the Hodges family, including Brother Hodges, Jesse Carroll Thornton, Jean Hodges McFarlane, and Bill Hodges. The family history quoted was written by Raymond Hodges's granddaughter Marie Hodges.

The comment about Captain Jesse by his daughter Louise came from a taped interview with her and her brother David in 1999. The comment that Captain Jesse "played out" came from Louise on the tape too. The interviewer, Charlotte Crist, hunted down the tape for me. David Hodges found humor in having been erroneously named for the "seventh son," and had a vanity license plate of 7TH SON.

Captain Jesse's skills as a tugboat captain were lauded by several Mathews men who sailed with him, including his grandson J. W. Corbett, in an interview in 2011. J.W. said no one but Raymond Hodges could handle a ship the way Captain Jesse could.

Jean and Bill Hodges recalled Captain Jesse employing five of his seven sons on a tugboat as officers. Jean described her father Dewey Hodges's efforts to recruit men from Mathews for jobs on his ship when he came home.

The descriptions of the Callis family came from the late Bill Callis, as well as from islanders Jack Rowe and Lottie Mitchem. The "Father Neptune" article appeared in the *Mathews Journal* on February 7, 1929.

Captain Mel Callis's reflections and sea tales appeared in the *GJ* on August 4, 1938.

As a newspaper reporter, I wrote stories about the drowning deaths of fishermen who had never learned to swim. Sadly, such deaths continue to happen.

The anecdote about George Hudgins leaving home during the fall harvest came from Stacy Hammond Jr. of Mathews.

The descriptions of the various jobs on a merchant ship are based on interviews with officers and crew, but a good overall explanation can be found in Glenn A. Knoblock's *African American World War II Casualties and Decorations in the Navy, Coast Guard and Merchant Marine* (2009).

The description of a hawsepipe came from David Sloane, a former cruise ship captain and now vice president, Maersk Line, Limited, Norfolk, Virginia.

The comments about the Bull Line's preference for Mathews men were released in a prepared statement by the company and printed in the *GJ* on February 7, 1929.

The cozy arrangement by which the Respess brothers from Gwynn's

Island did all of the Bull Line's hiring was described by Bill Callis, Jack Rowe, Clarence Collier Jr., and others in interviews. Bill Callis described Virgil Respess, and the process of getting a ship.

The account of the docking of FDR's presidential yacht came from the *GJ* on July 12, 1936.

The lonely widow's letter appeared in the *GJ* in March 1926.

The accounts of Mathews men going to sea out of desperation come from Guy Hudgins's daughter, Joseph Elliott's widow and daughter, and Walter Stillman's widow.

The list of perils of the sea came from boilerplate language in a maritime insurance policy I stumbled upon while working at Maersk Line, Limited, in Norfolk in 2009.

Reginald Deagle told me the monkey story in an interview in 2014. The submarine story came from the *GJ* on September 9, 1920.

The account of Lord Dunmore's defeat at Gwynn's Island is drawn from several sources, including *History and Progress*.

The information about the tide mill at Poplar Grove and John Lennon's subsequent purchase of the property is from the *GJ* on December 11, 1980, and November 3, 1983.

The accounts of Mathews's roles in America's wars are drawn largely from the *GJ* files through *History and Progress*. The reference to Mathews being rife with "guerillas and river pirates" came from a story from the *Philadelphia Inquirer* on October 13, 1863, and was reprinted in a compilation of Gloucester and Mathews newspaper articles by Joan Charles of the Gloucester Historical Society of Virginia in 2014.

Details about the belated German attempt to blockade the U.S. coast with U-boats in World War I came from John Terraine's *Business in Great Waters* (2009), pages 133–34.

Details of the story of Captain L. F. Borum's torpedoing in World War I came from a written account by Borum's family in the Gwynn's Island Museum in Mathews. Details of Captain Elvin "Bubba" Lewis's adventures during the Spanish Civil War came from an interview with his nephew

Raymond Owens, of Mathews, in 2014; and from articles in the *GJ* on January 27 and February 3, 1938.

I examined Mathews census records for 1910, 1920, 1930, and 1940 via www.ancestry.com.

I based my descriptions of the prewar and wartime Merchant Marine on interviews with mariners including Bill Callis, Brother Hodges, and Jack Rowe, and on books including Felix Riesenberg's *Sea War* (1956), Robert Carse's *The Long Haul: The U.S. Merchant Service in World War II* (1965), John A. Butler's *Sailing on Friday: The Perilous Voyage of America's Merchant Marine* (1997), John Bunker's *Heroes in Dungarees* (2006), and *The U.S. Merchant Marine at War 1775–1945*, edited by Bruce L. Felknor (1998). My information on the U.S. Navy's wartime shipbuilding program comes from Samuel Eliot Morison's *The Battle of the Atlantic, 1939–1943* (1947), pages 27–28.

My brief descriptions of the histories of the Bull Line, Moore-McCormack Lines, and the Ford Motor Company fleet come from, respectively, the article "Bull Line," by Lt. John K. Tennant of the U.S. Maritime Service, in the November 1949 *The Mast* magazine, published by the Maritime Service; a profile of Moore-McCormack on www.moore-mccormack .com, a Web site devoted to the history of the defunct company; and interviews with Jean Hodges and other family members of Mathews men who served on Ford ships.

The report on the Reverend Belch's sermon comes from the *GJ* on November 20, 1941. The current pastor of Gwynn's Island Baptist Church, the Reverend Ed Jordan, provided background on the church and a tour.

Accounts of the fire appeared in the *GJ* on December 4, 1941. A story about Japanese crab meat flooding the market and depressing blue crab prices for Mathews crabbers appeared in the *GJ* on January 23, 1941.

Chapter Two: The Devil's Shovel
Several commanders in the first wave of U-boats wrote about encountering the storm, but the quote is from Peter Cremer's *U-boat Commander* (1984),

pages 38–39. The information about the losses of U-boat lookouts to the sea came from Timothy Mulligan's *Neither Sharks Nor Wolves* (1999), pages 19–20. Mulligan's book uses extensive research to humanize the U-boat men and puncture myths about U-boats.

Commander Reinhard Hardegan's use of a tourist map and guidebook in his attack on U.S. shores is described in Michael Gannon's *Operation Drumbeat*, page 137. Gannon's groundbreaking book surprised me with its descriptions of the ease with which the U-boats operated in American waters and the Navy's slowness to act to protect merchant ships.

The description of Germany's secret use of a Dutch company to design and build the next generation of U-boats comes from Brayton Harris's *The Navy Times Book of Submarines* (1997), page 265.

Doenitz describes his thinking about sending U-boats to America in detail in his *Memoirs: Ten Years and Twenty Days* (1959), page 196. Doenitz's recollections of his experience in a sinking U-boat are found on pages 3 and 4. The characterization of his behavior at the asylum comes from Wolfgang Frank's *The Sea Wolves* (1955), page 16. Frank was Doenitz's propagandist during the war. Germany's maneuvers to continue developing submarines after World War I are described in Harris's *Navy Times Book of Submarines*, page 265.

The account of Doenitz reporting births to his men at sea comes from Mulligan's *Neither Sharks Nor Wolves*, page 184.

Among the books and documents I consulted for descriptions of U-boats and their workings were Cremer's *U-boat Commander*; Doenitz's *Memoirs*; E. B. Gasaway's *Grey Wolf, Grey Sea* (1970); Herbert A. Werner's *Iron Coffins: A Personal Account of the German U-boat Battles of World War II* (1969); Gannon's *Operation Drumbeat* (1990); Clay Blair's *Hitler's U-boat War* (2000); Harris's *Navy Times Book of Submarines*; and Wynn's *U-boat Operations of the Second World War* (1998). A good layman's explanation of the workings of sonar and radar in the U-boat war can be found in Admirel Daniel Gallery's *Twenty Million Tons under the Sea* (1956), pages 49–57. The book recounts the capture of the U-505.

The admonition that it is better to dive too soon comes from Gordon Williamson's *U-boat Tactics in World War II* (1990), page 56. The statistic about the ineffectiveness of torpedoes on the U-48 also comes from Williamson, page 43.

The wry observations of the fictitious U-boat commander in Lothar-Gunther Buchheim's novel *Das Boot* (1975) appear on page 52 of that book.

The information about Sir Arthur Conan Doyle's and Will Rogers's commentary on U-boats came from Harris's *Navy Times Book of Submarines*, page 234.

Werner's description of a depth charge attack is from his *Iron Coffins*, page 124.

Tin-can neurosis is described by Barrie Pitt in *The Battle of the Atlantic* (1977), page 72.

The fact that Doenitz gave his U-boats artificially high numbers to make the Allies think he had more than he did came from Edwin P. Hoyt's *The U-boat Wars* (2002), page 94.

My characterization of U-boat crews' political views is drawn in part from Mulligan's *Neither Sharks Nor Wolves*, as well as from U-boat commander Hans Georg Hess's recollections in Melanie Wiggins's *U-Boat Adventures: Firsthand Accounts from World War II* (1999), page 169. The account of a U-boat commander being denounced and executed comes from *Neither Sharks Nor Wolves*, pages 232–33.

The comparison of U.S. and German submarines comes from several sources, including an essay by Bernard Zimmermann on www.uboat.net.

The account of the U-boat's fatal toilet malfunction comes from Ronald Spector's *At War at Sea* (2001), page 243.

The account of Archie Gibbs, the American seaman who spent four days as a prisoner in a U-boat, comes from the *Virginian-Pilot* of Norfolk, July 27, 1942.

The figures on the Allied shipping losses at that point in the war come from Blair's *Hitler's U-boat War*, pages 418–19. The story about the "sightings" of Gunther Prien after his disappearance comes from Spector's *At*

War at Sea, page 239. The story about another U-boat officer checking on Prien in a prison camp came from Andrew Williams's *The Battle of the Atlantic,* pages 125–26.

My information about relatively few U-boat commanders accounting for most of the losses comes from Bernard Ireland's *The Battle of the Atlantic* (1993) and Mulligan's *Neither Sharks Nor Wolves,* pages 64 and 71.

Descriptions of how convoys are formed and structured came in part from interviews with Mathews mariners and from Felknor's *The U.S. Merchant Marine at War,* page 248.

My information about the role code breaking played in the U-boat war came from Stephen Budiansky's *Blackett's War* (2013); Spector's *At War at Sea,* page 239; Hugh Sebag-Montefiore's *Enigma: The Battle for the Code* (2000); John Winton's *Ultra at Sea* (1988); and Harris's *Navy Times Book of Submarines,* page 236.

The structure of a wolf pack is described, among many other places, in Doenitz's *Memoirs* and Williamson's *U-boat Tactics of World War II.*

Descriptions of the Germans' U-boat bunkers on the French coast can be found in Doenitz's *Memoirs,* notably on page 129, and in Randolph Bradham's *Hitler's U-boat Fortresses* (2003).

For a starting point and perspective on what was happening in the United States and elsewhere at stages of the U-boat war, I used Winston Groom's *1942* (2005).

Admiral Stark's comment that America was already at war in the autumn of 1941 comes from Gannon's *Operation Drumbeat* (1990), page 92.

Doenitz describes his frustration at not being able to send more U-boats to the United States in his *Memoirs.* Another good description of the U-boat force being pulled in all directions appears in Lisle A. Rose's *Power at Sea: The Breaking Storm, 1919–1945* (2007), page 308.

Hardegan's meeting with Doenitz and his preparations for departure to America are described in Gannon's *Operation Drumbeat,* and by Hardegan himself in his war diary, translated from German to English on www.uboatarchive.net. The text of Doenitz's message to his crews came from Ed Offley's *The Burning Shore* (2014), page 69.

The account of Hardegan's attack on the *Cyclops* and the U-123's cruise past New York comes from Williams's *The Battle of the Atlantic*, page 166, and Gannon's *Operation Drumbeat*, page 213.

The account of Hardegan's crude response to his victims' failure to realize they had been torpedoed comes from Thomas Parrish's *The Submarine: A History* (2004), page 253.

Chapter Three: Missing

The description of Henny Hodges is drawn from interviews with family members and neighbors, including Jesse Carroll Thornton, Jean Hodges, Brother Hodges, Stormy Heart Romaniello, Marlene Callis, and taped interviews with Louise and David Hodges. Jesse Carroll Thornton lived with Henny alone at Gales Neck in 1942, though he was only four years old.

Most of the Hodges family had been told that Jesse and Henny's infant son James Hodges died of tuberculosis. But Stormy Heart Romaniello said her mother, Louise Hodges, told her the toddler had died of burns after falling into the fireplace at the Hodges home in Norfolk. Death certificates including causes of death were not required by the Commonwealth of Virginia at the time.

The account of little Henrietta Hodges's death in an automobile accident comes from interviews with family members and a story in the *Mathews Journal* on May 30, 1918. My description of the fire comes from interviews with family members; a taped interview with Louise Hodges; and the *Mathews Journal* on December 3, 1931.

My information about Captain Ernest Thompson comes mainly through an interview with his son Ernest Travers Thompson, a retired U.S. Navy submariner from Mathews. Accounts of the sinking of the *Norvana* come from the NARA Record Group 38. Little documentation exists about the *Norvana* sinking because the ship vanished. But other ships' sinkings are described in survivors' statements, intelligence reports, and other documents. The movements of ships between ports during the war can be tracked through Ship Movement Cards, also in NARA Record Group 38.

Joseph Conrad's description of "overdue" and "missing" appear in his *The Mirror of the Sea*, pages 49 and 52. The exception to the grim record of "missing" ships comes from John R. Stilgoe's *Lifeboat* (2007), page 22. Hardegan described the torpedoing of the *Norvana* and her violent explosion in his war diary, translated into English on www.uboatarchive.net.

The *GJ* article on Thompson's loss and Blake's survival appeared on February 5, 1942.

The description of George Ernest Harrison comes partly from U.S. Census records, the *GJ*, and an interview with his relative, Grady Powell of Mathews. Powell also provided the letter from Harrison to his sister.

The account of the *Major Wheeler* sinking comes mainly from NARA Records Group 38. The description of the family's effort to get information comes from the *GJ*. The excerpt from the letter from the Bull Line to the navy secretary comes from Captain Arthur Moore's *A Careless Word . . . A Needless Sinking* (1998), page 330. Captain Moore's book is indispensible to anyone writing about the U.S. Merchant Marine in World War II. Another vital source of information is Robert M. Browning Jr.'s *United States Merchant Marine Casualties of World War II* (2011).

Accounts of mariners coming home after being thought dead can be found in John Bunker's *Heroes in Dungarees* (2006), pages 294–95.

The sinking of the *Lake Osweya* is described in NARA Record Group 38. Louise Hodges described her then husband's response to the sinking in a taped interview.

I obtained the list of vanished ships from Moore's *A Careless Word*, page 559, and tallied up the losses through Moore's book and NARA Record Group 38.

Thoughtful explanations of how submarines obliterated the prize rules can be found in Thomas Parrish's *The Submarine* and Bragton Harris's *Navy Times Book of Submarines*. Admiral Gallery's assertion about the cold-bloodedness of submarine warfare can be found in his *Twenty Million Tons Under the Sea*, page 12.

Much of my information about the Japanese submarine force came from interviews with Dr. Carl Boyd, history professor emeritus at Old Dominion University in Norfolk, Virginia, and coauthor of *The Japanese Submarine Force and World War II* (1995). Information about the U.S. submarine force's approach to Japanese merchant shipping came from Theodore Roscoe's *United State Submarine Operations of World War II* (1956) and Ann and John Tusa's *The Nuremberg Trial* (2010).

The account of Hitler's comments to the Japanese ambassador about killing merchant seamen came from Harris's *Navy Times Book of Submarines*, pages 302–3.

According to Timothy Mulligan's *Neither Sharks Nor Wolves*, page 213, historical records show only one instance of a U-boat commander's embracing Hitler's wishes. In March 1944, Heinz Eck of the U-852 opened fire on survivors on life rafts after interrogating them. Three of the castaways hid behind their rafts and survived to testify against Eck, who was hanged.

U-boat commander Otto Kretschmer's order to show mercy came from Mulligan's *Neither Sharks Nor Wolves*, page 196.

The information that 70 percent of merchant ships between 1940 and 1944 sank within fifteen minutes comes from Harris's *Navy Times Book of Submarines*, pages 302–3.

The accounts of U-boat captains offering help to lifeboat survivors come mainly from NARA Record Group 38. Moore's *A Careless Word* often describes such offers of aid in its summaries of ship sinkings.

The death of Wallace Albertson on the USS *Langley* was described in the *GJ* on April 9, 1942. The descriptions of the shortages of defenses for the East Coast of the United States come mainly from the Navy's *Eastern Sea Frontier War Diary*, from Michael Gannon's *Operation Drumbeat*, and Felknor's *The U.S. Merchant Marine at War*, pages 210–26. The description of the sailboat rigged to fire depth charges came from a 2004 interview with retired Coast Guardsman Theodore Mutro of Ocracoke Island, North Carolina.

Descriptions of Admiral Andrews's overwhelming responsibilities and his unsuccessful efforts to get help come from the *Eastern Sea Frontier War Diary*, Gannon's *Operation Drumbeat*, and Theodore Taylor's *Fire on the Beaches* (1958).

Morison's description of Admiral Andrews appears in Samuel Eliot Morison's *The Battle of the Atlantic*, volume 1 of his history of the U.S. Navy in World War II (1947), page 208. Descriptions of King come in part from Morison, page 130, as well as Gannon, Blair's *Hitler's U-boat War*, and Felknor. King's reluctance and slowness to organize convoys is described in Felknor, pages 210–26, as well as Gannon, Williams's *The Battle of the Atlantic*, Harris's *Navy Times Book of Submarines*, Bunker, Taylor, and Ed Offley's *The Burning Shore*. Blair defends King, saying he could not possibly have acted quicker than he did. Andrews's comment about his forces' helplessness against submarines can be found in the Preface to the *Eastern Sea Frontier War Diary*.

The strafing and bombing of whales was reported in the *Virginian-Pilot* on April 14, 1942. Theodore Taylor's comment in the footnotes comes from his *Fire on the Beaches*, page 36. The debacle of the USS *Dickerson* being attacked by a U.S. merchant ship is described in Homer H. Hickam Jr.'s *Torpedo Junction* (1989), pages 91–93. The U-boat commander's gleeful comments about shore lights on the U.S. East Coast came from Cremer's *U-boat Commander*, page 69; Morison's comment about shore lighting appears in his *The Battle of the Atlantic*, page 130. Felknor's *The U.S. Merchant Marine at War*, page 216, contains the text of Roosevelt's executive order giving the military the right to control "all lighting on the seacoast." The *GJ* editorial on coastal lights appeared on May 21, 1942.

U-boat commanders, including Reinhard Hardegan, wrote about taking pains to identify the vessels they sank, so that they could report back to Doenitz. Hardegan was one of those who carried a reference book from Lloyd's of London. The captured logbooks of U-boats show no indication of the commanders' receiving useful intelligence from spies on shore. The writer and former merchant mariner S. J. Flaherty, who wrote as "Ferocious" O'Flaherty, punctures the myth of loose lips sinking ships in his wry book *Abandoned Convoy* (1970). The telegram with the warning about not divulging the name of the missing man's ship came from Salome Hudgins of Mathews.

The double-whammy against the Allies of losing their access to secret German messages while the Germans gained access to theirs is described in Offley's *The Burning Shore*, page 83, as well as Stephen Budiansky's *Blackett's War*, Hugh Sebag-Montefiore's *Enigma: The Battle for the Code*, and John Winton's *Ultra at Sea*.

Navy Secretary Knox's absurd claims about U-boat sinkings appeared in newspapers all over the country, including *The New York Times*, March 22, 1942. Not all Americans bought into the propaganda. *Times* columnist Hanson W. Baldwin suggested that "the very nature of submarine warfare makes it difficult if not impossible to determine whether or not a submarine raider has been sunk. Frequently the Navy Department reports of encounters between surface ships and submarines have been misleading and overoptimistic." Admiral Simons's speech was covered by the *Virginian-Pilot* on April 2, 1942. Admiral Thomas Hoover's minimalist press remarks are described in Taylor's *Fire on the Beaches*, page 172.

The "bearable losses" assessment appears in the *Eastern Sea Frontier War Diary*, page 31.

The descriptions of the early war days in Mathews came from interviews with Clarence Collier Jr. and Elliott Hudgins.

Chapter Four: Professional Survivors

My description of Raymond Hodges comes mostly from interviews with members of the Hodges family, including his son Bill, Brother Hodges, Jesse Carroll Thornton, Stormy Heart Romaniello, Marlene Callis, and Louise and David Callis on tape. I also relied on several newspaper clippings tracking Raymond's career, including: the *Mathews Journal*, February 4, 1932; the *Mooremack News*, with permission from the *Christian Science Monitor*, December 1947; *Time* magazine, November 19, 1934; *The*

New York Times, September 1951; and *Critica*, of Buenos Aires, February 16, 1955.

Everyone in the Hodges family agreed Raymond dressed up when he went out, although his son Bill said Raymond dressed in jeans and denim shirts around the house. Bill Hodges described being whacked by his father with paint sticks. David Callis described Raymond's dressing-down of his brothers.

The Hodges girls may have been goaded by Raymond's son Bill, who tired of their questions and began concocting elaborate stories to watch their eyes widen. Bill may have originated the story that Dolly was formerly a dancer in the Ziegfeld Follies.

Numerous books describe the shipping lanes in World War II. Among the best are Gaylord T. M. Kelshall's *The U-boat War in the Caribbean* (1988); Melanie Wiggins's *Torpedoes in the Gulf: Galveston and the U-boats, 1942–1943* (1995); and Kenneth Wynn's *U-boat Operations of the Second World War.*

The description of the coordinated attack comes from Stanton Hope's *Tanker Fleet: The War Story of the Shell Tankers and the Men Who Manned Them* (1948), which on pages 54–55 describes the Dutch island of Aruba. Sir Thomas Holland made his remarks about the importance of manganese at a speech in London, reported by the Associated Press on July 24, 1942.

The descriptions of the *Mary*'s voyage and ultimate sinking are drawn from NARA Record Groups 38 and 26, and from interviews given by Robert Lee Brown and Allenby Grimstead to the *GJ* on April 23, 1942. Details are contained in the *GJ* notes. The notes are hundreds of pages of typewritten 1942 *GJ* reporters' notes and first drafts of stories, containing details not in the paper.

Details about Nicolai Clausen came from Kelshall's *The U-boat War in the Caribbean*, page 46, and Wynn's entry for the U-129.

Particulars of lifeboats, their food and water supplies, and other equipment, came from Phil Richards and John Banigan, *How to Abandon Ship* (1942), page 3. I recommend *How to Abandon Ship* for a wide range of

interesting observations about lifeboat survival in the U-boat war. Banigan
survived the sinking of the first U.S. ship in World War II, the *Robin Moor*.

The details about the refugee camp for mariners on Trinidad comes
from Felix Riesenberg's *Sea War*, page 18.

The information about pirates in the Windward Passage comes from
Angus Konstam's *Scourge of the Seas* (2001), pages 23–24, 80, and 97.

The description of Captain Walter Hudgins comes mainly from an
interview with his son Elliott Hudgins, and from a testimonial to him that
his family wrote for the Gwynn's Island Museum. The description of
Charles Davis comes mainly from his cousin Amelia Minter of North Carolina. The description of the attack on the *Barbara* is drawn from NARA
Record Groups 38 and 26, and from accounts in the *GJ* on April 9, 1942.

The dangers of working in the engine room are described in numerous
books. In Buchheim's novel *Das Boot*, the fictitious U-boat commander tells
his crew: "What a job working ten feet below the water line, knowing that at
any second a torpedo may tear open the ship's side without the slightest
warning? How often when on convoy the men must measure the thin plates
that divide them from the sea. How often they must surreptitiously try out
the quickest route to the deck, always with the taste of panic in their mouths,
and in their ears the rending scream of iron, the blast of the explosion, and
the roaring inrush of the sea. Not one second's feeling of security. Always
scared shitless, always waiting for the clanging of the alarm bell."

The account of radioman Lopez's experience came from www.usmm
.org, a Web site devoted to the U.S. Merchant Marine.

The information about the U-boat commander Ernest Bauer came
from Wynn's entry for the U-126.

The report that the Eastern Sea Frontier was the scene of half the
world's sinkings in March 1942 comes from the Navy's *Eastern Sea Frontier War Diary*, page 102. The interviews with the survivors of the *Marore*
appeared in the *Virginian-Pilot* of Norfolk on March 36, 1942. The description of the easy lifeboat voyage appeared in the *Virginian-Pilot*, May 5,
1943. The account of the nightmarish voyage of the survivors of the Belgian

freighter appeared in the *Virginian-Pilot* on February 24, 1942. The tally of ten sinkings for Stanizewski comes from www.usmm.org. The account of a ship's engineer constructing a still to produce drinking water from seawater appears in Bruce Felknor's *The U.S. Merchant Marine at War*, pages 319–20. The quote about the fortuitous zig comes from Roscoe's *United States Submarine Operations of World War II*, page 214.

Captain Jesse Hodges described his approach to avoiding U-boats to the *Washington Sunday Star* on September 6, 1942. Captain Homer Callis's approach was described by Jack Rowe and Lottie Mitchem of Gwynn's Island, as well as by Homer's son Bill Callis. Captain Elvin Lewis's approach was described by his nephew Raymond Owens of Mathews.

How to Abandon Ship also included a prayer for committing the dead to the sea: "Unto Almighty God we commend the soul of our brother departed, and we commit his body to the deep; in sure and certain hope of the Resurrection unto eternal life, through our Lord Jesus Christ; at whose coming in glorious majesty to judge the world, the sea shall give up her dead; and the corruptible bodies of those who sleep in him shall be changed, and made like unto his glorious body; according to the mighty working whereby he is able to subdue all things unto himself."

The information about Captain Levy Morgan comes from Jack Rowe of Gwynn's Island, U.S. Census records, and a memorial his family wrote to him in the Gwynn's Island Museum, as well as the *GJ* on March 26 and April 2, 1942. The complaint about Morgan's having to treat the crew carefully came from the first officer's interview with the Coast Guard in NARA Records Group 26, and the descriptions of the torpedoing and the grounding come from NARA Record Group 38, which in this case includes an intelligence report.

The descriptions of the merchant mariners' unique civilian, free-agent status come from numerous mariners, including Bill Callis, Jack Rowe, J. W. Corbett, and Brother Hodges. Riesenberg's comment appears in *Sea War* on page 22.

The information about Pegler's allegations about the Merchant Marine and the resulting libel case come from www.usmm.org, and the information about *Time*'s criticism of the Merchant Marine came from Riesenberg's *Sea War*, page 151. Helen Lawrenson's article in *Collier's*, "They Keep 'em Sailing," appeared on August 8, 1942. *The New York Times* editorial praising the U.S. Merchant Marine appeared on June 22, 1942.

My description of Captain Mellin Respess comes from interviews with Bill Callis, Jack Rowe, and Benny Fitchett of Mathews; Eleanor's friend Edward Judson; and U.S. Census records. Ship crew manifests accessed on www.ancestry.com show Mellin had sailed on the *Major Wheeler* several times in 1941.

The description of the voyage and sinking of the *Oakmar* came largely from NARA Record Group 38, and from the former German submariner Jochen Brennecke's *The Hunters and the Hunted: German U-boats 1939–1945* (2003), page 166.

The account of Mellin Respess visiting Eleanor's family on Gwynn's Island after being "quite ill in a hospital" comes from the *GJ* on April 30, 1942. The account of Mellin's last visit to the general store came from Benny Fitchett of Mathews, who also remembered being taught math at the island's only school by Mellin's wife, Eleanor.

Chapter Five: "Off Hatteras the Tankers Sink"

The account of the *E.M. Clark*'s sinking comes from NARA Record Group 38, and *Ships of the Esso Fleet* (1946), pages 144–48; Gerald Reminick's *Patriots and Heroes, Vol. 2* (2004), pages 72 and 183–84; and Bruce Felknor, *The U.S. Merchant Marine at War*, pages 200–201. The background on Boyd Dixon comes from an interview with his brother John Dixon of Gwynn's Island.

The description of the positive aspects of sailing on tankers comes from John Bunker's *Heroes in Dungarees*, page 188; Stanton Hope's *Tanker Fleet*; and Philip Kaplan's and Jack Currie's *Convoy* (1998) as well as from interviews with Captain Bill Callis and Jack Ward of Mathews, who commanded tankers after the war.

The descriptions of the dangers of burning oil and oil slicks come from the *Fire Fighting Manual for Tank Vessels* (1974) and Hope's *Tanker Fleet*, page 95, which describes the dangers of oil slicks to swimming men. The accounts of added perils in the footnote come from accounts of tanker sinkings in Captain Arthur Moore's *A Careless Word . . . A Needless Sinking*.

My accounts of the successes of Mohr and the U-124 are based in part on NARA Record Group 38 and Wynn's descriptions of U-124's activities. Mohr's poem also is quoted in several books, including Thomas Parrish's *The Submarine*, page 257.

My information about Nat Foster comes from U.S. Census records, letters in the George Betts collection at the Independence Seaport Museum in Philadelphia, and the *GJ* on March 22, 1942. The account of the *Muskogee*'s disappearance is based in part on documents in NARA Record Group 38, the Betts collection, and Wolfgang Frank's *The Sea Wolves*.

My description of Sam Dow comes mainly from U.S. Census records, crew manifests, and the *GJ* on April 9, 1942. The description of the sinking of the *Dixie Arrow* comes from NARA Record Groups 38 and 26; the *Virginian-Pilot* on March 29, 1942; *The New York Times* on March 29, 1942; Wynn's *U-boat Operations of the Second World War*; and the Maritime Commission's description of Oscar Chappell's actions in its award to him posthumously of the Merchant Marine Distinguished Service Medal. The description of the children of Hatteras seeing the pillar of smoke from the *Dixie Arrow* on their way to school comes from a 2004 interview with Gibb Gray, who was a boy on Hatteras Island in the village of Buxton in 1942.

The toll of tankers by the end of March comes from Clay Blair's *Hitler's U-boat War*, page 765. The accounts of fuel shortages in the northeastern United States come from Theodore Taylor's *Fire on the Beaches*, page 219. The information in the footnote about the tanker fleet comes from Blair, page 468.

The tanker losses prompted the construction of pipelines to carry oil from the Gulf of Mexico to the northeastern United States. The largest pipeline, nicknamed the Big Inch, was built in less than a year and finished in July 1943, according to Nathan Miller's *War at Sea*, page 294.

The account of the oil companies' concerns and suggestions comes from Michael Gannon's *Operation Drumbeat*, page 343. The description of the fake guns on the *Esso Baton Rouge* comes from Taylor's *Fire on the Beaches*, page 68. The fact that the tanker was sunk anyway came from Moore's *A Careless Word*, page 90. The account of Admiral King's request for a dimout rather than a blackout, and of the subsequent sinking off Atlantic City, New Jersey, comes from Gannon's *Operation Drumbeat*, page 344.

The account of Admiral Andrews organizing an escort fleet of small craft, and of Roosevelt's enthusiasm for it, comes from Parrish's *The Submarine*, page 258.

The text of Winston Churchill's comment to Harry Hopkins comes from Churchill's *The Hinge of Fate* (1950), the second volume of his five-volume series about World War II, page 110. The text of King's complaint about the British not bombing the U-boat pens comes from Edwin P. Hoyt's *U-boats Offshore* (1978), page 76.

The accounts of the British commando raid on the U-boat bunkers and the subsequent executions of French partisans come in part from Churchill's *The Hinge of Fate*, pages 121–22, and *The New York Times* on March 29, 1942.

The account of Rodger Winn's encounter with Admiral King and his staff is described in several books, including Stephen Budiansky's *Blackett's War*, pages 182–83. The report of the Navy's convoy plans comes from the *Eastern Sea Frontier War Diary*, page 111. Gaylord T. M. Kelshall points out the focus of the plan on available forces rather than need in *The U-boat War in the Caribbean*, page 17. Hitler's remark about "millionaires" and "beauty queens" came from Richard Overy's *Why the Allies Won* (1995), page 205. Hitler's boast came from Gannon's *Operation Drumbeat*, page 339.

My account of the *Atik* disaster came from Gannon's *Operation Drumbeat*, pages 322–28. My description of Hemingway's efforts to turn his fishing boat into a Q-ship came from Michael Reynolds's *Hemingway: The Final Years* (1999), pages 64–69, and Hilary Hemingway and Carlene Brennen's *Hemingway in Cuba* (2003), page 78.

I researched the story of the "lifeboat baby" in late 2004 and early 2005 while working for the *Richmond Times-Dispatch*. I got much of the story from interviews with the lifeboat baby, Jesse Roper Mohorovic, and his sister, Vesna Jurick, who was kind enough to translate from Croatian to English an account by her mother of the sinking and birth. Jesse had all the Navy documents about the sinking; the telegram his father received announcing his birth in a lifeboat; a copy of his ad-libbed birth certificate; and a map someone had given him showing the route his lifeboat had traveled between the sinking of the *City of New York* and the rescue of the lifeboat survivors by the USS *Roper*. Several members of the *Roper*'s crew talked with me, including Rhodes Chamberlain of New Mexico, who had a copy of the *Roper*'s logbook, a shipmate's diary, and other documents. The commander of the *Roper*, Hamilton Howe, left an oral history of his war experiences at East Carolina University. The story is also based on NARA Records Groups 38 and 26 and news accounts in *The New York Times*, the *International Herald Tribune*, and the *Virginian-Pilot*, as well as various tabloids. I interviewed Larry Atkinson, an oceanographer at Old Dominion University in Norfolk, about the characteristics of the Gulf Stream. The family of George Orner, who was in the lifeboat with the baby, sent me his account of the journey after my story was published in the newspaper. A Methodist missionary, Sarah King, also survived the sinking and published an account in the June 1942 issue of *The Methodist Woman* magazine, "My Experiences off Cape Hatteras." The fate of the last of the *City of New York*'s lifeboats was described in Felix Riesenberg's *Sea War*, page 75.

Lottie Mitchem described her nervousness in an interview on Gwynn's Island. Harry Hammond's respite from worry was described in the *GJ* on March 19, 1942.

The *East Indian*'s return was reported in the *GJ* on April 3. My description of the ship is based on interviews with Jean Hodges. The *East Indian*'s arduous voyage was described in M. Stanley MacLean's *13 Days Adrift* and reconstructed through the vessel's Ship Movement Card in NARA Record

Group 38. The departures of the crew are described by MacLean and in an interview with Walter Stillman's widow, Claire Stillman.

Dewey Hodges's illness was described by his daughter Jean. My description of Dewey Hodges comes significantly from Jean, but also from others who knew him in Mathews, including his nephews, Brother Hodges and Bill Hodges.

Chapter Six: Killing Ground to Battleground

I researched the story of the sinking of the U-85 in 2004–2005 while working on a story for the *Richmond Times-Dispatch*. I interviewed retired naval officer Kenneth Tebo, in Alexandria, Virginia. He was the young officer who first decided to pursue the radar and sonar target, and was on the bridge during the attack on the U-85 and the immediate aftermath. I also interviewed Rhodes Chamberlain of New Mexico, who provided a copy of the *Roper*'s logbook, the Navy's reports on the encounter, two shipmates' diaries, and other documents. I interviewed former *Roper* crewman Jacob DeWitt. I read the transcribed oral history of the *Roper*'s commander, Hamilton Howe, at East Carolina University. The civilian's account of the looting of the German bodies came from an article by John S. Van Gilder in the *Knoxville News Sentinel*'s Sunday Magazine on November 29, 1942. Doenitz comments about the ineffectiveness of destroyers patrolling for U-boats in his *Memoirs*, page 202.

The account of the *Gulfamerica* sinking comes from NARA Record Group 38; Hardegan's war diary translated on www.uboatarchive.net; Michael Gannon's *Operation Drumbeat*; Bruce Felknor's *The U.S. Merchant Marine at War*, page 205; and other sources. Hardegan's comment about improving Allied defenses came from Andrew Williams's *The Battle of the Atlantic*, page 176.

A great deal has been written about Liberty ships. I found some of the most interesting facts in Jim Marshall's article in *Collier's* magazine, "Hulls in a Hurry," on July 11, 1942. The material in the footnote about christening comes from another *Collier's* article, this one by Josef Israels II, "A Ship

Is Born," on August 28, 1943. I also drew from interviews with several Mathews mariners, including Bill Callis, Benny Fitchett, Reginald Deagle, Pete White, and Jack Ward; and from John Gorley Bunker's *Liberty Ships: The Ugly Ducklings of World War II* (1972), A. A. Hoehling's *The Fighting Liberty Ships* (1996), William F. Luthmann's *At Liberty* (1995), and Philip Kaplan and Jack Currie's *Convoy*.

Stephen Budiansky's quote about a "brutal calculus" comes from *Blackett's War*, page 185. The long list of World War II Liberty ship names is an entertaining read, at www.usmm.org/libertyships.html.

The information that Germany's intelligence service tripled its estimate of America's shipbuilding capacity comes from Ronald H. Spector's *At War at Sea*, page 239. Doenitz describes his new options in his *Memoirs*. The advantages of the milch cows are described in Wolfgang Frank's *Sea Wolves*, page 169.

The information about most of the ships lost in World War II dating back to the previous war comes from Axis Roland, W. Jeffrey Bolster, and Alexander Keyssar's *The Way of the Ship* (2008), page 303.

My description of the potential pleasures of a Caribbean mission comes from Gaylord T. M. Kelshall's *The U-boat War in the Caribbean*, page 85, and Melanie Wiggins's *U-boat Adventures*, page 50.

The account of the *Norlindo*'s sinking comes from NARA Record Group 38, which includes an intelligence report examining the Germans U-boat commander's level of generosity, and from Harro Schacht's war diary, translated from German into English on www.uboatarchive.net. The account of Schacht's subsequent torpedoing of the two tankers comes from Captain Arthur Moore's *A Careless Word*, pages 161 and 198.

The account of the torpedoing and grounding of the *Delisle* comes from NARA Record Group 38 and the *GJ* on August 20, 1942.

Much of my description of Genious Hudgins Jr. comes from interviews with his widow, Salome, and daughter, Vicki, as well as from others in Mathews. Salome and Vicki provided access to more than a dozen of Genious's letters, including the letter in which he reveals his fears to his sister.

The account of Genious surviving the sinking of the *Green Island* comes from his letters and from NARA Record Group 38. The account of the *Green Island*'s previous narrow escape comes from Felix Riesenberg's *Sea War*, pages 72–74.

Theodore Taylor offers a description of the 1940s Gulf Coast and the Mississippi River passes in *Fire on the Beaches*, pages 149–50.

The account of the *Virginia* sinking comes from NARA Record Groups 38 and 26; Schacht's war diary translated into English on www.uboat archive.net; Wynn's *U-boat Operations of the Second World War*; Robert Carse's *The Long Haul*, page 56; and Riesenberg's *Sea War*, page 114. Information about Frank White came from his nephew J. Edgar White of Portsmouth, and a tribute to White in the *Virginian-Pilot* on June 13, 1942, by reporter Harry P. Moore, with whom Frank White corresponded. The account of the courage of the swimming men comes from Wiggins's *Torpedoes in the Gulf*, page 56. The account of the *William C. McTarnahan* comes from Wiggins, page 85.

The account of the *Halo* sinking comes from NARA Record Group 38, including a six-page statement by Joseph Shackelford describing his experience, and a letter from the Mexican Gulf Oil Company suggesting ways to prevent future such disasters; the *GJ* on June 4, 1942, and July 2, 1942, in which Shackelford is quoted at length; on December 30, 1999, the *GJ* reporter's drafts; U.S. Coast Guard record of tanker losses; and Taylor's *Fire on the Beaches*, pages 163–67.

The account of the sinking of the *Gulfpenn* comes from NARA Record Group 38, the *GJ* on May 27, 1942, and *GJ* notes.

The account of Captain Borum's rescue of Belgian seamen in World War I comes from the *Mathews Journal*, May 5, 1919. The account of his rescue of the British seamen in World War II comes from the entry for Borum's ship, the *City of Birmingham*, on www.uboat.net, and from a brief history provided by the Borum family to the Gwynn's Island Museum.

The account of the *Elizabeth* sinking comes from NARA Record Group 38, which includes a Navy Armed Guard report on the voyage and an interview with Captain Walter Hudgins's son Elliott. The contents of the Davis telegram to his family came from an interview with his cousin Amelia Minter.

The *GJ* editorial complaining about the lack of a blackout appeared on May 21, 1942. The account of the pleasure-driving bust in Mathews came from the *GJ* on May 16, 1943. The *GJ* editorial finding reason for optimism in the Russian convoy's success appeared on April 16, 1942.

Chapter Seven: "Avoid Polar Bear Liver"

In writing about the rigors of the Murmansk Run, I drew from an interview with Bernard Stansbury, records on Russian convoys from NARA Record Group 38, and several other sources, including S. J. Flaherty's *Abandoned Convoy* (1970); Paul Kemp's *Convoy!* (2004); Theodore Taylor's *Battle in the Arctic Seas* (1976); B. B. Schofield's *The Russian Convoys* (1964); and Robert Carse's *A Cold Corner of Hell* (1969).

The political backstory to the Murmansk Run is described in detail in Churchill's *The Hinge of Fate*, which includes telling communications between Churchill and Stalin on pages 257 and 270–71. Churchill's comment that Bolshevism was "foul baboonery" came from Nicholas Bethell's *Russia Besieged* (1977), page 136, and the famous quote about being willing to help any enemy of Hitler's is printed on page 137.

The instructions for killing and eating polar bears are found on pages 139–40 of Phil Richards and John Banigan's *How to Abandon Ship*.

My description of Captain Guy Hudgins is drawn from interviews with his daughter Diana Swenson and her husband, Art, in Mathews. The account of Guy's voyage to Murmansk with PQ-15 comes from that interview; a detailed account of the trip in Samuel Duff McCoy's *Nor Death Dismay* (1944); Felix Riesenberg's *Sea War*, page 139; Carse's *A Cold Corner of Hell* and *The Long Haul*; Kemp's *Convoy!*; NARA Record Group 38; and the *GJ* on July 2, 1942.

The account of PQ-16's voyage to Murmansk comes from *GJ* interviews with Charles Edwards and Charles Majette on August 6, 13, and 27,

1942, and *GJ* notes; my interview with Pearl and Fay Hutchinson, Cecil Ripley's sister and niece, of Mathews; Riesenberg's *Sea War*, page 139; Carse's *A Cold Corner of Hell* and *The Long Haul*; Kemp's *Convoy!*; and NARA Record Group 38. Joe Diggs's letters were provided by his relative Gary Brownlee of Mathews.

My description of James Ashberry came from an interview with his younger brother, Vernon, in Mathews. The account of the *City of Alma*'s sinking came from a *GJ* interview with James Ashberry on August 20, 1942; NARA Record Group 38; and the U.S. Maritime Administration's account of the actions of a third mate who won a medal for heroism for helping Ashberry right the boat and then rescue several shipmates. The *GJ* reporter's notes contained Ashberry's disparaging remark about Mathews, which did not appear in the paper.

A detailed account of the U-701's mine laying appears in Ed Offley's *The Burning Shore*. The details about the mining of the *Robert C. Tuttle* come from NARA Record Group 38. The description of Forrest's experience on the *Tuttle* comes from an interview he gave the *GJ* on June 25, 1942, and *GJ* notes. Forrest still believed at the time that his ship had been torpedoed rather than mined. Several residents of Virginia Beach still remember watching the mined ships exploding offshore. Doenitz's boast came from Taylor's *Fire on the Beaches*, page 177.

Descriptions of the U-boat landings of saboteurs, and the results, appear in Clay Blair's *Hitler's U-boat War*, pages 602–05, and many other books, as well as on the FBI's Web site.

The account of the *Millinocket*'s sinking comes from NARA Record Groups 38 and 26, Wynn, and the *GJ* on July 9, 1942. The paper subsequently printed the poem Captain Lewis Callis had written about Gwynn's Island.

The account of the *Manuela*'s sinking comes from NARA Record Group 38 and an interview by the *GJ* with Godsey on July 7, 1942. Captain Rodney Callis recalled the summer of 1942 along the coast in an interview with the *GJ* on December 30, 1999.

Marshall's message to King and King's reaction came from Michael

Gannon's *Operation Drumbeat*, page 391, and Carse's *The Long Haul*, page 100. Roosevelt's comment comes from Felknor, page 226.

Numerous members of the Hodges family, including Brother Hodges, Jesse Carroll Thornton, Jean Hodges, and David Callis described a Hodges "dining" to me. The size of a Hodges meal is described by John A. Fox in "Virginia Seamen Give Their Lives to Keep Our Ships Afloat," in the *Washington Sunday Star* on September 6, 1942. Bill Hodges remembered the dining in June in particular, and the large number of sea captains present. Jean Hodges recalled her father's call back to the sea from Ford and his efforts to get the *Onondaga* crewed and ready. Genious Hudgins Jr.'s daughter, Vicki, found a document in which her father is offered a different job at lesser pay just before signing on with Dewey Hodges.

The disaster of PQ-17 is described in numerous books, one of the best being Flaherty's *Abandoned Convoy*.

The description of the return trip of Convoy PQ-16 from Murmansk comes from *GJ* interviews with Charles Edwards and Charles Majette on August 6, 13, and 27, 1942; *GJ* notes; Carse's *A Cold Corner of Hell* and *The Long Haul*; NARA Record Group 38; and Navy Armed Guard reports. Information about Captain Joe Diggs came from interviews with Pearl Hutchinson and Gary Brownlee of Mathews. Brownlee provided a letter from Charles Edwards about Diggs's death, as well as some of Diggs's heavily censored letters to his family in Mathews.

Chapter Eight: Catastrophe

The account of the *Ruth* sinking came from NARA Record Groups 38 and 26; *GJ* notes; a *Richmond Times-Dispatch* article on July 22, 1942; and *GJ* articles on July 16 and 23, 1942. Information about Mel Callis came from his nephew Bill Callis, as well as Benny Fitchett, Clarence Collier Jr., and Jack Rowe of Mathews. Mel Callis's comments about Mathews and mermaids appeared in the *GJ* on August 4, 1938. Information about Perry Collier came from his grandson, Clarence Collier Jr.

I learned of the existence of Ashley Clinton Williams from Glenn A.

Knoblock's *African American World War II Casualties and Decorations* (2009), pages 542–43, and found more about him in U.S. Census records for 1920 and 1930. Knoblock's book describes the discrimination African American mariners faced in the first half of the twentieth century.

The account of the attack on the *Thomas McKean* comes from NARA Record Group 38, which includes lengthy reports on an intelligence investigation that led nowhere, and the official statements of Roland Foster and the ship's first assistant engineers, printed in their entirety in Daniel Gallery's *Twenty Million Tons Under the Sea*, pages 125–40. Gallery wrote his book when the official statements of hundreds of ships' officers were in NARA's records. NARA has since destroyed those statements, retaining only summaries of the statements of the survivors of sunken ships. The account of the attack also draws on *GJ* notes and the *GJ* on July 23 and August 6, 1942.

Captain L. F. Borum's second sinking in two world wars was described in NARA Record Groups 38 and 26, including a Navy Armed Guard report, and through information provided by the Borum family to the Gwynn's Island Museum.

The account of the *Norlandia* sinking comes from NARA Record Groups 38 and 26 and an interview with Captain Herbert Callis's daughter Joan Marble. The description of Callis's previous rescue of men from another ship comes from Captain Nicholas Manolis's *We at Sea* (1949).

Information about the *Onondaga*'s voyages through the Caribbean comes from her Ship Movement Card in NARA Record Group 38 and in Genious Hudgins's letters to his wife, Salome. Mellin Respess's joining the *Onondaga* as a passenger in Puerto Rico was described by Jean Hodges and Jack Rowe, among others.

The descriptions of Leslie Hodges are based on interviews with several members of the Hodges family, including Jean Hodges, Brother Hodges, Jesse Carroll Thornton, Betty Fernald, and Stormy Heart Romaniello, as well as family friends such as Edwin Jarvis, and a taped interview with Louise Hodges. The description of Stacy Hammond comes in part from interviews with his son Stacy Hammond Jr. in Mathews. The account of the sinking of the *Oneida* comes from NARA Record Groups 38 and 26, *GJ* notes, and the *GJ* on July 30, 1942.

My description of Spencer Hodges comes from interviews with his son Spencer Jr. as well as other members of the Hodges family, and others in Mathews who knew him later as the county sheriff. Spencer Jr. remembered the trips with his father to break the news of Leslie's death to Henny.

Accounts of the memorial ceremony at the Gwynn's Island drawbridge come mostly from *GJ* notes and the *GJ* story on July 23, 1942.

I reconstructed the *Onondaga*'s voyages through her Ship Movement Card in NARA Record Group 38, Genious Hudgins's letters to Salome, and Dewey Hodges's last letter to his family on July 23, 1942. Dewey's letter, as noted earlier, is entered in Norfolk Circuit Court in Norfolk, Virginia, as Dewey's last will and testament.

The sinking of the *Onondaga* is described from interviews with Russell Dennis's son Russell Dennis Jr., who provided the text of Dennis's telegram to Mathews after the sinking. The account relies on NARA Record Groups 38 and 26; Wynn's *U-boat Operations of the Second World War*; *The New York Times*; the *Virginian-Pilot*; *GJ* notes and the *GJ* on July 30, 1942; Norfolk Circuit Court Probate case files for October and November 1942; and the U.S. District Court decision by Judge John Paul in *Hodges v. New York Life Insurance Co.*, March 2, 1948.

Jack Musick, a shark biologist and author from Virginia, provided background about sharks and shark fishing economics and methods for particulars about the Carillos and the *Donatella*.

The surviving records do not specify exactly when the shark fishermen found the remains. Jenkins's letter says the fishermen found them shortly after the sinking and that they included flesh and bone. A large shark would digest flesh in its stomach within a day or two of consuming it, but the shark's digestive tract could contain flesh for as long as a week, and fishermen gutting a shark would open its digestive tract as well as its stomach. The exact timing of the fishermen's catch does not affect the chain of events.

The family's reaction to the anonymous call came from Jean Hodges, who was present when the call came. Spencer Hodges Jr. recalled accompanying his father to break the news of Dewey's death to Henny, as he had done with Leslie's death.

The story on Mathews in the *Washington Sunday Star* appeared on September 6, 1942. A *Baltimore Sun* feature on the losses on Gwynn's Island had appeared on August 9, 1942. The *Sun* story, "Torpedoes Strike on Gwynn's Island," by William B. Crane, prompted a Mathews man to write to the paper to point out that the island was not the only part of Mathews that had suffered terrible losses.

The descriptions of the evolution of the interlocking convoy system come from Samuel Eliot Morison's *The Battle of the Atlantic*, pages 254–57 and 260. The statistic about the decline in sinkings in the Eastern Sea Frontier comes from Michael Gannon's *Operation Drumbeat*, pages 388–89. Admiral Andrews's remarks come from the Navy's *Eastern Sea Frontier War Diary*.

Doenitz's reflections on withdrawing his U-boats from U.S. waters are described in his *Memoirs*, pages 236–38.

Chapter Nine: "Please Don't Tell Me"

The account of Homer's last voyage on the *Mae* comes from the *Mae*'s Navy Armed Guard commander's report on convoy TAW-12 in NARA Record Group 38. The description of Captain Homer Callis and his short-lived effort to go ashore comes from interviews with his son Bill Callis, Jack Rowe, Benny Fitchett, and Lottie Mitchem on Gwynn's Island. The description of Nancy Callis comes from the same people, as well as Bill Callis's daughter, Lisa Callis. Nancy Callis told the *GJ* on December 30, 1999, that she had felt that her neighbors regarded her as the angel of death. Bill Callis recalled his big brother, Homer Callis Jr., advising him to choose the Merchant Marine over the Navy.

The information about Homer Sr.'s replacement, Captain Willard Hudgins, comes from his son, Buster Hudgins, as well as Lottie Mitchem, Bill Callis, and Jack Rowe.

The description of Lester Smith is based on interviews with his widow, Lottie Mitchem, and his friends Bill Callis and Jack Rowe. The account of the *Mae* sinking comes from NARA Record Groups 38 and 26 and interviews in the *GJ* with Lester Smith.

The account of Will Hunley's going to sea comes from his children, Jimmy and Rebecca Hunley; from an interview in the *GJ* with Hunley and David Hodges upon their joint retirement from the sea on January 11, 1979; and from an interview Hunley gave the *Glo-Quips* paper in Gloucester County, Virginia, on August 14, 1974. The account of the sinking of the *Commercial Trader* comes from NARA Record Groups 38 and 26, including a Navy Armed Guard report; a detailed written account of the sinking by Captain Hunley, provided by his son, Jimmy; *GJ* notes; the *GJ* stories on November 19, 1942, and January 11, 1979; and the *Glo-Quips* account.

The account of the *Steel Navigator* sinking comes from NARA Record Group 38; *GJ* notes; a *GJ* interview with Hall on November 24, 1942; Robert M. Browning Jr.'s *United States Merchant Marines Casualties of World War II*, page 188; and Wynn's *U-boat Operations of the Second World War*.

The letters noting Lester Smith's recovery were shared with me by his widow, Lottie Mitchem, and in some cases printed in the *GJ*.

Genious Hudgins Jr.'s widow, Salome, and daughter, Vicki, shared the letters she received from the Navy and from well-wishers. They also described Salome's reaction and refusal to believe Genious was dead.

Edna Hodges's attempts to have her husband, Captain Dewey Hodges, declared legally dead so the family could access accounts in his name are described in the October 15, 1942, proceedings in the Probate section of Norfolk, Virginia, Circuit Court.

The description of the first part of the *East Indian*'s voyage comes from M. Stanley MacLean's forty-page *13 Days Adrift* and a detailed account by Charles Edwards of Gloucester; *GJ* notes; and the *GJ* on January 14, 1943, and December 30, 1999. The sea snakes are indeed highly venomous but pose little threat to humans because their teeth are not designed for biting us.

The description of Wolfgang Luth comes from Jordan Vause's *U-boat Ace: The Story of Wolfgang Luth* (1990); Jocher Brennecke's *The Hunters and the Hunted*, pages 196–99; and Timothy Mulligan's *Neither Sharks Nor Wolves*. The account of the sinking and subsequent lifeboat voyage comes from NARA Record Group 38, including a Naval Armed Guard report; Brennecke, pages 196–99; *GJ* notes; the *GJ* on November 26 and December 3, 1942, and January 7, 1943; my interview with Clayton's son Rick Hammond; and MacLean's *13 Days Adrift*.

The text of Doenitz's *Laconia* order comes from Ann and John Tusa's *The Nuremberg Trial*, page 186.

A lifeboat crammed with frightened, hungry, thirsty people was an incubator for conflict. Writers and filmmakers have turned the lifeboat drama into a genre. A short story by John Steinbeck formed the basis for Alfred Hitchcock's 1944 film *Lifeboat*, in which American, British, and German castaways schemed and struggled to the death. More recent examples include Charlotte Rogan's novel *The Lifeboat*, in which a woman chooses sides between a ship's officer and others who challenge his leadership, and Yann Martel's novel *Life of Pi*, in which a young Indian man shares a lifeboat with a ferocious Bengal tiger.

The letter from R. M. Jenkins describing the Carillos's discovery of the rings in the shark's belly is dated October 22, 1942—almost three months after the sinking. The letter makes it clear that Jenkins investigated the situation as soon as the Carillos brought the rings and remains into port. The most likely explanation for the time lag is that Jenkins initially wrote to the wrong shipping companies. Edna Hodges's lawyer first heard about the letter from a law school classmate who worked for the Lykes Brothers shipping line.

The entire text of Jenkins's letter was printed by both the *Virginian-Pilot* and the *Ledger-Dispatch* of Norfolk on November 7, 1942. The story was picked up by United Press and the Associated Press and reprinted in newspapers around the country, including the *Richmond Times-Dispatch*, where Henny Hodges most likely read it under the headline, "Shark's Body

Yields Rings, Man's Remains." The *American Weekly* of Great Britain printed a story on the ring in the shark in 1943.

The account of Edna discussing the family's options with her daughters comes from her daughter Jean, who took part in the discussion.

The descriptions of the Hodges daughters come from members of the Hodges family, including Brother Hodges, Jesse Carroll Thornton, Louise and David Hodges (on tape), Stormy Heart Romaniello, Marlene Callis, and Betty Fernald, as well as Edwin Jarvis.

The account of the Hodges daughters' approaching their father and brothers to ask them to stop sailing the deep ocean comes from Brother Hodges, who overheard his parents discussing the daughters' request at the dinner table.

The description of Coleman Hodges comes largely from his daughter Betty Fernald, but also from members of the Hodges family, including Brother Hodges, Jesse Carroll Thornton, Louise and David Hodges (on tape), Stormy Heart Romaniello, and Marlene Callis, as well as Edwin Jarvis.

Roosevelt's and Churchill's strategy sessions have been described in numerous books. My favorites are Churchill's *The Hinge of Fate* and Rick Atkinson's *An Army at Dawn* (2002). Atkinson's great trilogy about the American armies in the European war never overlooks the role of the Merchant Marine in sustaining them.

The estimate of the supply needs of American soldiers in Europe comes from Benjamin W. Labaree et al., *America and the Sea: A Maritime History* (1998), page 582.

Chapter Ten: Counterattack

The account of Captain Guy Hudgins's voyage in Operation Torch comes from NARA Record Group 38, including a Naval Armed Guard report; Samuel Duff McCoy's *Nor Death Dismay*; and an interview with Guy's daughter and son-in-law, Diana and Art Swenson. Rick Atkinson's *An Army at Dawn* offers a detailed account of all three prongs of the North Africa invasion. Hutson Hudgins's excited accounts of the invasion came from *GJ* notes and the *GJ* article of December 10, 1942. The account of the German intelligence failure regarding Operation Torch and the U-boats' preoccupation with attacking a routine convoy instead comes from Doenitz's *Memoirs*, pages 275–77. The account of the four troop transports being torpedoed off Morocco comes from Robert Carse's *The Long Haul*, page 151.

The account of Captain Raymond Hodges's voyage to Malta on the *Mormacmoon* comes from interviews with Raymond's son Bill; the "Malta War Diary," which I accessed at www.naval-history.net/xDKWD-Malta1942a.htm; and Jim Whalen's *Last of the Boom Ships* (2000).

The descriptions of Malta draw in part on Philip Kaplan and Jack Currie's *Convoy* and Sam Moses's *At All Costs* (2007). Raymond's austere meal with the governor was described by his son Bill Hodges. The dismal success rate of ships trying to reach Malta between February and August comes from Kaplan and Currie's *Convoy*, page 165. Dr. Carl Boyd, the specialist on Japanese submarines from Old Dominion University in Norfolk, offered perspective on Japanese submarines in the Indian Ocean.

The story about the U-boat's picking up a weather report from Duluth comes from Theodore Taylor's *Fire on the Beaches*, page 46. The account of trawler captains staying in port comes from the *GJ* on August 20, 1942.

The information about the Hodges family holiday gatherings comes from the *GJ*'s neighborhood sections for December 1942 and 1943. The descriptions of the quiet Christmases with mariners at sea came from numerous Mathews mariners. The descriptions of Captain Robert Gayle's Christmas came from a *GJ* story on December 26, 1985. Jack Rowe provided the account of Gayle's ship nearly colliding with a U-boat in the fog. Gayle's daughter Beverly described his personality. The *GJ* editorial about the holidays appeared on December 24, 1942.

Good descriptions of Roosevelt's and Churchill's discussions and strategy between North Africa and Sicily are in Churchill's *The Hinge of Fate* and Atkinson's *An Army at Dawn*.

The account of the *Collingsworth* sinking comes from NARA Record Groups 38 and 26 and the *GJ* on February 25, 1943. The account of the sinking of the *Roger B. Taney* comes from NARA Record Groups 38 and 26. The account of the sinking of the *Benjamin Harrison* comes from NARA Record Groups 38 and 26, as well as from the *GJ* on May 6, 1943.

The circumstances of Grand Admiral Erich Raeder's demotion are described in Samuel Eliot Morison's *The Atlantic Battle Won, May 1943–May 1945* (1954), page 57.

The descriptions of how castaways can read natural clues comes from Harold Gatty's fascinating *The Raft Book* (1943), pages 7–12 and 39–44. The captain of the *Roger B. Taney* paid attention to the natural signs as Gatty suggests, but he erred in thinking that the sight of a butterfly meant land was near. Gatty writes that butterflies, unlike shore birds, often stray too far out to sea and die.

The figure of 430 subs and the heavy toll on the two convoys in mid-March comes from Ed Offley's *Turning the Tide* (2011), pages 42 and 53. The account of the back-and-forth battles between U-boats and convoy escorts comes from Doenitz's *Memoirs*, page 328.

Doenitz's declaration that the attack on the two convoys was his greatest success comes from his *Memoirs*, pages 329–30.

The Allied counteroffensive against U-boats has been the subject of several books, including Michael Gannon's *Black May* (1989), Offley's *Turning the Tide*, David Syrett's *The Defeat of the German U-boats* (1994), and Vice Admiral Sir Peter Gretton's *Crisis Convoy* (1974). The counteroffensive has been described in numerous other books, including the British Ministry of Defence's history of the U-boat war, *The U-boat War in the Atlantic* (1989), Taylor's *Fire on the Beaches*, Riesenberg's *Sea War*, Lisle A. Rose's *Power at Sea: The Breaking Storm, 1919–1945* (2007), Clay Blair's *Hitler's U-boat War*, and Doenitz's *Memoirs*.

The contributions of British physicists to antisubmarine warfare in World War II are detailed in Stephen Budiansky's *Blackett's War*, notably on page 143. The significance of microwave radar is described in Barrie Pitt's *The Battle of the Atlantic* (1977), page 183. Doenitz's comment about aircraft being unable to destroy U-boats came from Pitt's *The Battle of the*

Atlantic, page 182. A U-boat's disadvantage against planes is clearly explained in Gaylord T. M. Kelshall's *U-boats in the Caribbean*, page 153. The
advantages of new, more powerful depth charges set to explode at U-boats'
maximum depth are described in Offley's *Turning the Tide*, page xiv. The
advantages of the destroyer escort (DE) and escort carrier are described in
Bruce Felknor's *The U.S. Merchant Marine at War*, pages 230–33 and Michael Gannon's *Operation Drumbeat*, pages 392–93. Morison's *The Atlantic Battle Won* describes how the DE came to exist, pages 35–36. Admiral
Gallery, who led a hunter-killer group, describes such groups' structure
and operations in his *Twenty Million Tons Under the Sea*. The fact that
hunter-killer groups became the most prolific U-boat destroyers after mid-
1943 comes from Gannon's *Operation Drumbeat*, page 392.

Raymond Hodges's letter to his parents was printed in the *GJ* on May
13, 1943. The account of Convoy HX-232 comes from British Admiralty
records, and Records Group 38. Syrett's *The Defeat of the German U-boats*
points out the paradox that each side was monitoring the other's messages
while never imagining its own messages were being monitored.

The information about the mounting U-boat losses comes from the
Ministry of Defence's *The U-boat War in the Atlantic*; Morison's *The Atlantic Battle Won*, page 11; and Blair's *Hitler's U-boat War*. Lisle describes
the death of Doenitz's younger son, Peter, on page 319 of *Power at Sea*. Blair
describes the fate of Doenitz's older son, Klaus, in *Hitler's U-boat War*, page
569. David Fairbank White describes Doenitz's personal attachment to his
U-boats and crews in *Bitter Ocean*, page 232. John Terraine quotes Doenitz's decision to fight on in *Business in Great Waters* (2009), page 616. Rose
describes Doenitz's decision to keep sending U-boats to sea in *Power at Sea*,
page 319. Morison quotes Doenitz's upbeat message to his U-boat crews in
The Atlantic Battle Won, pages 83–84, and Hitler's views on page 59.

Chapter Eleven: The Conveyor Belt

The account of the *Robert Rowan* sinking comes from an interview with
Bernard Stansbury, NARA Record Group 38, and Wynn. The account of

the disastrous Allied parachute drop appears in Robert Wallace's *The Italian Campaign* (1978), page 25.

Ernie Pyle's observations about the size of the Sicily invasion fleet came from *The Italian Campaign*, page 18. The account of the *Timothy Pickering* explosion came from Captain Arthur Moore's *A Careless Word*, page 281, and Felknor, pages 277–78. The description of Navy Armed Guard assignments as undesirable comes from Bernard Stansbury and from the August 7, 1943, *Collier's* magazine article, "We Man the Deck Guns," by Ensign Robert C. Ruark, USNR.

Doenitz describes his reluctance to send U-boats into the Mediterranean "mousetrap" in his *Memoirs*, pages 160–61 and 366. Herbert Werner's dispirited comment appears in his *Iron Coffins*, page 177.

The account of Captain Homer Callis's new ship and new assignment in the Mediterranean comes from interviews with his son Bill Callis and the Ship Movement Card for the *Cape Mohican* in NARA Record Group 38. Homer's granddaughter, Lisa Callis, provided the letter from Homer to Nancy.

The account of the torpedoing of the *Cape Mohican* comes from interviews with Bill Callis; NARA Record Group 38, including a Navy Armed Guard report; and the *GJ* on March 16, 1943. The fact that the torpedoing was the fourth for the *Cape Mohican*'s radio operator comes from the radioman's account on www.usmm.org.

Captain Herbert Callis's encounter with *Collier's* magazine writer Quentin Reynolds in Moscow is described in Reynolds's article, "It Happens in Moscow," on August 21, 1943. Accounts of Captain Callis's voyage to Murmansk on the *Thomas Hartley* come from an interview with Callis's daughter Joan Marble (who also provided a copy of the certificate Callis received for his ordeal) and from the Navy Armed Guard report of the voyage in NARA Record Group 38. The account of Callis's voyage to Murmansk came mainly from a Navy Armed Guard report. The fact that a crew member was put ashore as a "mental case" comes from the Russian Convoys file in NARA Record Group 38.

Accounts of the Germans' efforts to ruin the port of Naples to prevent the Allies from using it came from Rick Atkinson's *The Day of Battle* (volume 2 of the *Liberation Trilogy*) (2007), pages 2 and 242, and Wallace's *The Italian Campaign*, pages 77–78.

The account of the Allied mustard gas disaster at the Italian port of Bari is described in several books, including Gerald Reminick's *Nightmare in Bari* (2001).

The information on the increased production of Liberty ships in 1943 comes from Philip Kaplan and Jack Currie's *Convoy*, page 68. The statistic about the cargo numbers in October 1943 comes from Reminick's *Patriots and Heroes*, page 130.

The account of the mining and sinking of the *Delisle* comes from NARA Record Group 38. Paul Grubb's account of rescuing Captain Clendaniel on the *Delisle* appears in *GJ* notes and in a *GJ* story on November 18, 1943. Galza's account of rescuing Clendaniel—as well as a different one-legged mariner on a previous voyage of the *Delisle*—is described by the U.S. Maritime Commission in its narrative accompanying the award to Galza of the Distinguished Service Medal. Clendaniel's hometown paper, the *Brooklyn Eagle*, gave a different account of the return of Clendaniel's artificial leg in its February 27, 1944, edition. John Bunker's *Heroes in Dungarees* offers yet another version on pages 298–99. The background about Paul Grubb came from an interview with his younger sister Jane Grubb of Minnesota.

The account of the *Esso Providence* fire and Winder's heroics comes from *Ships of the Esso Fleet*, pages 486–91, and from the *GJ* on April 6, 1944, based on a war correspondent's reporting from Italy.

Jack White's experiences were described in the Mathews County High School newspaper, *Anchors Aweigh*. Jack Ward of Mathews described his experiences exploring inland Italy in interviews with me.

The Allied amphibious invasion at Anzio is described in numerous books, including Atkinson's *The Day of Battle*. Churchill's wry comment about the whale appears in his *Closing the Ring*, page 488. The descriptions of the terrifying German railroad guns come from *The Day of Battle* and Wallace's *The Italian Campaign*, page 179. The admiral's remarks to the merchant captains appear in Samuel Eliot Morison's *Sicily, Salerno and Anzio* (1954), page 370. Livesay's comments come from *GJ* notes.

The description of the disbanding of the airplane watchers and Eleanor Respess's christening of the *John Russell Pope* both come from the *GJ* on October 7, 1943. The account of the explosion at the mine depot comes from the *GJ* on November 21, 1943. The description of Paul Grubb's reaction to the explosion comes from an interview with his sister Jane Grubb.

The account of Bernard Stansbury's posting to the *Penelope Barker* and the ship's subsequent torpedoing on the Murmansk Run come from an interview with Stansbury; the *GJ* on May 3, 1944; and NARA Record Group 38, including a Navy Armed Guard report.

The account of stockpiling munitions at Anzio for the eventual Allied breakout comes from Wallace's *The Italian Campaign*, pages 187–88. The story of the *Paul Hamilton* explosion comes from NARA Record Group 38; the article "One Torpedo—580 Men—7000 Tons of Explosives," by Jim W. Dean, on www.veteranstoday.com, April 20, 2011; the *GJ* on May 10, August 17, 1944; and the family's remembrances of Billups in the Gwynn's Island Museum.

Bill Callis' experiences in the Normandy invasion came from an interview with him, and from the *President Monroe*'s Ship Movement Card in NARA Record Group 38.

The account of the capture of the U-505 comes from Daniel Gallery's *Twenty Thousand Tons Under the Sea*. The report that Admiral King was furious about the capture comes from Clay Blair's *Hitler's U-boat War*, vol. 2, page 553.

The captain of the Liberty ship *Cyrus McCormick*'s description of the crowded English Channel on D-Day comes from Bunker's *Heroes in Dungarees*, page 282. Doenitz's orders to his U-boats to defend Normandy against the D-Day invasion come from Werner's *Iron Coffins*, page 213, and Doenitz's *Memoirs*, page 422. The toll on U-boats on D-Day comes from

Doenitz's *Memoirs*, pages 422–23. Morison pronounces his verdict on the U-boats in *The Atlantic Battle Won*, page 63. The description of Randolph Payne's experiences on Omaha Beach comes from an interview with his daughter, Renee Arga-Bright. Bill Callis described his experiences at the port of Cherbourg in an interview with me. The total of supplies delivered to American troops at Omaha Beach in June comes from Bunker's *Heroes in Dungarees*, page 285.

Eisenhower's quote about the importance of the U.S. Merchant Marine to the Allied war effort comes from www.usmm.org.

The increasing losses of U-boats are described in Doenitz's *Memoirs*, page 420. The destruction of the U-107, U-515, and U-575 is described in Wynn's *U-boat Operations of the Second World War*.

Lester Smith's homecoming and his enthusiasm for returning to sea were described by his widow, Lottie Mitchem, in an interview with me. Raymond Hodges's son Bill described Raymond's suggestion that he join the Merchant Marine. Horace Hodges described his announcement to his mother that he was going to sea. Coleman's promotion to captain of the *Edward A. Savoy* was described by his daughter Betty Fernald. J. W. Corbett described his arrival and the *Edward A. Savoy* in an interview with me.

Chapter Twelve: War's End

My account of Coleman Hodges's achievement of his goal of becoming captain comes from interviews with his daughter Betty Fernald and J. W. Corbett, as well as the *Edward A. Savoy*'s Ship Movement Card in NARA Records Group 38. The description of J.W. comes from interviews with him and with other members of the Hodges family who knew him, including Brother Hodges and Jesse Carroll Thornton.

The statistics about the declining danger of the Murmansk Run came from the Masters, Mates & Pilots newsletter of July 1945. The account of the *Edward A. Savoy*'s voyage to Murmansk comes from NARA Records Group 38; records from the British Admiralty in London; Kemp's *Convoy!*, page 210–12; and interviews with J. W. Corbett and Coleman Hodges's daughter Betty Fernald.

The account of the Hodges anniversary festivities comes from the *GJ* on December 16, 1944, and from interviews with Jesse Carroll Thornton, Stormy Heart Romaniello, and Marlene Callis. Raymond's letter to Captain Jesse and Henny was provided by Jesse Carroll Thornton.

Jack Rowe described his meeting with Homer Callis Jr. in the Pacific in interviews with me.

The experiences of Captain Raymond Hodges and Captain Homer Callis in convoys come from NARA Records Group 38, including a Navy Armed Guard report.

The descriptions of the port of Antwerp come in part from Atkinson's *The Guns at Last Light: Volume III of the Liberation Trilogy* (2013), pages 330–32, and John Bunker's *Heroes in Dungarees*, page 287. J. W. Corbett described his experiences with V-1 rockets in Antwerp in interviews with me. Captain Rodney Callis's experience in Antwerp is described in the Naval Armed Guard report for his ship, the *Edward A. White*. The explanation of the origin of the "V" in V-2 comes from Richard Overy's *Why the Allies Won*, page 239. Atkinson describes the V-2 disaster at the movie theater in *The Guns at Last Light*, page 333.

The account of Raymond Hodges's first visit home since early 1942 comes from interviews with Raymond's son Bill Hodges, Jesse Carroll Thornton, and Stormy Heart Romaniello, as well as the *GJ* on March 8, 1945.

Bill Callis told me about his reaction after joining a ship and finding Lester Smith on the crew.

Bernard Stansbury described his reaction to his second sinking in a row.

The Masters, Mates & Pilots comment on Roosevelt's death comes from the MMP newsletter for May 1945.

A detailed account of the sinking of the USS *Monaghan* in Typhoon Cobra can be found in Bob Drury and Tom Clavin's *Halsey's Typhoon* (2007).

The description of kamikaze attacks in general, and specifically the attack on the USS *Hazelwood*, comes from Robin L. Rielly's *Kamikaze Attacks of World War II* (2010). Homer Sr.'s subsequent letters to his wife, Nancy, were provided to me by Homer's granddaughter (and Bill Callis's daughter), Lisa Callis. Bill Callis described his phone conversation with his mother regarding his brother's death.

Doenitz describes his unexpected discovery that he was the next führer, and explains his actions afterward, in his *Memoirs*. The sinking of the *Black Point* and its attacker is described in Lawrence Paterson's *Black Flag: The Surrender of Germany's U-boat Forces* (2009). The text of Doenitz's parting message to his U-boat commanders comes from Clay Blair's *Hitler's U-boat War*, vol. 2, pages 699–700. The account of a U-boat commander cutting his wrists in Boston comes from the *Virginian-Pilot*, via the Associated Press, on May 19, 1945. The account of the two U-boats fleeing to Argentina comes from Timothy Mulligan's *Neither Sharks Nor Wolves*, page 237, and from *Black Flag*. The text of the Bull Line's radiogram announcing the German surrender comes from Captain Walter Hudgins's son Elliott Hudgins, who has a copy of the radiogram. Elliott Hudgins also provided a copy of the U.S. Maritime Commission's radiogram explaining to mariners that Germany's surrender merely shifted the full focus of the war to the Pacific.

Accounts of the captured U-505 drawing crowds in Norfolk and elsewhere come from the *Virginian-Pilot* on June 30 and July 5, 1945.

Captain T. O. Rainier's experiences on the *Cape Victory* at the end of World War II came from interviews with his granddaughter Joan Marble (the daughter of Captain Herbert Callis, who was stranded in Murmansk with the Forgotten Convoy); in the *GJ* on November 16, 1950; and Paul Tibbets's *Return of the Enola Gay* (1998), page 187.

The account of William Franklin Hale's death on the USS *Indianapolis* came from his daughter, Betsy Stewart of Mathews, and from Richard F. Newcomb's *Abandon Ship! The Saga of the USS Indianapolis, the Navy's Greatest Sea Disaster* (2001).

The account of Mathews's reaction to the war's end comes from interviews with people in Mathews and from the *GJ* on August 16, 1945, the same day the editorial appeared.

The listed casualty rates of U.S. merchant mariners during World War II have changed over the years, reflecting the absence of a centralized records system and the frequent changes of crew on merchant ships. Immediately after the war, the Maritime Administration estimated the losses of merchant mariners at 5,638. Today the nonprofit group American Merchant Marine Veterans (AMVV) and www.usmm.org estimate that roughly 9,300 U.S. merchant mariners lost their lives in the war, including men who died after the war of war injuries. Using 9,300 as the total for losses, the Merchant Marine's casualty rate is slightly higher than that of the U.S. Marine Corps. The Merchant Marine and Marine Corps rates are much higher than those of any other branch of the service, although the Army lost by far the most men. The casualty rates of various branches of the U.S. armed forces in World War II come from Bruce Felknor's *The U.S. Merchant Marine at War*, page 331.

The information about the U-boat casualty rates comes from Mulligan's *Neither Sharks Nor Wolves*, page 251–52.

The figures on the U.S. Merchant Marine's accomplishments come from *The U.S. Merchant Marine at War: A Report of the War Shipping Administration to the President, January 15, 1946*. Admiral King's quote comes from www.usmm.org. The account of the parade comes from the *Virginian-Pilot*, through the Associated Press, on October 1, 1945.

Churchill's quotes come from *The Hinge of Fate*, page 125, and Stephen Budiansky's *Blackett's War*, page 141. Churchill's memorable quotes about U-boats also include, "The U-boat attack was our worst evil. It would have been wise for the Germans to stake all upon it. In politics, when you have got hold of a good thing, stick to it." And, less elegantly, "This mortal danger to our lifelines gnawed my bowels."

Rohwer's comment about the seriousness of King's error in failing to establish a convoy system sooner comes from Nathan Miller's *War at Sea*, page 296; Michael Gannon's comment is from *Operation Drumbeat*; and

Middlebrook's is from Alex Roland et al., *The Way of the Ship*, page 305. Blair defends King on page 692 of the first volume of his *Hitler's U-boat War*. Blair was so incensed by Gannon's criticism of King that he called out Gannon by name in *Hitler's U-boat War*.

The accounts of Raymond Hodges and other Mathews mariners quickly shifting to new cargoes after the war come from Brother Hodges, Bill Hodges, Benny Fitchett, Reginald Deagle, Pete Smith, and others in Mathews. The Maritime Commission's estimate that most of the war equipment in Europe would go to the Pacific came from the MMP newsletter of June 1945.

The accounts of Raymond Hodges's voyages to bring home U.S. troops came from interviews with his son Bill Hodges and the *Mormacmoon's* Ship Movement Card in NARA Record Group 38. The description of Captain Frank Boyer's voyages comes from the Motorun neighborhood sections of the *GJ* between 1944 and 1946. The fact that the mariners also brought home the bodies of American service members came from Rick Atkinson's *The Guns at Last Light*, pages 639–40.

Brother Hodges described his encounter with his uncle Raymond in Odessa in interviews with me.

Chapter Thirteen: Legacy

The account of Jesse and Henny's move to Hudgins is based on interviews with Jesse Carroll Thornton and Brother Hodges and the *GJ* on August 30, 1945. The description of Captain Jesse Hodges's forced retirement from the sea came from Jesse Carroll Thornton, Brother Hodges, Stormy Heart Romaniello, Marlene Callis, and the *GJ* on August 25, 1957.

Jean Hodges described the family's retreat from the Hodges dinings. The account of the young seaman approaching Bernard Pierson's father comes from information provided by the Pierson family to the Gwynn's Island Museum, and from an interview with Jack Rowe of Gwynn's Island. The account of William Burton Gay's parents learning of his fate comes from the *GJ* on October 25, 1945. The account of Captain Otis Levering Callis's death comes from the *GJ* on December 6, 1945. The account of

Salome Hudgins's change of mind comes from an interview with her and her daughter, Vicki.

The accounts of the Nuremberg trials come from Ann and John Tusa's *The Nuremberg Trial*, in particular pages 355–60. Biddle's dissenting view is found on page 461. The description of Doenitz's attitude comes from *Collier's* magazine, September 22, 1945. Admiral Gallery's view is on pages 298–99 of his *Twenty Million Tons Under the Sea*.

My description of Travers Thompson's postwar career in the U.S. submarine service comes from an interview with him.

The account of Benny Fitchett's anxious visit to the old German battleship in Gdynia, Poland, comes from an interview with him.

My descriptions of Mathews's entry into the postwar world come from interviews and from the following issues of the *GJ* in 1946: January 24, January 31, February 7, February 28, March 21, August 8, August 15, September 13, October 3, October 11, November 6, and November 14.

The planners of the monument had few contacts in the Mathews black community and most likely were unaware that a black mariner from Mathews had been killed on the *Ruth*. Ashley Clinton Williams's family had moved from Mathews a decade before the war.

The story of Will Hunley's unusual way of wishing goodnight to his children comes from his son, Jimmy Hunley.

The account of the Mathews Day celebration in 1946 comes from the *GJ* on October 3, 1946. The *Richmond Times-Dispatch* editorial about Mathews was reprinted in the *GJ* on that day. The subsequent letter from the captain of the USS *Mathews* appeared in the *GJ* on November 14, 1946.

My account of Edna Hodges's unsuccessful efforts to have Dewey's death and the sinking of the *Onondaga* declared an accident comes from the *Virginian-Pilot* on February 17, 1948, and March 5, 1948; the written ruling by U.S. District Court Judge John Paul in *Hodges vs. New York Life Insurance Co.*, March 2, 1948; and an interview with Jean Hodges. The description of Edna's and her children's life after the war comes from interviews with Jean Hodges.

Details of Homer Callis's final days and his wife Nancy's life afterward came from Bill Callis and his daughter, Lisa Callis, who provided the letter from her grandfather.

The description of Eleanor Respess's life after the war came from interviews with Bill Callis and Eleanor's friend David Judson.

Lester Smith's widow, Lottie Mitchem, described his life after the war, with Jack Rowe and Bill Callis providing additional details. The description of Lester's last summer mornings with his daughter and granddaughter comes from the *GJ* on July 2, 1987.

Jesse Carroll Thornton, Jesse Hodges's grandson, described Captain Jesse's last days and his funeral, as well as Henny's decision not to attend.

My account of Raymond's days as a cruise ship captain comes mainly from his son Bill Hodges, who also provided a translation of an article about his father that appeared in *Critica*, the Buenos Aires newspaper, on February 16, 1955. Several articles about Captain Raymond Hodges also appeared in the Moore-McCormack company newsletter, the *Mooremack News*. The account of Raymond's final days and burial at sea comes from Bill Hodges.

The description of Coleman Hodges's short life after the war comes primarily from his daughter Betty Fernald, but also from a taped interview with his brother David and sister Louise, and interviews with Jesse Carroll Thornton, Brother Hodges, and Marlene Callis.

The account of Henny Hodges's death comes mostly from her grandson Jesse Carroll Thornton.

The descriptions of the physical remnants of the U-boat war came from my visits to those places. MIT spokesman Kurt Hasselbalch explained how the *Roper*'s anchor reached the school. Pete Smith described a cruise on the *Jeremiah O'Brien* and provided background documents.

The account of the explosion and deaths aboard the *Snoopy* came from the Associated Press on July 24, 1965. The account of the nonfatal torpedo discovery off Rhode Island came from the *New Bedford Standard-Times* on May 30, 1998. The story of the U-869 is beautifully told by Robert Kurson in *Shadow Divers* (2005). The story of Ballard's expedition and the

Navy's reconsideration of what sank the U-166 comes from the Public Broadcasting System's NOVA program "Nazi Attack on America," broadcast on May 6, 2015. The section about divers and government protection of wrecks is based on interviews with several wreck divers, including Jim Bunch of North Carolina; John Broadwater, former director of NOAA's Monitor National Marine Sanctuary; and Lauren Heesemann, research coordinator for the Monitor sanctuary.

The account of George Betts's sleuthing and his efforts to contact the families of men lost on the *Muskogee* comes primarily from a collection of Betts's personal papers. He donated the papers to the Independence Seaport Museum in Philadelphia, which keeps them in its archives. The collection also contains newspaper clippings and photographs.

In 2004 I communicated through an interpreter with a U-85 crewman's cousin, Dr. Hansjuergen Fresenius, in Northeim, Germany, about his views of the U-boat sinking. Fresenius was among those who made the trip from Germany to Hampton to visit the Germans' graves.

The information about the sinking of the HMT *Bedfordshire* comes primarily from L. VanLoan Naisawald's *In Some Foreign Field* (1997), which describes the sinking and aftermath in detail. I have attended the memorial service for the British seamen on Ocracoke Island, North Carolina, and also visited the graves of British seamen on Hatteras Island.

When I interviewed Jesse Roper Mohorovic in 2004 for a story for the *Richmond Times-Dispatch* about his lifeboat birth, I was surprised to discover that I had interviewed him a decade earlier while he was a shipping company executive. I had been writing a story about the decline of the U.S. Merchant Marine. Jesse did not mention his lifeboat birth to me at that time.

My description of the Merchant Marine's decline and its current state comes from my experience working at Maersk Line, Limited, of Norfolk, from 2009–2014, during part of which time the company was considered the largest employer of U.S. merchant mariners, and from an interview with Captain T. Christian Spain, national assistant vice president, government relations, for the American Maritime Officers (AMO) union in

Washington, D.C. I further consulted Maersk Line vice president David Sloane, Jeff Brandt of the U.S. Coast Guard's National Maritime Center, and Morris Harvey, president of American Merchant Marine Veterans (AMMV), a nonprofit advocacy group for merchant mariners. I also drew from Benjamin W. Labaree's *America and the Sea*, René De La Pedraja's *The Rise and Decline of U.S. Merchant Shipping in the Twentieth Century* (1992), and Alex Roland et al., *The Way of the Ship*.

The description of efforts to persuade Congress to grant mariners veteran status, and currently to approve lump-sum payments, comes from Morris Harvey and Saaren "Sindy" Raymond of AMMV, and H. Gerald Starnes's self-published book, *Torpedoed for Life* (2013).

Sonny Richardson provided a unique perspective on Mathews. He has roots in the maritime community—his middle name is Hudgins and his father was a docking pilot like Captain Willie Hodges; he has served in local elective office; and now he sells real estate in Mathews.

I have visited the Gwynn's Island Museum numerous times to examine its trove of photos and artifacts about the Mathews mariners in World War II. The museum was where I started. The Mathews Maritime Foundation museum is assembling its own collection of exhibits and artifacts.

The description of Bill Callis comes from numerous interviews with him and his daughter, Lisa. A fictional treatment of Bill Callis's life, and specifically his behavior when he came home from the sea, appears in the title story of Mark Richard's collection of short stories, *The Ice at the Bottom of the World* (1986). Richard gave the Bill Callis character the name Bill Doodlum, and Mathews County the name Doodlum County.

My descriptions of Mathews County men gravitating to the tugboat business come from interviews with Sonny Richardson, David Callis, and Jimmy Hunley in Mathews.

I have attended Hodges family gatherings at the invitation of Brother Hodges and Jesse Carroll Thornton, and have visited Gales Neck with Brother, Jesse, and Jean Hodges, and other family members, with the permission of the historic trust that now owns the property.

BIBLIOGRAPHY

Atkinson, Rick. *An Army at Dawn: Volume I of the Liberation Trilogy*. New York, Henry Holt & Company, 2002.

———. *The Day of Battle: Volume II of the Liberation Trilogy*. New York, Henry Holt & Company, 2007.

———. *The Guns at Last Light: Volume III of the Liberation Trilogy*. New York, Henry Holt and Company, 2013.

Bethell, Nicholas. *Russia Besieged*. Alexandria, VA, Time-Life Books, 1977.

Blair, Clay. *Hitler's U-boat War*. 2 vols. New York, Modern Library, 2000.

Blanchard, Fessenden Seaver. *A Cruising Guide to the Chesapeake, Including the Passages from Long Island Sound Along the New Jersey Coast and Inland Waterway*. New York, Dodd, Mead and Company, 1968.

Boyd, Carl, and Akihiko Yoshida. *The Japanese Submarine Force and World War II*. Annapolis, MD, Naval Institute Press, 1995.

Bradham, Randolph. *Hitler's U-boat Fortresses*. Westport, CT, Praeger, 2003.

Brennecke, Jochen. *The Hunters and the Hunted: German U-boats 1939–1945*. Annapolis, MD, Naval Institute Press, 2003.

British Ministry of Defence. *The U-boat War in the Atlantic*. London, Her Majesty's Stationery Office, 1989.

Browning, Robert M., Jr. *United States Merchant Marine Casualties of World War II*. Jefferson, NC, McFarland & Company, Inc., 2011.

Buchheim, Lothar-Gunther. *Das Boot*. New York, Alfred A. Knopf, 1975.

Budiansky, Stephen. *Blackett's War*. New York, Alfred A. Knopf, 2013.

Bunch, Jim. *Germany's U-85: A Shadow in the Sea*. Nags Head, NC, Deep Sea Press, 2003.

Bunker, John. *Heroes in Dungarees*. Annapolis, MD, Naval Institute Press, 2006.

Bunker, John Gorley. *Liberty Ships: The Ugly Ducklings of World War II*. Annapolis, MD, Naval Institute Press, 1972.

Butler, John A. *Sailing on Friday: The Perilous Voyage of America's Merchant Marine*. Washington, DC, Brassey's, 1997.

Carse, Robert. *A Cold Corner of Hell*. New York, Doubleday & Company, 1969.

———. *The Long Haul: The U.S. Merchant Service in World War II*. New York, Norton, 1965.

Cheatham, James T. *The Atlantic Turkey Shoot: U-boats off the Outer Banks in World War II*. West Columbia, SC, Wentworth Printing Corporation, Inc., 1990.

Chewning, Alpheus J. *The Approaching Storm: U-boats off the Virginia Coast During World War II*. Lively, VA, Brandylane Publishers, 1994.

Churchill, Winston. *The Hinge of Fate*. Boston, Houghton Mifflin, 1950.

———. *Closing the Ring*. New York, Houghton Mifflin Company, 1951.

Cremer, Peter. *U-boat Commander*. Annapolis, MD, Naval Institute Press, 1984.

Cruikshank, Jeffrey L., and Chloe G. Kline. *In Peace and War: A History of the U.S. Merchant Marine Academy at Kings Point*. Hoboken, NJ, John Wiley & Sons, 2008.

De La Pedraja, René. *The Rise and Decline of U.S. Merchant Shipping in the Twentieth Century*. New York, Twayne Publishers, 1992.

Doenitz, Karl. *Memoirs: Ten Years and Twenty Days*. Annapolis, MD, Naval Institute Press, 1959.

Drury, Bob, and Tom Clavin. *Halsey's Typhoon*. New York, Grove/Atlantic, Inc., 2007.

Duffus, Kevin. *War Zone*. Raleigh, NC, Looking Glass Productions, Inc., 2012.

Felknor, Bruce L. *The U.S. Merchant Marine at War, 1775–1945*. Annapolis, MD, Naval Institute Press, 1998.

Flaherty, S. J. *Abandoned Convoy*. Jericho, NY, Exposition Press, 1970.

Frank, Wolfgang. *The Sea Wolves*. New York, Rinehart & Company, 1955.

Freeman, Robert H. *The War Offshore*. Ventnor, NJ, Shellback Press, 1987. Contains *Eastern Sea Frontier War Diary* [National Archives & Records Administration].

Gallery, Daniel. *Twenty Million Tons Under the Sea*. New York, Warner Books, 1956.

Gannon, Michael. *Black May*. New York, Harper Collins, 1989.

———. *Operation Drumbeat*. New York, Harper Perennial, 1990.

Gasaway, E. B. *Grey Wolf, Grey Sea*. New York, Ballantine Books, 1970.

Gatty, Harold. *The Raft Book: Lore of the Sea and Sky*. New York, George Grady Books, 1943.

George, Rose. *Ninety Percent of Everything*. New York, Henry Holt & Co., 2013.

Gloucester County Historical Society. *History and Progress: Mathews County, Virginia*. The Mathews County Historical Society, Inc., 1982.

Gretton, Peter. *Crisis Convoy*. London, Pernell Book Services, 1974.

Groom, Winston. *1942*. New York, Grove Press, 2005.

Harris, Brayton. *The Navy Times Book of Submarines: A Political, Social and Military History*. New York, Berkley Publishing Group, 1997.

Hemingway, Ernest. *Islands in the Stream*. New York, Scribner, 1970.

Hemingway, Hilary, and Carlene Brennen. *Hemingway in Cuba*. New York, Rugged Land LLC, 2003.

Herbert, Brian. *The Forgotten Heroes: The Heroic Story of the United States Merchant Marine.* New York, Tom Doherty Associates LLC, 2004.

Hickam, Homer H., Jr. *Torpedo Junction.* New York, Dell Publishing, 1989.

Hoehling, A. A. *The Fighting Liberty Ships.* Kent, OH, Kent State University Press, 1996.

Hope, Stanton. *Tanker Fleet: The War Story of the Shell Tankers and the Men Who Manned Them.* London, Anglo-Saxon Petroleum Company, 1948.

Hoyt, Edwin P. *The U-boat Wars.* New York, Cooper Square Press, 2002.

———. *U-boats Offshore.* New York, PEI Books, 1978.

Ireland, Bernard. *Battle of the Atlantic.* Annapolis, MD, Naval Institute Press, 1993.

———. *War at Sea 1914–45.* London, Cassell, 2002.

Kaplan, Philip, and Jack Currie. *Convoy.* Annapolis, MD, Naval Institute Press, 1998.

Katz, Robert. *The Battle for Rome.* New York, Simon & Schuster, 2003.

Kelshall, Gaylord T. M. *The U-boat War in the Caribbean.* Annapolis, MD, Naval Institute Press, 1988.

Kemp, Paul. *Convoy!* Edison, NJ, Castle Books, 2004.

Knoblock, Glenn A. *African American World War II Casualties and Decorations in the Navy, Coast Guard and Merchant Marine.* Jefferson, NC, McFarland & Company, Inc., 2009.

Konstam, Angus. *Scourge of the Seas.* Oxford, Osprey Publishing, 2001.

Kurson, Robert. *Shadow Divers.* New York, Ballantine Books, 2005.

Labaree, Benjamin W. et al. *America and the Sea: A Maritime History.* Mystic, CT, Mystic Seaport Museum, Inc., 1998.

Land, Emory Scott. *Winning the War with Ships.* New York, Robert M. McBride Co., Inc., 1958.

Luthmann, William F. *At Liberty.* Chapel Hill, NC, Professional Press, 1995.

MacLean, M. Stanley. *13 Days Adrift.* St. Petersburg, FL, privately printed, 1943.

Mathews County Historical Society. *Mathews County Panorama.* Mathews County Historical Society, Inc., 2000.

Manolis, Nicholas. *We at Sea.* New York, Anatolia Press, 1949.

McCoy, Samuel Duff. *Nor Death Dismay.* New York, Macmillan Company, 1944.

McPhee, John. *Looking for a Ship.* New York, Farrar Straus & Giroux, 1990.

Miller, Nathan. *War at Sea.* New York, Scribner, 1995.

Moore, Arthur. *A Careless Word . . . A Needless Sinking.* New York, American Merchant Marine Museum, 1998.

Morison, Samuel Eliot. *The Battle of the Atlantic, 1939–1943.* Vol. 1 of *History of United States Naval Operations in World War II.* Annapolis, MD, Naval Institute Press, 1947.

———. *Sicily, Salerno and Anzio, January 1943–June 1944.* Vol. 9 of *History of United States Naval Operations in World War II.* Annapolis, MD, Naval Institute Press, 1954.

———. *The Atlantic Battle Won, May 1943–May 1945.* Vol. 10 of *History of United States Naval Operations in World War II.* Boston, Little, Brown and Company, 1984.

Moses, Sam. *At All Costs.* New York, Random House, 2007.

Mulligan, Timothy. *Neither Sharks Nor Wolves: The Men of Nazi Germany's U-boat Arm, 1939–1945.* Annapolis, MD, Naval Institute Press, 1999.

Naisawald, L. VanLoan. *In Some Foreign Field*. Raleigh, NC, North Carolina Division of Cultural Resources, 1997.

Newcomb, Richard F. *Abandon Ship! The Saga of the USS Indianapolis, the Navy's Greatest Sea Disaster*. New York, HarperCollins, 2001.

Offley, Ed. *The Burning Shore*. New York, Basic Books, 2014.

———. *Turning the Tide*. New York, Basic Books, 2011.

Overy, Richard. *Why the Allies Won*. New York, W. W. Norton & Co., 1995.

Parrish, Thomas. *The Submarine: A History*. New York, Viking, 2004.

Paterson, Lawrence. *Black Flag: The Surrender of Germany's U-boat Forces*. Minneapolis, MN, Zenith Press, 2009.

Pitt, Barrie. *The Battle of the Atlantic*. Alexandria, VA, Time-Life Books, 1977.

Powell, James R., and Alan B. Flanders. *Wolf at the Door*. Richmond, VA, Brandylane Publishers, Inc., 2003.

Reminick, Gerald. *Nightmare in Bari*. Palo Alto, CA, Glencannon Press, 2001.

———. *Patriots and Heroes*, Vol. 2. Palo Alto, CA, Glencannon Press, 2004.

Reynolds, Michael. *Hemingway: The Final Years*. New York, W. W. Norton & Company, 1999.

Richard, Mark. *The Ice at the Bottom of the World*. New York, Anchor Books/Random House, Inc., 1986.

Richards, Phil, and John Banigan. *How to Abandon Ship*. Baltimore, Cornell Maritime Press, Inc., 1942.

Rielly, Robin L. *Kamikaze Attacks of World War II: A Complete History of Japanese Suicide Strikes on American Ships, by Aircraft and Other Means*. Jefferson, NC, McFarland & Company, Inc., 2010.

Riesenberg, Felix. *Sea War*. New York, Rinehart and Company, Inc., 1956.

Rigge, Simon, with the editors of Time-Life Books. *War in the Outposts*. Alexandria, VA, Time-Life Books, 1980.

Rohwer, Jurgen. *Axis Submarine Successes 1939–1945*. Annapolis, MD, Naval Institute Press, 1983.

Roland, Alex, W. Jeffrey Bolster, and Alexander Keyssar. *The Way of the Ship*. Hoboken, NJ, John Wiley & Sons, Inc., 2008.

Roscoe, Theodore. *United State Submarine Operations of World War II*. Annapolis, MD, United States Naval Institute, 1956.

Rose, Lisle A. *Power at Sea: The Breaking Storm, 1919–1945*. Columbia, University of Missouri Press, 2007.

Schofield, B. B. *The Russian Convoys*. Philadelphia, Dufour Editions, 1964.

Sebag-Montefiore, Hugh. *Enigma: The Battle for the Code*. New York, John Wiley & Sons, 2000.

Snow, Richard. *A Measureless Peril*. New York, Scribner, 2010.

Spector, Ronald H. *At War at Sea*. New York, Viking, 2001.

Standard Oil Company. *Ships of the Esso Fleet*. New Jersey, Standard Oil Company, 1946.

Starnes, H. Gerald. *Torpedoed for Life: World War II Combat Veterans of the U.S. Merchant Marine*. New York, CreateSpace, 2013.

Stilgoe, John R. *Lifeboat*. Charlottesville, VA, University of Virginia Press, 2007.

Syrett, David. *The Defeat of the German U-boats.* Columbia, University of South Carolina Press, 1994.

Taylor, Theodore. *Battle in the Arctic Seas.* New York, Sterling Point Books, 1976.

———. *Fire on the Beaches.* New York, W. W. Norton & Company, 1958.

Terraine, John. *Business in Great Waters.* South Yorkshire, UK, Pen and Sword Military Press, 2009.

Tibbets, Paul. *Return of the Enola Gay.* Columbus, OH, Mid Coast Marketing, 1998.

Tusa, Ann, and John Tusa. *The Nuremberg Trial.* New York, Skyhorse Publishing, 2010.

U.S. Coast Guard. *Fire Fighting Manual for Tank Vessels.* Coast Guard Publication 329, January 1974.

U.S. War Shipping Administration. *The U.S. Merchant Marine at War: A Report of the War Shipping Administration to the President, January 15, 1946.* Washington, DC, 1946.

Vause, Jordan. *U-boat Ace: The Story of Wolfgang Luth.* Annapolis, MD, Naval Institute Press, 1990.

Wallace, Robert. *The Italian Campaign,* Alexandria, VA, Time-Life Books, 1978.

Walling, Michael G. *Bloodstained Sea: The U.S. Coast Guard in the Battle of the Atlantic, 1941–1944.* New York, International Marine/McGraw-Hill, 2004.

Werner, Herbert A. *Iron Coffins: A Personal Account of the German U-boat Battles of World War II.* New York, Da Capo Press, 1969.

Whalen, Jim. *Last of the Boom Ships.* Bloomington, IN, 1st Books Library, 2000.

White, David Fairbank. *Bitter Ocean.* New York, Simon & Schuster, 2006.

Wiggins, Melanie. *U-boat Adventures: Firsthand Accounts from World War II.* Annapolis, MD, Naval Institute Press, 1999.

———. *Torpedoes in the Gulf: Galveston and the U-boats, 1942–1943.* College Station, Texas A&M University Press, 1995.

Williams, Andrew. *The Battle of the Atlantic.* New York, Basic Books, 2003.

Williamson, Gordon. *U-boat Tactics in World War II.* Oxford, Osprey Publishing, 1990.

Winton, John. *Ultra at Sea.* New York, William Morrow and Co., 1988.

Wynn, Kenneth. *U-boat Operations of the Second World War, Volume I: Career Histories, U1–U510.* Annapolis, MD, Naval Institute Press, 1998.

I found these Web sites especially helpful: www.usmm.org, www.ancestry.com, www.convoy.web, www.naval-history.net, www.uboat.net, and www.uboatarchive.net.

INDEX

The Ghost Ships of Archangel

The Arctic Voyage That Defied the Nazis

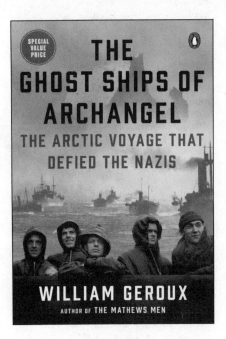

On the fourth of July, 1942, four Allied ships traversing the Arctic split from their decimated convoy to head further north into the ice field of the North Pole. The convoy had started as a fleet of thirty-five cargo ships carrying $1 billion worth of war supplies to the Soviet port of Archangel—the only help Roosevelt and Churchill had extended to Joseph Stalin to maintain their fragile alliance against Germany. At the most dangerous point of the voyage, the ships had received a startling order to scatter and had quickly become easy prey for the Nazis.